MULTIMEDIA MODELING

Towards Information Superhighway

MULTIMEDIA MODELING

Towards Information Superhighway

Singapore   14 – 17 November 1995

editors

Tat Seng Chua & Hung Keng Pung
(The National University of Singapore, Singapore)

Tosiyasu L Kunii
(The University of Aizu, Japan)

World Scientific
Singapore • New Jersey • London • Hong Kong

Published by

World Scientific Publishing Co. Pte. Ltd.

P O Box 128, Farrer Road, Singapore 9128

USA office: Suite 1B, 1060 Main Street, River Edge, NJ 07661

UK office: 57 Shelton Street, Covent Garden, London WC2H 9HE

British Library Cataloguing-in-Publication Data
A catalogue record for this book is available from the British Library.

MULTIMEDIA MODELING
Towards Information Superhighway

ISBN   981-02-2502-4

Printed in Singapore.

Preface

Effective human face-to-face communication uses a variety of senses, including aural, visual, mental abstraction, touch and feels. Our model of the world is also multi-sensory. Our interaction with our environment often involves recalling, relating and understanding information of multiple medium types and senses. Computers were originally designed to process only alpha-numeric data, which covers a small aspect of human communication system. Over the years, the computers were improved to work with graphics, image and, more recently, audio and video. Virtual reality added touch and feels to the human-computer interface. The process of integrating multiple senses and media into computer systems accelerated recently, following the development of higher resolution graphics adapters, faster processors, high-speed networks, large capacity storage devices, and better multimedia information processing techniques. These developments lead to the emergence of interactive multimedia systems that encompass the fields of computing, telecommunication and broadcasting. This has broaden the applications of multimedia from the traditional areas of information organization, presentation and learning, to the new fields of simulation and virtual reality. Applications that have benefited from the introduction of multimedia include: training, demonstration of products for sales or inventory, education, computer-aided design and engineering, medicine, weather, and entertainment.

The term "multimedia" is used to denote the integration of information of multiple medium types, including text, image, graphics, video and audio. Up until now, multimedia technology has been focused on processing the "atoms" (or "forms") of the media, rather than their semantic contents. Most such systems emphasize on the presentation, transmission, storage and processing of raw multimedia data, where everything is converted into streams of low-level bits and bytes. Such systems lack capabilities for users to perform high-level tasks on the media, such as the analysis and manipulation of the medium contents. The media used in this form are known as passive media.

In contrast, an active medium permits the users to interact and manipulate its contents to carry out useful tasks such as the retrieval of additional information, and the control of real-world entities. An active medium must encode, in addition to its raw data, a model describing its semantic contents. The model can be mapped to the reality by direct mapping. With such mapping, we are able to interact directly with objects appearing in, say, a video display to interrogate their semantic contents, and to control other related tasks. The concept of an active medium offers significant improvement in information communication and processing. However, it places stringent requirements on multimedia information systems.

Current multimedia systems are far from the ideal, where all media are active, first class entities. We know little about representation, indexing, interaction and retrieval of non-textual media, especially for images, audio and video. Little is even known about the basic semantic units that characterize non-textual media. Without such knowledge, it is difficult to develop consistent model to represent the contents of these media for the purpose of analysis, indexing and retrieval. It is also difficult to develop effective content analysis techniques to discover their contents. The integration of multimedia and computer graphics to create a simulated world of real and synthetic objects also requires the development of new techniques and models.

This volume is devoted to the discussion of effective modeling of multimedia information and systems for a wide range of applications. It aims to provide common modeling frameworks for integrating the diverse field of multimedia information. The volume contains 28 technical articles. The articles are grouped into 10 chapters. The first chapter contains 3 articles covering issues of next generation multimedia systems. It sets the direction for the rest of the articles. The remaining 9 chapters cover major issues of current research interests. They are: Modeling Multimedia Systems and Standards; Image Retrieval; Interactive Multimedia; Multimedia Synchronization; Networked Multimedia; Music Analysis and Performance System; JEPG and Model-based Image Coding; 3D Geometric Modeling; and, Multimedia Systems and Applications.

The majority of the articles describe, in various levels of details, the modeling issues of multimedia information and systems. It is perhaps the only book that devotes entirely to this important but much neglected topic. It is hoped that this volume will help propel research towards this rich and exciting field.

All articles contained in this volume were selected, after vigorous peer reviews, for presentation at the second international conference on Multi-Media Modeling (MMM'95) held in Singapore on 14-17 November 1995. The conference brought together researchers from the fields of multimedia, computer graphics, computer vision, database, information retrieval and computer communication. Future MMM conferences are planned on an annual basis in France (1996) and Singapore (1997).

We are grateful to the authors for submitting the papers, and the reviewers for their considerable efforts in reviewing the papers on time. We would also like to acknowledge the supports of our sponsors and co-organizers for making this conference possible. Finally, special thanks are due to conference organizing committee, and in particular, Mrs Veronica Ho, for helping to put this conference together.

T.S. Chua
H.K Pung
T.L. Kunii

Table of Contents

Chapter 10: Multimedia Systems and Applications

Chapter 1

Towards Next Generation Multimedia Systems

Next Generation Multimedia: the Ideal and the Real

Tosiyasu L. Kunii and Yoshihisa Shinagawa

Abstract

Up to now, multimedia technology has been focused on transmitting various information via computer networks; everything is converted to data and is transmitted. Such information has been virtual; i.e., the information remains in the realm of synthetic worlds, and at its best, transmitted to the real world in audio-visual (AV) forms. It presents virtual realities. This is the reality of current multimedia. This paper proposes the ideal: the next generation multimedia that use the multimedia data for controlling the real world. The information is mapped to the reality by direct mappings. For example, we can use direct-control robots or direct-control micro machines. The control data can be transmitted via CrossoverNets whose prototype installations have been completed at five hundred sites and have been in daily use for ten years.

1 Passive vs Active Multimedia

Long before computers came into being, multimedia instruments already existed: books. They can contain texts as well as pictures and drawings. Most of the actual uses of multimedia today are still limited to the uses as *electronic books*; i.e., textual and image information is shown from secondary storages or is transferred via computer networks. Let us call such multimedia *passive multimedia*. Although the current bandwidth of most networks is not broad enough to transfer video data without delays, we include time-varying images in this type of multimedia.

Passive multimedia can create virtual worlds. They can bring us to the places we cannot actually go. The virtual reality has enabled us to experience such worlds. We can walk through virtual buildings or human bodies [12], or move our bodies in different environments [5]. They cannot, however, physically affect the real worlds around the users. This is the reality of current multimedia. Their benefit is that the users can get the information of the virtual worlds interactively without going to libraries or stores.

The ideal future multimedia will be *active multimedia* in contrast to the current passive multimedia; The multimedia data will be used for controlling the real world. The information is mapped to the reality by direct mappings. For example, we can use direct-control robots or direct-control micro machines. The applications of such direct mappings include remote medical examination, educational systems, home automation and controlling facilities in intelligent buildings. The data can be transmitted via CrossoverNets [4, 7] whose prototype installations have been completed at five hundred sites and have been in daily use for ten years.

2 CrossoverNet

CrossoverNet is a multimedia local area network (LAN) that allows two-way communication of both digital and analog data among two arbitrary nodes connected to it. Analog audio-visual (AV) information such as cable televisions (CATV) can be incorporated into CrossoverNet. The broadcasting and the communication systems are integrated in one single framework. The head-end [7] called the *intelligent head-end* (IHE's) enables the dynamic channel exchange and converts one frequency into another. It can be connected to ATM and CATV networks, and it is equipped with MPEG2 decoders and encoders to exchange time-varying images [3, 6].

Several digital and analog channels can be placed in a single broad-band cable, and digital information can be embedded in analog information in such a way as the character-multiplexing broadcast. Digital information on the digital channels can control analog information on the analog channels. For example, we can send digital control codes to AV devices to control how and where analog information should be used. The ability of CrossoverNet to exchange analog data has enabled flexible office automation and flexible manufacturing [6].

In CrossoverNet, a connection has either a digital or an analog attribute, corresponding to digital and analog data communication, respectively. The former is called the *digital data* (DD) *connection* and the latter *audio visual* (AV) *connection*. The nodes in CrossoverNet are divided into the *network nodes* (NN) and the *station nodes* (SN). The SN is connected to devices. A *subnet segment* is the minimal unit of the network. It consists of several SN and one NN. The NN connects the subnet segment to the network. The NN can dynamically exchange the connections of the NN and SN, namely NN-SN and NN-NN. This allows CrossoverNet to change its topology dynamically. For example, it can take the configurations of a bus, bridge, a ring (see Fig. 1) etc.

CrossoverNet is constructed based on the OSI reference model [15]. The protocol of the network layer, for example, starts at the state where DD connection is established by the transport layer. The protocol then enters into the AV connection

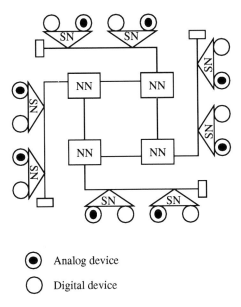

Analog device

Digital device

Figure 1: A CrossoverNet configuration of a ring [7]

establishment phase when an AV connection request is issued from the upper layer.

3   Top-Down Educationwares

At present, we are developing educational softwares (educationwares) in which users understand the contents in a top-down way, in contrast to the contemporary bottom-up education. The backbone network of the top-down educationware will be Crossover-Net. It is called the *MOVE* (Multimedia Open network and Virtual reality for new Education) project. Users first understand the applications of theories and then gradually goes down to the logical aspects of the theories. In this way, users do not lose sight of the meanings of their study.

The current example themes of the educationwares are algebraic topology, and differential topology and geometry. Usually, such theories are very abstract and hard to understand. They are, however, necessary to develop softwares such as computer-aided design (CAD) [9], image understanding, medical image processing [10, 11], and geographical information systems [1, 14]. The top-down educationwares first show the applications of the theories such as CAD and medical image processing, and allow the users to see where the theories are used in the applications interactively by visualizing the theoretical concepts [2]. For example, to check to see whether the CAD data represents manufacturable objects or to understand the shapes of the objects in medical images, topological computation is very useful.

The information used in the MOVE project is in reality limited to AV forms. As the ideal, direct-control robots are to be used to teach the theories of manifolds, kinematics, forward/inverse dynamics and robotics. Medical education is prepared also to be covered by using direct-control micro-machines. Tele-medical cares (e.g., [8]) are also considered in the same way by combining the tele-existence technology [13] with CrossoverNet.

4   Controlling Home Automation

In the ideal, all house hold appliances and AV devices may contain computers inside connected by wireless LAN's. It, however, requires a lot of time before such networks are realized. A much easier way to control house hold appliances and AV devices is to take advantage of the infra-red light remote controllers. Contemporary house hold appliances such as air conditioners, lights, and AV devices such as TV sets and CD / video players are very often equipped with such remote controllers. One example of taking advantage of the remote controllers is the G-code TV program recorder. It decodes and converts the G-code to the time and the channel number of the TV program to be recorded, and controls a video recorder by the infra-red light remote controller.

The infra-red light remote controllers have a standard signal format. Such remote controllers can be incorporated into one controller connected to CrossoverNet.

5   Conclusions

We have proposed the next generation multimedia that actively interact with and then control the real world. This aspect of multimedia should be advanced further in combination with the tele-existence techniques. The security problems will become very serious and should be studied extensively at the same time.

6   Acknowledgements

We would like to express our gratitude to Prof. Senro Saito of the University of Aizu and Dr. Yukari Shirota of Ricoh Software Division for providing us with detailed information of CrossoverNet.

References

1. T. Ikeda, T. L. Kunii, Y. Shinagawa, and M. Ueda. A geographical database system based on the homotopy model. In T. L. Kunii and Y. Shinagawa, editors, *Modern Geometric Computing for Visualization*. Springer-Verlag, 1992. To appear.

2. T. L. Kunii, H. Hioki, and Y. Shinagawa. Visualizing highly abstract mathematical concepts: a case study in animation of homology groups. In *Mulitimedia Modeling (Proc. First International Conference on Multi-Media Modeling)*, pages 3–30. World Scientific, Singapore New Jersey London Hong Kong, 1993.

3. T. L. Kunii, S. Saito, M. A. M. Caprez, and L. F. Caprez. Beyond the next generation multimedia network: CrossoverNet/G2. In Sung Yong Shin and Tosiyasu L. Kunii, editors, *Proc. Pacific Graphics '95*, pages 43–62. World Scientific, 1995.

4. T. L. Kunii and Y. Shirota. Crossover net : A computer graphics/video crossover lan system. *The Visual Computer*, 2(2):78–89, 1986.

5. T. L. Kunii and L. Sun. Dynamic analysis-based human animation. In T. S. Chua and T. L. Kunii, editors, *Computer Graphics Around the World (Proc. CG International '90)*, pages 3–15. Springer, Tokyo Berlin Heidelberg New York London Paris Hong Kong, 1990.

6. S. Saito, T. L. Kunii, and K. Yamauchi. A real-time coordinated multimedia architecutre − a flexible office automation and flexible manufacturing viewpoint −. In *Proc. MmNet'95*, 1995. In press.

7. S. Saito, H. Yoshida, and T. L. Kunii. The crossovernet lan system using an intelligent head-end. *IEEE Trans. on Computers*, BC-38(8):1076–1085, 1989.

8. F. Sauer and R. Kabuka. Multimedia technology in the radiosity department. *Proc. ACM Multimedia 94*, pages 263–269, 1994.

9. Y. Shinagawa, Y. L. Kergosien, and T. L. Kunii. Surface coding based on Morse theory. *IEEE Computer Graphics and Applications*, 11(5):66–78, September 1991.

10. Y. Shinagawa and T. L. Kunii. Constructing a Reeb graph automatically from cross sections. *IEEE Computer Graphics and Applications*, 11(6):44—51, November 1991.

11. Y. Shinagawa and T. L. Kunii. Using surface coding to detect errors in surface reconstruction. In T. L. Kunii and Y. Shinagawa, editors, *Modern Geometric Computing for Visualization*, pages 227–240. Springer-Verlag, 1992.

12. Y. Shinagawa, T. L. Kunii, Y. Nomura, T. Okuno, and Y-H. Young. Automating view function generation for walk-through animation. In N. Magnenat-Thalmann and D. Thalmann, editors, *Proc. of Computer Animation '90*, pages 227–237. Springer, Tokyo Berlin Heidelberg New York London Paris Hong Kong, 1990.

13. S. Tachi, K. Tanie, K. Komoriya, and M. Kaneko. Tele-existence (I): Design and evaluation of a visual display with sensation of presence. In *Proc. 5th International Symposium on Theory and Practice of Robots and Manipulators*, 1984.

14. S. Takahashi, T. Ikeda, Y. Shinagawa, T. L. Kunii, and M. Ueda. Extracting features from discrete geographical elevation data with topological integrity: Algorithms for extracting critical points and constructing topological graphs. In *Proc. Eurographics '95*, 1995. In press.

15. H. Zimmerman. OSI reference model - the OSI model of architecture for open systems interconnection. *IEEE Trans. Commun.*, COM-28:425–432, 1980.

MODELING ISSUES IN COMPUTER VISION AND MULTIMEDIA

S.L. TANIMOTO

Department of Computer Science and Engineering
Box 352350, University of Washington
Seattle, WA 98195, USA

Modeling has slightly different meanings in the application areas of computer-aided design ("synthetic modeling"), image and speech understanding ("natural modeling"), and information retrieval ("derivative modeling"). Techniques are described for modeling sensed data in computer vision, and the possibilities for applying them in derivative modeling are discussed. Issues for the design of tools to support interactive modeling are raised. Applications of derivative modeling in educational activities based on image processing are discussed.

1 Introduction

1.1 Multimedia

The integration of digital representations of images, sound, designed objects and other data is known as *multimedia*. Multimedia objects such as interactive movies, educational courseware, and tours through virtual worlds, can be stored on magnetic and optical disks, and they can be transmitted over networks. Of particular importance in the creation and use of these documents or interactive objects are the methods by which the computer bits represent the sensory signals or component objects or the way in which one pattern of bits represents another. These methods are called *modeling*.

This paper divides modeling techniques into three categories and describes how techniques from one area may be reapplied to another.

1.2 Modeling

Let us divide modeling in multimedia into three broad types:

1. Representations of artificial objects being designed or explored. This kind of modeling is common in computer graphics, computer-aided design, animation, simulation of 3-D dynamical systems such as highway traffic flow, speech synthesis, and computer-generated music. Let us call this *synthetic modeling*.

2. Representations of objects in the real world, computed from sensor outputs. Such modeling includes highly compressed images from cameras,

parameters output by robot vision systems, coded speech, and results of neural network and other analyzers that are fed data from sensors. This sort of modeling is done in computer vision and speech understanding. In contrast to synthetic modeling, we can call this *natural modeling*, whether or not the objects being represented are from nature or are man-made.

3. Representations of computer-based documents for purposes other than that of the original document. This kind of modeling includes the creation of document signatures, index entries, content descriptions, representations for browsing, and the like. The documents being modeled may themselves be models of either the synthetic or natural sort. This document modeling we can call *derivative modeling*, in order to stress the distinction between the model of the document and the document itself, which may be a model.

In this paper, the emphasis is on issues related to natural modeling and derivative modeling. Modeling for computer-aided design is discussed relatively little. Natural modeling has been a concern of researchers in computer vision for over three decades. The computer vision community has explored a great variety of modeling techniques, and these can be found in the literature. Derivative modeling has begun to attract a lot of attention in the past two years, as a result of massive quantities of information becoming available world-wide on the Internet (see, for example, Greenhalgh[3]). Although derivative modeling techniques are not yet very well developed, the techniques from natural modeling show promise in contributing to a technology of derivative modeling.

Another dimension on which to examine the modeling process is the automatic/manual dimension. For purposes of discussion, let us identify three points (or perhaps better called fuzzy regions) on this axis:

1. fully manual model creation.

2. interactive model creation by a human using computer tools.

3. fully automatic model generation,

Most synthetic modeling is done largely by a human designer using relatively low-level computer tools, such as drawing tools, 3-D tools for constructive solid geometry, etc. In computer vision, most models are obtained from sensed images by fully automatic algorithms. In derivative modeling, both automatic and manual indexing techniques are common. Derivative modeling could benefit greatly from improved tools to permit interactive index construction and interactive content modeling.

This paper begins with an overview of a selected set of natural modeling techniques from computer vision. It then proceeds to discuss how they may be applied in derivative modeling. Needs for interactive tools are identified. Finally, applications of multimedia in education are discussed, and problems of content description (part of the derivative modeling challenge) are addressed.

2   Natural Modeling in Computer Vision

Natural modeling techniques are those that produce appropriate coded digital representations of sensory data such as scanned images, digitized sound, or 3-D data from laser rangefinders. A great variety of natural modeling techniques have been developed by computer vision researchers in their efforts to develop computers that "see" or that perform useful image analysis tasks such as factory inspection, microscope slide analysis of human cells, or conversion of architectural blueprints into computer-assisted-design geometry files.

In this section, we consider a few of these modeling techniques, beginning with the hierarchical representation of images. This highlights the issue of appropriate resolution, which is pervasive in modeling.

2.1   Image Representation

Images digitized by scanners, vidicon cameras, CCD cameras and the like are most commonly stored in the computer as two-dimensional arrays of numbers or of triples of numbers, each number representing a pixel brightness value, or each triple of numbers representing the values of the red, green, and blue components of a pixel. Implicit in such a representation are several modeling decisions: the vertical and horizontal resolution believed appropriate for the image as well as the gray-scale or color-scale resolution believed appropriate. The resolution selected is either a system default or is chosen so as to capture all or most of the essential information without wasting too much space or incurring unneccessarily lengthy computation times.

One breakthrough in image representation for computer vision which occurred between 1975 and 1985 was the development of *multiresolution* methods. The use of such methods makes the algorithm designer very conscious of the tradeoffs between accuracy on the one hand and time and space on the other. Multiresolution representations permit resolution for a particular processing step to be chosen dynamically during the run, rather than in advance, and the resolution used may be different at every step of the algorithm.

Two important methods of multiresolution image representation are exponential pyramids and wavelet expansions. An *exponential pyramid*, or "pyramid" is an image representation which includes a sequence of 2-dimensional images at increasing degrees of spatial resolution. It can be defined more formally as a mapping from a "hierarchical domain" to a range of pixel values. A *cell* is defined to be a vector of three integers: (k, i, j). Such a cell is said to be at level k, "row" i, and "column" j. Now, given a particular positive integer L, the *hierarchical domain* having $L + 1$ levels is the set of cells

$$\{(k, i, j) \text{ such that } 0 \leq k \leq L, \text{ and } 0 \leq i \leq 2^k - 1, \text{ and } 0 \leq j \leq 2^k - 1\}.$$

A *pyramid* is a function which maps a hierarchical domain to some range. For a range of $\{0, 1\}$, we say the function is a *binary pyramid* or a *bit pyramid*. Other ranges give us byte pyramids, word pyramids, color pyramids, feature pyramids, etc. Figure 1 illustrates a byte pyramid for a monochrome image.

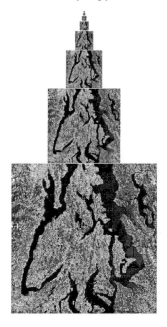

Figure 1: A byte pyramid for a monochrome image of Puget Sound. Image analysis algorithms may dynamically move among levels of resolution with such a representation.

Pyramids not only permit the use of an appropriate level of resolution in particular processing steps in image processing,[5] but they can facilitate progressive transmission of images and image browing with fast response. An interesting kind of pyramid use in computer vision is to provide an interconnection structure for a set of parallel processors. An architecture with such an interconnection scheme is called a "pyramid machine." A pyramid machine can perform many image processing operations very rapidly, and it can also offer the convenient application of pyramid data structures in algorithms. An example of such an algorithm is the "pyramidal Hough transform."[9]

Wavelet expansions permit an integration of space-domain, frequency-domain, and multiresolution techniques, and therefore they provide a wider variety of representations than exponential pyramids do. The fundamental concepts of wavelet representation are the use of a "wavelet basis" of component images and the expansion of a given image in that basis. The most popular wavelet basis for images is the Haar basis, which is the product of vertical and horizontal 1-D Haar bases. Wavelet expansions are typically used in image compression and texture analysis. Later, we describe the use of wavelets in an image query-by-contents systems.

2.2 *Shape*

Shape is the visual property that seems most important in human recognition of things — artists such as Picasso have been able to draw rather sparse contours with just the right curvature to create the unmistakable percept of a face in the mind of an observer. Two-dimensional shape modeling methods fall into categories such as boundary representations, grammatical methods, scalar features such as the convexity ratio, and Fourier transforms of boundary curves.

In addition to the issue of the effectiveness with which a particular shape method models the objects in an image, there is an important question of how databases of such features should be indexed. In the 3-D object recognition approach called "geometric hashing," a large index structure is constructed from a database of 3-D models in such a way that lots of partial clues in a new image to be recognized can be combined into a prioritization of the models in the database in terms of how they match the new image.[2]

2.3 *Texture*

Describing the microstructure of images has been something of a black art. The many techniques developed for texture analysis may have applications in indexing, too, and for that reason, we mention one of them. When K. Laws[7] designed his texture transformations that produced "texture energy" maps, he was to some extent anticipating the uses of wavelets to describe images. The 5×5 "Laws masks" he developed have wavelet-like characteristics. The more recent wavelet work puts texture analysis into the broader context of multiresolution image representation and gives designers more options for image modeling.

2.4   Series Expansions

The fundamental concept here comes from linear algebra, but it finds application in image representation, modeling, and compression. As have one-dimensional signals, images have been modeled as summations of periodic patterns, and they have been expanded in Fourier series, Hadamard transforms, and all manner of 2-D "vector space" bases. Wavelets, mentioned earlier, are generally used in collections that are bases for wavelet series expansions.

In the last five years, the Karhunen-Loève transformation has been rediscovered in the context of face image modeling. Kirby and Sirovich[6] and Pentland and his associates[8] have developed the concept of "eigenfaces" — particularly significant eigenvectors of the covariance matrix of a population of face images.

2.5   Relational Representations

While modeling of images with features and transforms can highlight certain information, modeling at a more symbolic level is needed in applications that must make logical inferences about the objects in images. At this "higher" level of modeling in computer vision, one finds representations that consist of entities and relationships among them. For example, an analysis of an image producing regions made up of pixels can also produce a graph structure that explicitly represents the adjacency relationships between pairs of regions. A sample is shown in Figure 2. If the regions (or the corresponding graph nodes) are interpreted semantically, then we have a symbolic representation of the image. Typically used for recognition, such symbolic descriptions may have potential use in information retrieval systems as well.

Computer vision modeling techniques such as those described above have mainly been used in recognition algorithms. They have the potential to be used now in information retrieval, as well. However, the challenges of derivative modeling are somewhat different from those of natual modeling, and these differences must be recognized as one goes about trying to apply the natural modeling techniques.

3   Challenges of Derivative Modeling

Whereas natural modeling produces computer representations of signals obtained by sensors of the outside world, the input to a derivative modeling process is not a natural signal but an artifact or document already represented inside the computer. The objective is to derive a new, possibly partial and incomplete representation of the artifact, so that information about the artifact

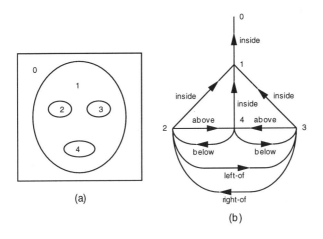

Figure 2: (a) Result of region analysis, and (b) relational representation.

can be used in new ways. Typical of such uses are document management, information retrieval, and browsing by humans or software agents.

3.1 Image Retrieval Problem

Of growing importance, because of the masses of multimedia data coming online with the World-Wide Web, are techniques for identifying and retrieving "appropriate" information objects on the Web. The Web is a complex and relatively unstructured information base jointly "administered" by tens or hundreds of thousands of people. Information placed on the Web for one purpose and one intended audience may be useful by them or by others for that or other purposes, if they can find it and evaluate it in a timely manner.

Information can be retrieved using two fundamentally different kinds of queries: semantic specifications (e.g., with SQL) and by content (using software that evaluates similarity of documents or parts of documents).

An interesting example of image retrieval by contents is the wavelet-based querying system of Jacobs et al[4]. In this system, a distributed database of images (consisting of a collection of World-Wide Web Uniform Resource Locators) is indexed by creating a table of "signatures." Each image has it signature computed by performing a Haar-basis wavelet expansion of the image in each of the Y, I, and Q color components, and then the 60 coefficients having greatest magnitude in each component are quantized to the binary scale $\{-1, +1\}$, and saved. Querying is done by taking a sketched image (or a scanned image) as the query, performing a similar transformation on the query image, and then matching the signature of the query against signatures in the index. A quasi-distance metric (an asymmetric measure of similarity) based on the number of matching wavelet coefficients is computed to assess the degree to which an indexed image agrees with the query.

This method has been tested with a distributed database of 20,000 images. It is able to rank the images in order of similarity to the query in a matter of milliseconds, and then display postage-stamp-sized representations of the top 20 images in another second or so. It was found that if the user is allowed to look at a postcard or other small representation of the image and to practice drawing queries for a few minutes, then the user can be quite effective in obtaining the desired image.

Interesting issues that have arisen in the development and testing of this system include the automatic determination of an appropriate set of weights with which to bias the contributions of the different wavelet coefficients. Jacobs and his collaborators found that low-frequency wavelet coefficients should be weighted more heavily than high-frequency coefficients in order for the matching function to best conform to the intentions of users. An issue for future research is the design of parameterizable matching functions that permit users to specify how their queries should be matched against database entries.

Another issue is the design of the index of signatures to permit rapid selection of the entries most closely matching the queries. Jacobs et al use one list of image identifiers for each color component and wavelet basis image that actually occurs with coefficient -1 in any of the database's signatures. There are also lists for images having $+1$ coefficients. The signature of the query image can then be rapidly compared to those in the database.

With the given signature and matching mechanisms, users must usually enter queries that are "correct" in certain respects, in order to retrieve specific images they desire. For example, the matching is relatively sensitive to color and to correct placement of gross visual transitions within the image frame. The matching is neither color invariant (although a monochrome matching mode is available which limits the signature comparisons to the intensity component of the Y-I-Q representation) nor translation invariant. Consequently, users need to learn how to use the system effectively through practice.

3.2 Databases for Computer Vision

Another group of derivative modeling issues comes up in the context of databases. Two kinds of issues here are: (1) how the database should be structured, and (2) what the user should see on the screen.

3.3 Indexing

An index helps users or software systems locate particular pieces of information by providing a list or other concise representatoin of a set of items, such that search is made easy for the user. Designing the entries or signatures of documents is one important derivative modeling issue. For academic papers, titles, abstracts or summaries provide good index entries. For images, content descriptions in natural language text or postage-stamp sized miniatures of the images may be good entries. For automatic retrieval of documents by software, various signature representations may be appropriate derivative models. While checksums are not much good for retrieval but good for verification of document integrity, more detailed signatures of documents may be useful. Selected components of transforms, limited content descriptions, and perhaps excerpts or reduced-resolution renditions may be appropriate.

In addition to containing the right information, an index must have it organized properly. Whereas alphabetical orderings are standard for textual indexes, image indexes typically do not have well-understood orderings, and multimedia databases will face even more complicated questions about index ordering. If an acceptable ordering is available, additional structuring of the index can provide performance gains during query processing. One such structuring takes advantage of the triangle inequality property for distance metrics[1].

Berman's work makes clear that not only should indexes be designed with particular distance functions or families of distance functions in mind, but the distance functions themselves should be carefully designed for the classes of retrieval problems for which they will be used.

3.4 Designing Distance Functions

If multimedia document signatures are themselves complex objects, then particular strategies for designing distance functions for them are needed. Signatures may often be regarded as vectors, each of whose components comes from a different kind of space. Distance functions can be designed as weighted sums of component distances[10]. If particular components are graphs, then we may use relational distances based on graph matching. Distance functions for "comparing apples and oranges" can also be intelligently designed in terms of path lengths in concept hierarchies.

In addition to the issues of how a distance function is made up of components of various sorts, an important issue is how users can be given tools to design their own distance functions for matching of multimedia objects. Key here is the design of interfaces to distance function design systems.

Another issue concerned with distance function design is symmetry versus asymmetry. A distance metric must satisfy a symmetry property: $d(x,y) = d(y,x)$. In query-by-content systems, distance functions are sometime intentionally asymmetric. This reflects a fundamental asymmetry in the relationship between query and database entry. In image query-by-content systems, queries are often constructed objects (synthetic models) and tend to be simple, lacking detail, because it would be too time-consuming for a user to specify unnecessary details just to pose the query. Asymmetry is also manifest in the nature of the retrieval process: a query must be general enough to catch any database entries in the subset of interest to the user; one query should be able to match many different potential targets. Wildcard constructs and variables are necessarily on the query side and not the database entry side. These differences between useful query functions and traditional metrics suggest the need for a definitive study of distance functions for query-by-content retrieval.

3.5 Content Description Languages

While natural modeling techniques can be adapted for derivative modeling and therefore assist in information retrieval of multimedia objects containing patterns similar to those in a query, query by content methods will be even more effective when content can be described accurately at a high linguistic level.

In the realm of educational multimedia, content description must be tied to curriculum structures and user models. The design of content description languages will be an important computer-science issue in the coming decade.

4 Derivative Modeling for Educational Multimedia

4.1 Motivation

As the World-Wide Web grows, lots of educational multimedia resources are coming online. Learners and educators will need good ways to access them and index them.

4.2 Modeling Educational Content

One method for derivative modeling of educational multimedia material is using domain models in the "curriculum network" family. Using an "educational progress net" or EPN, curriculum and multimedia document content can be modeled using a common form and set of conventions for meaning. An EPN consists of a set of nodes and a set of arcs. The nodes represent concepts or skills, and the arcs represent prerequisite relationships. The nodes and arcs are labeled with textual descriptions of the skills concepts or learning transitions that they represent. In the project "Mathematics Experiences Through Image Processing" at the University of Washington, EPNs are being used for content modeling in mathematics education.[11] An interactive tool called the Pixel Calculator supports the introduction of image processing ideas in an 8-th grade (14-year old student) context. The METIP Programming Environment extends this to a high-school/early-undergraduate level of mathematics and computing.

Developing accurate content descriptions currently requires a lot of manual work. However, as tools increase in functionality, and as experience with the content description language grows, we expect that more an more of the modeling process can be made interactive and eventually automated.

5 Summary

Modeling has been classified into three types: synthetic, natural, and derivative. Natural modeling techniques, which turn images and sounds into more appropriate or abstract patterns, have been developed to great sophistication in computer vision and speech understanding. However, they can be adapted for information retrieval and other derivative modeling applications, provided that these adaptations are well thought out and coordinated with solutions of problems in distance function design and index design. Query-by-content techniques will benefit greatly from natural modeling techniques, but their greatest promise can only be fulfilled provided content-description languages and tools are perfected.

Additional Information

More information about the application of image processing in education is available on the World-Wide Web at the following URL:
http://www.cs.washington.edu/research/metip/

Acknowledgements

Discussions with L. Shapiro and D. Johnson helped establish a context for some of the ideas described in this paper. The aforementioned research on learning mathematics via image processing has been supported in part by NSF Grant No. MDR-9155709.

References

1. A. Berman. A new data structure for fast approximate matching. Technical Report 94-03-02, Department of Computer Science and Engineering, University of Washington. Seattle WA. (1993).

2. O. Faugeras. *Three-Dimensional Computer Vision: A Geometric Viewpoint* (Cambridge, MA: MIT Press, 1993).

3. M. Greenhalgh, *Real-Time Imaging*,1, 33-47 (1995).

4. C. Jacobs, A. Finkelstein, and D. Salesin, *Proceedings of SIGGRAPH'95* (Los Angeles, CA, August 6-11, 1995).

5. J.-M. Jolion and A. Rosenfeld, *A Pyramid Framework for Early Vision* (Dordrecht, Netherlands: Kluwer Academic Publishers, 1994).

6. M. Kirby and L. Sirovich. *IEEE Trans. on Pattern Analysis and Machine Intelligence*, **12**, 103-108 (1990).

7. K.I. Laws. *Textured Image Segmentation*. Ph. D. dissertation, (Los Angeles, CA: University of Southern California, 1980).

8. A. Pentland, B. Moghaddam, and T. Starner. *Proceedings of the IEEE Conference on Computer Vision and Pattern Recognition*, 84-91 (Seattle, WA, June 21-23, 1995).

9. S.L. Tanimoto, *Proceedings of the IAPR Workshop on Computer Vision: Special Hardware and Industrial Applications*, 229-232 (Tokyo, Japan, October 12-14, 1988).

10. S.L. Tanimoto, *The Elements of Artificial Intelligence Using Common Lisp*, 2nd Ed. (New York: W.H. Freeman, 1995).

11. S.L. Tanimoto, *Proceedings of the 1995 IFIP World Conference on Computers in Education*, 805-814 (Birmingham, UK, July 23-28. London: Chapman & Hall, 1995).

VLNET: A NETWORKED MULTIMEDIA 3D ENVIRONMENT WITH VIRTUAL HUMANS

IGOR SUNDAY PANDZIC[1], TOLGA K. CAPIN[2],
NADIA MAGNENAT THALMANN[1], DANIEL THALMANN[2]

[1] *MIRALAB-CUI*
University of Geneva
24 rue de General-Dufour
CH1211 Geneva 4, Switzerland
{ipandzic,thalmann}@cui.unige.ch

[2] *Computer Graphics Laboratory*
Swiss Federal Institute of Technology
CH1015 Lausanne, Switzerland
{capin,thalmann}@lig.di.epfl.ch

ABSTRACT

Virtual environments define a new interface for networked multimedia applications. The sense of "presence" in the virtual environment is an important requirement for collaborative activities involving multiple remote users working with social interactions. Using virtual actors within the shared environment is a supporting tool for presence. In this paper, we present a shared virtual life network that supports collaboration of distant users by integrating virtual humans and different media.

Keywords: Multimedia, Virtual Life, Computer Animation, Networked Multimedia, Virtual Actors.

1. Introduction

Increasing hardware and network performance together with software technology make it possible to define more complex interfaces for networked multimedia applications. 3D virtual environments are increasingly popular tools as intuitive interfaces for these applications. In addition, a *networked* virtual environment can provide a natural shared environment, by supporting interactive human collaboration and integrating different media in real-time in a single 3D surrounding. It supports awareness of and interaction with other users; and it provides an appropriate mechanism for interaction with the environment by supporting visual mechanisms for data sharing and protection.

Research in networked virtual environments can be divided into two classes:

- To increase the performance of the system by providing faster simulation and display as well as decreasing network overhead,

- To provide a more realistic environment, in terms of visual representation of the environment, and by improving the interaction mechanisms through physical realism or behavioral realism.

Providing a behavioral realism is a significant requirement for systems that are based on human collaboration, such as Computer Supported Cooperative Work (CSCW) systems. Networked CSCW systems also require that the shared environments: support awareness of other users in the environment, provide mechanisms for different modes of interaction (synchronous vs. asynchronous, allowing to work in different times in the same environment), provide a comfortable interface for gestural communication, supply mechanisms for customized tools for data visualization, protection and sharing. An interface designed for cooperative work should take these requirements into account.

Virtual environments can provide a powerful mechanism for networked CSCW systems, by their nature of emphasizing the *presence* of users in the virtual world. This can be accomplished through the support of:

- representing the users and special-purpose service programs by 3D actors in the virtual environment,

- mechanisms for the users to interact with each other in the natural interface via facial interaction and body gestures of their virtual actors,

- mechanisms for the users to interact with the rest of the virtual environment through complex and realistic behaviors such as walking and grasping,

- user-customized tools for editing grasped objects, depending on the object type (e.g. images, free-form surfaces).

There has been an increasing interest in the area of networked virtual environments recently [5,6,13,17]. These systems discuss the task issues, and less work has been done on supporting the immersive properties [10,16], including the users' sense of presence in the shared environment through representation of the whole body and gestural communication with other users or autonomous actors. The aim of *VLNET (Virtual Life Network)* is to provide a networked 3D environment that provides mechanisms for increasing collaboration among distant partners by supporting the sense of presence, and integrating different media and virtual humans in the same virtual world.

The paper starts with the properties of the system: the environment, methods for modeling and animation of virtual actors in this environment, facial interaction support, communication model and further improvements using autonomous actors. Then we discuss the implementation aspects of the system and list current applications in use. Finally, we present our concluding remarks and expectations for future improvements.

2. Properties of the System

The VLNET system provides a networked shared virtual environment that allows multiple users to interact with each other and their surrounding in real time. The users are represented by 3D virtual human actors with realistic appearances and articulations, with similar movements to their actual bodies.

In addition to user-guided actors, the environment can also be extended to include autonomous human actors which can be used as a friendly user interface to different services such as navigation. Virtual humans can also be used in order to represent the currently unavailable partners, allowing asynchronous cooperation between distant partners.

The environment incorporates different media: sound, 3D models, facial interaction among the users, images represented by textures mapped on 3D objects, and real-time movies. Instead of having different windows or applications for each medium, the environment integrates all information in a single 3D surrounding, with a similar view of the actual world.

2.1. The Environment

The objects in the environment are classified into two groups: fixed (e.g. walls) or free (e.g. a chair). Only the free objects can be picked, moved and edited. This allows faster computations in database traversal for picking. In addition to the virtual actors representing users, the types of objects can be: 3D models of objects, image texture-mapped polygons representing documents in the virtual world, etc. Figure 1 shows a general view of an example environment. Once a user picks an object, she can reposition or edit the object. Each type of object has a user-customized program corresponding to the type of object, and this program is spawned when the user picks and requests to edit the object.

2.2. Virtual Actors

In the environment, each participant is represented by a 3D virtual body that resembles the user. Each user sees the virtual environment through the eyes of her body. The user controls the movement of her virtual actor by various input devices, such as spaceball, mouse. Stereo display devices such as shutter glasses and head-mounted displays can also be used for more immersive virtual worlds.

It is not desirable to see solid-looking floating virtual actors in the environment; the actors should have realistic appearance and motion. There are numerous methods for controlling motion of synthetic actors. A motion control method specifies how the actor is animated and can be classified according to the type of information it privileged in animating the synthetic actor. The nature of the privileged information for the motion control of actors falls into three categories:

- The first approach corresponds to methods heavily relied upon by the animator: rotoscopy, shape transformation, keyframe animation. Synthetic actors are *locally controlled* by the input of geometrical data for the motion.

- The second way is based on the methods of kinematics and dynamics. The input is the data corresponding to the complete definition of motion, in terms of forces, torques, constraints. The task of the animation system is to obtain the trajectories and velocities by solving equations of motions. Therefore, one can say that the actor's motions are *globally controlled.*

- The third type of animation is called *behavioral animation* and takes into account the relationship between each object and the other objects. The control of animation can also be performed at task-level, but one may also consider the actor as an autonomous creature. The motion of the actor is controlled by providing high-level directives indicating a specific behavior without any other stimulus.

Each category can be used for guiding virtual actors in the virtual environment, however it is important to provide appropriate interfaces for controlling all motions. No method alone is convenient to provide, only by itself, a comfortable interface to accomplish all the motions; therefore it is necessary to combine various techniques for different tasks.

For the current implementation, we use local methods for the users to guide their virtual actors for navigating in the virtual environment and picking objects using various input devices; and behavioral animation for realistic appearance based on these inputs and the behavioral parameters, such as walking for navigation and grasping for picking. This set of behaviors can easily be extended, however these behaviors are sufficient to perform everyday activities, providing minimum set of behaviors to interact with the environment.

The walking motion is used for navigation, guided by the user interactively or automatically generated by a trajectory for autonomous actors. This model is based on the Humanoid walking model [1], and includes kinematical personification depending on the individuality of the user [2]. The participant uses the input devices to update the transformation of the virtual actor's eye position. This incremental change in position is used by a *walking motor* to update the joint values of the virtual body. The joint values for the knees, arms, and the body are updated, using the individual parameters of the user as well as the biomechanical experimental data for real walking [1].

For the grasping motion, we apply the inverse kinematics within the right arm of the virtual actor. The participant uses the input devices, such as spaceball or dataglove, to update the position and orientation of the actor's right hand. Based on this input, the posture of the right arm is computed within the joint limit constraints, for realistic appearance. Although there are multiple ways for final posture of right arm, the grasping motor considers the normal posture of grasping. It would be

Fig. 1. The environment integrates different media in a single stream

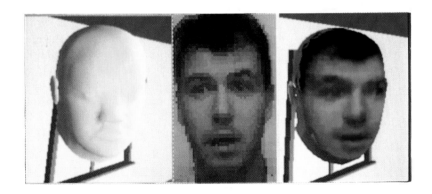

Fig. 2. Mapping of face image on virtual face

possible to apply a physically correct method for arm movement, however our concern is more on the visual appearance of the grasping motion.

2.3. Facial Gestures

Face is one of the main streams of interaction among humans for representing intentions, thoughts and feelings; hence including facial expressions in the shared virtual environment is almost a requirement for efficient interaction. In addition, face becomes an important factor for differentiating other participants naturally in multi-user environments. Although it is also possible to utilize a videoconferencing tool among the users in a separate window, it is more appropriate to display the facial gestures of the users in the face of their 3D virtual actors in order to provide a better interaction among participants.

We include the facial interaction by texture mapping the user's face image on the virtual actor's head. To obtain this, the subset of the image that contains the user's face is selected from the captured image and is sent to other users. To capture this subset of image, we apply the following method: initially the background image is stored without the user. Then, during the session, video stream images are analyzed, and the difference between the background image and the current image is used to determine the bounding box of the face in the image. This part of the image is compressed using the SGI Compression Library MVC1 compression algorithm. Finally, the image is sent to the other users after compression. There is a possibility to send uncompressed gray-scale images instead of using compression, which is useful if the used machines are not powerful enough to perform compression and decompression without a significant overhead. However, with all the machines we used this was not necessary. If this option is used, the compression can be turned on/off on the sending side, and the receiving side recognizes automatically the type of images coming.

At the receiving side, an additional service program is run continuously in addition to the VLNET program: it continuously accepts the next images for the users and puts to the shared memory. The VLNET program obtains the images from this shared memory for texture mapping. In this way, communication and simulation tasks are decoupled, decreasing the overhead by waiting for communication.

Currently, we are using the simplified object for representing the head of users' virtual actors (Figure 2). This is due to the fact that the complex virtual actor face requires additional task of topologically adjusting the texture image to the face of the virtual actor, to match the parts of the face.

2.4. Communication Architecture

We exploit a distributed model of communication, therefore each user is responsible for updating its local set of data for the rendering and animation of the objects.

There is always one user that determines the environment. The other users are "invited" and do not need to specify any parameters, all the data is initially loaded over the network to the local machine when the user is connected to the shared environment. There exists one server responsible for transmitting the actions to the participants.

The communication is asynchronous. The information about the users' actions are transmitted to the server as the actions occur. The actions can be changing position or orientation of the actors, joint changes in the virtual bodies, as well as grasping or releasing an object. The actions are sent to the other users by the server in terms of new orientations of the updated objects in space, or other possible changes such as modification to the objects.

Note that the architecture requires the broadcasting of the data from the server to all the users in the system. This can create a bottleneck if there are a lot of users in the environment. To overcome this problem, we plan to exploit a communication mechanism that makes use of the geometric coherence of interactions among the virtual actors in the three-dimensional environment. This solution is based on the aura and nimbus concepts, proposed by Fahlen and Stahl [4] in order to emphasize the awareness among the entities in the virtual environment. *Aura* (possibly, but not necessarily, of a sphere or a cylinder shape) refers to the subspace where an object has potential to interact with others. In order for two objects to interact, their auras should intersect. Furthermore, if the auras intersect, then a test whether the *focus* (possibly a frustum) of the first object intersects with the *nimbus* (possibly of sphere shape) of the second object. Focus represents the subspace where the object draws its attention. Nimbus refers to the space where the object makes an aspect of itself available to other users. If the focus of the first user intersects with the nimbus of the second object, then it is assumed that the user is attracted to the object.

We make use of the aura and nimbus concepts as follows: When the data is to be sent from a server to a participant, the sending program tests if the nimbus of the sending user intersects with the focus of the receiving user's virtual actor. The intersection means that the actors are near to each other, therefore the server sends the change to the receiving user. If there is no intersection with one other actor's focus, it can be assumed that the actor is too far and does not need the extensive knowledge of the source user, therefore the change is not sent every time step. However, for consistency, it is necessary to send the local position data every k frames. The k value could be computed using the distance between the two actors, however we assume a constant k for the initial implementation.

2.5. *Autonomous Virtual Actors*

It is also possible to include additional virtual autonomous actors in the environment, which represent a service or a program, such as guiding in the navigation. As these virtual actors are not guided by the users, they should have sufficient behaviors to act autonomously to accomplish their tasks. This requires building behaviors for motion, as well as appropriate mechanisms for interaction.

Animation of autonomous actors is an active area of research [15]. A typical behavioral animation system consists of three key components:

- locomotor system,

- the perceptual system,

- the organism system.

The perceptual system should be improved through the synthetic vision [9] for percepting the whole world, and appropriate mechanisms for interaction. Interaction with the virtual actors is also an active research area, and this should take into account multi-modal properties for communication.

3. Implementation Issues

For the virtual environment to be realistic, it should be fast enough for providing feedback in real-time; otherwise it is not comfortable to use. Therefore, we currently make use of the state-of-the-art technology discussed below to achieve currently utmost performance, but it is widely accepted that these platforms will be popular in a few years' time. There are three ways for speeding-up the system performance: display, communication, simulation.

For fast display, we make use of the IRIS Performer environment. Performer provides an easy-to-use environment to develop real-time graphics applications. It can extract the maximum performance of the graphics subsystem, and can utilize multiple processors in the workstation for graphics operations. Therefore, it is an appropriate platform to increase the performance of display part of the system. In addition, it provides efficient mechanisms for collision detection, and supports a variety of popular file types.

The network overhead can also have a significant effect, especially with increasing number of users. Therefore, it is important to provide low-latency high-throughput connections. The ATM network is one of the most promising solutions to the network problem, therefore we are experimenting our system over the ATM pilot network, provided to the Swiss Federal Institute of Technology and University of Geneva, by

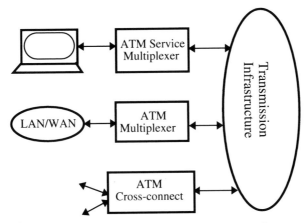

Fig. 3. Network Topology, ATM Overlay Network

Swiss Telecom (Figure 3). The ATM technology, based on packet switching using fixed-length 53-byte cells, allows to utilize videoconferencing, video-on-demand, broadcast video. The quality of service is achieved on demand, and guarantees a constant performance. The network has full logical connectivity at the virtual path level and initially supports PDH 34 Mbit/s and SDH 155 Mbit/s links. The pilot provides point to point links in the first phase. Multipoint links are supposed to be added in the future, allowing more efficient multiple-user virtual environments. In addition, distributed virtual reality interface will allow to investigate new opportunities for different traffic and Quality of Service requirements.

In addition to the display and network parts, the simulation part should also be performed efficiently using appropriate mechanisms. As discussed before, we make use of the HUMANOID system for modeling and real-time animation of virtual actors. The HUMANOID environment supports the following facilities:

- real-time manipulation of virtual actors on a standard graphics workstation,

- a way of accelerating the calculations using a dedicated parallel machine or by distributing the calculation load on several workstations,

- a flexible design and management of multiple humanoid entities,

- skin deformation of a human body, including the hands and the face,

- a multi-layer facial animation module,

- collision detection and correction between multiple humanoid entities,

- several motion generators and their blending: keyframing, inverse kinematics, dynamics, walking and grasping.

4. Applications

As already discussed, VLNET is a general-purpose system. As various widely-used file formats are supported, it is easy to create a shared environment consisting of already developed models with other computer modeling programs, such as AutoCad, Inventor, etc. In this section, we present some experimental applications currently available with our system (Figure 4):

- Teleshopping: The VLNET system is currently used by Chopard Watches, Inc., Geneva to collaboratively view and interact with the computer-generated models of the recently-designed watches with the remote customers and colleagues in Singapore, and Geneva. The models had already been developed using Auto-Desk program, and these were easily included in the virtual environment, with the help of 3DS (3D Studio) reader for Performer.

- Business: Experiments are continuing for building a virtual room involving distant users to be able to have a meeting, with the aid of images and movies to be able to discuss and analyze the results.

- Entertainment: The VLNET environment is also used for playing chess between various distant partners; and puzzle solving by two users. These models have been created using the IRIS Inventor system.

- Interior design: Currently experiments are continuing on furniture design by s customer and the sales representative to build a virtual house. The model has been created using the WaveFront package.

5. Conclusions and Future Work

In this paper, we have presented a system which provides an efficient and visually effective way for human collaboration. Currently, the system implementation is under progress, and when completed, it will provide a satisfactory virtual environment for interactive cooperation. We believe that integrating virtual humans and different media in a single virtual environment provides a feeling of presence of users.

Further improvements are to include physical models for interaction, more visual realism by integrating already-developed body deformations module, natural language interface with the virtual actors, sound rendering. These new properties will require

Fig. 4. Applications of the VLNET Environment

powerful processors. We also intend to integrate VLNET to the framework of dVS and DIVE to be able to support more platforms.

6. Acknowledgements

The research is partly supported by ESPRIT project HUMANOID (P 6079), Swiss National Foundation for Scientific Research, Silicon Graphics, the Federal Office of Education and Science, and the Department of Economy of the State of Geneva. We would like to thank Riccardo Camiciottoli for his 3D Studio driver for Performer, and the assistants of LIG and MIRALAB for their collaboration in models and libraries.

7. References

1. R. Boulic, T. K. Capin, Z. Huang, P. Kalra, B. Lintermann, N. Magnenat-Thalmann, L. Moccozet, T. Molet, I. S. Pandzic, K. Saar, A. Schmitt, J. Shen, D. Thalmann, *The Humanoid Environment for Interactive Animation of Multiple Deformable Human Characters*, Proceedings of Eurographics '95, 1995.

2. R. Boulic, N. Magnenat-Thalmann, D. Thalmann *A Global Human Walking Model with Real Time Kinematic Personification*, The Visual Computer, **6(6)**,1990.

3. j. Cassell, C. Pelachaud , N. Badler, M. Steedman, B. Achorn, T. Becket, B. Douville, S. Prevost, M. Stone, *Animated Conversation: Rule-Based Generation of Facial Expression Gesture and Spoken Interaction for Multiple Conversational Agents*, Proceedings of SIGGRAPH'94, 1994.

4. L. E. Fahlen, O. Stahl, *Distributed Virtual Realities as Vehicles for Collaboration*, Proceedings of Imagina '94, 1994.

5. M. A. Gisi, C. Sacchi, *Co-CAD: A Collaborative Mechanical CAD System*, Presence: Teleoperators and Virtual Environments, **3(4)**, 1994.

6. M. R. Macedonia, M. J. Zyda, D. R. Pratt, P. T. Barham, Zestwitz, *NPSNET: A Network Software Architecture for Large-Scale Virtual Environments*, Presence: Teleoperators and Virtual Environments, **3(4)**, 1994.

7. N. Magnenat-Thalmann, *Tailoring Clothes for Virtual Actors*, Interacting with Virtual Environments, MacDonald L., Vince J. (Ed), 1994.

8. I. S. Pandzic, P. Kalra, N. Magnenat-Thalmann, Thalmann D., *Real-Time Facial Interaction*, Displays, **15(3)**, 1994.

9. O. Renault, N. Magnenat-Thalmann, D. Thalmann, *A Vision-based Approach to Behavioral Animation*, The Journal of Visualization and Computer Animation, **1(1)**, 1990.

10. C. Rich, R. C. Waters, C. Strohecker, Y. Schabes, W. T. Freeman, M. C. Torrance, A. R. Golding, M. Roth, *Demonstration of an Interactive Multimedia Environment*, IEEE Computer, **27(12)**, 1994.

11. J. Rohlf, J. Helman, *IRIS Performer: A High Performance Multiprocessing Toolkit for Real-Time 3D Graphics*, Proceedings of SIGGRAPH'94, 1994.

12. M. Slater, M. Usoh, R. Geeas, A. Steed *Creating Animations Using Virtual Reality ThatcherWorld: A Case Study*, Proceedings of Computer Animation 95, 1995.

13. S. Stansfield, *A Distributed Virtual Reality Simulation System for Simulational Training*, Presence: Teleoperators and Virtual Environments, **3(4)**, 1994.

14. Swiss Telecom, *ATM Pilot Services and User Interfaces*, Swiss Telecom, 1993.

15. D. Thalmann, *Automatic Control and Behavior of Virtual Actors*, Interacting with Virtual Environments, MacDonald L., Vince J. (Ed), 1994.

16. D. Travis, T. Watson, M. Atyeo, *Human Psychology in Virtual Environments*, Interacting with Virtual Environments, MacDonald L., Vince J. (Ed), 1994.

17. D. Zeltzer, M. Johnson, *Virtual Actors and Virtual Environments*, Interacting with Virtual Environments, MacDonald L., Vince J. (Ed), 1994.

Chapter 2

Modeling Multimedia Systems and Standards

DESIGN OF MULTIMEDIA PROTOCOLS
BASED ON
MULTIMEDIA MODELS

Michel DIAZ

LAAS du CNRS
7, avenue du Colonel Roche
31077 TOULOUSE Cedex - FRANCE
diaz@laas.fr

ABSTRACT

This paper presents a multilevel methodology for the design of distributed multimedia systems. The corresponding approach is based on the use of an adequate model at both layers, the application layer and the communication layer.

Although more complex solutions could be selected, the model given here is based on an extension of time Petri nets. It allows the application users to easily describe the behaviours of multimedia information and their synchronisation constraints.

After presenting the model, it is shown how it can be used to define and design the most adequate protocols needed to be implemented to transfer general multimedia objects. How the corresponding protocols can be handled is given by defining a generic and application dependent multimedia connection for transferring data between remote communicating processes. This connection, called a Partial Order connection, is a multimedia extension of usual Connection Oriented and ConnectionLess concepts. Furthermore, located at the Transport layer, it defines a new architecture for multimedia distributed systems.

Index terms:

Distributed multimedia systems, Time, Timed Petri Nets, Specification, Modelling, Multimedia Information and objects, Synchronisation, Multimedia protocols, Partial order connections

I. INTRODUCTION

A design methodology developed in the CESAME project [1] for designing distributed multimedia systems is given in this paper. It presents how the global architecture is based on the use of a formal model, an extension of time Petri nets, as this model allows the users to easily describe multimedia information.

After presenting the model, it is then shown how this model can be used to define and implement the most adequate protocols needed to transfer general multimedia objects. How the corresponding protocols can be handled is given by defining a generic and application dependent transfer connection between remote communicating processes. This connection, called a Partial Order connection (POC), is a multimedia extension of the usual Connection Oriented and ConnectionLess concepts and protocols. It is located at the Transport layer and leads to the definition of a new architecture for multimedia distributed systems.

In multimedia systems, flows of data, voice and video images need to be synchronised. For instance, audio and video streams must jointly fulfil isosynchrony and maximum jitters. While designing multimedia applications for isolated computers or systems is a rather simple task, it appears that building distributed multimedia architectures is much more complex. This is because the multimedia synchronisation requirements of the objects, needed at the sending and the receiving sites, must be enforced in spite of the transfers through the (set of) network (s).

The basic design assumption of the approach presented here is as follows : in order to be able to receive and reassemble complex multimedia objects, the receiving entity must be aware of a model representing the synchronisation constraints that characterise the (sent and received) multimedia objects.

Of course, such an assumption requires the selection of an adequate model. This paper first presents in Section II how Petri Nets have been extended to represent multimedia objects, how they handle streams and capture the basic synchronisation constraints of multimedia and hypermedia objects. As they are powerful and well understood by users, Time Petri nets [3] (TPNs) have been extended to express the specificity of media-based objects. Object Composition Petri Nets [10] (OCPNs), Time Stream Petri Nets [13] (TSPNs) for multimedia objects and Hierarchical TSPNs [16] (HTSPNs) for hypermedia objects have been proposed to precisely model these complex behaviours. Their common Petri net basis will be used as the starting point of the methodology presented here. Formal models have been shown of interest for designing existing protocols [17] . Of course, other models, in particular Estelle [18,20] and LOTOS [19] with some adequate time extension [21] could have been used, but as it will be seen later on, these Petri net extensions first capture at the user level the needed constraints and second can easily provide communication parameters for implementing adequate communication protocols.

Section III then presents how such models can be used for protocols. Current protocols use either connectionless (CL) or connection-oriented (CO) approaches. A new concept, a Partial Order Connection (POC), has been defined. It will be seen that CL and CO approaches are two specific cases of the much more general POC concept presented here. More precisely, a POC is an end-to-end connection that provides a partial order service where the objects can be delivered to the users in a order different from the sending order. How this new concept has emerged and a definition of reliable and unreliable POCs have been given. It will be finally shown how such a generalised connection, a multimedia transport connection, can be defined and how multimedia objects can be handled in an integrated way. This leads to the definition of a new sophisticated multimedia architecture for multimedia distributed systems.

II. THE EXTENDED PETRI NET MODELS

II-1- Time Petri nets

The first two Petri net based models that include explicit values of time are Time Petri Nets [2,3] and Timed Petri Nets [4,5].

Timed Petri Nets [4] are derived from Petri Nets by associating one firing duration with each transition of the net. An equivalent model is obtained by adding one time value to the places [5], where this value indicates the time the tokens have to stay in their corresponding places before being able to be removed by a firing.

Time Petri Nets (TPNs), more general than Timed Petri nets, have been proven quite convenient for defining [3] and verifying [6,7] temporal constraints. Time Petri Nets are Petri nets where two values of time, (t^{min}, t^{max}), are associated with transitions. Assuming that transition t is being continuously enabled,

t^{min} is the minimal time that must elapse, starting from the time at which transition t is enabled, until t can fire,

and t^{max} is the maximum time during which transition t can be enabled without being fired.

Times t^{min} and t^{max} are values relative to the moment at which transition t is enabled. If t has been enabled at time T , then t, even if it is continuously enabled, cannot fire before time $T+t^{min}$ and must fire before or at the latest at time $T+t^{max}$, unless it is disabled earlier by the firing of another transition.

This model can of course define imperfect timings because the firing may occur inside a given interval (that can be (0, infinity) at the maximum as it is the case for usual untimed Place-Transition Petri nets).

The semantics of TPNs are given in [6,7] which also present a formal way of analysing them. In this approach the state of a TPN is a pair S = (M,I) where M is a marking and I is a set of inequalities.

II-2- The OCPN model

A structured Petri net model associating a time value to each of its places, called OCPN, has been proposed [9,10] for multimedia objects : this model allows the users to describe the timed synchronisation of multimedia objects. It uses a set of seven primitives that are sufficient to characterise all possible temporal relative positions of two intervals [8], and these primitives define composition rules usable to build complex models by composing simple ones.

Based on these constructs, timed place Petri nets can represent any temporal relationship between two intervals. OCPNs are obtained by composing in a serial-parallel way timed place Petri nets using these seven temporal constructs. OCPNs represent an ideal behaviour of multimedia objects.

Let us first consider the untimed Petri nets related to OCPNs. For this, Figure 1-a presents an application having a set of multimedia windows. The multimedia object, to be eventually transmitted as considered in this paper, consists of sub-media, these sub-media being numbered from 1 to 1004, where 1 represents a logo, 2 and 3 still pictures, 4 a text and 5 to 1004 two video sequences. The simple Petri net representing this object is given in Figure 1-b. It can be seen that a relationship appears between the windows and the parallel flows of the Petri nets. Time values can be associated to places. If the video rate is 25 frames/s, then the total presentation time is 20 s for the 500 video frames. Then the other non video places should also receive a time of 20 s, while the video places must last 40 ms. Note that a presentation starts for its given corresponding duration as soon as the corresponding place is marked, i.e. the window appears on the display for its duration when the place receives a token.

38

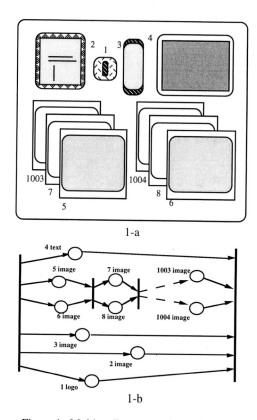

1-a

1-b

Figure 1 : Multimedia presentation and model

II-3- The TSPN and HTSPN models

In TPNs time is local to transitions as the (implicit) timer of a transition starts only when the transition is enabled, i.e. when all its input places have received a token. This is too strong for multimedia systems where timers have been associated to places in OCPNs for complete locality.

Time Stream Petri Nets [11,12,13] (TSPNs) , also using the composition primitives of OCPNs extend OCPNs first by using intervals (t^{min} , t^{max}) enriching the previous nominal values, these three values being associated to arcs and not to places, and, second, by defining a sophisticated firing type for each transition of the net.

In such a model :
- a place represents the processing of a multimedia object and its display to the user during the interval of time (t^{min} , t^{max}),
- an arc gives its timing constraints related to its couple (ingoing place, output transition), indicating the minimal, nominal and maximal duration of the corresponding presentation of the multimedia object, the firing date being related to the synchronisation of its outgoing

transition,
- a transition represents the synchronisation of all its input flows, each of them being represented by one input arc.

Note that, as an extension of TPNs, when a token is received by a place at time T, it remains in the place during an amount of time defined by one value inside the couple (t^{min}, t^{max}). This amount is dependent on the outgoing arcs of the places and on the firing conditions of the transitions related to these arcs. So the firing of a transition is defined by the couples of all arcs entering it, and during the timed dynamic behaviour of the net, depends on these couples and on the time T at which the places receive the tokens.

As it follows that some mismatches between all the arcs firing conditions may occur, TSPNs enforce the continuity of the multimedia objects by defining a firing type for each transition, inside a set of nine possibilities :
{ AND, WEAK-AND, STRONG-OR, OR, MASTER, AND-MASTER, WEAK-MASTER, STRONG-MASTER, AND-MASTER }.
These rules allow the specifier to make precise if the firing of the transition, i.e. the flow synchronisation, is controlled by the first, the last or the master flow.

The previous model has then being extended for handling hypermedia documents, leading to the HierarchicalTSPN model [14,15,16].
As a consequence, the HTSPN model includes :
    - the possibility of defining hyper links for defining and expressing link navigations, as in hypertexts,
    - to represent the hierarchy of different layers of synchronisation, where three layers seem now necessary, the atomic, composite and link synchronisation layers,
    - to keep (the interests of) the TSPN models in composite places, including the representation and handling of hierarchical, link related timing constraints.
    Finally this model has been extended by typing the places to represent the real data constituting the hypermedia objects.

Using hierarchical -composite- places is of importance, as a composite place can represent a TSPN. So a link, represented by a link place, can for instance be synchronised with one composite place, this composite place being equivalent and representing a TSPN : this is simply done by having these two places as inputs of the same transition.
Such a link can be used for instance to force the firing of this common transition : this firing can stop the presentation of this TSPN and start another different one by marking another (composite) place.
It can be understood that in such a case the global presentation, as seen by the user, will be composed of two sub-presentations, the first one being the one before the action of the link, and the second one being the one that runs after the action of the link.

    Let us now consider how these models can be related to a set of adequate protocols for the interactive remote access to complex multimedia or hypermedia objects.

III. PARTIAL ORDER PROTOCOLS FOR MULTIMEDIA OBJECTS

Of course, in the general case, the multimedia objects and their presentations must be transferred from the server site to the remote interactive site by using protocols. Usual data transfer protocols use either connectionless (CL) or connection-oriented (CO) paradigms. A new concept, a Partial Order Connection (POC), has been proposed : a POC concept provides a conceptual link between present connectionless and connection-oriented protocols. Connectionless and connection-oriented protocols appears to be two extreme specific cases of this new concept.

There exists strong time requirements related to multimedia systems [22,24,26,28] and as a consequence high speed multimedia protocols are needed and have to be implemented [23,25,27]. Partial orders have been used in different contexts [30,31,32] but never to design protocols and to build distributed architectures.

A POC [33,34,35,36] is an end-to-end connection where the sent information, the messages, can be delivered to a receiving entity in a order that is different from their sending order. The difference between the sequential sending and the different possible sequential receptions define the selected partial order. In particular, these different possible receptions lead to transfer speed-up and resources savings at both sending and receiving sides.

III-1- From CL and CO connections to POCs

In CL datagram services, as UDP, the sent protocol data units (PDUs) are not related to each other and errors are not recovered. CO protocols, as TCP, enforce a reliable delivery of protocol data units based on a sequential numbering of the PDUs. It has been proposed to classify CL and CO protocols as follows [36] :

a) CL protocols provide their users with :
    no reliability and no order, as PDUs are independent.
b) CO protocols provide their users with :
    a total reliability, as lost, out-of sequence or duplicated PDUs are detected and recovered, and a total order as PDUs are delivered in sequence to the receiving user entity, in accordance with the sequential sending order.

It follows that protocols can be classified, Figure 2-a according to two axes :
    - one reliability axis, R, graduated from no to full reliability,
    - one order axis, O, graduated from no to total order.
CO protocols, having $O=1$ and $R=1$, define one point at the upper right corner, and CL protocols, having $O=0$ and $R=0$, define one point at the lower left corner (2-b). It may be noticed that a complete set, the indicated surface, of protocols appears (2-c).

It is easy to understand the reliability axis as a given reliability corresponds to more or less losses of protocol data units. As multimedia objects as video sequences can tolerate losses, i.e. a few images can be lost without deteriorating the presentation, the different reliability possibilities, depending on the number of images those loss is accepted, follow.

What is more difficult to understand is the meaning and the importance of the order axis. To do so, let us consider the upper segment R-POC on Figure 2-d, where reliability is always equal to 1, but where order can vary from no order to total order.
If this segment has a meaning, then a partial order will be useful. Let us now consider Figure 1-b, i. e. the Petri net representing the multimedia object. Then, as we are looking for it, it appears that this model represent a partial order between the places, i.e. between the pieces of information to be sent. As a consequence, the partial order of the multimedia object can be used to implement a partial order multimedia protocol directly related to this object.
This shows the interest of defining multimedia partial order protocols, as these protocols can be directly connected to the objects that are to be transmitted through the network.

Let us now show the interest of these defined partial orders. For this it is needed to consider now together Order and Reliability.
To characterize more precisely the concept of a POC, let us further discuss order through the example of Figure 1. On the sender side, as the PDUs will be sent sequentially, they should

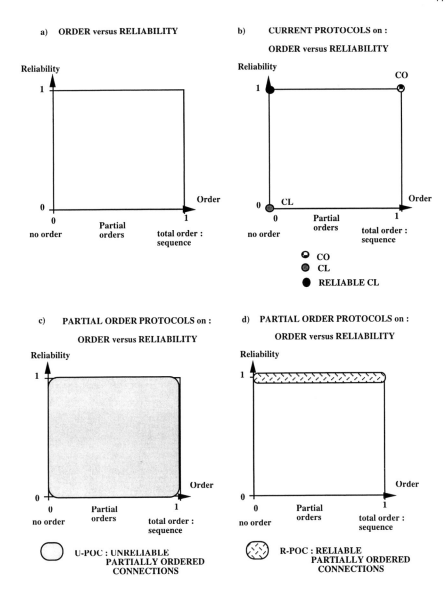

Figure 2 : Order, Reliability and Connections

be transmitted using the obvious sequence : 1; 2; 3;... etc... Let us suppose now that the first PDU, number 1, is lost. So, if a reliable delivery is needed then retransmission has to occur. Then, usually, the following PDUs are not saved and all the sequence has to be retransmitted, which increases the needed bandwidth and delay of the network.

Note that those constraints become more important when the transfer speed increases and the delay decreases, which is the case for high speed protocols.

Let us now consider the Petri net of Figure 1 where it appears that sub-media 1, 2, 3, 4, 5, 6 are not tightly related : for instance, as 1 and 2 are in parallel, as shown by the Petri net, they can be received and displayed in any order : 1 before 2 or 2 before 1, without any consequence for the presentation to the user.

Let us assume that PDUs are equal to Service Data Units (SDUs) for simplicity. Now if the receiving protocol is able to understand that PDUs 2 and 3 are independent, then it knows that these two PDUs can be made available to its service user in any order, and in case of lost of PDU 1, then PDU 2 can be delivered to the user instead of being received again later.

This is precisely what partial order protocols do. It follows that the partial order reduces the dedicated amount of memory buffers and furthermore gives a better delay to the user.

As a consequence, it appears that multimedia applications, consisting of texts, images, sounds and video, do require partial order services and that these partial orders can be used to improve the performance of the communication software. Note that partial order protocols also give to the application software a way of defining its constraints in terms of application dependent transfer parameters, here reliability and order.

It has been proposed to characterize [35,36] by the set of the linear extensions of a partial order, the difficulty inherent to implement this partial order by a network. This is because the linear extensions of the partial order are a set of sequences that can be accepted by the receiving entities and users : the more sequences the user can accept, the simpler it will be to implement the corresponding software.

This is because, for an unordered service consisting of n PDUs, there are n! possible delivery orderings that satisfy the service as any order can be accepted by the receiving service user. On the other hand, a sequential total ordering means that only one delivery order, the same as the one that has been used by the sender, can be accepted by the receiving user, and for any other received orderings the sending and receiving entities will have to take time and resource consuming appropriate actions.

As the number of those acceptable delivery orderings is the number of linear extensions of the partial order, it is proposed to use it as a characterization of the facility to actually implement the connection : the larger the number of linear extensions is, the easier it is to design the network.

Structured solutions for calculating the number of linear extensions and associated metrics are given in [35,36].

III-2- Establishing a POC

Implementing a POC first means to make the partial order known to the communicating entities. The POCs and the corresponding POC protocols have been located in the Transport layer. Then any partial order transfer needs in the general case to establish a connection. This follows from the fact that the receiving entity must be aware of the partial order (of the model) and the transmitted messages must follow an end-to-end basis.

To use the most adequate partial order connection, it is proposed to transmit the user defined partial order, i.e. in this case the Petri net, to the transport entity. This partial order will be used, when establishing the PO connection, by sending it to the remote receiving entity. The sending transport entity opens one connection with the remote transport entity and, during the establishment of the connection its sends as a connection parameter, the partial order, coding it in the best way, for instance as a graph.

Upon receiving the graph, the receiving entity builds a local representation of the Petri net to be used in order to accept and deliver, to the user, the received PDUs. Of course, the SDUs, or sub-objects, are delivered to the user not in the order they have been sent but in accordance with the partial order defined by the Petri net. For instance, in Figure 1, all SDUs represented by Places 1, 2, 3, 4, 5 and 6 can be delivered to the user as soon as they are received, i.e., whatever the order they are received from the network.

As in the most general case such a model could also be used at the application layer, the corresponding locations of the model inside the global architercture is given in Figure 3. Figure 3-a gives the model just before the establishment of the connection. After being transferred to the remote transport entity during the connection establishment phase, the model can also be transmitted to the remote application entity, as shown in Figure 3-b.

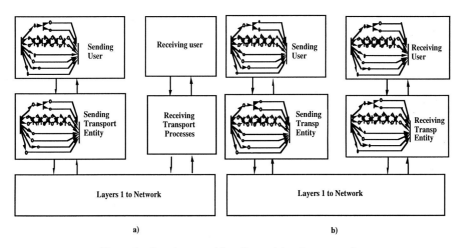

Figure 3 - Opening a multimedia partial order connection

This concept allows the communication system to conceptually cut the gap existing between specifying the application constraints and implementing the communication protocols.

If linear extensions are a proper characterisation of the network protocols, then the partial order transfer given here is the most optimized transfer for the corresponding application, i.e., the application defined by the partial order.

This is because : a) if the network allows other linear extensions, then it may deliver sequences that are incoherent with the object synchronization as wrong transfer sequences can be accepted ; b) if the network allows less linear extensions, then in this case, it may have to take time and resource consuming appropriate actions, due to the recovery of errors for instance, that would have not been necessary because of the missing sequences.

III-3- A new multimedia Transport architecture

Architecture is a quite important issue in distributed systems [41,43] and it is well known in multimedia systems that multimedia objects are constituted of different media and of course that these media have different quality and speed requirements [42,4,4,45,46]. This becomes particulary important when distributed systems are considered.

In such a case, when building architectures, the best designs should be the ones that use the underlying network in the most efficient way. This can be done if the multimedia objects are decomposed into different subparts, each of these subparts defining a dedicated and adequate quality of service for its transfer.

Furthermore, due to the errors that exist during the transfer inside the network, the objects will be desynchronized and a resynchronization at the receiving site in needed.

It has been proposed in [38,39] to define a new transport architecture based on multimedia POCs, in charge of handling the transmission errors and the deliveries to the user. As a consequence, a multimedia partial order Transport entity manages a set of monomedia connections, where each of these monomedia connections provides a given quality of service corresponding to its corresponding part of the multimedia object.

The structure of the multimedia transport protocol appears in Figure 4, where it is shown that the multimedia Petri net is used in the transport layer to control and implement the synchronisation needed between the different monomedia connections.

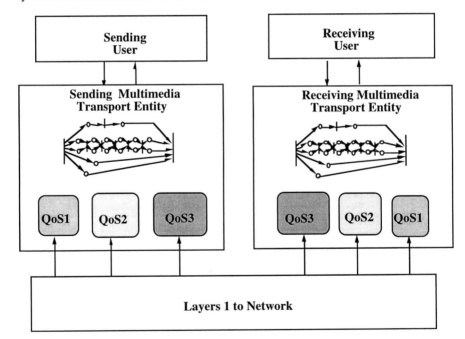

Figure 4 - Architecture of the Multimedia Transport Entity

As a consequence, a POC transport :
1- delivers the SDUs in an order compatible with the partial order,
2- delivers the SDUs as soon as possible, decreasing delays and jitters.

As an example, suppose that a monomedia Transport connection C_i has a reliability parameter Q_i, where Q_i gives the maximum number of PDUs that can be lost without being recovered.

Two different implementations can be defined [38,39] :

a) Reliability management per media

The protocols do not deliver a received SDU on a connection if its delivery is forbidden by a not already received SDU on another connection. Then :
• of course, a SDU is delivered if its loss is coherent with the reliability of its connection, and furthermore
• it is delivered when it is deliverable with regard to the multimedia partial order.

b) Reliability management per group of media

The protocol may now deliver a given SDU on a connection C_i even if this delivery generates the loss of one or more SDUs on another connection, C_j, which means that :
• of course when the SDU is deliverable with respect to the reliability of its connection C_i
• but also when it generates one loss or a few losses on C_j, but when these losses are in accordance with Q_j, the reliability figure of this connection C_j.

It follows that implementation b) delivers the SDUs at an earlier date than implementation a).

The case of two different multimedia connections appears in Figure 5 where each partial order multimedia transport connection is characterized and controlled by its synchronisation model.

III-4- Integrating TSPNs

The interest of TSPNs comes from the fact that they include intervals and that these intervals can be used to decrease the timing constraints on the multimedia objects. These intervals make simpler the asynchronous implementations. These implementations will have to fulfil the specified interval, and this becomes easier when "the intervals of validity" increase.

Networks being asynchronous, they also become simpler to implement when intervals of validity exist and are large. By giving its maximum acceptable intervals, the users also indirectly specify their minimum constraints on the network, which is of high interest for any distributed processing.

As computers are asynchronous, it seems more appropriate to implement the synchronisation constraints at the highest level of the architecture [47] . This is shown in Figure 6 where time synchronisation is done under the passive part of the system, i.e. the part of the system that does not modify any more the time synchronisation.

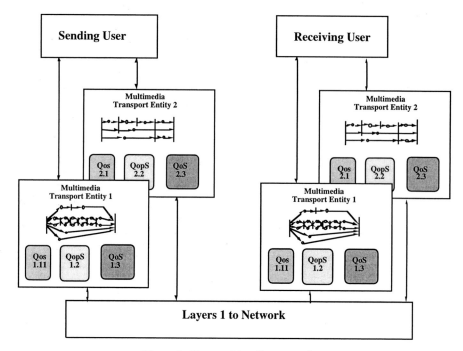

Figure 5 - Two multimedia connections

The interests of HTSPNs come from the fact that they represent the composition of different multimedia presentations.

Of course, a complex application will need different multimedia presentations to be integrated and synchronized. Each of them will be represented by a TSPN, by a model and so by a partial order. As a consequence, a set of different partial orders will be needed during a complex application. As it has been seen, all of them, based on the user choices, will have to be transmitted to the remote transport entity and to be handled by this remote transport entity for implementing the optimized transfer.

As a consequence, the partial order and the Petri net will have to be dynamically modified, and more complex protocols are needed. These protocols must include negotiation and re-negotiation of partial orders inside an already established connection. This is the work under current development.

IV. CONCLUSION

This paper introduces a methodology for designing multimedia distributed systems by using a model representing the multimedia objects.

The TSPN model is defined by extending time Petri nets, using intervals on arcs instead of in transitions and by defining new firing rules to enforce the firing time semantics. TSPNs and HTSPNs are able to model multimedia objects at different levels of granularity.

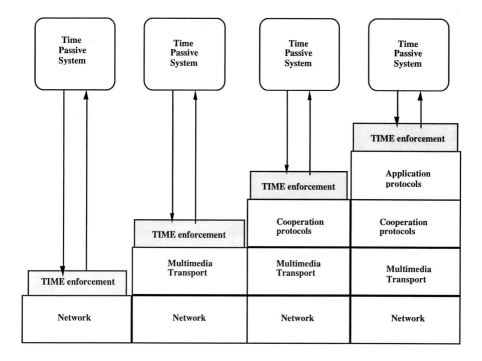

Figure 6 - Handling time

It has been shown how TSPNs can be used as a basis for implementing the most suitable communication connection for sending complex multimedia objects.

The general notion of connection has been investigated. It led to a new concept, the concept of a partial order connection, that extends the previous concepts of connectionless and connection-oriented protocols.

The ideas underlying partial order connections have been presented and it has been shown how these partial order connections are much more general than the usual CL or CO connections.

It has also been shown how such general connections can be defined by the application layer and how their definition at the application level can be transferred to the communication software, in the transport layer, leading to a new communication architecture.

ACKNOWLEDGEMENTS

This work has been developed under grant 92 1B 178 from CNET - France Telecom as part of the CESAME project on the design of High Speed Multimedia Cooperative Systems. The author would like to thank everyone who participated in this work, mainly P. Amer, Ch. Chassot, A. Lozes, Ph. Owezarski and P. Sénac.

48

REFERENCES

1. M. Diaz, G. Pays, *The CESAME project: Formal Design of High Speed Multimedia Cooperative Systems*, Special issue on CESAME, Annals of Telecommunications, May-June 1994.
2. P. Merlin, *A study of the recoverability of computer system*, Thesis, Computer Science Dept., University of California, Irvine, 1974.
3. P. Merlin, D.J. Farber, *Recoverability of communication protocols*, IEEE Transactions on Communications, COM-24, (9), Sept. 1976.
4. C. Ramchandani, *Analysis of asynchronous concurrent systems by timed Petri nets*, Project MAC, TR 120, MIT, Feb. 1974.
5. Sifakis, *Use of Petri nets for performance evaluation in measuring modelling and evaluating computer systems*, Performance Evaluation of Systems using nets" Net Theory and Application, LNCS, 1980.
6. B. Berthomieu, M. Menasche, *An enumerative approach for analysing Time Petri Nets*, 9th World Computer Congress, IFIP'83, Paris, France, September 1983
7 B. Berthomieu, M. Diaz, *Modeling and verification of Time Dependent Systems using Time Petri Nets*, IEEE Tr on Sotware Engineering, Vol 17, N° 3, March 1991.
8. J. F. Allen, *Maintaining knowledge about temporal intervals*, Comm. of the ACM, 26, (11), November 1983, pp 832-843
9. Little (T.), Ghafoor (A.). *Network Considerations for Dist'd Multimedia Objects Composition and Communication.* IEEE Network Magazine, (November 1990), 32-49.
10. Little (T.), Ghafoor (A.). *Synchronization and Storage Models for Multimedia Objects.* IEEE J on Selected Areas in Comm., (April 1990), 8(3), 413-427.
11. M. Diaz, P. Sénac. *Time Stream Petri Nets, a Model for Multimedia Streams Synchronization.* In Proc. of the First International Conference on Multi-media Modelling - Vol.1, Singapore, November 1993, World Scientific, Tat-Seng Chua & T. L. Kunii Editors, 1993, pp 257-273.
12. M. Diaz, P. Sénac. *Time Stream Petri Nets, a Model for Timed Multimedia Information.* 15th International Conference on Application and Theory of Petri Nets, June 1994, Zaragoza, Springer-Verlag, R. Valette Editor, pp 219-238, 1994.
13. P. Sénac, M. Diaz, P. de Saqui Sannes. *Toward a Formal Specification of Multimedia Synchronization Scenarios*, Annales des Télécommunications, Tome 49, no. 5-6, pp 297-314, May-June 1994.
14. P. Sénac, P. de Saqui Sannes, R. Willrich. *Hierarchical Time Stream Petri Nets: a Model for Hypermedia Systems.* 16th Int Conf on Application and Theory of Petri Nets, June 1995, Torino,. LNCS 935, Springer, G. de Michelis & M. Diaz Editors, pp 451-470, 1995.
15. P. Sénac, R. Willrich, M. Diaz. *Hypermedia Synchronization Modeling: a Case Study.* In proc. of ED-MEDIA'95 World Conference on Educational Multimedia and Hypermedia, pp 585-590, Graz, 1995.
16. P. Sénac, M. Diaz, A. Léger, P. de Saqui Sannes. *Modeling Logical and Temporal Synchronization in Hypermedia Systems.* To appear in IEEE Journal on Selected Areas in Communications, 1995.
17. M. Diaz, C. A. Vissers, *SEDOS, Software environment for the design of open distributed systems*, IEEE Software Magazine, November 1989.
18. M. Diaz, J. P. Ansart, J. P. Courtiat, P. Azema, V. Chari, Editors, *The Formal description techniques Estelle*, North-Holland, 1989.
19. P. Van eijk, C. Vissers, M. Diaz Editors, *The Formal description techniques LOTOS*, North-Holland, 1989.
20. S. Budkowski, P. Dembinski, *The Formal Specification Technique Estelle*, Computer Networks and ISDN Systems, North Holland, 1987.
21. Courtiat J.P., Cruz de Oliveira, *About Time Non-determinism and Exception Handling*

in a Temporal Extension of LOTOS, IFIP Int Conf on Protocol Specification, Testing and Verification, Vancouver, June 1994, North Holland, Vuong & Chanson Editors.

22. Courtiat J.P., Cruz de Oliveira R., Rust da Costa Carmo L., *Towards a new Multimedia Synchronisation mechanism and its Formal Definition*, ACM Multimedia'94, San Francisco, October 1994.

23. DOERINGER (W. A.), DYKEMAN (D.), KAISERSWERTH (M.), MEISTER (B. W.), RUDIN (H.), WILLIAMSON (R.). *A survey of light-weight transport protocols for high-speed networks*. IEEE Transactions on Communications (Nov. 1990), **38**, n° 11.

24. Pehrson B., Pink S., *Multimedia and high speed networking in MultiG*,Computer Networks and ISDN Systems, 21, pp 315-319, 1991.

25. Danthine (A.), Baguette (Y.), Leduc (G.), Leonard (L.). *The OSI95 connection-mode Transport service - the enhanced QoS*. 4th IFIP Conference on High Performance Networking, Liège, Belgium, Dec. (14-18) 1992.

26. Dairaine L., Santoso H., Horlait E., *Deterministic and statistical intra-flow synchronization services*, Proceedings of the IEEE MICC Conference, 2-4 Novembre 1993, Kuaka Lumpur, Malaysia.

27. Rust da Costa Carmo L.F., Courtiat J.P., *Implementing intra-stream synchronization by means of conditional dependency expressions*, 5th IFIP Conference on High Performance Networking, Grenoble, Juin 1994, LNCS, n° 712, 1993

28. Santoso H., Dairaine L., Fdida S., Horlait E., *Preserving temporal signature: a way to convey time constrained flows*, Proc. of GLOBECOM'93, Houston, Texas, Novembre 1993

29. Rust da Costa Carmo L.F., Courtiat J.P., Cruz de Oliveira R., *A new mechanism for achieving inter-stream synchronization in multimedia communication systems*, IEEE Int Conf on Multimedia Computing and Systems, Boston, May 1994.

30. Lamport (L.). *Time, Clocks and the Ordering of Events in a dist'd System.CACM*, (July 1978), 21(7),558-565.

31. Ajuha (M.). *FLUSH Primitives for Asynchronous Dist'd Systems*. Info Processing Letters. (February 1990), 34(1), 5-12.

32. Shafer (K.), Ahuja (M.). *Process-channel(agent)-Process Model of Asynchronous dist'd Communication*. In Proc. ICDCS 12, Yokohama, Japan, (June 1992), 4-11.

33. Amer (P.D.), Chassot (C.), Connolly (T.), Diaz (M.). *Partial Order Transport Service for Multimedia Applications: Reliable Service* - 2nd High Performance Distributed Computing Conf. (July 1993) - Spokane, Wash..

34. Amer (P.D.), Chassot (C.), Connolly (T.), Diaz (M.). *Partial Order Transport Service for Multimedia Applications: Unreliable Service* - INET '93 3rd International Conference, San Francisco, CA, (August 17-20 1993).

35. Diaz (M), Lozes (A.), Chassot (C.), Amer (P. D.). *Partial Order Connections : A new concept for High Speed and Multimedia Services and Protocols*. Annals of Telecommunications, May-June 94, tome 49, n°5-6.

36. Amer (P. D.), Chassot (C.), Connolly (C.), Conrad (P.), Diaz (M.). *Partial Order Transport Service for Multimedia and other Applications*. IEEE/ACM Transactions on Networking, Oct. 1994, vol.2, n° 5.

37. Diaz (M), DRIRA (K.), Lozes (A.), Chassot (Ch.) *Definition and Representation of the Quality of Service for Multimedia Systems*. 6th International Conference on High Speed Networking, HPN'95, Palma de Mallorca (Balearic Islands), Spain, September 11-15, 1995.

38. Chassot (C.), Diaz (M.), Lozes (A.). *From the Partial Order Concept to Partial Order Multimedia Connections*. First International HIPPARCH workshop, INRIA Sophia Antipolis, December 15-16, 1994.

39. Chassot (C.), Diaz (M.), Lozes (A.). *From the Partial Order Concept to Partial Order Multimedia Connections*. Extended version of preceding paper, To appear in Journal on

High Speed Networking, 1995.
40. Diaz (M), DRIRA (K.), Lozes (A.), Chassot (Ch.) *Definition and Representation of the Quality of Service for Multimedia Systems.* 6th International Conference on High Speed Networking, HPN'95, Palma de Mallorca, Spain, September 11-15, 1995.
41. D. D. Clark, D. L. Tennenhouse, *Architectural Considerations for a New Generation of Protocols,* SIGCOMM'90 Symp, September 1990, Computer Communication Review, Vol 20, N° 4,September 1990.
42. Campbell (A.), Coulson (G.), Hutchison (David.). *A Multimedia Enhanced Transport Service in a Quality of Service Architecture.* 4th Int work on Network and OS Support for Digital Audio and Video. November 3rd -5th 1993. Lancaster, UK.
43. Tennenhouse (D.L.). *Layered Multiplexing Considered Harmful. Protocols for High-Speed Networks,* Elsevier Science Publishers B.V. (North-Holland).
44. Besse L., Dairaine L., Fédaoui L., Tawbi W., Thai K., *Towards an architecture for distributed multimedia applications support,* IEEE ICMCS, Boston, USA, Mai 1994.
45. Campbell (A.), Coulson (G.), Hutchison (D.). *A Multimedia Enhanced Transport Service in a Quality of Service Architecture.* 4th International workshop on Network and Operating Systems Support for Digital Audio and Video, Nov. (3-5) 1993, Lancaster, UK.
46. Leopold (H.), Campbell (A.), Hutchinson (D.), Singer (N.). *Towards an integrated quality of service architecture (QoS_A) for distributed multimedia communications.* 4th IFIP Conference on High Performance Networking, Liège, Belgium, Dec. (14-18) 1992.
47. Ph Owezarski, M. Diaz, P. Sénac, *Modélisation et implémentation de Mécanismes de Synchronisation multimédia dans une application de visioconférence* (in French), Colloque CFIP, Rennes, Mai 1995, Hermès, C. Jard-P. Rolin Editeurs, 1995

ON CONCEPTUAL MODELING FOR INTERACTIVE MULTIMEDIA PRESENTATIONS

ELINA MEGALOU[*]
and
THANASIS HADZILACOS

Computer Technology Institute and
[*]*Dept. of Computer Engineering and Informatics, University of Patras,*
P.O. Box 1122, GR-26110, Patras, Greece
E-mail: {megalou, thh} @cti.gr

ABSTRACT

The design of an interactive multimedia presentation is best left to the creative director, normally not a computer professional. This design however, involves complex synchronisation, interactivity and control flow aspects, the standard tools for which - such as Petri nets- have not been developed with such users in mind. This is why special-purpose rapid prototyping tools are often used -with successful though limited results. We propose a different approach particularly suitable for the design of whole classes of similar multimedia titles: to utilise -a slightly extended version of- the models used for conceptual database modeling which have been designed to be understandable by non computer professionals. We point out how the process of design of interactive multimedia presentations is related to conceptual database modeling. We present the modeling primitives necessary for multimedia as extensions applicable to any semantic or object-oriented model, using OMT as an example. We design MHEG-compatible metaclasses of common generic composite multimedia objects. Finally, examples of how this methodology has been used in practice are presented as an argument for its applicability.

1. The Setting

1.1. What the paper is all about

Interactive multimedia presentations are a special type of information systems. One aspect that is special about them is that their specifications as applications are given by a non-computer specialist, whence a need for special-purpose design tools. Rather than develop new tools for user-guided design of multimedia titles, we extend -in the direction of accommodating the requirements of multimedia titles- semantic data models which have proven their practicality in lay hands. Thus, the contribution of the paper is to provide those minimal extensions to semantic and object-oriented models needed for multimedia, in a natural and standard-complying way.

To develop an information system one must first design it, by building an application model. Such a model represents at the same time the real world and the computer system to be developed. Consider for example a multimedia application for tourism for the end-user to browse through vacation resorts and make reservations. Its design includes a representation of the real world (e.g. hotel H has so many rooms with such and such prices) and a representation of the computer system (e.g. 5″ video clips will be presented on the upper right quarter of the screen along with suitable narration, interruptable by pressing any one of three "buttons" each of which has the following functionality:...).

Traditionally the model of an application is developed by computer professionals who consult with a domain knowledge provider -often indiscriminately and inaccurately referred to as "the user"- for the representation of the real world and then work by themselves for the representation of the computer system guided by appropriate principles of efficiency and ergonomics. Since the domain scientist, in general not a computer professional himself, bears the responsibility of correctness of the outside world representation, the models used allow such a verification. *Conceptual data modeling* is the representation of the static aspects of the real world relevant to the application in a way which is formal and suitable for unambiguous translation to computer manipulatable form and yet understandable to the domain knowledge provider; thus conceptual modeling uses no computer metaphors. The models used go by the name of semantic or object-oriented and are based on fundamental ontological concepts such as "entity", "attribute", and "relationship" well established before the advent of computing technology. For the design of the computer system on the other hand, no such restrictions apply: esoteric tools such as Petri nets [3], or labelled directed graphs are used to fit the representational needs. And herein lays the challenge for the design of multimedia titles: it is a non-computer professional, namely the creative director, who must specify not only the outside world (such as hotels and rooms) but also the workings of the application (screen layout and interactivity of buttons). To this we should add that the look and feel of the application (its presentation and interactivity) is not simple; rather it is often the essence of that particular computer system complexity.

The advent of powerful object-oriented models brought about two major changes in database modeling: First is the unification of static and dynamic aspects; and second is that a single model can be used for both the outside world and the computer system representation. Although several dissimilar object-oriented models exist, their differences do not affect the present work. We shall use OMT [25] as a concrete model, without affecting the generality or applicability of our methodology.

The development of interactive multimedia presentations calls for the integration of two distinct production lines: that of a movie and that of a computer application. So, good multimedia title production requires teamwork by scarce and expensive professionals from both fields. Since title production is at the end of the day the responsibility of the creative director, computer engineers should mainly produce the tools to facilitate his work. In [11], a methodology was proposed and applied for the efficient production of whole series of similar multimedia presentations. The basic idea is the generic specification of the title series content, interactivity and control flow. There, this was done by narrative specifications and special-purpose hand-filled forms, from which an OMT model was derived. Here we take the methodology one step further and formalize it. We use, in as much as possible, the same models and techniques used in classical applications for conceptual modeling of the outside world (based on concepts which have proven to be understandable and usable: entities, relationships, attributes, isa hierarchies, aggregations and grouping, augmented with minimal constructs for temporal synchronization (for composite multimedia objects), spatial synchronization (for screen layout) and interactivity. This is detailed in Section 2.2. We provide conceptual modeling primitives exemplified via OMT, to be used as add-ons to any model and use them to present MHEG-compatible generic classes for common composite multimedia objects, (Sections 2.3, 2.4 and 2.5). Finally, in Section 2.6, we include some examples of actual use.

1.2. Conceptual Modeling and Multimedia

The first stage in the life cycle of a computer application, or an information processing system, is requirements analysis. This results in a set of desiderata for the application, expressed in natural language, possibly including charts, pictures, regulations, equations or sketches. For this set of requirements to be transformed into computer executable code, it must undergo a set of transformations the first of which is a formal design.

From flow charts to OMT, modeling has evolved to serve the different types of applications from the elementary input-transformation-output to the interactive editor and the operating system -each with a different type of complexity. Interactive multimedia presentations need sophisticated models both for the outside world presentation and for the application itself -while the algorithms and processes involved are usually simple.

For data-intensive applications, which normally include a database, data modeling consumes a substantial part of the design effort. Database design is roughly divided into three stages, the conceptual, the logical and the physical design. (Older taxonomies made a simpler division into logical and physical, using conceptual as a synonym to logical, which is a source of considerable confusion; still others [5] propose a further subdivision into semantic, conceptual, logical and physical, a view we will not follow here.) Traditionally, the reason given for distinguishing database design from the rest of the application model is that data modeling captures the static aspects of the application. Recent, object-oriented, models have integrated static and dynamic aspects in a single model.

We should point out three distinct usages of "static":

- Data types whose instance does not depend on time (such as numbers, and pictures) are called static as opposed to time-based data types (such as sound, video and animation). It is in this sense that multimedia types are sometimes defined as *dynamic* data types [13][24].
- A static, as opposed to schema-evolving, database is one whose structure does not change.
- Object oriented models consider both object characteristics (such as colour) and object behaviour (such as the ability to change colour) to be object attributes. The former are called static properties while the latter dynamic (methods).

Although conceptual data models abound, the representational concepts used boil down to three: entity sets (object classes), attributes thereof and relationships among them.

Attributes are represented in a variety of ways, not always explicitly. Some models may allow characterizations of attributes (such as: key, unique, mandatory, computable, etc.). Relationships may again be represented explicitly or implicitly; most models allow some characterizations of relationships, usually their cardinality and may distinguish some special, structural relationships such as the Isa, IsPartof and IsMemberof (also known as generalization, aggregation and grouping). It is important to notice that these are not computer related categories; rather they are generally understandable concepts.

The most well known such model is the Entity-Relationship model [6], with several variations, and is the simplest of semantic data models. Object-oriented models, in addition to incorporating these concepts, allow for the handling of the dynamic aspects of the application, the so-called behaviour of objects in the framework of the same model. OMT is relatively recent but well developed and widely accepted.

Concluding, we propose to use semantic concepts and object oriented models for the design of interactive multimedia applications because:

- The representation must be understandable by non computer professionals and these concepts have been proven to be suitable for this.
- The concepts are basically adequate and need only simple and natural extensions.

1.3. Related Work

This work is based on research in conceptual database design (such as [5][6][22]) and in multimedia modeling (such as [13][15][18,19][21]). Among the various semantic and object-oriented models, we consider IFO [1] and OMT [25] as prototypical. For non-standard application areas (such as Geographic Information Systems and Temporal Databases) extensions to these models have been proposed in order to model aspects such as position, topological relationships and time [14][27][8,9,10][28][24]. For the representation of the dynamic aspects of a system, including process synchronization, control flow, data flow and interactivity, models, such as PetriNets [3] and State Diagrams [25] are used.

In the multimedia literature, the issue of conceptual modeling has been addressed under different views and abstraction levels: Much of this research focuses on multimedia documents. Meghini & al. in [21] propose an extension of the ODA (a model for document architecture that integrates the representation of a document's structure -logical model- with its presentation formats -layout model-) for document content. Klas & al. in [15] approach multimedia modeling via objects, introducing metaclasses i.e. "objects that represent data model concepts and can be employed to add to a kernel data model new modeling primitives". In [2], multimedia presentations are considered as hierarchical compositions of temporal objects and a hierarchical composition model for handling time dependencies within multimedia systems is discussed.

Significant work in the area of multimedia data modeling has been done by Gibbs. In [13], based on the observation that media objects (e.g. video, audio) are arranged in temporal sequences (e.g. frames, samples), a model is proposed with temporal sequences as the main abstraction for time-based media and three general structuring mechanisms, namely interpretation, derivation and composition (specification of spatial and/or temporal relationships within a group of objects).

The research by Little constitutes an important contribution to multimedia conceptual modeling, focusing on multimedia presentation and synchronization. [17] is a survey on conceptual models for multimedia synchronization, including temporal-intervals, process models (for process synchronization, using language-based models or graph-based models), user interaction (Petri net based HyperText) and temporal abstractions (when temporal models are deficient). In [18], using the term "time-dependent data" for data whose values and delivery time matter, Little and Grafoor propose temporal-interval-based models to capture the timing relationships in multimedia presentations and to manage them within a database. In [20] Petri Nets are extended in order to represent the synchronization of multimedia entities, by adding time and resource attributes, resulting in the Object Composition Petri Net. The need of a database schema "for the storage of the multimedia presentation, capable to preserve the semantics of the Petri net" is pointed out. The proposed synchronization schema constitutes a generic extension of various models; it is based on node type templates (terminal, non-terminal, metatype) and allows for temporal relationships between two non-terminal nodes as attributes to templates.

A standardized solution for the definition of multimedia classes is given by MHEG[1], whose objective is to develop standard representations and encodings for general purpose interchange of multimedia and hypermedia information [16][23].

Finally, a distinction between database and application is made by Rumbaugh in [26] though not explicitly for multimedia applications. Rumbaugh, differentiates application objects, which represent user-visible aspects of an application (e.g. the flight reservation display screen) from domain objects (e.g. flight) and defines the concept of presentation as an application object. Presentation represents the arrangement of semantic data "such that the user can perceive and interact with it". The need for additional information concerning presentation parameters, layout structure and view constructing information, is also noted. To control the application and its interactions with the outside world (user interfaces, schedulers etc.) a special object (controller) is introduced.

2. Extending Modeling Primitives

2.1. Complex objects in interactive multimedia presentations

In the real world we conceive of entities associated with each other to form more complex ones in a vast variety of ways; linguistically we say that the similar entities "constitute" the more complex one -the inverse relationship is "consists of". When modeling, on the other hand, we must select just a few basic constructs which will allow the recursive formation of complex objects from simpler ones. Semantic data models [1][5][22] use two such constructs: aggregation (an object consists of its parts) and

---

[1] MHEG Standard (ISO DIS 13522-1) issued by ISO IEC JTC1/SC29/WG12 group

grouping (an object is a set of other objects). The inverse relationships, namely IsPartOf and IsMemberOf, are the two distinct types of "constitute" available in most semantic and object-oriented data models.

In multimedia applications dealing with complex objects is fundamental: a single data type (such as a piece of video or animation) may consist of several simpler ones (frames in this case); a true multimedia object consists of several simpler monomedia objects (pictures, narration, and text for instance); a multimedia *scene* is a complex of multimedia objects assembled on the screen under various spatial and temporal relationships; a multimedia presentation is a assembly of such scenes woven in a complex whole through the *Interactivity* of the scenes.

So in multimedia applications we have: the standard notion of "consists" -a hotel consists of its picture and the number of rooms with their prices; a *"spatial* consists" -a scene consists of two non-overlapping pictures and text on the bottom of the screen; a *"temporal* consists" -a slide show consists of a sequence of slides; and an *"interactivity* consists" -a presentation consists of 4 scenes in a sequence determined by the way the user presses the buttons on the scenes. Notice that there are two concepts of temporal: "time based" data such as a video clip and "time dependent" objects such as a synchronized narration and slide show.

It is clear therefore that the plain concepts of aggregation and grouping will not be sufficient. In [27] it is noted that when dealing with spatial objects, i.e. those whose position in space matters to the information system, it is often the case that if objects A, B and C constitute object X, then the position of A, B and C is a subset of the position of X. Thus they introduce *spatial aggregation* and *spatial grouping*, as simple extensions to modeling primitives for conveying this extra piece of information. We shall adopt this proposal and extend it to temporal and interactivity aggregation and grouping.

2.2. *Modeling Constructs for Building Composite Multimedia Objects Classes*

2.2.1. *Temporal Relationships*

In [5], Brodie & al. define aggregation as a form of abstraction in which a relationship between objects is considered to be a higher level aggregate object. Every instance of an aggregate object class can be decomposed into instances of the component object classes, which establishes a part-of relationship between objects.

In [4], the playout duration of a multimedia object during presentation is represented by a *temporal interval* which is defined by two end points or instances.

In our model multimedia objects have a special attribute called "playout duration", whose domain is the set of temporal intervals. We define temporal-aggregation as an aggregation in which the playout duration of the composite object is determined by the playout durations of the constituents.

If C is an aggregation of c_1, c_2,..... c_n, then it is a *temporal aggregation* if $\tau = \tau_1 \cup \tau_2 \cup$ .... τ_n, where τ is the playout duration of C and τ_i is the playout duration of c_i for $1 \leq i \leq n$. Note that not all aggregations where some of its constituent objects have temporal attributes, constitute a temporal aggregation. Consider for example a car, as an aggregation of its parts (body, engine, etc.). Although the car and its parts may have lifetime attributes, the lifetime of the car is likely to be different than the union of those of its parts.

Finally, in the context of multimedia applications a temporal-aggregation implies parallel temporal relationships as it represents an assembly of temporal-intervals usually assigned to different audiovisual channels (an audiovisual channel is a "logical-space" for media streams e.g. an audio channel is a logical space for audio streams; different portions of the screen area can be viewed as different visual channels).

Grouping is defined in [5] as that form of abstraction in which a relationship between similar objects is considered to be a higher level set object. An instance of a set object class can be decomposed into a set of instances of the member object classes and this establishes a member-of relationship between a member object and a set object.

Similarly to temporal aggregation, we define temporal grouping, as the grouping where the playout duration of the aggregate object has value equal to the union of the temporal intervals of the playout durations of the constituent objects.

If C is a grouping of $c_1, c_2, \ldots c_n$, then it is a ***temporal grouping*** if $\tau = \tau_1 \cup \tau_2 \cup \ldots \tau_n$, where τ is the playout duration of C and τ_i is the playout duration of c_i for $1 \leq i \leq n$. Notice again that not all groupings of objects with temporal aspects are temporal groupings.

In the context of multimedia applications, similar objects are those of the same type and at the same audiovisual channel. Consequently, temporal grouping implies serial (sequential) temporal relationships.

Temporal Integrity Constraints. Presentational temporal integrity constraints are conditions that express mandatory temporal relationships among presentation objects (static temporal integrity constraints), or allowable operations on temporal relationships (dynamic temporal integrity constraints).

Given any two time-intervals, there are thirteen distinct ways in which they can be related [4][18], namely *before, meets, overlaps, during, starts, finishes, and equals* and their reverse relationships. Before and meets, represent sequential temporal relationships, while overlaps, during, starts, finishes and equals represent parallel temporal relationships. Equal represents synchronous temporal intervals. Presentational temporal integrity constraints can be expressed by these thirteen temporal relationships, and combinations thereof utilizing the operators $\in, \exists, \forall, \neg, \wedge, \vee, \Rightarrow, \Leftrightarrow$ (e.g. before $\vee$ meets). It is often the case however in multimedia application design that the characterizations sequential, parallel, and synchronous are sufficient.

2.2.2. *Spatial Relationships*

Spatial relationships, both geometric and topological, have been studied extensively in mathematics and recently in the context of Geographic Information Systems [8,9,10]. In [14] topological relationships are used to define topological integrity constraints for the design of spatial applications. Geographic objects are assumed to have a special attribute, *position,* which models their shape, size location and orientation in space. In [27] spatial aggregation (respectively: spatial grouping) is defined for geographic applications as aggregation (respectively: grouping) of spatial objects with the position of the aggregate object being the union of the positions of the constituents.

In multimedia presentations we can view visual objects (e.g. photographs, video) as spatial objects whose *presentational position* models the screen portion they occupy.

Following [27] we define spatial-aggregation as an aggregation in which the presentational position of the composite object is determined by the presentational positions of the constituents. If C is an aggregation of c_1, c_2,.... c_n, then it is a *spatial aggregation* if $p = p_1 \cup p_2 \cup$ .... p_i where p is the presentational position of C and p_i is the presentational position of c_i for $1 \leq i \leq n$. Spatial aggregation denotes "screen partitioning".

Similarly we define spatial grouping, as the grouping where the presentational position of the aggregate object is the union of the presentational positions of the constituent objects. If C is a grouping of c_1, c_2,.... c_n, then it is a *spatial grouping* if $p = p_1 \cup p_2 \cup$ .... p_i where p is the presentational position of C and p_i is the presentational position of c_i for $1 \leq i \leq n$. Spatial-grouping denotes "collection of display areas".

Spatial Integrity Constraints : Given two spatial objects (points, lines and regions) there are sixteen distinct ways in which they can be related [10][14]. Although any combination of them can be used to express spatial integrity constraints, spatial-overlap (S-OVERLP) and full-screen (S_FULLSCR) are sufficient for most multimedia presentations.

2.2.3. *Interactivity*

In multimedia presentations, "interactivity" captures the possibilities offered to the user in order (a) to navigate through the multimedia presentation (b) to retrieve the desired information and (c) to control the flow of the presentation. In fact, as in the majority of the interactive applications, user-interaction is the basic factor that directs the control flow of the application; thus, interactivity must be explicitly described in the application design. This description includes the definition of the interaction facilities, -called either *interaction constructs* or *input objects*- and the linkage mechanisms.

Interaction facilities are objects, usually visual ones, with a special attribute, *interactivity*. The domain of the attribute is subsets of triplets (e_i, c_j, a_k), where e_i is an *event*, c_j is *condition*, and a_k is an *action*. A set of triplets models the behaviour of an interaction facility to external stimuli under certain conditions.

We define interactivity-aggregation, as an aggregation in which the interactivity of the composite object is determined by the interactivity of the constituents. If C is an aggregation of f_1, f_2,.... f_n, then it is a *interactivity aggregation* if $i = i_1 \cup i_2 \cup$ .... i_i where i is the interactivity of C and i_i is the interactivity of f_i for $1 \leq i \leq n$. Interactivity-aggregation denotes "partitioning of interaction possibilities".

Similarly we define interactivity grouping, as the grouping where the interactivity of the aggregate object is the union of the interactivity of the constituent objects. If C is a grouping of f_1, f_2,.... f_n, then it is an *interactivity grouping* if $i = i_1 \cup i_2 \cup$ .... i_i where i is the interactivity of C and i_i is the interactivity of f_i for $1 \leq i \leq n$. Interactivity-grouping denotes "collection of interaction possibilities".

The interactivity of the scene is usually the interactivity of its constituents objects. However, a scene may have additional linkage mechanisms so, the interactivity of the constituents objects participate to, but not totally comprise, the interactivity of the scene. Moreover, the linkage mechanisms associated with an input object of a scene, are valid either during the whole presentation (tied up with the input object and may belong to various scenes), or only during the scene's presentation time (tied up with the scene).

Interactivity Integrity Constraints: In addition to spatial-integrity constraints (S-OVERLP, S-FULLSCR) that can be applied also to assemblies of interaction constructs due to their spatial extend, there exist constraints that stem from particular interactivity properties, such as: the interactive constructs of a scene are usually overlapped, they are organized in priority hierarchies, or they have constraints on their simultaneous validity. For the conceptual modeling, we consider three most frequently used constraints: (a) I-HIER: denotes hierarchy of interaction constructs (b) T-OP/T-TR : denotes opacity or transparency of the interaction constructs of a scene (i.e to allow or prohibit the transmission of events to the underlying objects) and (c) I-EXCL: denotes mutually exclusive interaction constructs.

Linkage Mechanisms: For highly interactive applications, the description of the linkage mechanisms coincides with the application control flow. The specification of the control flow of an interactive multimedia presentation, includes the definition of *states* - which represent presentation intervals-, of *events* -which are external stimuli- and of *actions*, which represent state transitions. Flow charts, although simple and user-understandable, are inadequate, being suitable for sequential rather than event-driven applications. Time Petri nets and various types of automata, do suffice, but they are too complex for the creative director to use. State diagrams seem to be the best fit for our purposes. An example of using state diagrams to model the control flow of interactive multimedia applications is given in section 2.7 based on the OMT Dynamic model notation (a collection of state diagrams)

2.3. Extensions to OMT Object Model Notation

The object-oriented approach has proved to be most appropriate for the conceptual modeling of multimedia applications [11][13[15]. The extensions presented in the previous section are generic; they can be used with any semantic model which has the minimal functionality of allowing the construction of complex objects from simpler ones. We shall illustrate this with the widely used Object Modeling Technique (OMT)[2] [25].

---

[2] The OMT methodology can be applied throughout the system development life cycle and in order to construct visual projections of the system, uses three kinds of models: the Object Model, the Dynamic Model, and the Functional Model.

The proposed extensions on the OMT Object Model graphical notation are summarized in Fig. 1. Grouping, in OMT, is called "the multiplicity association construct".

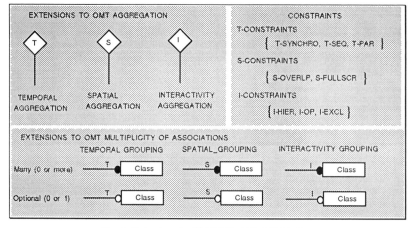

Fig. 1. Extensions to OMT Object Model Notation

2.4. Associating semantics with the use of MHEG classes at the conceptual level.

Conceptual design is followed by logical and physical design, where classes are defined in detail and implemented. For the definition of classes of multimedia objects there is a standard, namely MHEG [16][23]. MHEG[3] defines object classes, from which objects can be instantiated by the object designer and interchanged between applications.

It is important to have a conceptual modeling schema that can be readily transformed to a computer program; given the MHEG standard, it is sensible to conform the conceptual modeling of interactive multimedia applications to MHEG principles. To this end:

- we show how MHEG is related to semantic models used for the conceptual modeling of interactive multimedia applications.
- we associate semantics with the use of MHEG classes at the conceptual level.

A global view of the class hierarchy defined by MHEG and other MHEG-related activities [7] is shown in Fig. 2. The representation is based on the OMT object model notation.

---

[3] The MHEG standard defines a classification of structures corresponding to units of multimedia/hypermedia (MH) information to be interchanged and results in autonomous and reusable information structures which are generic to MH applications. The following classes are defined: Content, Multiplexed Content, Composite, Action, Link, Script, Descriptor Class, Container Class. Run-time objects are defined for the purpose of reusing objects in different presentations[23]

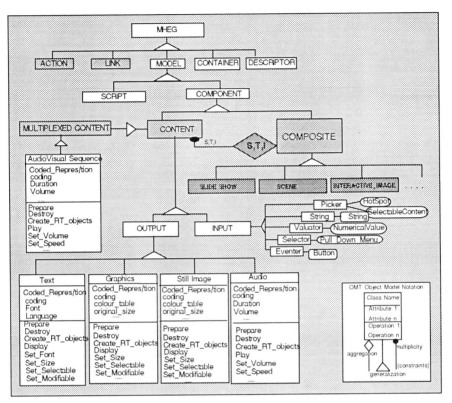

Fig. 2. Extended-OMT model of MHEG Class Hierarchy

MHEG is addressed to application developers and object designers, in order to create interchangeable, open applications. From the view of the "domain knowledge provider", only those classes that represent user-oriented concepts, such as a photo, a piece of text, a button, a scene or a slide show, make sense at the conceptual level.

The MHEG classes which with semantics added , correspond to those concepts are:

(a) **MHEG Content Class** and **MHEG Multiplexed Content**, which correspond to simple or multiplexed media objects (photo, video etc.)

(b) **COMPOSITE Class**, which corresponds to complex objects (e.g. slide show). Those classes can be modeled using our extended semantic model.

(c) **MHEG Link and Action Classes** include the description of the application's interactivity; at the conceptual level, their representation by state diagrams suffices. MHEG Script class and MHEG Container class are meaningful only to object designers. In Fig. 2 shaded boxes represent MHEG classes related to the conceptual level design and the proposed extensions to the MHEG hierarchy scheme. SlideShow, Scene and

InteractiveImage associate semantics to the MHEG composite classes and are described in the following subsection.

2.5. *MHEG-complying Composite Multimedia Objects*

Some types of composite multimedia objects are very common in interactive multimedia presentations. Here is how to model them using OMT extended notation within MHEG principles:

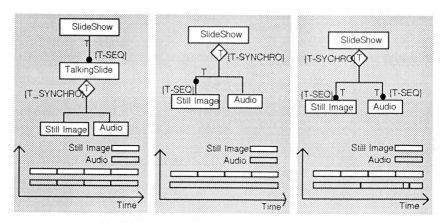

Fig. 3. Modeling SlideShow using extended OMT notation

SlideShow is used to describe an ordered sequence of slides synchronized with a sequence of music and/or narration. Several "versions" of SlideShows fit to this definition; each one corresponds to a composite multimedia object with slightly different structure. Fig. 3 shows three representative slide shows, along with their time-axis representations.

InteractiveImage is an association of a Still Image with a group of spatially-arranged active-areas (hotspots).

Scene is the area where visual objects are assembled for presentation. "Scene" is a spatial aggregation of visual objects, either input, such as buttons or output, such as text, still images, graphics and video. A scene may have playout duration; however, the positions of its components do not change during its presentation. Fig. 4 shows how we model a Scene and an Interactive Image using the extended OMT. The scene example is part of a multimedia tourist presentation (project "Aegean"[12]). The interactive map at the background has geographic places as active hotspots. The Scene consists of two screen portions dedicated to slide shows and a number of thematic and control buttons. The slide show presentations and the audio have the same duration.

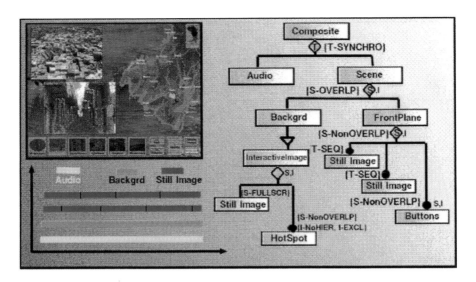

Fig. 4. Modeling a Composite Object (extended OMT)

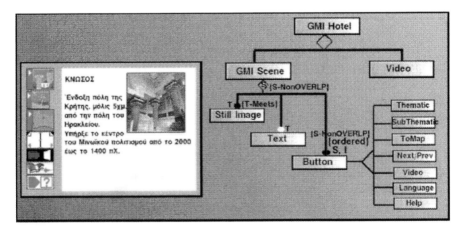

Fig. 5. Modeling a tourist multimedia object (extended OMT)

2.6. An Example

The example shows the applicability of our principles for user-guided multimedia conceptual modeling. We model (part of) an interactive tourist multimedia application

(GMI project [11]), using the extended OMT object model -to capture structural aspects, spatiotemporal synchronization and integrity constraints- (Fig. 5) and the OMT Dynamic model -to capture the user navigation and control flow- (Fig. 6). A GMI Hotel is a real world object; structurally, each hotel has a number of photos, zero or more pieces of text, and a video. For presentation sake, each hotel appears with an information page (GMI scene) and a Full Screen Video, while the transition from one state to the other is done through the Video button.

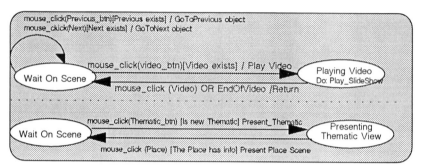

Fig. 6. The Control Flow of a tourist multimedia object (OMT Dynamic Model)

3. Conclusions

Several factors affect the broad acceptance of a new modeling technique; ease of personnel retraining is a major one. This is why we tried to find ways of using existing and well established models, looking for those minimal extensions needed for interactive multimedia presentations and implementing them as add-ons -rather than propose completely new special-purpose models.

In the design of multimedia applications, and in particular of interactive multimedia presentations, the usual role of the domain knowledge provider, which is to state the requirements and verify that the conceptual design of the system is a correct abstraction of the real world, must be extended to the working of the application itself. The creative director must design the spatiotemporal synchronization and the interactivity of the multimedia objects that participate in the application as well as its control flow. For this, two types of tools have hitherto been available: rapid prototyping -suitable but limited- and design tools originally constructed for the computer specialist -rather a different species from creative directors.

The design structures available for general-purpose conceptual modeling are suitable for multimedia but not sufficient. We proposed adding temporal, spatial and interactive dimension to them. We showed that this fits well with both general object oriented models -using OMT as a specific example- and with multimedia standards such as MHEG

We are applying our methodology to the design and development of series of multimedia titles for tourism and corporate presentations. But, of course, only the broader acceptance of our proposal may constitute an indication of success. We should like to develop CASE tools to accompany our methodology, again as extensions to standard CASE tools. Another direction of our research is the general set of multimedia applications, not just interactive multimedia presentations. Finally more research is needed in order to fully and mathematically capture the interactivity aspects.

Acknowledgment

This work has drawn on unpublished work by Nectaria Tryfona and Th. Hadzilacos on Spatial Information Systems [27].

4. References

1. S. Abiteboul and R. Hull, *IFO: A Formal Semantics Database Model*, ACM Transactions on Database Systems, 1987, 4, pp. 525-565.
2. P. Ackerman, *Direct Manipulation of Temporal Structures in a Multimedia Application Framework*, Proc. of ACM Multimedia '94.
3. T. Agerwala , *Putting Petri nets to work*, IEEE Computer, Dec. 1979.
4. J.F. Allen, *Maintaining Knowledge about Temporal Intervals*, Com. of the ACM, Vol. 26, No. 11, 1983, pp. 832-843.
5. M. L. Brodie, *On the Development of Data Models*, in *On Conceptual Modeling*, M.L.Brodie, J. Mylopoulos, W.J. Dchmidt (editors), (New York: Springer-Verlag), 1982.
6. P.S. Chen, *The Entity-Relationship Model: Toward a unified view of Data*, ACM Transactions on Database Systems, 1976, 1, pp. 9-36.
7. *Dynamic Distributed Document Script*, Austrian Research Center, Seibersdorf, MHEG Related activities, Proc. of International MHEG Workshop, Berlin, August 1994.
8. J. M. Egenhofer and R. J. Herring, *Categorizing Binary Topological Relationships Between Regions, Lines and Points in Geographic Databases*, Orono, ME: Department of Surveying Engineering, University of Maine, 1991.
9. J. M. Egenhofer, K. K. Al-Taha, *Reasoning about Gradual Changes of Topological Relationships*, Lecture Notes in Computer Science (Berlin:Springer-Verlag), Theories and Methods of Spatio-temporal Reasoning 1992, 639, pp. 252-268.
10. J. M. Egenhofer and R. J. Herring, *A Mathematic Framework for the Definition of Topological Relationships*, Proc. of the 4th International Symposium on Spatial Data Handling, Zurich, Switzerland, 1990, pp 803-813.
11. D. Gardelis, Th. Hadzilacos, P. Kourouniotis, M. Koutlis, E. Megalou, *Automating the generation of multimedia titles*, Proc.of the 10th International Conference on Advanced Science and Technology (ICAST'94), "Entering the 21st Century - Multimedia Information Systems", Chicago, USA, March 1994.

12. D. Gardelis, Th. Hadzilacos, M. Koutlis, E. Megalou, *Experiences from the developement of a multimedia tourist POIS*, Proc. of Greek Computer Society's Multimedia Workshop, Athens 1992

13. S. Gibbs, Ch. Breiteneder, D. Tsichritzis, *Data Modeling of Time-Based Media*, University of Geneva, Switzerland.

14. Th. Hadzilacos and N. Tryfona, *A Model for Expressing Topological Integrity Constraints in Geographic Databases*, Springer-Verlag, Lecture Notes in Computer Science, vol 639, Theories and Methods of Spatio-temporal Reasoning, 1992.

15. W. Klas, E. Neuhold, M. Schrelf, *Using an object-oriented approach to model multimedia data*, Computer Communications, vol. 13, no 4, May 1990.

16. F. Kretz, F. Colaitis, *Standardizing Hypermedia Information Objects*, IEEE Communications Magazine, May 1992.

17. T.D.C Little, A. Grafoor, C.Y.R.Chen, C.S. Chang, P.B. Berra, *Multimedia Synchronization*, IEEE Data Engineering Bulletin, Vol. 14, No. 3, Sept. 1991, pp 26-35.

18. T.D.C Little and A. Grafoor, *Interval-Based Conceptual Models for Time-Dependent Multimedia Data*, Transactions on Knowledge and Data Engineering, Vol. 5, No. 4, Aug. 1993.

19. T.D.C Little and A. Grafoor, *Spatio-Temporal Composition of Distributed Multiemdia Objects for Value-Added Networks*, Computer, October 1991.

20. T.D.C Little and A. Grafoor, *Syncronization and Storage Models for Multimedia Objects*, IEEE Journal On Selected Areas in Communications, Vol. 8, No. 3, Apr. 1990.

21. C. Meghini, F. Rabitti, C. Thanos, *Conceptual Modeling of Multimedia Documents*, IEEE Computer, Oct 1991.

22. B. S. Navathe, *Evolution of Data Modeling for Databases*, Communications of the ACM, Vol. 35, No. 9, Sept. 1992.

23. *OMHEGA*, ESPRIT project 8339, Proc. of International MHEG Workshop, Berlin, August 1994.

24. N. Pissinou and K. Makki, *On Temporal Modeling in the Context of Object Databases*, SIGMOD RECORD, Vol. 22, No. 3, Sept. 1993.

25. J. Rumbaugh, M. Blaha, W. Premerlani, F. Eddy, W. Lorensen, *Object-Oriented Modeling and Design*, Prentice Hall, 1991.

26. J. Rumbaugh, *Objects in the Twilight Zone, How to find and use application objects*, JOOP, 1993.

27. N. Tryfona and Th. Hadzilacos, *Conceptual Data Modeling for Geographic Applications: Models and Tools*, C.T.I. Technical Report - 95.02.7, Computer Technology Institute, Patras, 1995.

28. M. Worboys, H. Hearnshaw, D. Maguire, *Object-Oriented Data modeling for Spatial Databases*, International Journal of Geographic Information Systems, 4,4, pp. 369-383, 1990.

MODELING TECHNIQUES FOR HYTIME

LLOYD RUTLEDGE, JOHN F. BUFORD, AND JOHN L. RUTLEDGE

Distributed Multimedia Systems Laboratory
Department of Computer Science
University of Massachusetts - Lowell
One University Avenue
Lowell, MA 01854-2881 USA
URL: http://dmsl.cs.uml.edu
E-mail: {lrutledg,buford,jrutledg}@cs.uml.edu

ABSTRACT

Hypermedia/Time-based Structuring Language (HyTime) defines constructs for representing general hypermedia document concepts. Building documents with HyTime can be difficult because it uses many constructs and has an intricate relationship with its parent language Standard Generalized Markup Language (SGML). Further, HyTime inherits from SGML the establishment of document models as well as the document instances that follow them. In this paper we introduce some techniques for modeling how HyTime and SGML constructs contribute to the structure of documents and document models. We also introduce a defined set of "meta-HyTime constructs", which correspond to the semantic concepts HyTime constructs represent. Diagramming notations are provided in conjunction with these techniques as a tool for aiding document developers in understanding and communicating their use of HyTime.

1. Introduction

Hypermedia/Time-based Structuring Language (HyTime)[3,7] is an international standard for defining hypermedia document structure. This structure is described in terms of presentation-independent concepts considered universal to hypermedia processing. These concepts are specified using the constructs HyTime provides. They are specified with Standard Generalized Markup Language (SGML)[5,7], which defines the structure of documents in general. This separation between SGML and HyTime constructs within documents implies a layering in the authoring of HyTime documents.

SGML provides for the defining of both document models and the document instances that conform to them. HyTime inherits this capability. As such, SGML and HyTime document authors are concerned not only with the creation of documents but also with the designing of the general structures for the class of documents in which each fits. The specification of document models is part of the two standards. This provides an independent means of verifying a document's conformance to a particular model, thus facilitating the interchangeability of documents between applications using that model. The separation of document models from document instances implies another layering in the authoring of HyTime documents.

In this paper we introduce *meta-HyTime constructs*. Each meta-HyTime construct represents a general hypermedia concept that HyTime constructs describe. The HyTime standard document provides a strict definition of its constructs but does not strictly define the concepts those constructs represent. Since different HyTime constructs can be used to represent the same concepts, it is often convenient to model documents and in terms of these more general concepts instead of the specific HyTime constructs representing them. In this paper we introduce the specification of such concepts, which we call meta-HyTime constructs. This separation between HyTime and meta-HyTime constructs introduces another layering in the authoring of documents.

In earlier work we have used a diagram notation for describing SGML and HyTime documents and models[2]. Such diagrams are useful tools in the development of document models and instances. In this paper we describe some diagramming formalisms for representing HyTime documents on various levels of the layers described above, including that of meta-HyTime constructs.

2. Background

2.1. SGML

Standard Generalized Markup Language (SGML)[5,7] is an international standard for defining the textual encoding of document structure and content. SGML defines a set of constructs that build the markup that is placed with the content of a textual document file. This markup delimits the text content into containers called *elements*. In addition to text, elements can contain other elements or a combination of other elements and text. An element also has a *generic identifier* (GI) that states the element's type name. SGML also defines *attributes* that are associated with and describe elements. Each attribute has a name and a value. Two particularly useful types of attributes are the *unique identifier* (ID) and the *unique identifier reference* (IDREF). An ID attribute gives its element a unique name within the document. An IDREF attribute has as its value the ID of some other element in the document, thus representing a reference to the element. Together these constructs provide the hierarchical structure of a document, descriptive information about portions of the document, and the inclusion in the document of external resources and information.

Particular classes of documents are defined by SGML document type definitions (DTDs). Each SGML document must be associated with a particular DTD. A DTD defines a set of element types that can be used in conforming SGML documents. Regular expressions describing the valid contents of each element type are provided in the DTD. It also defines the set of attributes that can be used with each element type. Processing a document instance with its DTD can check the validity of the document format.

The driving philosophy behind SGML is that documents should be represented in a way that is independent of their means of presentation. The result is that an SGML document can be used by a variety of applications for a variety of purposes without having to be re-edited. This characteristic of SGML use also facilitates the processing of documents by SGML applications not designed for that document's set.

2.2. HyTime

Hypermedia/Time-based Structuring Language (HyTime)[3,7] is an international standard for defining the SGML encoding of hypermedia document structure. HyTime defines a set of primitives, called *architectural forms*, that represent the hypermedia aspects of a document. These aspects include multi-directional and multiply anchored hyperlinking, descriptive, flexible, and powerful document object locating, and the scheduled placement of document objects along measured axes.

HyTime extends SGML by defining how instances of these architectural forms are built from SGML constructs. An SGML element is recognized as conforming to a particular HyTime architectural form through its *HyTime architectural form attribute*. When assigned to an element, it establishes that element as a HyTime element. The name of this attribute is typically "HyTime". Its value is the name of the architectural form to which the element conforms. A HyTime element of a particular form also has other attribute assignments particular to that form. This collection of HyTime attributes defines the hypermedia semantics that a particular element conveys.

There are two types of HyTime architectural forms: the *element type form (ETF)* and the *attribute list form (ALF)*. Each HyTime element is recognized, through the HyTime architectural form attribute as described above, as conforming to one ETF. A particular set of HyTime attributes is defined for each ETF. Each ETF also uses the HyTime attributes defined for a group of ALFs. The attributes of one ALF can be shared by multiple ETFs.

HyTime is divided into six modules, each of which represents an area of hypermedia structuring. These modules are named *base, measurement, location addressing, hyperlinking, scheduling*, and *rendering*. In this paper we focus on modeling constructs from the hyperlinking and location addressing modules. Some constructs from the base module are also used. Hyperlinking module constructs are used to describe the hypertext relationships that exist between different document portions. Location addressing module constructs establish document portions as accessible for use with other constructs such as those that define hyperlinks.

HyTime's role in document processing is similar to SGML's. Both enable presentation-independent document formatting, both enhance document portability, and applications of both typically expect and apply their own semantics to composites of the constructs of the two languages.

3. Document Model Diagramming

In this paper we introduce document diagramming notations for six aspects of HyTime documentation. These six aspects are:

- The SGML parsed document
- The SGML DTD

- The HyTime meta-DTD
- The HyTime document constructs
- The HyTime-defined document model
- The meta-HyTime constructs

The first five of these diagram notations is illustrated in the subsections ahead using the HyTime document in Example 1. The diagramming of meta-HyTime construct usage is described in Section 4, also using Example 1.

The HyTime code in Example 1 represents a basic hypertext document. This document contains the string "this cites this". Its HyTime constructs encode a hyperlink connecting the first "this" and the second "this". The hyperlink is considered as of type "citations". The first "this" substring is encoded as the "start" of the link, and the second "this" as the link's "end". Hypertext traversal is allowed in any direction between the two words.

The ETFS used in this document are *HyTime document (HyDoc), suppress-HyTime (sHyTime), independent link (ilink), data location (dataloc)* and *dimension list (dimlist).* The root element of any HyTime document conforms to the HyDoc ETF. It establishes the document as using HyTime constructs. The sHyTime ETF establishes an element as having no HyTime semantics and not requiring HyTime processing. Such elements do, however, still use the attributes of certain ALFs. The ilink ETF is used to establish a hypertext relationship between different parts of a document. A dataloc element defines a portion of an element's content as accessible to HyTime constructs. Without location ETFs such as dataloc, a part of a document could only be referenced if it was an element with an ID

```
<!DOCTYPE  book [
<!ELEMENT  book - O (citation|location|text)*>
<!ATTLIST  book    HyTime   (HyDoc)    #FIXED    HyDoc>
<!ELEMENT  citation - O EMPTY>
<!ATTLIST  citation  HyTime    (ilink)     #FIXED    ilink
                     anchors   IDREFS    #REQUIRED
                     anchrole  CDATA     #FIXED    "start end"
                     HyNames  NAMES     #FIXED    "anchors linkends">
<!ELEMENT  location - O (dims)>
<!ATTLIST  location  HyTime    (dataloc)   #FIXED    dataloc
                     id        ID        #REQUIRED
                     locsrc    IDREF     #REQUIRED
                     quantum   (norm)    #FIXED    norm
                     reftype   CDATA     #FIXED    "locsrc text">
<!ELEMENT  (text|dims) - O (#PCDATA)>
<!ATTLIST  text    id      ID        #IMPLIED>
<!ATTLIST  · dims   HyTime   (dimlist)   #FIXED    dimlist>]>
<book>
<citation anchors="frstword lastword">
<location id=frstword locsrc=phrase><dims>1 1
<location id=lastword locsrc=phrase><dims>-1 1
<text id=phrase>this cites this
```

Ex. 1: Code for a small HyTime document.

attribute assigned to it. Finally, a dimlist can be contained in a location element such as a dataloc to specify the measurements defining a portion of an element's data.

In the Example 1 document, dataloc elements are used to make the "this" substrings accessible as distinct document objects. An ilink element uses these datalocs to establish a hypertext relationship between the two substrings. Since the element containing the string has no special HyTime semantics, it is defined as an sHyTime element. Finally, all of these elements are contained in a HyDoc to establish the document as a HyTime document.

The following five subsections show how modeling and diagramming techniques can be used to convey and illustrate this usage of SGML and HyTime. Section 4 shows how to use these techniques with meta-HyTime constructs.

3.1. SGML Parsed Document Diagramming

The text in a DTD and document instance is parsed to generate the representation of a document's structure. This representation of SGML constructs accounts for elements, their generic identifiers, their attribute assignments, their contents, and the referencing of other elements.

The key for SGML parsed document diagrams is in Figure 1. A box is drawn for each element instance. The generic identifier for each element is typed in its box. Below an element's box is typed its attribute assignments that result from the parse. Some of these assignments may have been fixed in or defaulted from the DTD. Others may have been explicitly defined in the document instance. Solid lines connect elements to their contents. Sometimes this content is text; other times it is other elements. Dashed arrows connect IDREF attributes to the elements they reference.

The SGML parsed document diagram for Example 1 is shown in Figure 2. It shows that the root element of the document tree is a book element. Further, the book element is depicted as containing a citation followed by two location elements and a text element. The location elements in turn each contain dims elements. Attribute assignments are included under the these elements. Also demonstrated is that three of these elements contain text strings. Finally, the id reference from the citation element to a text element is shown.

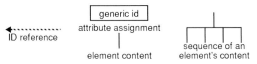

Fig. 1. SGML parsed document diagram key.

72

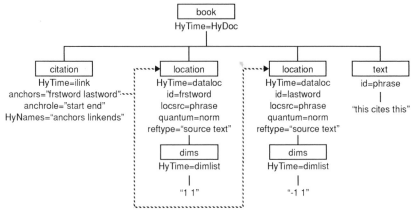

Fig. 2. SGML parsed document diagram for Example 1.

3.2. SGML DTD Diagramming

An SGML DTD describes the possibilities and restrictions for documents that conform to it. It identifies the types of elements that can exist. It also specifies, using a regular expression-based syntax, what elements of each type are allowed to contain. Further, a DTD provides attribute declarations for each element type that describe what attributes elements can have, what their values can be, and what their default values are.

The key for SGML DTD diagrams is in Figure 3. This notation is similar to that for SGML parsed documents. Element generic identifiers are put in boxes, attributes are described underneath those boxes, and solid lines connect boxes to content. With DTD diagrams, however, each box corresponds to an element type rather than an element instance. The text directly underneath these boxes depict DTD attribute declarations rather than assignments. Finally, content is described using content models rather than as explicit sequences.

The graphical notation for content models provides all the information given in the content models of SGML code. Element types can be grouped together as sequences or or-groups. Multiple occurrences of elements and groups can be shown. A depiction for SGML inclusion sets is also provided.

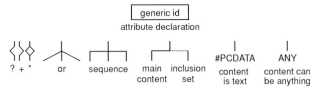

Fig. 3. SGML DTD diagram key.

The SGML DTD diagram for Example 1 is shown in Figure 4. It shows how book elements can contain any number of citation and text elements in any order. It also displays that the latter element types contain text data.

3.3. HyTime Meta-DTD Diagramming

The syntax of HyTime documents is defined in the standard by the HyTime meta-DTD. It shows what patterns of SGML constructs in documents comprise HyTime constructs. This relationship of SGML constructs to patterns of HyTime constructs is complex. We have found in helpful in our work to represent the meta-DTD diagrammatically. Such diagrams are useful tools for illustrating how HyTime constructs arise from SGML and how HyTime constructs relate to one another.

The structure of the meta-DTD is characterized by the existence of two types of objects: element type forms (ETFs) and attribute list forms (ALFs). Both of these types of forms have SGML-defined declarations for HyTime attributes. There are a number of relationships that exist between forms of these types. Each ETF can contain a certain pattern of elements conforming to other ETFs. The textual representation of this pattern is based on SGML content model notation. Each ETF uses the attributes of particular ALFs. Another type of relationship is that a HyTime ID attribute can be restricted to referencing only elements of certain ETFs.

The key for HyTime meta-DTD diagrams is in Figure 5. As with the previous two diagram notations, each box corresponds to the concept of an element. This notation introduces a new icon for representing ALFs: the smoothed box. Both ETF and ALF icons have attribute declarations under them in the same fashion used for SGML DTD diagrams.

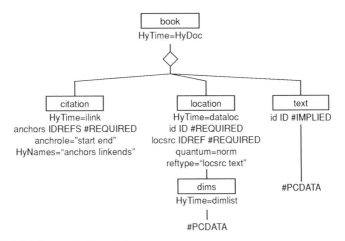

Fig. 4. SGML DTD diagram for Example 1.

74

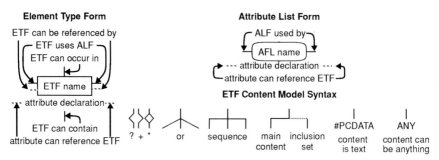

Element Type Form

ETF can be referenced by

ETF uses ALF

ETF can occur in

ETF name

attribute declaration

ETF can contain

attribute can reference ETF

? + *   or   sequence   main inclusion   #PCDATA   ANY
                        content set

                        content   content can
                        is text   be anything

Attribute List Form

ALF used by

AFL name

attribute declaration

attribute can reference ETF

ETF Content Model Syntax

Fig. 5. HyTime meta-DTD diagram key.

The content model notation used for relating ETFs to each other is also taken from the DTD diagram notation. Dashed arrows associate IDREF attributes to the ETFs they are restricted to referencing. IDREF attributes with no arrows have no such restrictions.

The complete meta-DTD diagram is rather large and complex. The portion of the HyTime meta-DTD diagram that is relevant for Example 1 is shown in Figure 6. The root element of any HyTime document must conform to the *HyTime Document (HyDoc)* element type form, as it does in the example document. A HyDoc element can contain any combination of many ETFs, including *contextual link (clink)*, *data location (dataloc)*, *dimension list (dimlist)*, and *suppress-HyTime (sHyTime)* elements. This diagram also shows a dataloc element as being able to contain a dimlist element. Also, the ALFs *all-id* and *all-ref* can be used by any HyTime element.

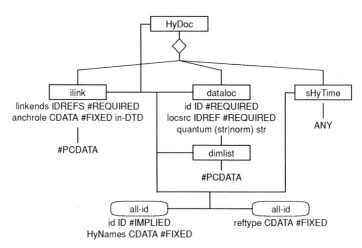

Fig. 6. Portion of the HyTime meta-DTD diagram that is relevant for Example 1.

Here we show the ilink attributes that are used in our sample document. The *link ends (linkends)* attribute contains id references to the anchors of this link. The *anchor roles (anchrole)* attribute assigns a role name to each anchor. A dataloc element is required to have an ID attribute, as shown in the diagram. It also must have a *location source (locsrc)* attribute, which specifies an element within the document to which the dataloc's address is to be applied. This address is the dataloc's text contents, which specify numbers indicating the tokens of a location source's text contents are to be located. The *quantum* attribute specifies how these tokens are to be established and counted. There are no restrictions on what sHyTime elements contain.

All the ETFs use the ALFs *all-id* and *all-ref*. The all-id ALF establishes some attributes that any HyTime element can use. Here we show the definition of the ID attribute, which is the same as the SGML ID attribute. The HyNames attribute can reassign for its element an SGML attribute with a particular name as being a HyTime attribute of a different name. The *reference type (reftype)* attribute of the all-ref ALF places restrictions on the types of elements that an IDREF attribute can reference. The use of these attributes will be illustrated in the subsections ahead.

3.4. HyTime Document Construct Diagramming

The HyTime standard specifies a collection of constructs that can be recognized from processing SGML documents. SGML elements can be recognized as instances of HyTime element type forms. Attributes of these elements are sometimes recognized as HyTime attributes. Because ID attributes are considered HyTime attributes and some HyTime attributes are IDREFs, many unique identifier references will be recognized as HyTime constructs.

The key for HyTime document construct diagrams is in Figure 7. This diagram notation is very similar to that for SGML parsed documents. One difference is that the text within each element box is not the element's generic identifier but the name of the ETF it conforms to. The GI of an element is put between angled lines above the element's attribute specifications. Another difference is that the HyTime attributes of each element are given in italics, while the SGML-only attributes remain in normal text.

The HyTime document construct diagram for Example 1 is shown in Figure 8. It demonstrates that the seven elements are recognized as instances of the HyDoc, ilink, dataloc, dimlist, and sHyTime ETFs. The first HyTime attribute under the ilink element is named "linkends" because that is its HyTime name. The SGML name for that element, "anchors", is shown in an SGML-only attribute assignment at the bottom of the list. This reassignment was specified by the value of the HyNames attribute for the ilink. Since the other attributes have the same SGML and HyTime names, they only need to be listed once.

76

Fig. 7. HyTime document construct diagram key.

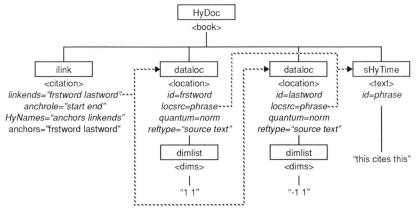

Fig. 8. HyTime document construct diagram for Example 1.

3.5. HyTime-defined Document Model Diagramming

HyTime only defines the recognition of constructs within SGML parsed documents. The use of SGML DTD constructs to define the meta-DTD can be confusing because HyTime neither specifies a single DTD nor the conformance of DTDs. Further, DTD constructs alone cannot specify all the constraints that would make all of its documents HyTime conforming. However, the designing of DTDs for HyTime documents is still important. A DTD can often specify some constraints that enforce HyTime-conformance. Wary DTD developers can avoid unnecessarily permissive DTDs. DTD writers must also avoid making their DTDs HyTime-preventing. DTDs for classes of HyTime-conforming documents are often called *HyTime DTDs (HDTDs)*.

The designing of HyTime DTDs is also important because some HyTime constructs can be used to contribute to the specification of a document model. Typically, such constructs define restrictions on allowable instances of certain other constructs. The *ID reference element type (reftype)* HyTime attribute is an example of such a construct, and is used in Example 1. When assigned for an element, reftype specifies that a particular IDREF attribute can only reference elements of certain types. If this attribute is declared in the DTD as fixed, then the same restriction applies to all instances of that element type. Such a global restriction could be considered part of the model for that document. HyTime has other constructs that can contribute to document model specifications, such as lexical typing and property defining. When constructs like these are fixed in a DTD, they can be considered as contributing to the document model defined by the HDTD.

We have developed a diagram notation for representing the document models defined by HDTDs. The key for HyTime-defined document model diagrams is in Figure 9. It borrows icons from the diagram notations for both SGML DTDs and the HyTime meta-DTD. It contains the data within a DTD diagram with some modifications and the addition of HyTime-define document model information. One modification is that the box icons contain ETF names instead of generic identifiers. However, each box still corresponds to an element type, and the generic identifier is placed under the box above the attribute declarations. One addition is the use of dotted arrows to associate IDREF attribute declarations to the element types they are restricted by reftypes to referencing.

The HyTime-defined document model diagram for Example 1 is shown in Figure 10. It shows the information within the DTD diagram from Figure 4. The ETF names are added, as is the reftype-defined restriction that the locsrc attribute can only reference text elements.

4. Meta-HyTime Constructs

The modeling and diagramming of five aspects of HyTime documentation have been described in Section 3. In this section we introduce a sixth aspect, that of *meta-HyTime constructs*. HyTime defines constructs for representing some general hypermedia concepts. However, it does not formalize the concepts themselves. Often multiple HyTime constructs represent the same generic concepts. Such groups of constructs are differentiated by the syntactic context in which they are applied rather than by the general concept they represent. It is helpful to identify these concepts when considering a document in terms of its general hypermedia structure but independently of its HyTime syntax.

In this section we introduce *meta-HyTime constructs*, which correspond to these syntax-independent concepts. For each meta-HyTime construct identified, a diagram notation for it and a specification of the HyTime constructs patterns that comprise it are given. These constructs enable document developers to model and structure their

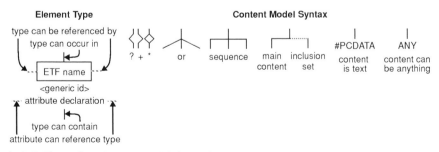

Fig. 9. HyTime-defined document model diagram key.

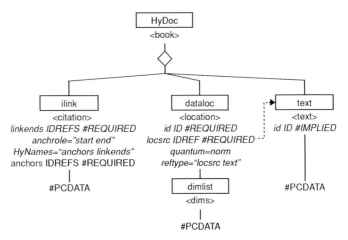

Fig. 10. HyTime-defined document model diagram for Example 1.

documents in terms of these general hypermedia concepts instead of just in terms of specific HyTime constructs. Here we continue to use the code from Example 1 as the basis for sample diagrams. Sample meta-HyTime constructs for hyperlinking and location addressing are introduced as a demonstration of how meta-HyTime constructs in general can be created and applied. The code Example 1 in the previous section is used here to illustrate their use.

4.1. Hyperlinking

The most important HyTime-defined concept in Example 1 is the hyperlink. It is the concept that associates the first "this" with the second. The ilink ETF was used to represent this hyperlink, but other HyTime constructs could have been used to represent equivalent and similar hyperlinks. One meta-HyTime construct is the *hyperlink*. It is derived from the usage of the clink form. It can also be derived from the usage of Hytime constructs *independent link (ilink), aggregate link (agglink)*, and *span link (spanlink)*.The components of the hyperlink meta-construct are derived from the ilink ETF. The ilink ETF defines all the hyperlinking semantics definable by any of the other HyTime link construct.

The ilink ETF and its attributes define certain hyperlinking semantics. These include the *link type*, the *anchors*, the *significance of each anchor in hyperlink*, and the link's *traversability*. The link type is a single word that describes the class of the link. In SGML/HyTime syntax this word is the generic id of the hyperlink element. The anchors themselves are determined by the *linkends* attribute as a list of ID references to the anchors. The *anchor roles (anchrole)* attribute assigns to each anchor a name describing its role in the hyperlink. The significance of each anchor can be further specified by the *link end terms (endterms)* attribute, which references for each anchor a document subtree describing that anchor. Finally, the allowable directions of traversal through the anchors are determined by the *external access traversal rule (extra)* and *internal access traversal rule (intra)* attributes.

The key for meta-HyTime hyperlink construct diagrams is in Figure 11. This key provides for the specification of the hyperlink itself, the type of the link, its anchors, their roles, and the directions in which they can be traversed to and from along the hyperlink. The meta-HyTime hyperlink construct diagram for Example 1 is shown in Figure 12. The ilink element with the GI of "citation" is displayed as a hyperlink of link type "citation". Its anchors are defined as the locations specified by the dataloc elements. The modeling of this locations' resolution is described in the next subsection. The anchor names for the link are "start" and "end". Bidirection traversal to and from both anchors is allowed.

4.2. Location Addressing

There any many element type forms in the location addressing module of HyTime. The primary differences between them are in how they use SGML and HyTime syntax and semantics to specify the location of objects. They are similar in that they all specify the location of some document object. We have found two meta-HyTime constructs useful for representing the general hypermedia significance of location elements within a document structure. The two constructs are the *resolved location* and the *extra-SGML object*.

A *resolved location* meta-HyTime construct associates a location element with the document object it locates. Here, the box containing the ETF name for a location element is colored gray to make it visually distinct. A thick gray line with a gray arrowhead at its end connects this box with the graphical representation of the object it locates. This makes it easy for the viewer of a document structure diagram to follow a HyTime-defined reference through a sequence of location specifications to its destination.

When a location resolves to an object defined using SGML, its graphical representation is a thick gray arrow pointing to the icon representing the located SGML construct. However, HyTime location addressing can locate objects not defined using SGML

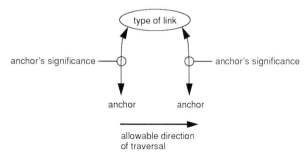

Fig. 11. Meta-HyTime hyperlink construct diagram key.

constructs. These include the *data location address (dataloc)* ETF, which resolves to a portion of data content rather than to an SGML construct. Such located objects are represented by the *extra-SGML object* meta-HyTime construct. An extra-SGML object is depicted as a gray box surrounding the diagram portion representing the located object.

Figure 12 has a diagram with hyperlink and location address meta-HyTime constructs. The boxes for the two dataloc elements are colored gray to indicate they are location addresses. A large gray arrow connects these boxes the words they locate.

5. Related Work

HyTime database research has been performed as GMD-IPSI in Darmstadt, Germany. They have described how the layering of HyTime over SGML affects the model for HyTime processing[1]. A general model of hypertext has been proposed by the Dexter group[6]. The Dexter model defines constructs that can be used to describe any hypertext document or system, enabling comparison between different systems. Another model, Hypertext Design Model (HDM), has been proposed for representing hypertext applications has been proposed[4].

6. Conclusion

This paper described some techniques for modeling the use of SGML and HyTime constructs in defining document structure. Diagram notations were provided for depicted the models created. These modeling techniques and their diagram notations reflect the various layers of construct definition from which SGML and HyTime encoding can be viewed. modeling and diagraming schemes were presented for the SGML encoding of

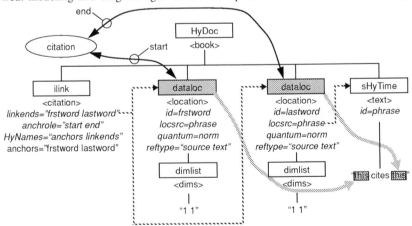

Fig. 12. Meta-HyTime hyperlink and location address construct diagram for Example 1.

document instances, the SGML encoding of document models, the HyTime meta-DTD, the HyTime encoding of document instances, and the HyTime encoding of document models.

This paper also introduced meta-HyTime constructs for representing the general hypermedia concepts HyTime constructs encode. These meta-HyTime constructs enable another layer of modeling and diagramming document structure. This meta-HyTime layer models documents in terms of their general hypermedia structure rather than in terms of the specific HyTime constructs that encode this structure. Modeling and diagramming with this layer assists document developers in understanding and communicating how HyTime constructs contribute to a document's general hypermedia composition.

7. References

1. Boehm, Klemens, Aberer, Karl, and Neuhold, Erich, "Administering Structured Documents in Digital Libraries", *Advances in Digital Libraries*, eds., Adam, N.R., Bhargava, B., and Yesha, Y., Springer, Lecture Notes in Computer Science, 1995.

2. Buford, John F., Rutledge, Lloyd, Rutledge, John L., and Keskin, Can, "HyOctane: A HyTime Engine for an MMIS", *Multimedia Systems*, vol. 1, no. 4, February 1994 pp. 173–185.

3. DeRose, Steve J., and Durand, David G., *Making Hypermedia Work: A User's Guide to HyTime*, Kluwer Press, 1991.

4. Garzotto, Franca, Paolini, Paolo, and Schwabe, Daniel, "HDM — A Model-based Approach to Hypertext Application Design", *ACM Transactions on Information Systems*, vol. 11, no. 1, January 1993, pp. 1–26.

5. Goldfarb, Charles F., *The SGML Handbook*, Oxford University Press, 1991.

6. Halasz, F., and Schwartz, M., "The Dexter Hypertext Reference Model", *Communications of the ACM*, vol. 37, no. 2, February 1994, pp. 30–39.

7. International Standards Organization, *Hypermedia/Time-based Structuring Language (HyTime)*, ISO/IEC IS 10744, 1992.

8. International Standards Organization, *Standard Generalized Markup Language (SGML)*, ISO/IEC IS 8879, 1986.

TRACE CALCULUS AND THE SPECIFICATION
OF OBJECT BEHAVIORS

LI YANG

Institute of Systems Science, National University of Singapore
Heng Mui Keng Terrace, Kent Ridge, Singapore 0511
Phone: (+65)772-6743, Fax: (+65)774-4990, E-mail: yangli@iss.nus.sg

ABSTRACT

The coming multimedia applications of information systems present new challenges to data modeling, at the modeling of both structures and behaviors of objects. The design of a distributed multimedia application involves many temporal problems related to the processing, transportation, storage, retrieval and presentation of data. A formal approach to semantic specification of objects and their behaviors is proposed. Object behaviors are described by traces, i.e. sequences of actions on the object. A trace calculus is proposed based on the linear temporal logic. Its integration with the algebraic modeling approach is discussed. Object state transitions can be mapped into relations on the trace structure. Dynamic behaviors of objects can be specified with axioms and inference rules. The specification is shown through an example. This provides a starting point from which more general characteristics of objects, such as encapsulation, aggregation and synchronization, can be formally described.

1. Introduction

Traditional database design methodologies are not appropriate for the requirements of new database applications such as multimedia information systems, mobile databases, and CAD/CAM. Among these new technical challenges, the specification and verification of object behaviors have to be of main interest for system designers and users. The interest in object behaviors is growing in part due to recent concerns with: the behavior description of systems in the area of conceptual modeling[1,2,15]; the dynamic aspects and synchronization of multimedia databases[6,10,11]; and the manipulation of rather complex entities in object migration[17]. In the area of database design there has been a constant interest in object specifications and tools. These specifications and tools provide the necessary means for abstraction and modularization. However, they are not useful till now when dealing with object behaviors as opposed to structures.

In this paper, objects are assumed as timely evolving entities. Objects have temporal existence in the sense that they can be created, can evolve and can be destroyed, if ever. The major property of objects is that they have internal states, and changes of states will generate observable behaviors[3]. In general, this essence of abstraction has two characteristics: it is invested with object attributes — usually consisting of tangled family of relationships with other objects and nested claims and rights to them; secondly and more crucially, it can have its behaviors changed depending on external requests(actions) made to it or, indirectly, to objects to which it is beholden. We assume that the first action sent to an object is to create it, with the subsequent actions update the object. In this point of view, an object in its current state can be described by a sequence of actions sent to it, i.e. by an object trace. The whole life cycle of an object is a sequence of actions it receives from the beginning to the end.

This paper is devoted to the development of basic concepts and tools for the specification of behaviors in addition to that of structures, as a more adequate alternative to the traditional structure techniques for conceptual modeling. Rather than the study of object workflows[13,16] which do not consider object structures, we extend the algebraic modeling mechanism by adding attribute symbols and actions. Attributes, whose values may be changed by actions, are different from functions. With the algebras on object signature as semantic domain, object state transitions can be mapped into relations on the Kripke interpretation structure. Dynamic behaviors of objects can be specified with axioms and inference rules of trace calculus. By adding further restrictions on the models allowed by trace calculus, various properties of objects can be specified hierarchically.

The paper is organized as follows: Section 2 presents the syntax of the proposed approach. Section 3 discusses its semantics. Section 4 gives some trace laws. A formal system for trace calculus is given in Section 5. Section 6 shows how to specify the multimedia synchronization of objects through an example.

2. Syntax of Trace Calculus

We introduce a language $\mathcal{L}_{Trace}$ about object traces on the basis of many-sorted logic and first-order linear temporal logic[7,8,12]. It allows us to construct a logic system to describe dynamic properties of objects. Objects referred here are dynamically evolving entities which have internal states and observable behaviors.

The algebraic approach to formal specification starts from signatures. In order to specify object behaviors, we extend the conventional signatures with action symbols and attribute symbols. An object signature Σ is a quad-tuple $\Sigma = \langle S, F, A, E \rangle$, where S is a set of sorts and F is a set of function symbols. $\langle S, F \rangle$ is a signature in conventional sense[18] to describe data contexts of objects which are independent on object states. A is a set of attribute symbols sorted by $S^* \times S$. Interpretations of attribute symbols may vary from time to time, i.e. depend on states of the object. E is a set of action symbols sorted by S^*. Constants are usually represented by nullary function symbols. Variables in programming languages can be represented by nullary attribute symbols.

Assuming E (the set of action symbols) as a sort, we have the ΣE-signature $\langle SE, FE \rangle$ (the free extension of the signature $\langle S, F \rangle$) where $SE = S \cup \{E\}$ is the extension of the set S with E, and FE is a set of symbols sorted by $S^* \times SE$, the extension of function symbols F with action symbols, i.e. $\forall \omega \in S^*, s \in SE$, if $s \in S$

then $FE_{\omega,s} = F_{\omega,s}$, otherwise $FE_{\omega,E} = E_{\omega}$.

Let us consider a media player example: A media player in its simplest form has three types of objects: PROVIDER, PLAYER and BUFFER. PROVIDER provides information into the BUFFER. PLAYER gets the information from the BUFFER and puts it to an appropriate output device. The signature PROVIDER in its simplest form may be

ObjectSignature PROVIDER =
    Sorts: ITEM, BOOL
    Functions:
        true, false: BOOL
        /* other boolean functions */
    Attributes:
        item: ITEM
        waiting: BOOL
    Actions:
        retrieve(ITEM)
        put(ITEM)
End

The attribute *item* is a piece of data that the provider currently deals with. Attribute *waiting* indicates whether the provider is now waiting to put the data into buffer. The value of these attributes will vary from time to time.

The signature PLAYER and BUFFER are:

ObjectSignature PLAYER =
    Sorts: ITEM, BOOL
    Attributes:
        item: ITEM
        waiting: BOOL
    Actions:
        play(ITEM)
        get(ITEM)
End

ObjectSignature BUFFER =
    Sorts: ITEM, INT
    Attributes:
        count: INT
    Actions:
        get(ITEM)
        put(ITEM)
End

These objects are "abstract" in the sense that we do not aware of their implementations. They can be further refined to more specific objects. For example, BUFFER can be implemented as an array or a queue or whatever else.

Let X be an S-sorted set of free variables, $X = \{X_s | s \in S\}$. For every sort $s \in SE$ the set, $T(\Sigma, X)_s$, of *terms* of sort s is the least set containing: 1. every $x \in X_s$; 2. *Init* $\in T(\Sigma, X)_E$ if $s = E$, *Init* is called the *initial action term*; 3. $f(t_1, \ldots, t_n)$ where $f \in FE_{\langle s_1 \times \ldots \times s_n \rangle, s} \cup A_{\langle s_1 \times \ldots \times s_n \rangle, s}$ and $t_i \in T(\Sigma, X)_{s_i}$ for $1 \leq i \leq n$; 4. $[a]t$ where $a \in T(\Sigma, X)_E$ and $t \in T(\Sigma, X)_s$; 5. $[Init]t$, $\mathbf{X}t$ and $\mathbf{X}^- t$ where $t \in T(\Sigma, X)_s$. $\mathbf{X}$

is a temporal operator which means "next" and $\mathbf{X}^-$ means "previous". Terms in $T(\Sigma, X)_E$ are called *action terms*.

Let $\Sigma = \langle S, F, A, E \rangle$ be an object signature, an *atomic formula* has either the form $t_1 = t_2$ where $t_1, t_2 \in T(\Sigma, X)_s$ are terms of $s \in SE$, or *enabled*(a) where $a \in T(\Sigma, X)_E$. Σ-*formulas* are built from atomic formulas using the conventional and temporal operators. Formally, the set $F(\Sigma, X)$ of Σ-formulas is the least set containing: 1. every atomic formula; 2. $[a]p$ where $a \in T(\Sigma, X)_E$ and $p \in F(\Sigma, X)$; 3. formulas with temporal operators: i.e. $\mathbf{X}p$, $p\mathbf{U}q$, $\mathbf{X}^-p$ and $p\mathbf{U}^-q$ where $p, q \in F(\Sigma, X)$; 4. formulas with first-order operators: i.e. $\neg p$, $p \to q$ and $\forall x : s\ p$ where $p, q \in F(\Sigma, X)$, and $x \in X_s$ is a free variable in p. In Σ-formulas, $\mathbf{X}, \mathbf{U}$ means "next", "until". The superscript "$-$" means "reverse the time order". Further operators are as usual considered as abbreviations: $p \wedge q \stackrel{\triangle}{=} \neg(p \to \neg q)$, $p \vee q \stackrel{\triangle}{=} \neg p \to q$, $p \leftrightarrow q \stackrel{\triangle}{=} (p \to q) \wedge (q \to p)$, $\mathbf{t} \stackrel{\triangle}{=} p_0 \vee \neg p_0$ (with some particular atomic formula p_0), $\mathbf{f} \stackrel{\triangle}{=} \neg \mathbf{t}$, $\mathbf{F}p \stackrel{\triangle}{=} \mathbf{t}\mathbf{U}p$ ("sometimes"), $\mathbf{G}p \stackrel{\triangle}{=} \neg(\mathbf{F}\neg p)$ ("always"), $p\mathbf{B}q \stackrel{\triangle}{=} \neg(\neg p\mathbf{U}q)$ ("before"), $\mathbf{F}^-p \stackrel{\triangle}{=} \mathbf{t}\mathbf{U}^-p$, $\mathbf{G}^-p \stackrel{\triangle}{=} \neg(\mathbf{F}^-\neg p)$, and $\exists x : s\ p \stackrel{\triangle}{=} \neg\forall x : s\ \neg p$.

3. Semantics of Trace Calculus

The semantics of $\mathcal{L}_{Trace}$ is given by extending the Kripke structure of first-order linear temporal logic.

3.1. Semantic Domain

Given a ΣE-algebra $\mathcal{A}$, $\mathcal{A}_E$ gives interpretation of action symbols in E, and consequently $\mathcal{A}_E^*$ gives interpretation of sequences of actions. Elements of $\mathcal{A}_E$ are called actions, elements of $\mathcal{A}_E^*$ are called traces. For traces, we introduce following notations: ϵ stands for the empty trace; $\omega \cdot a$ represents a trace ω followed by an action a; $|\omega|$ is the length of trace ω, which is defined as $|\epsilon| = 0$ and $|\omega \cdot a| = |\omega| + 1$; ω_i stands for the i-th action in ω; and $^i\omega$ refers to the prefix of ω with a length i.

The interpretation of terms and formulas is given by the extension of Kripke structure of first-order linear temporal logic. It is given by a ΣE-algebra, a mapping, and relationships among actions and traces. ΣE-algebra gives the interpretation of attributes; the mapping gives values of attributes in traces; and the relationship specifies whether an action is enabled after a given trace. Formally, A Σ-interpretation has the form $\mathcal{I} = \langle \mathcal{A}, \mathcal{F}, \mathcal{E} \rangle$, where $\mathcal{A}$ is a ΣE-algebra, $\mathcal{F}$ is a mapping $\mathcal{F}(f) : \mathcal{A}_E^* \to (\mathcal{A}_{s_1} \times \ldots \times \mathcal{A}_{s_n} \to \mathcal{A}_s)$ for all $f \in A_{\langle s_1 \times \ldots \times s_n \rangle, s}$, and $\mathcal{E} \subset \mathcal{A}_E^* \times \mathcal{A}_E$ describes relationship among actions and traces. The relationship gives possible valid sequences of actions on an object before the execution of a specific action.

A trace structure $\mathcal{K} = \langle \mathcal{I}, v, \omega \rangle$ consists of a Σ-interpretation $\mathcal{I} = \langle \mathcal{A}, \mathcal{F}, \mathcal{E} \rangle$, a valuation of variables in $\mathcal{I}$, $v = \{v_s\}_{s \in SE}$, where $v_s : X_s \to \mathcal{A}_s$, and a trace ω. Here we use traces rather than sequences of states[14] in conventional temporal structure.[*]

3.2. Interpretation of Terms

Given an object signature $\Sigma = \langle S, F, A, E \rangle$ and its Σ-interpretation $\mathcal{I} = \langle \mathcal{A}, \mathcal{F}, \mathcal{E} \rangle$, a *valuation* of a set X of variables in $\mathcal{I}$ is $v = \{v_s | s \in SE\}$, where v_s is a mapping from X_s to the semantic domain $\mathcal{A}_s$. Let $v : X \to \mathcal{I}$ be a valuation, its extension v_i^* (the valuation of terms in the state s_i) on a trace ω is defined as follows:

1. $\forall x \in X_s, v_i^*(x) = v(x)$;

2. $\forall f \in FE_{\langle s_1 \times ... \times s_n \rangle, s}$, and $t_i \in T(\Sigma, X)_{s_i}$ for $1 \le i \le n$, we have
   $v_i^*(f(t_1, \ldots, t_n)) = f^{\mathcal{A}}(v_i^*(t_1), \ldots, v_i^*(t_n))$;

3. $\forall f \in A_{\langle s_1 \times ... \times s_n \rangle, s}$, and $t_i \in T(\Sigma, X)_{s_i}$ for $1 \le i \le n$, we have
   $v_i^*(f(t_1, \ldots, t_n)) = \mathcal{F}_i(f)(v_i^*(t_1), \ldots, v_i^*(t_n))$;

4. if $a \in T(\Sigma, X)_E, a \ne Init$ and $t \in T(\Sigma, X)_s$, then
   $$v_i^*([a]t) = \begin{cases} v_{i+1}^*(t) & \text{if } v_i^*(a) = \omega_{i+1} \\ v_i^*(t) & \text{otherwise} \end{cases} ;$$

5. if $t \in T(\Sigma, X)_s$, then $v_i^*([Init]t) = v_0^* t$;

6. if $t \in T(\Sigma, X)_s$, then $v_i^*(\mathbf{X}t) = v_{i+1}^* t$;

7. if $t \in T(\Sigma, X)_s$, then $v_i^*(\mathbf{X}^- t) = v_{i-1}^* t,\ i > 0$;

Similarly, the assignment $\mathcal{K}_i(F)$ of a formula F in the state s_i can be defined inductively as follows.

1. $\mathcal{K}_i(t_1 = t_2) = \mathbf{t}$ iff $v_i^*(t_1) = v_i^*(t_2)$

2. $\mathcal{K}_i(enabled(a)) = \mathbf{t}$ iff $({}^i\omega, v_i^*(a)) \in \mathcal{E}$

3. $\mathcal{K}_i(\neg p) = \mathbf{t}$ iff $\mathcal{K}_i(p) = \mathbf{f}$

4. $\mathcal{K}_i(p \to q) = \mathbf{t}$ iff $\mathcal{K}_i(p) = \mathbf{f}$ or $\mathcal{K}_i(q) = \mathbf{t}$

5. $\mathcal{K}_i([a]p) = \mathbf{t}$ iff $\begin{cases} \mathcal{K}_{i+1}(p) = \mathbf{t} & \text{if } v_i^*(a) = \omega_{i+1} \\ \mathcal{K}_i(p) = \mathbf{t} & \text{otherwise} \end{cases} ;$

6. $\mathcal{K}_i([Init]p) = \mathbf{t}$ iff $\mathcal{K}_0(p) = \mathbf{t}$

---

[*]Actions are transitions of states, i.e. $s_0 \xrightarrow{a_0} s_1, \ldots, s_i \xrightarrow{a_i} s_{i+1}, \ldots$ (s_i is the i-th state, a_i is the action issued at the state s_i, and it causes transition of the state s_i to s_{i+1}). Clearly, we can use the trace $Init\, a_0 a_1 \ldots$ to represent the transition of states $s_0 s_1 \ldots$. $Init$ stands for the creation of an object which is always the first action on the object.

7. $\mathcal{K}_i(\mathbf{X}p) = \mathbf{t}$ iff $\mathcal{K}_{i+1}(p) = \mathbf{t}$

8. $\mathcal{K}_i(p\mathbf{U}q) = \mathbf{t}$ iff $\exists j \geq i$ such that $\mathcal{K}_j(q) = \mathbf{t}$ and $\mathcal{K}_k(p) = \mathbf{t}$ for every $k, i \leq k < j$

9. $\mathcal{K}_i(\mathbf{X}^-p) = \mathbf{t}$ iff $i > 0, \mathcal{K}_{i-1}(p) = \mathbf{t}$

10. $\mathcal{K}_i(p\mathbf{U}^-q) = \mathbf{t}$ iff $\exists j \leq i$ such that $\mathcal{K}_j(q) = \mathbf{t}$ and $\mathcal{K}_k(p) = \mathbf{t}$ for every $k, j < k \leq i$

11. $\mathcal{K}_i(\forall x\, p) = \mathbf{t}$ iff $\mathcal{K}_i'(p) = \mathbf{t}$ where $\mathcal{K}' = (\mathcal{I}, v', \omega)$ satisfies $v'(y) = v(y)$ for every $y, y \neq x$.

A formula p is called *valid* in a trace structure $\mathcal{K}$ (denoted by $\models_\mathcal{K} p$) and $\mathcal{K}$ is called a model of p if $\mathcal{K}_i(p) = \mathbf{t}$ for every $i \geq 0$. p is called valid (denoted by $\models p$) if $\models_\mathcal{K} p$ holds for every trace structure $\mathcal{K}$ on Σ. p follows from a set Γ of formulas (denoted by $\Gamma \models p$) if $\models_\mathcal{K} p$ holds for every $\mathcal{K}$ with $\models_\mathcal{K} q$ for every $q \in \Gamma$. A set Γ of formulas is called *satisfiable* if there is some $Trace_\Sigma$-structure $\mathcal{K}$ such that $\models_\mathcal{K} p$ holds for every $p \in \Gamma$. A formula p is called satisfiable if $\{p\}$ is satisfiable. For satisfiability, we have the following facts:

Fact 1 *If $\forall q \in \Gamma, \models q$ and $\Gamma \models p$, then $\models p$*

Fact 2 *$p_1, \ldots, p_n \models q$ iff $(\models \mathbf{G}p_1 \wedge \cdots \wedge \mathbf{G}p_n) \to q$*

Fact 3 *If $\Gamma \models p$ and $\Gamma \models p \to q$, then $\Gamma \models q$*

Fact 4 *If $\Gamma \models p$, then $\Gamma \models [a]p$ and $\Gamma \models [Init]p$*

Fact 5 *$\models p$ iff $\neg p$ is not satisfiable*

4. Trace Laws

We show that the logic laws in first-order temporal calculus are still valid for traces. A formula $p(p_1, \ldots, p_n)$ (of $\mathcal{L}_{Trace}$) is called *tautologically valid* if it results from a tautology $p(x_1, \ldots, x_n)$ (of first-order temporal logic, $\mathcal{L}_{FLTLB}$) by consistently replacing atomic formulas $x_1, \ldots, x_n$ of p by formulas $p_1, \ldots, p_n$ of $\mathcal{L}_{Trace}$.

Theorem 6 *Every tautologically valid formula is valid.*

Proof sketch. Let $p^* = p(p_1^*/p_1, \ldots, p_n^*/p_n)$ be a substitution of $p_1, \ldots, p_n$ of p by trace formulas $p_1^*, \ldots, p_n^*$, $\mathcal{I}$ be a Σ-interpretation, v a valuation, and $\omega = s_0, \ldots, s_i, \ldots$ be an object trace. For $i \geq 0, 1 \leq j \leq n$, we define the valuation $\mathcal{M}_i(p_j) = \mathcal{K}_i(p_j^*)$, where $\mathcal{M} = (S, v, \beta)$ is a first-order temporal structure corresponds to $\mathcal{K}$ where S is the corresponding ΣE-algebra, and β is the interpretation of $\mathcal{F}$ on the trace $\omega = s_0 s_1 \ldots s_i \cdots$. By induction, we will have $\mathcal{M}_i(p) = \mathcal{K}_i(p^*)$. If p is a tautology, then $\mathcal{M}_i(p) = \mathcal{K}_i(p^*) = \mathbf{t}$. $\square$

Hence, we may use all tautologies of first-order temporal logic as "logical laws" in trace calculus. Suppose a formula q follows from some formulas $p_1, \ldots, p_n$ in the first order temporal logic. If we substitute consistently formulas in $p_1, \ldots, p_n$ and q

with trace formulas, we should not destroy the logical relationship. Let $p_1, \ldots, p_n, q$ be trace formulas (of $\mathcal{L}_{Trace}$), q is called a *tautological consequence* of $p_1, \ldots, p_n$ if the formula $p_1 \wedge \ldots \wedge p_n \rightarrow q$ is tautologically valid. The desired result is:

Corollary 7 *If q is a tautological consequence of $p_1, \ldots, p_n$, then $p_1, \ldots, p_n \models q$.*

These are logical laws in $\mathcal{L}_{Trace}$ coming from the "classical part" of the temporal logic. Surely there are also temporal logical laws in $\mathcal{L}_{Trace}$ concerning trace operators. We give in Appendix A quite an extensive list of formulas all of which we claim to be valid without proving these facts.

A term t is said to be *substitutable* for a variable x in a formula p if its substitution for x in p does not create new occurrences of attributes symbols in the scope of temporal operators ($\mathbf{X}, \mathbf{F}, \ldots$) and action operators ($[Init], [a]$), and the local variables in t do not bounded by substitution. If t does not contain any local variable, it is clear that t is substitutable for any x in p. The following facts are obvious:

Fact 8 *If a term t is substitutable for a variable x in p, then $\models \forall x \, p \rightarrow p(t/x)$*

Fact 9 *If there is no free occurrence of action symbol a in p, then $\models \forall a[a]p \rightarrow (\mathbf{X}p)$*

Fact 10 *If there is no attribute symbol in p, then $p \leftrightarrow [Init]p$ and $p \leftrightarrow [a]p$*

Fact 11 *Let $a \in T(\Sigma, X)_E$ and $x \in X_s$, if there is no free occurrence of x in a, then*
$$\models \forall x[a]p \leftrightarrow [a](\forall x \, p)$$

Fact 12 $\models \forall x[Init]p \leftrightarrow [Init](\forall x \, p)$

5. Trace Axiomatization

Following the semantics of trace calculus, we give a formal system in Appendix B for the derivation of formulas. The system is a sound one.

Theorem 13 (Soundness) *Let p be a formula and Γ a set of formulas. If $\Gamma \vdash p$, then $\Gamma \models p$*

Proof. By induction on the assumed derivation of p from Γ. □

Theorem 14 (Deduction Theorem) *Let p, q be formulas, p is closed, and Γ a set of formulas. If $\Gamma \cup \{p\} \vdash q$, then $\Gamma \vdash [Init]\mathbf{G}p \rightarrow q$.*

Proof. By induction on the assumed derivation of q from $\Gamma \cup \{p\}$. □

The converse assertion holds obviously without any restrictions:

Fact 15 *If $\Gamma \vdash [Init]\mathbf{G}p \rightarrow q$, then $\Gamma \cup \{p\} \vdash q$*

Example: For the Media Player example, the set of axioms for PROVIDER may be as follows:

The effect of the action $retrieve(i)$:

p1: $[retrieve(i)]item = i$

p2: $[retrieve(i)]waiting = \mathbf{t}$

The effect of the action $put(i)$:

p3: $[put(i)]waiting = \mathbf{f}$

Initial condition:

p4: $[Init]waiting = \mathbf{f}$

The prerequisite of the action $retrieve(i)$:

p5: $enabled(retrieve(i)) \rightarrow waiting = \mathbf{f}$

The prerequisite of the action $put(i)$:

p6: $enabled(put(i)) \rightarrow (item = i) \wedge (waiting = \mathbf{t})$

Dynamic constraints:

p7: $waiting = \mathbf{t} \rightarrow \mathbf{F}put(item)$

In fact, axioms as pi:$[retrieve(i)]item = i$ should be strictly written as $enabled(retrieve(i)) \rightarrow ([retrieve(i)]item = i)$. We get the abbreviation by only specifying constraints that should be satisfied by actions enabled under the state.

In the same way, the set of axioms for PLAYER is:

y1: $[play(i)]waiting = \mathbf{f}$

y2: $[get(i)]item = i$

y3: $[get(i)]waiting = \mathbf{t}$

y4: $[Init]waiting = \mathbf{f}$

y5: $enabled(play(i)) \rightarrow (item = i) \wedge (waiting = \mathbf{t})$

y6: $enabled(get(i)) \rightarrow waiting = \mathbf{f}$

y7: $waiting = \mathbf{t} \rightarrow \mathbf{F}play(item)$

The set of axioms for BUFFER is:

b1: $[put(i)]count = count + 1$

b2: $[get(i)]count = count - 1$

b3: $[Init]count = 0$

b4: $enabled(put(i)) \rightarrow (count < size)$

b5: $enabled(get(i)) \rightarrow (count > 0)$

b6: $enabled(put(i)) \rightarrow \mathbf{F}enabled(get(i))$

It is worth to mention that we only give here prerequisites for the execution of actions. Because the description of communications is based on the sharing of action names, different objects may share the same name of action. If we use a sufficient description for execution of actions, different descriptions may conflict with each other in composition of objects. Hence we assume that all external conditions of actions are satisfied when we describe an object. What we need to describe are only the prerequisite for that object.

6. Aggregation and Synchronization: an Example

Objects can be composed into a "larger" object — aggregated object. A system is an aggregated object in the sense that it contains component objects. There are many interactions among these components in a system[4]. The most usual interaction is the sharing of objects — one component object is shared by several other objects; or sharing of actions — several objects are synchronized by an action[11]. This mechanism is especially important to have different media synchronized for multimedia applications.

In the media player example, PROVIDER and BUFFER share the same action *put*. Such a sharing can be represented as an auxiliary object whose signature has nothing but the action *put*. The system composed of PROVIDER and BUFFER is the minimum system that contains PROVIDER, BUFFER and the auxiliary object. Now we give a system SYSTEM which is composed of PROVIDER, PLAYER and BUFFER. These components share the actions *get* and *put*. The signature is as follows:

ObjectSignature SYSTEM = ITEM + BOOL + INT

    Sorts:
    Functions:
    Attributes:
        Provider.item, Player.item: ITEM
        Provider.waiting, Player.waiting: BOOL
    Actions:
        retrieve(ITEM)
        play(ITEM)
        put(ITEM)
        get(ITEM)
End

According to CCS[5,9], each action of an object has channel to communicate with others. Parameters in action symbols are unified during communication. Such communications require simultaneous participation of objects involved — the synchronization of actions. For convenience, we assume that the synchronization mechanism is based on the same name of action symbols. Consequently, the description of a system is the same as a single object. With such an approach, we need some renaming of action symbols when we construct the description of systems from the descriptions of component objects.

Axioms of SYSTEM are obtained from the axioms of PROVIDER, BUFFER and PLAYER by proper renaming. For conciseness, we write the action a to stand for the atomic formula $enabled(a)$ if it does not cause confusion.

The effect of the action *retrieve*(i):

p1: $[retrieve(i)]Provider.item = i$
p2: $[retrieve(i)]Provider.waiting = \mathbf{t}$

The effect of the action *play*(i):

y1: $[play(i)]Player.waiting = \mathbf{f}$

The effect of the action *put*(i):

p3: $[put(i)]Provider.waiting = \mathbf{f}$

b1: $[put(i)]Buffer.count = Buffer.count + 1$

The effect of the action $get(i)$:

y2: $[get(i)]Player.item = i$

y3: $[get(i)]Player.waiting = \mathbf{t}$

b2: $[get(i)]Buffer.count = Buffer.count - 1$

Initial condition

p4: $[Init]Provider.waiting = \mathbf{f}$

y4: $[Init]Player.waiting = \mathbf{f}$

b3: $[Init]Buffer.count = 0$

The prerequisite of the action $retrieve(i)$:

p5: $enabled(retrieve(i)) \rightarrow Provider.waiting = \mathbf{f}$

The prerequisite of the action $play(i)$:

y5: $enabled(play(i)) \rightarrow (Player.item = i) \wedge (Player.waiting = \mathbf{t})$

The prerequisite of the action $put(i)$:

p6: $enabled(put(i)) \rightarrow (Provider.item = i) \wedge (Provider.waiting = \mathbf{t})$

b4: $enabled(put(i)) \rightarrow (Buffer.count < size)$

The prerequisite of the action $get(i)$:

y6: $enabled(get(i)) \rightarrow Player.waiting = \mathbf{f}$

b5: $enabled(get(i)) \rightarrow (Buffer.count > 0)$

Dynamic constraints:

p7: $Provider.waiting = \mathbf{t} \rightarrow \mathbf{F}put(Provider.item)$

y7: $Player.waiting = \mathbf{t} \rightarrow \mathbf{F}play(Player.item)$

b6: $put(i) \rightarrow \mathbf{F}get(i)$

There is a problem when several objects communicate with one object independently and request the same action of the object. Independent communication requires different action names for different objects, whereas synchronization needs the same action symbol between communicating objects. To avoid conflict, we can extend the signature and description of the object by adding action symbols and corresponding axioms. For example, we can add action symbols $get1(item)$ and $get2(item)$ to BUFFER, the corresponding axioms are:

(ab1) $get1(i) \rightarrow get(i)$

(ab2) $get2(i) \rightarrow get(i)$

(ab3) $\neg(get1(i) \wedge get2(i))$

(ab4) $get(i) \rightarrow get1(i) \vee get2(i)$

Axioms (ab1) and (ab2) are the renaming of get; (ab3) represents the mutual exclusion between $get1$ and $get2$; and (ab4) stops any further extension of BUFFER.

7. Concluding Remarks

This paper presents the use of object traces and temporal logic in the specification of objects and their behaviors. The objects we discussed are objects with internal states and external observable behaviors. Structures of objects and inheritance are not considered. Our objective is the complete integration of structural (relationships and attributes) and dynamic (events and behaviors) aspects in the sense that a semantic abstraction would provide a uniform way of dealing both aspects, putting an end to the separation between the description of structures and of behaviors.

We should stress that the presentation of trace calculus leaves no room for discussing further details and other developments. Some interesting things were not reported herein due to space limitations. These works include the following:

- Objects in the general sense have certainly more overall characteristics, in addition to the primitive properties on traces. These characteristics include the encapsulation of objects and concurrency properties such as safety, liveness and fairness. By adding further restrictions on the models allowed by trace calculus, these characteristics can also be specified.

- One important feature of objects to specify is structurization (or inheritance). Because it is the property among different objects, we intend to discuss it in object category. By introducing an institution of objects, we will give the semantic interpretation of inheritance. It is expected that stepwise refinements and type-specific transactions can be specified by the mechanism.

- Based on the proposed theory, we intend to design an object description language. It is expected a comprehensive language which describes various aspects of objects mentioned above. At this point, object description language gives us a modeling mechanism for multimedia objects. By giving mechanisms to describe static/dynamic aspects, it provides a basis for multimedia system design.

- Finally, we are also looking at further developments of the language for transaction specifications, message passing, and of tools to support system design, such as model checkers based on a concrete execution mechanism of specifications.

Appendix A

The following are logical laws in $\mathcal{L}_{Trace}$ related to temporal operators. For detailed discussion, see [19].

Duality law:
T1 $\neg[a]p \leftrightarrow [a]\neg p$
Idempotency law:
T2 $[Init][Init]p \leftrightarrow [Init]p$
Distributivity laws:
T3 $[a](p \to q) \leftrightarrow [a]p \to [a]q$

T4 $[a](p \land q) \leftrightarrow [a]p \land [a]q$

T5 $[a](p \lor q) \leftrightarrow [a]p \lor [a]q$

Monotonicity law:

T6 $p \to q \models [a]p \to [a]q$

Absorbability laws:

T7 $[a][Init]p \leftrightarrow [Init]p$

T8 $\mathbf{X}[Init]p \leftrightarrow [Init]p$

T9 $\mathbf{G}[Init]p \leftrightarrow [Init]p$

T10 $\mathbf{F}[Init]p \leftrightarrow [Init]p$

T11 $\mathbf{X}^-[Init]p \leftrightarrow [Init]p$

T12 $\mathbf{G}^-[Init]p \leftrightarrow [Init]p$

T13 $\mathbf{F}^-[Init]p \leftrightarrow [Init]p$

T14 $[Init]\mathbf{G}p \leftrightarrow (\mathbf{G}p \land \mathbf{G}^-p)$

T15 $[a]p \to (p \lor \mathbf{X}p)$ *if $a \neq Init$.*

T16 $(p \land \mathbf{X}p) \to [a]p$ *if $a \neq Init$.*

Appendix B

This is a formal system for the derivation of trace formulas.

Axioms:

(taut) all tautologically valid formulas of $\mathcal{L}_{FLTLB}$,

(a1) $p \to [a]p$ if there is no attribute symbol in p

(a2) $[a][Init]p \leftrightarrow [Init]p$

(a3) $\mathbf{X}[Init]p \leftrightarrow [Init]p$

(a4) $\mathbf{X}^-[Init]p \leftrightarrow [Init]p$

(a5) $\neg[a]p \leftrightarrow [a]\neg p$

(a6) $[a](p \to q) \leftrightarrow [a]p \to [a]q$

(a7) $\forall x\, p \to p(t/x)$ if t is substitutable for x in p,

(a8) $[Init]\mathbf{G}p \leftrightarrow \mathbf{G}p \land \mathbf{G}^-p$

(a9) $\forall a\, [a]p \to \mathbf{X}p$

(a10) $\forall x\, [a]p \to [a]\forall x\, p$, if there is no free occurrence of x in a.

Inference Rules:

(mp) $p, p \to q \vdash q$

(nex) $p \vdash \mathbf{X}p$

(las) $p \vdash \mathbf{X}^- p$

(act) $p \vdash [a]p$

(emp) $p \vdash [Init]p$

(inv) $[Init]p, p \to \mathbf{X}p \vdash p$

(ind) $p \to q, p \to \mathbf{X}p \vdash p \to \mathbf{G}q$

(indp) $p \to q, p \to \mathbf{X}^- p \vdash p \to \mathbf{G}^- q$

(gen) $p \to q \vdash p \to \forall x \, q$ if there is no free occurrence of x in p

As similar to that of the linear temporal logic, we would like to abbreviate purely classical derivation steps by using "cut" rules. This is performed by the following derived rule:

(prep) $p_1, \ldots, p_n \vdash q$ whenever q is a tautological consequence of $p_1, \ldots, p_n$,

References

1. S. Abiteboul, P. C. Kanellakis, and E. Waller. Method schemas. In *Proceeding of ACM SIGMOD International Conference on Principles of Database Systems*, pages 16–27, 1990.
2. P. Chen. The time dimension in the entity-relationship model. In *Proceeding of IFIP World Congress 86*. Elsevier Science Publishers B.V. (North-Holland), 1986.
3. J. Fiadeiro and A. Sernadas. Specification and verification of database dynamics. *Acta Informatica*, 25(6):625–661, 1988.
4. S. Gibbs. Composite multimedia and active objects. In *Proceedings of OOPSLA '91 Conference*, 1991.
5. C. A. R. Hoare. *Communicating Sequential Processes*. Prentice-Hall International Series in Computer Science. Prentice-Hall, London, 1985.
6. P. Hoepner. Synchronizing the presentation of multimedia objects. *IEEE Computer Communications*, 15(9):557–564, November 1992.
7. F. Kröger. *Temporal Logic of Programs*. EATCS Monographs on Theoretical Computer Science. Springer-Verlag, Berlin, 1987.
8. D. Long. A review of temporal logics. *Knowledge Eng. Rev.*, 4:141–162, 1989.

9. R. Milner. *A Calculus of Communicating Systems*, volume 92 of *Lecture Notes in Computer Science*. Springer-Verlag, New York, 1980.

10. C. Nicolaou. An architecture for real-time multimedia communication systems. *IEEE Journal on Selected Areas in Communication*, 8(3):391–400, April 1990.

11. M. J. Perez-Luque and T. D. C. Little. Temporal models for multimedia synchronization. In *Proc. Interactive Multimedia over Networks*, Palma de Mallorca, Spain, July 1994.

12. A. Pnueli. The temporal of programs. In *Proceeding of the 18th FOCS*, pages 46–57, 1977.

13. V. R. Pratt. Action logic and pure induction. In J. van Eijck, editor, *Logics in AI: European Workshop JELIA'90*, volume 478 of *Lecture Notes in Computer Science*, pages 97–120. Springer-Verlag, September 1990.

14. G. Saake. Descriptive specification of database behaviour. *Data & Knowledge Engineering*, 6(1):47–73, 1991.

15. A. Sernadas and C. Sernadas. Object-oriented specification of databases: an algebraic approach. In *Proc. VLDB*, pages 107–116, Brighton, England, 1987.

16. M. P. Singh, G. Meredith, C. Tomlinson, and P. C. Attie. An event algebra for specifying and scheduling workflows. In *Proc. 4th Inter. Conf. on Database Systems for Advanced Applications*, pages 53–60, Singapore, 1995. World Scientific.

17. J. Su. Dynamic constraints and object migration. In *Proc. VLDB*, pages 233–242, Barcelona, Spain, 1991.

18. M. Wirsing. Algebraic specification. In *Formal Models and Semantics*, volume B of *Handbook of Theoretical Computer Science*, pages 675–788. Elsevier Science Publishers B.V. (North-Holland), 1990.

19. L. Yang. Semantic specification and modeling of multimedia database objects. Technical report, Institute of Systems Science, National University of Singapore, April 1995.

Chapter 3

Image Retrieval

Automatic Shape Indexing and Rapid Multimedia Retrieval Using Intelligent STIRS Signatures

Rosemary Irrgang

CSIRO Division of Information Technology
Locked Bag 17, N. Ryde NSW 2113, Australia
Tel: 3253156, Fax: 3253101
Email: irrgang@syd.dit.csiro.au

Abstract

A shape signature technique based on the Hough transform, has been developed to allow automatic shape indexing and rapid retrieval of noisy images and video frames. The matching process involves only computation of a one dimensional correlation.

1 Introduction

Automatic indexation of large multimedia databases is a topic currently under intensive study. Most existing multimedia systems require users to produce text descriptions of each image or video sequence for indexing and retrieval. This works well only if all future retrieval applications can be specified in advance. Recently a number of automated and semi automated content based indexing schemes have been reported which use statistical measures of features such as colour, texture and directionality [Denslow et al 1993], [Chua 1994] and [Niblack 1993]. Niblack's system also supports a crude shape indexing method which assumes that shapes are noise free binary images which do not contain occlusions. The indexing technique uses shape features such as area, circularity, eccentricity and moment invariants which do not uniquely characterise the shape. In addition shape boundaries are assumed to be previously specified. The research documented below aims to produce a shape signature based on the Hough transform for a more accurate description of shapes in images. The new technique developed is well suited to large database indexing applications as it allows rapid matching of two shape signatures by computing only a one dimensional correlation. The enhanced algorithm has been used successfully for content based indexing and retrieval from a case base of aerospace images, and a commercial image base of landscape scenes.

The Hough transform is recognised as a powerful tool in shape analysis which gives accurate results even in the presence of noise and occlusions [Leavers 1993]. The technique has been generalised to detect analytic curves and arbitrary shapes [Ballard 1982], [Leavers 1993]. The STIRS (Scalable Translation Invariant Rotation to Shifting) matching technique was originally developed by Pao and Li [Pao 1992]. The technique can be applied to curves of arbitrary shape and allows the translation, rotation and intrinsic parameters of the curve to be decoupled.

The STIRS technique uses delineating tangents to describe the shape boundary and also calculates the equivalent of distances between each pair of parallel tangents. The signature produced is a table containing the angles of the delineating tangents and the distances between parallel pairs. The granularity of the signature can be selected to give either a detailed or a more approximate signature. The novel methods produced during this project allow application of the STIRS technique to noisy discontinuous images. In addition, the improved techniques overcome problems encountered when applying the standard STIRS technique to images containing multiple objects or large noise effects. A new technique for calculation of distances between the tangents has also been derived. This method overcomes problems with inaccurate distance calculations caused by quantisation effects, which are particularly severe when the delineating tangent pairs are not exactly parallel.

In the original STIRS shape matching reference, the authors [Pao 1992] suggest that shapes may be considered to be similar if a significant peak is obtained when test and reference signatures are correlated at various rotation angles. However they fail to give a measure of significance. To overcome this problem, a new technique has been developed which allows normalised significance testing of the shape matching results. A normalised metric is essential in an automated system, as the numeric values of peak heights show a large variation, which is dependent on both noise effects and the complexity of the shape boundaries.

Original enhancements which can be applied to a number of Hough transform methods, have also been developed. Standard Hough techniques use binary edge data, that is, edges are represented by a one, with the rest of the image set to zero. In addition, the direction of each edge is not used by the standard algorithms. The new methods allow use of all of the grey shade values, and the edge directions are also taken into account. In addition knowledge added and statistical techniques are used to improve the decision process. For example, locally derived context knowledge is used to select optimal tangent pairings, and statistical techniques are employed to determine which gradient discontinuities are most likely to lie on a shape edge.

Shape signatures produced by the new STIRS technique are well suited to the indexing of large multimedia databases as the signature is a highly condensed representation. In addition, comparing signatures of test and database images involves only a fast one dimensional correlation. For very large databases, it is also quite simple to calculate both a coarse and a fine grained signature with little increase in computation time. The coarse representation can then used for a first pass elimination of strongly dissimilar database images.

1.1 *Noise Effects*

Two types of image noise can be distinguished. The first type, occurs randomly at each pixel and can usually be characterised by a Gaussian distribution. Such noise may be due to random corruption of the data during analog to digital conversion and is easily handled. The second type of noise, correlated noise, is far more problematical. If the image contains multiple features then the resulting transform space is a composite of the distributions associated with each feature instance, and the effect may be that a number of small insignificant peaks combine to produce a large peak. Grimson and Huttenlocher [1990] point out that, where complex recognition tasks are to be implemented, the probability of false peaks can be very high.

One method [Li 1989] which seeks to alleviate the effects of correlated noise adds connectivity checks to the Hough transform technique. The method, is a modified Hough transform which performs contiguity checks in a simple and efficient way. Unfortunately Li's paper discusses only the application of the straight line Hough transform and there is no obvious extension of the connectivity checking method to curves of arbitrary shape.

1.2 *Knowledge Driven Strategies*

After an extensive review of recent literature on Hough techniques, Leavers [1993] notes that it is becoming increasingly obvious that many of the excessive computational demands of the method can be significantly reduced by using knowledge driven strategies to monitor and moderate the transformation process. A complete world knowledge base is not required in most applications. For an arbitrary curve, what is relevant for the object recognition problem is the location, rotation angle, and scale of the curve in the image relative to the stored template. The input of simple knowledge about the object's known orientation and/or fixed scale features, allows these properties to be exploited, thereby restricting the possible angles and scales of the template candidates, and reducing the dimension of the problem. The development of algorithms which exploit even simple knowledge about the class of image objects, appears to be a worthwhile step towards a more intelligent image analysis process.

2 STIRS Signatures

The STIRS method uses the polar coordinate (ρ, θ) representation of the classical Hough transform [Ballard 1982]. A shape signature is obtained from the ρ, θ space by computing the distance between pairs of parallel lines tangent to the shape, ie. those with the same θ values. The resultant transform is then a signature of the shape. If the size of the test object is known, we can also optimise the search by discarding points with ρ values that are larger than the maximum diameter of the object. The signature possesses the following properties:

- It is invariant to translation of the shape in the image plane.
- Rotation of the shape in the image plane corresponds to circular shifting of θ in the signature.
- If the shape is scaled by a factor S in the image plane, the signature will be scaled by the same factor.

Once the scale factor has been determined, matching two signatures is only equivalent to computing a one dimensional correlation. The height and location of a peak, if one is found, indicates the similarity and orientation of the test object with respect to the reference object. Knowing the orientation of the test object, the location can be found using an inverse transform from the $\theta - \rho$ space to the x-y plane. The observation was made by Pao [1992], that the same translation term, has been added to all points in the θ_i th column of the array. This translation term can be eliminated by storing the distances between pairs of points of the array that are in the same column, which is equivalent to measuring the perpendicular distances between pairs of parallel tangents to the curve. Storage is saved as one dimension of the accumulator array is not required.

The STIRS signature method appears well suited for use in multimedia indexing and retrieval because it allows recognition of shapes with varying scales and orientations on memory limited machines, and also offers savings in computation time. Calculation of the range for both θ and ρ is also a simple process using this formulation, which allows generally applicable quantization algorithms to be produced.

2.1 *Shape Matching Using the STIRS Signature*

In the discrete domain, the straight line Hough transform is computed for a finite number of values of theta. If the theta and rho axes are quantised into m_θ and m_ρ levels respectively, the transform can be represented by a two dimensional array of size m_θ x m_ρ. Pao [1992] uses a Boolean array, however this discards information about the number of points in each cell, which can be used to improve the accuracy of the shape recognition process. The enhanced implementation was designed to use all of the available information, which required modification of the original correlation algorithm devised by Pao et al [1992].

2.2 *Problems With the Original STIRS Method*

A number of problems with the original STIRS method have been identified. Firstly, it is difficult to calculate delineating tangents accurately if the image is noisy, particularly if the edges are discontinuous. In addition the method is not suited to shapes which have no parallel tangents, (eg. triangles) while bodies with sharp corners are difficult to represent accurately. Lines extraneous to the body of interest and complex noise errors also make identification inaccurate. Improvements have been implemented to address a number of these problems. The addition of case based context knowledge [Irrgang 1994] is also supported to ensure appropriate quantisation parameters are used and to limit the search space during computation of the STIRS signature

3 Enhancements to Hough Techniques for Detection of Curves of Arbitrary Shape

A number of novel enhancements to the original Hough signature technique [Pao et al 1992] have been added, these include:

(1)   Detection of Connected Edge Sections of Arbitrary Shape

A new "snake" technique to detect connected edge points with reasonable accuracy, using knowledge added techniques has been derived (Accepted for publication [Irrgang 1996]). The technique allows a more reliable computation of the direction of tangents incident at points along the edge of each shape in the image, and also facilitates the removal of isolated segments produced by noise in the image. The novel method derived is applicable to curves without a known analytic representation.

The new connectivity algorithm is a two stage process. During stage one, the most probable continuation for each edge point is computed, using an N step lookahead process [Irrgang 1994 (b)] and an energy function. The energy function is defined to use edge gradient magnitudes and directions, information about the length and curvature of the contiguous edge so far, and context knowledge where this is available. The appropriate energy function can be retrieved from the case base, with a default energy function employed in the absence of context knowledge. The algorithm evaluates the energy function at neighbouring pixels to compute the most probable N step lookahead path at each pixel location. The stage one process terminates wherever the energy function violates a threshold value. Once edge points have been grouped into sets of connected edge pixels or edgels, a higher level stage two process using the same N step lookahead algorithm can be invoked to produce longer connected edge segments. Energy thresholds can be relaxed during the higher level process if additional evidence exists to indicate connectivity, for example a pixel lying between two long connected edge sections is probably part of the edge.

(2)   Knowledge Enhanced Detection of Tangents Delineating Shapes

The N step lookahead algorithm [Irrgang 1996] is used to compute tangents delineating each shape in the image. The initial lookahead search is restricted to a small N (3 in the case illustrated in Fig. 1). A larger N could be used to give a smoothing effect but details of the image may be lost. At each probable edge point, an N step lookahead search is commenced to find the most probable edge continuation point, using knowledge about the colour or intensity on either side of the edge, edge gradient direction and edge gradient magnitude. After each search one more point is added to the edgel. If a sufficient number of connected points can be found, the average direction of the edgel is used to calculate the slope of the tangents to selected points on the edge section. Isolated edge points can be discarded.

(3)   Improved Pairing of Parallel Tangents on Opposite Sides of the Shape

Pao [1992] suggests 3 methods for the selection of tangent pairs, viz.
• Select all possible combinations of pairs of points in the same column of the (ρ,θ) table, (equivalent to pairs of locations of parallel tangents).
• Select pairs of points such that one of the points has the maximum or minimum ρ value.
• Select points from each column at random. If the scaling factor of the object is known, points whose ρ value difference is greater than the known object size can be discarded.

Problems occur with each of Pao's three suggestions. Firstly, joining all possible point combinations is computationally expensive and ensures that if multiple shapes occur in the image they will all be linked together. The difficulty with Pao's second suggestion is that, if multiple objects are present, selection of the maximum distance between tangents biases the algorithm towards joining points on two different objects, as these points are likely to be most widely separated. Joining the two closest points usually leads to the linking of two contiguous points which are on the same side of the object.

The third suggestion is more practical. However, if object scales are not known, multiple objects would probably be linked. If multiple objects are present, linking edge points on shape A, to edge points on shape B produces a noisy reference signature which could make shape recognition difficult or even impossible. Cross linking of objects should generally be avoided, however, such avoidance is difficult in a cluttered noisy image. Images containing correlated noise can present additional problems. An example is shown in Fig.1, which shows an image which contains an aircraft and a bright reflection of a section of the aircraft wing and other objects. Naturally the wing is highly correlated with its reflection. The tangent pairing is performed without using the new context knowledge enhancements to the STIRS algorithm and the results are poor, with many tangents joined to noise objects outside the aircraft image boundary. The image shown in Fig. 1 is useful later as a test of the robustness of the modified STIRS technique, as the shape of the plane with its tapered wings, presents few parallel sections for the tangent pairing algorithm.

Fig. 1 Without the Use of Context Knowledge Enhancements, a Noisy STIRS Tangent Pairing is Produced for Aircraft Image

3.1 *Improved Methods for Detection of Opposite and Parallel Tangents*

Pao selected delineating tangents without using global and context knowledge. The new method described in this paper, for the identification of optimal tangent pairs employs simple context and generic knowledge to select the delineating tangents. For example, the grey shade intensity gradient direction values at each edge location are employed to ensure that a tangent is linked to another parallel tangent which lies on the opposite side of the object (with an opposite shading gradient change). In addition, with the new algorithm, edge gradient directions on opposite sides of the image are assumed to differ approximately by an amount of Pi radians (180 degrees). This assumption holds for any object whose edges are either darker or lighter than the background. An adjustable fuzzy threshold is used to allow for varying amounts of noise in the image.

To avoid cross linking of multiple objects, a further context based constraint has been added to the new algorithm. The default assumption is made that the interior of the shape is lighter than the background, this assumption holds well for smoke tunnel images and for the aircraft images used in this project, however a switch can be set if the reverse situation applies. Using this assumption, the average grey shade intensity computed along a line joining tangents on opposite sides of any reasonably convex body, should be lighter than the background. In the majority of cases, lines joining tangents in two separate image features must cross an area of darker background which produces an average line intensity value below the threshold so that the join will be rejected. A software routine calculates the average (avcol) grey shade or colour intensity along the line joining two parallel tangents. The value of avcol is then compared with the region around each edge to estimate whether or not the line crosses background regions. Another option allows the computation of the percentage of pixels along the joining line, which are below a threshold grey shade value. An additional constraint can optionally be imposed to ensure that no edge point can be linked to more than one other edge point. The algorithm selects the closest unused parallel edge point which is located on the opposite side of the shape. The closest point is selected as a further precaution against cross linking of multiple shapes. The method used avoids discretization or "bucketing effects" with both the selection of tangents with similar Theta values, and the calculation of the Rho differences, by storing the original exact values of Theta and Rho, and using these exact values in all comparisons. Bucketed values are used only as indices in the accumulator array.

The results obtained using the improved STIRS algorithm will be detailed in the following sections. Fig. 2 below illustrates how a STIRS shape index is computed.

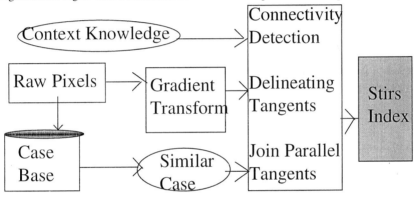

Fig. 2 Calculation of STIRS Shape Index

The process is described in two separate stages. In stage one, calculation of the delineating tangents and STIRS signatures using the improved algorithms will be outlined. Results obtained for applications using simple shapes will be detailed first, followed by a discussion of complex noisy images. Lastly, results of the stage two process, which involves matching of the signatures for test and reference images, will be described.

3.2 Results Using the New Algorithm for Calculation of Simple STIRS Signatures

The algorithm was tested using Cassini Oval shapes (Fig. 3). An edge gradient transform was firstly used to calculate edge locations around each shape. The transform computed both edge gradient magnitudes and directions for each edge location. The N step lookahead algorithm was then applied to detect connected edge points which in turn were used for calculation of the tangents delineating the shape. The results of the parallel tangent pair detection algorithm, are illustrated in Fig. 3 in which the white lines join pairs of parallel tangents detected by the algorithm. The method was also tested with other simple curves such as the rectangle and circle shown in Figs. 4 and 5 respectively. Application of the algorithm is straightforward with these simple images, as noise is produced only by random quantising effects. Once appropriate tangent pairs have been

Fig. 3 Characteristic Tangents and Parallel Tangent Pairs for Cassini Oval Image

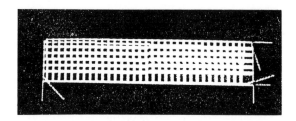

Fig. 4 Characteristic Tangents and Parallel Tangent Pairs for Rectangle

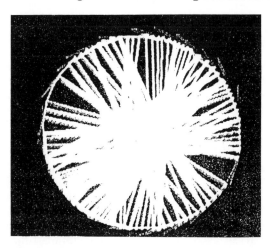

Fig. 5 Characteristic Tangents and Parallel Tangent Pairs for Circle

identified, the distance between tangents can be computed. The original method used by Pao [1992] calculates differences between rho values as an estimate of this distance, which can be inaccurate when paired tangent lines are not quite parallel. A new formulation, which gives improved accuracy has been used. The equation to calculate the distance between the two tangents (rdiff) is given below:

$$\text{rdiff} = \frac{\text{abs}(x_2 \cos(\theta_1) + y_2 \sin(\theta_1)) - \rho_1 + \text{abs}(x_1 \cos(\theta_2) + y_1 \sin(\theta_2) - \rho_2)}{2}$$

....Eq. (1)

where θ_1 and θ_2 are the theta values for tangents 1 and 2 respectively, and (x_1, y_1) and (x_2, y_2) are the points of incidence of the tangents with the shape. The distance is stored in an accumulator indexed by quantised rho and theta values. The set of theta, rho and accumulator (kd) values constitutes the STIRS signature of a shape. Table 1 shows an example of the Hough signatures obtained for two rectangles, one of which is rotated through 90 degrees. Theoretically two rows only should be produced, with theta values of 26 and 38. However, two rows are actually produced with theta values of 26 and differing rho values, as a result of discretization errors.

Table 1 STIRS Signature for Rectangle and Rotated Rectangle

Rectangle Shape Theta	Rectangle Shape Rho	Rectangle Shape Accumulator	Rotated Rectangle Theta	Rotated Rectangle Rho	Rotated Rectangle Accumulator
26	6	26	26	27	11
26	7	39			
38	26	11	38	6	65

The algorithm was found to be extremely robust when applied to simple shape images such as the Cassini ovals and rectangles described above. Changes in parameter settings had very slight effect on peak heights and later computations of orientation, and errors detected could be attributed to discretization effects.

3.3 Results of STIRS Signature Computations for Noisy Images

Fig. 6 shows the results of the identification of parallel tangent pairs in a rotated version of the noisy aircraft image in Fig. 1. A comparison of Figs. 1 and 6 indicates a marked improvement in the tangent pair identification results. This improvement can be attributed to two factors. Firstly, an improved version of the N step lookahead algorithm was used, which also relaxed constraints on the multiple use of edge points, producing a larger number of delineating tangents. Secondly, the improved context based constraints described above were added to the tangent linking routine. This eliminated much of the noise which was generated by crosslinking to noise objects. Fig. 6 shows a processed image for a fuzzy scene containing assorted razors also using the new method.

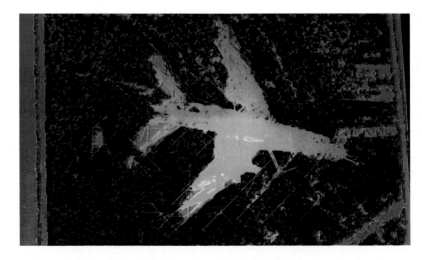

Fig. 6 Linked Parallel Tangent Pairs for Original Aircraft Image

Fig. 7 Linked Parallel Tangent Pairs for Razor Image

4 Shape Matching Using STIRS Signatures

An improved version of the matching algorithm proposed by Pao [1992] is used to compare the signatures of test and reference images, the algorithm also computes the difference in orientation of the two images. The main improvement in the new algorithm is that numeric values in the accumulator array, representing the number of linked tangents at each (rho, theta) location, are used to calculate the shape matching metric, where the original version, uses only binary values. To calculate the rotation of the test pattern, the reference signature (with wraparound) "slides" over the test template. The position at which maximum correlation occurs corresponds to the amount of rotation. The position of the peak value detected gives the quantised theta value corresponding to the difference in orientation. A modified version of the algorithm above is used for shape matching using STIRS signatures. Results with a score greater than zero, obtained using the modified matching algorithm for a comparison of the rotated (60 degrees) and unrotated Cassini images are plotted in Fig. 8. The histogram shows the differences in theta values on the X axis and the scores obtained with the matching algorithm on the Y axis. A peak can be observed for a theta difference of 8. For this test, 360 degrees were quantised into 50 buckets, which means that each bucket represents 7.2 degrees. The orientation of the rotated shape is therefore calculated to be between 57.6 (8x7.2) degrees and 64.8 degrees. A finer quantisation grid could be used for the Cassini images to give a more exact result.

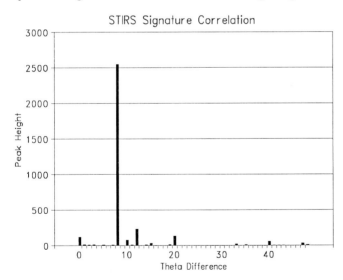

Fig. 8 Scores Obtained From Signature Comparison for Cassini Ovals

Table 2 gives the results obtained for a STIRS signature comparison of the rotated (90 degrees) and unrotated rectangles. The difference in orientation between the two rectangles, computed from Table 2 is calculated to lie between 86.4 degrees (12 x 7.2) and 93.6 degrees (13 x 7.2).

Table 2 Scores From STIRS Signature Comparison of Rotated and Unrotated Rectangles

THETA1 - THETA2	SCORE
12	16065

A number of simple image objects were tested at varying orientations from zero to 180 and the STIRS algorithm performed well with all of these, computing the orientation correctly within the quantisation limits chosen. The method of computation of scale and translation differences used was identical with the technique documented by Pao [1992]. The results of testing on simple image objects indicate that the Hough signature computation technique performs well, correctly identifying objects in images and concurrently computing the difference in orientation between the test and reference shapes. Complex noisy objects, or objects with tapered or irregular shapes and few parallel edges which are discussed next, appear to present more of a challenge as the signature produced may not adequately define the object.

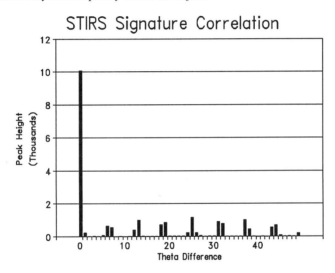

Fig. 9 Peak Detected for STIRS Comparison of Test Shape and Reference Aircraft Image

Fig. 9 illustrates the STIRS signature correlation results for the comparison of unrotated test and reference aircraft images. The X axis represents orientation differences and the peak height (Y axis) gives a measure of the significance of the STIRS comparison. The strong peak detected indicates that the test shape is an instance of the reference shape.

4.1 Results of Shape Matching for Noisy Images

Table 3 lists the results of shape matching using rotated and unrotated versions of the aircraft image shown in Figs. 1 and 6 respectively, with variations in the gradient magnitude parameter. Tests 2 and 3 used different rectangular regions of the test image for the comparison, a gradient threshold of 0.2 standard deviations and a rotated test image. The lower gradient threshold allows detection of more edge points on the shape but with a corresponding increase in noise edges detected. Tests 1 to 3 used all possible candidate points for detection of corresponding parallel tangents, while tests 4 and 5 linked only the closest parallel tangents located on opposite sides of the shape. Test 5 used an unrotated image as the test input, while all the other tests used a rotated test image.

Pao [1992] states that the test image can be considered as an instance of the reference image if a "significant" peak is detected, however the term "significant" needs to be more precisely defined. The height of the peak detected by the new STIRS signature matching algorithm was found to be a function of both the number of edge points used and the number of linked tangents in the image. The new algorithm normalises peak heights by matching both test and reference image signatures with themselves at a lag of zero, to give a maximum possible STIRS correlation for each. The match between test and reference image is then normalised by dividing the peak STIRS score obtained by the smaller of the autocorrelation values, to give a percent of maximum peak height. The additional computational cost involved in calculating two correlations using 50 points, at a single lag value was slight. Table 3 shows the results obtained with test and reference signature matching under the conditions described above. Higher peak heights were obtained by using all possible point combinations, but all of the tests produced significant peak heights. The difference in orientation between test and reference signature is listed in quantised form in the last column of Table 3. All of the tests also correctly calculated a difference in rotation between test and reference images. (The values of 37 represent an orientation in the range -86.4 to -93.6 degrees which includes the correct value of -90 degrees).

Table 3 Results of STIRS Matching for Rotated and Original Aircraft Images

Test Number	Gradient Magnitude Threshold	Test Image Rotation in Degrees	STIRS Matching Peak Height	STIRS Maximum Peak Height	Percent of maximum Peak Height	Computed Theta Difference (Quantised)
1	0.2	-90	19930	44150	45.14	37
2	0.2	-90	20439	44150	46.29	37
3	0.6	-90	21155	39832	53.11	37
4	0.6	-90	2861	10062	28.43	37
5	0.6	0	10062	10062	100.0	0

5 Discussion

Results obtained with the improved STIRS signature technique for shape recognition are encouraging. The addition of context based connectivity checking to the detection of characteristic tangents allows the method to be used on images containing edge discontinuities and noise. Context based constraints added to the algorithms for detection of parallel tangents have been demonstrated to greatly decrease the number of crosslinking errors which were originally observed in images containing multiple objects or significant noise effects. Enhancements to the original signature comparison algorithm allow retention of additional information on the number of lines represented by each accumulator cell. Normalisation of the peak height measure has also been added, which assists with the assessment of the significance of the results of shape comparisons.

The discussion so far has assumed that in scenes containing multiple objects, an ideal signature is produced by linking parallel tangents only within a single object. However, in some applications, object relativities must be preserved. For example, in the comparison of two street scenes, relative locations of buildings provide salient information. Where relativities must be preserved, crosslinking of objects is a desirable feature of the signature based indexing, rather than a problem. In the latter case, tests using landscape images indicated that quite fuzzy images can produce good results.

The most useful aspect of the STIRS method for image base retrieval, is that rapid matching of two signatures is possible by computing only a one dimensional correlation. Additional time savings can be achieved by the use of a coarser grained image for first pass matching, followed by a finer detail match of promising candidate images. This technique is recommended where the scale is unknown.

6 Conclusion

Retrieval of stored images and case information from the case base using only an image as the input query is a goal of this research. Other researchers for example, [Niblack et al 1993] have added a form of shape indexation which requires operators to manually trace around shapes of interest in each image. Such an onerous requirement would render the system unusable for all but the most dedicated of users.

Shape recognition metrics are required to be relatively fast, as large image data bases may have to be searched. There is a less stringent requirement, however for accuracy, as retrieval of a few irrelevant images in conjunction with the correct one is normally not a serious problem. The Hough reference signature techniques, with their reduced computational requirements, appear to be promising candidates for incorporation into an image similarity metric which incorporates shape. Tests of retrieval using Hough signature comparisons on the limited set of case base images in the VITAL system [Irrgang 1994] has successfully retrieved the correct image in each trial, although a number of other similar images also produce peaks. Further testing on a larger image data base will be required for thorough investigation of the use of the technique for a more generic image similarity based retrieval. However the technique is currently a valuable addition to text based retrieval on the existing multimedia case base.

Use of the context based boundary detection and delineating tangent calculations allows shapes to be isolated without any requirement for users to trace relevant shapes. Boundary detection, tangent linking and shape signatures for all the images in the case base can be calculated and stored as part of the case base index. The reduction of shape matching to a one dimensional correlation allows high speed retrieval.

Further research is planned in which the shape metrics can be combined with other relevant measures such as colour, texture and directionality. Higher level concepts for use in indexation are also under study. For example some images have a strong geometric component, containing predominantly straight lines and sharp angles, while another group (eg landscapes) may be classed as fractal images. Indexing schemes which contain such meta level concepts are also part of an ongoing research thrust, which should provide more intelligent content based image retrieval in the future.

REFERENCES

Dana H. Ballard and C.H.Brown, "Computer Vision", Prentice Hall 1982.

S. Denslow, Z. Zhang, R. P. Thompson, and C.F.Lam, "Statistically Characterized Features for Directionality Quantitation in Patterns and Textures", Pattern Recognition, Vol. 26, No. 8, pp. 1193-1205 1993.

W.E.L.Grimson and D.P Huttenlocher, "On the sensitivity of the Hough Transform for Object Recognition", IEEE Pattern Anal. and Machine Intelligence, 10(3), 1990, 255-274.

Rosemary Irrgang and Henry Irrgang, "A Case Based System for Adaptive Image Understanding", The Second World Congress on Expert Systems, Lisbon Portugal, Jan. 1994, CD-ROM, "Moving Toward Expert Systems Globally In The 21st Century", Macmillan New Media, Cambridge MA, USA.

Rosemary Irrgang "A Case Based System for Adaptive Image Understanding", PhD. Thesis Sydney University Dept. of Aeronautical Engineering, Aug.1994 (b).

Rosemary Irrgang and Henry Irrgang, "An Intelligent Snake Growing Algorithm for Fuzzy Shape Detection", to appear in Proc. of The Third World Congress on Expert Systems, Seoul, Feb. 1996.

V. F. Leavers, "Which Hough Transform?", Survey, CVGIP: Image Understanding, Vol. 58. No. 2, Sep. pp 250-264 1993.

H. F. Li, D. Pao and R. Jayakumar, "Improvements and Systolic Implementation of the Hough Transformation for Straight Line Detection", Pattern Recognition, Vol. 22, No. 6 pp. 697-705, 1989.

W. Niblack, R.Barber, W. Equitz, M. Flickner, E. Glasman, D. Petkovic, P. Yanker, C. Faloutsos, "The QBIC project: Querying Images by Content Using Colour, Texture, and Shape", Computer Science, Feb. 1 1993.

Derek C. W. Pao, F. Li, and R. Jayakumar, "Shapes Recognition Using the Straight Line Hough Transform: Theory and Generalisation", IEEE Transactions on Pattern Analysis and machine Intelligence, Vol. 14, No. 11, Nov. 1992.

Paul Suetens, Pascal Fua, Andrew J. Hanson, "Computational Strategies for Object Recognition", ACM Computing Surveys, Vol. 24, No 1, 5-61, March 1992.

Tat-Seng Chua, Swee-Kiew Lim and Hung-Keng Pung, "Content -based Retrieval of Segmented Images", to appear in Proc. ACM Multimedia Conference, San Francisco, October 1994.

IMAGE INDEXING AND RETRIEVAL
BASED ON COLOUR HISTOGRAMS

YIHONG GONG

School of Electrical and Electronic Engineering
Nanyang Technological University, Nanyang Ave, Singapore 639798
Email: eygong@eygong.eee.ntu.ac.sg

and

CHUA HOCK-CHUAN, GUO XIAOYI

School of Electrical and Electronic Engineering
Nanyang Technological University, Nanyang Ave, Singapore 639798

ABSTRACT

While general image understanding is difficult, it is relatively easy to capture some primitive image properties, such as colour histograms, and use these properties to index or search for an image in an image database. In this paper, we present an image database system, in which images are indexed and retrieved based on colour histograms. We address the problems inherent in colour histograms created by conventional methods. We then propose a new method to create colour histograms which are compact in size and insensitive to minor illumination variations such as highlight and shading. We also propose an indexing scheme (based on a two-layer hierarchical tree) to encode the histograms into a numerical key; so as to simplify and speed-up the searching process. Our system supports query methods based on user-provided sample image and system-provided templates. Experiments on our system have shown favourable results.

1.   Introduction

As data storage becomes cheaper today, databases are evolving. Not only have they become more popular, they have also grown in size and variety. Multimedia databases that encompass texts, sounds, still images, and video motion pictures are getting popular. Hence, there is an increasing demand for new database techniques that not only organise and manage multimedia data, but also able to sift through the enormous volume of data to extract useful information.

Efforts have been made on extending traditional database techniques to support multimedia databases, particularly in applications such as medical image archives and geographic information system. At this moment, the most common technique for integrating images into databases is to store images together with some descriptive texts or keywords. Image retrievals are performed by solely matching the query texts with the stored keywords. This approach is exclusively text-based and uses no visual information of the underlying image. There are many problems associated with this approach. Firstly, automatic generation of descriptive keywords from images (i.e., image understanding) is currently beyond our reach. Hence, keywords have to be assigned and entered into the system manually. Not only is this indexing process time consuming due to the enormous volume of images, but it is also subjective. A retrieval attempt will fail if a user forms a query based on a different set of keywords, or the query refers to the image contents which were not described in the database. Secondly, some visual properties, such as textures and shades, are difficult or nearly impossible to be described with text.

Therefore, an image database system with visual content-based indexing and retrieval capabilities is imperative. Retrieving images would become easier if the query can be formed in terms of visual properties or pictorial items, such as texture patterns, colour and shape of objects, or sample images. In this paper, we present an image database system in which images are indexed and retrieved based on colour histogram.

2.   Previous Works

Various image visual properties have been exploited for content-based image indexing and retrieval. Kato and Hirata [1] extracted contours from artistic colour paintings, and retrieve paintings by matching an outline sketch of the desired painting provided by the user with the contour images stored in the database. Swain [2] used the colour histogram to measure the similarity between a sample image provided by the user and the images stored in the database. A incremental intersection scheme was also devised to reduce the running cost of the histogram match. More comprehensive studies can be found in [3] and [4] which derived visual properties of an image, such as colour, shape, texture, and histogram; and used them in content-based indexing and retrieval.

The major drawback for sketch-matching is that it requires the user to provide a fairly accurate outline sketch, because the sketch-matching process is relatively sensitive to translational, rotational, and size variations. Furthermore, it is difficult to retrieve images containing the same set of objects but captured from a different viewpoint, or images which do not contain regions with clear boundaries such as texture areas.

Image indexing and retrieval based on colour histograms are simple and yet effective. Histograms are invariant to translation and rotation about the viewing axis. They change slightly with change in viewing angle, scale and occlusion. It is reported that a 3-D object can be adequately represented by a small number of histograms [2]. Colour histogram is therefore adopted in our system as the primitive image property for image indexing and retrieval.

3.   Image Histogram Creation

The most common method for creating a histogram is to equally subdivide the RGB colour space into a number of small bins, and then count the number of pixels falling into each of these bins. The main problem for this approach is that colours from two adjacent histogram bins reveal only trivial difference. A small change in illumination conditions, or influence of noise can cause pixels to drift from one bin to an adjacent bin. As a result, two similar images may have two different sets of histogram bins. Matching these histogram bins (used by [2]) would fail to retrieve all the similar images from the database (this has been observed from our experiments). Furthermore, a large number of bins makes the task of image indexing difficult.

To overcome the problems, it is necessary to subdivide the colour space in such a way that colours with similar perceptual nature are grouped together in the same histogram bin. Different histogram bins must possess distinguishably different colour perception. Histograms created using this approach will be robust to changes in illumination, and provide more accurate similarity measure between images. Moreover, dividing colour space based on colour perceptual nature can greatly reduce the number of bins required, and therefore easier for indexing.

A colour space representing colours along the human perceptual dimensions is crucial in segmenting colours based on colour perceptual similarity. The RGB colour space, although widely used in colour processing systems and hardware monitors, does not carry direct semantic information about the colour. For instance, a person cannot visualise a colour given its (R,G,B) triplet. Furthermore, equal geometric distances in the RGB colour space do not generally correspond to equal perceptual changes in colour.

Contrary to the RGB colour space, the empirically defined Munsell colour space describes colours in terms of hue (the colour type), value (brightness) and chroma (saturation) - three semi-independent ttributes related to the human perception of colour. This capability of separating the luminant and chromatic components of a colour is extremely useful in handling images under non-uniform illuminating conditions such as highlight, shading, and strong contrast. Our experiments have shown that hue is least affected by changes in illumination, while chroma and value may show distinguished changes [5]. Furthermore, colours in the HVC space are arranged in such a way that equal geometric distances correspond to equal perceptual differences.

Many methods have been proposed to mathematically transform between the RGB and the Munsell colour spaces. Our experiments have shown that the MTM (Mathematical Transform to Munsell) [6] gives the best approximation to the Munsell colour space. The transform is done through the following three phases:

a. Transform from (R,G,B) to (X,Y,Z)

$$X = 0.607R + 0.174G + 0.201B \tag{1}$$
$$Y = 0.299R + 0.587G + 0.114B \tag{2}$$
$$Z = 0.066G + 1.117B \tag{3}$$

b. Transform from (X,Y,Z) to (M_1, M_2, M_3)

$$H_1 = 11.6\{(X/X_0)^{\{1/3\}} - (Y/Y_0)^{\{1/3\}}\} \tag{4}$$
$$H_2 = 11.6\{(Y/Y_0)^{\{1/3\}} - (Z/Z_0)^{\{1/3\}}\} \tag{5}$$
$$H_3 = 11.6((Y/Y_0)^{\{1/3\}} - 1.6 \tag{6}$$
$$M_1 = H_1 \tag{7}$$
$$M_2 = 0.4 * H_2 \tag{8}$$
$$M_3 = 0.23 * H_3 \tag{9}$$

c. Transform from (M_1, M_2, M_3) to (H,V,C) (Munsell colour space)

$$H' = \text{Arctan}(M_2/M_1) \tag{10}$$
$$S_1 = \{8.88 + 0.966 * \cos(H')\} * M_1 \tag{11}$$
$$S_2 = \{8.025 + 2.558 * \sin(H')\} * M_2 \tag{12}$$
$$H = \text{Arctan}(S_2/S_1) \tag{13}$$
$$V = 11.6(Y/Y_0)^{\{1/3\}} - 1.6 \tag{14}$$
$$C = \{(S_1)^2 + (S_2)^2\}^{\{1/2\}} \tag{15}$$

After the transformation of colour spaces, the HVC colour space is to be subdivided into bins based on colour perceptual natures. We have empirically divided the HVC colour space into 11 bins as shown in Table 1. We choose to divide the colour space rather roughly as we found that trivial colour differences contribute little to the content-based image retrieval process. This is because in a real world scene, a pure object colour is most likely diverged to a certain extent due to non-uniform illuminating conditions such as shading, highlight, reflection, and strong contrast. Two images with the same visual content but taken with minor differences in illuminating conditions should not be considered as different images.

The side effect for this approach is that the probability of retrieving irrelevant images (or false positives) might increase. These false positive matches can be largely reduced by introducing a secondary similarity measure to complement the histogram metrics. In our system, optional secondary match using average H, average V, and average C values is available.

In order to match images with different sizes, we normalise the pixel count in each histogram bin by the total number of pixels in the image.

Colour histogram holds information on the colour distribution, but lacks locality information. In addition, the histogram for the entire image tends to miss small image regions that produce no strong peaks in the histogram. These problems can be overcome by subdividing an image into sub-areas; and create a histogram for each of the sub-areas (i.e. local histograms). The more sub-areas we have, the more accurate is the locality information; but more memory would be required to store the histograms. Trade-off between memory requirement and the precision of the locality is to be made. In our system, in addition to the histogram for the entire image (global histogram), we divide the image into 9 equal sub-areas (3 x 3) which are numbered from 0 to 8 in a left-right, top-down manner. A local histogram is created for each sub-area. During a retrieval process, user has the choices of matching only the global histogram, or all the nine local histograms, or combination of them.

Table 1: Range of the colour zones

Colour Name	Hue (degree)	Value	Chroma
Red	0~36	4~9	1.5~30
	36~64	4~9	1.5~30
Orange	64~112	4~8	9~30
Yellow	80~1112	9~10	1.5~30
Skin Color	36~64	4~9	1.5~15
	64~112	4~8	1.5~9
Green	112~196	4~10	1.5~30
Cyan	196~256	6~8	1.5~30
Blue	256~512	4~8	1.5~30
Purple	312~359	4~8	1.5~30
Black	-	<3	-
Gray	-	4~8	<1.5
		3~4	-
White	-	>9	<1.5

The average H, average V and average C values of all the histogram bins are computed and stored along with the image in the database in a tree structure (see section 4). For more stringent colour matching, a secondary match based on these average values can be carried out, after the primary histogram match. This hierarchical approach allows users to impose more controls on the matching process.

4.   Image Indexing

A numerical index-key is created for each histogram. This approach turns the computational intensive histogram matching process into an easy numerical index-key search.

In histogram matching, the absolute values of the pixel count, the H, V and C attributes for the histogram bins are not important. Arbitrary group numbers are assigned and used instead. The normalised pixel count in the histogram bins is assigned into 9 groups as shown in Table 2. Similarly, we divide the H, V and C axes into 9, 4 and 4 groups respectively, with interval of $40°$, 2.5 and 7.5. During the histogram matching, comparisons are made by using these group numbers instead of the absolute values.

Table 2: Group number for the normalized pixel count

Group Number	Range (%)
0	$[0 \sim 5)$
1	$[5 \sim 15)$
2	$[15 \sim 25)$
3	$[25 \sim 35)$
4	$[35 \sim 45)$
5	$[45 \sim 55)$
6	$[55 \sim 65)$
7	$[65 \sim 75)$
8	$[75 \sim 100]$

In our system, a two-layer tree structure in which each leaf node of the top B^+-tree is associated with an independent B^+-tree (Figure1) is devised to facilitate both the histogram-match and average H, V, and C values match. B^+-tree is adopted because it can be implemented easily on secondary storage [8], which is crucial in large-scale databases.

The numerical index key consists of two parts as shown in Figure 2. The first part of the key contains 36 bits. The first three bits represent the number of the sub-area from which the histogram is created. Every three consecutive bits in the remaining key . represent the group number of the normalised pixel count (Table 2) in the 11 histogram bins. Similarly, 7 bits are used to represent the average H, V and C group numbers of the histogram bins in the second part of the key as shown in Figure 2. Specifically, bit 0 to 2, 3 to 4, 5 to 6 represent the group number of the average H, V and C respectively.

The first part of the numerical key is used to transverse the top B^+-tree. Since images with the same histogram configuration have the same first part of the key, they are stored in the same leaf node of the top tree, hence in the same second layer B^+-tree associated to that leaf node. Matching based on the average H, V and C values is performed by utilising the second part of the numerical key in the second-layer B^+-tree. All the images stored in the second-layer tree will be fetched if matching of the average HVC values is not requested. Assuming that M part-one and N part-two numerical keys are stored in the top and the second layers respectively, this search process takes $O(\log_k M + \log_k N)$, where k is the number of branches from each non-leaf node in the tree [8].

5. User Interfaces

Two scenarios have been assumed for histogram-based image queries:
a.   User has a sample image, and would like to search the database for images that resemble the entire or only highlighted portion of the sample image.

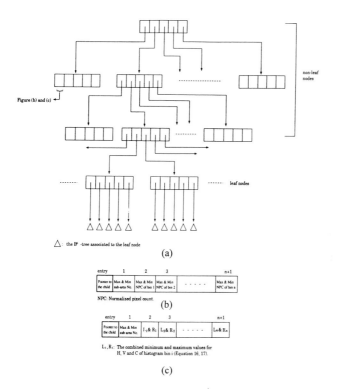

Figure 1: The configuration of the two-layer $B^+ - tree$ structure: (a): the tree structure; (b): the configuration of the non-leaf nodes in the top tree; (c): the configuration of the non-leaf nodes in the second layer tree.

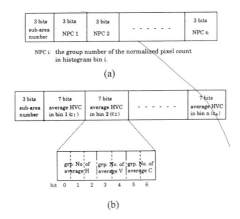

Figure 2: Format of the index key; (a): the first part of the index key; (b): the second part of the index key.

b.   User has a vague idea of the desired images in mind. He can vividly remember the background or the colour composition of certain regions in the image.

Two query methods are developed based on the above two scenarios:
a.   Query by user-provided samples;
b.   Query by combining system-provided templates.

5.1   *Query by User-Provided Samples*

Examples are shown in Figure 3 and Figure 4. The user can choose to use the entire image, or highlight a portion of the sample image for database query. The global histogram for the entire image would be created. If the entire sample image is chosen, nine local histograms (one per sub-area) would be created. If a portion of the sample image is specified, only local histogram for the sub-areas which are covered would be created. In addition, user can choose to enable or disable the secondary match based on the average H, V, and C values.

5.2   Query by Combining System-Provided Templates

Template for common objects such as sky, forest, lawn, brick wall, rocks, and sand beach are provided and can be expanded. User can select these templates and make modifications on these templates. An example is shown in Figure 5. It consists of a template display area, a template list, and coloured labels showing the colour configuration of the selected template. User can select templates from the template list and modify the colour composition of the selected template by adjusting the R, G, or B scalars. User can then place the template on any of the sub-areas.

6.   Experimental Results

The proposed system is implemented using X/Motif and C on SUN-SPARC platform. The database is currently populated by more than 300 colour images with a variety of image contents.

Figure 3 shows an example of image retrieval based on the global match of user-provided sample image. It can be observed from (b) that all the retrieved images contain colour content quite similar to the query sample.

Figure 4 demonstrates the effect of image retrieval based on both the histogram match and the average HVC match. In (a), the blue sky of the sample image was outlined as the query pattern. (b) and (c) show the images retrieved without and with the secondary average HVC match respectively. It can be observed that (b) contain the similar patterns to the query image, but with relatively larger variations in colours, while (c) possess closer brightness and saturation.

(a)

(b)

Figure 3: An exmaple of the image retrieval based on the global match method; (a): the sample image; (b): the retrieved images.

124

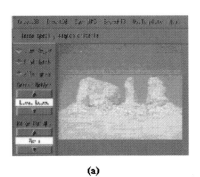

(a)

(c)

(b)

Figure 4: The effect on an image retrieval with and without secondary match of the average HVC values; (a): the sample image; (b): the images retrieved without secondary match; (c) the images retrieved with secondary match.

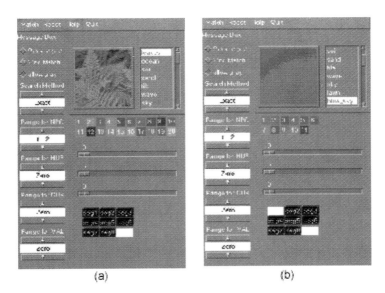

(a)   (b)

(c)

Figure 5: An example of the image query by combination of the system provided templates; (a): template *leaves* is selected and positioned at *seg9*; (b): template *blue-sky* is selected and positioned at *seg1*; (c): the retrieved images.

Figure 5 illustrates query by combining system-provided templates. In this example, two templates, namely, *leaves* and *blue-sky*, were selected from the template list, and positioned at *seg9* and *seg1* respectively (Figure 5(a), (b)). Consequently, two images containing similar patterns to the two templates at the specified locations were retrieved (Figure 5(c)).

7. Conclusion

A image database system with content-based image indexing and retrieval capabilities based on colour histogram is built. Our experiments have shown that the system is effective and robust especially in retrieving images with under non-uniform illuminating conditions. Our future work includes incorporating other image properties, such as shape, texture and orientation, to improve the indexing and retrieval capabilities.

8. References

[1]   T.Kato, T.Kurita and H.Shimogaki, Intelligent Visual Interaction with Image Database Systems - Toward the Multimedia Personal Interface, *Journal of Information Processing of Japan*, Vol.14, No.2, p134-143, 1991.

[2]   M.J.Swain, Interactive Indexing into Image Databases. *SPIE*, Vol.1908, 1993.

[3]   W.Niblack, R.Barber, W.Equitz and etc, The QBIC Project: Querying Images By Content Using Colour, Texture, and Shape. *SPIE*, Vol.1908, 1993.

[4]   Y.H. Gong and M.Sakauchi, An Object-Oriented Method for Colour Video Image Classification Using the Colour and Motion Features of Video Images. *ICARCV'92*, Singapore.

[5]   Y.H.Gong and M.Sakauchi, A Method of Detecting Regions with Specified Chromatic Features. *ACCV'93*, Japan, 1993.

[6]   M. Miyahara and Y. Yoshida, Mathematical Transform of (R,G,B) Colour Data to Munsell (H,V,C) Colour Data. *Journal of the Institute of Television Engineers, Japan*, Vol.43, No.10, pp.1129--1136, 1989.

[7]   M.J.Swain and D.H.Ballard, Colour Indexing. *International Journal of Computer Vision*, Vol.7, No.1, 1991.

[8]   F.R.McFadden, J.A.Hoffer and Srinivasan, Database Management. *Cummings, Inc*, 3rd Edition, 1988.

Using a Conceptual Graph Framework for Image Retrieval[a].

Mourad Mechkour, Catherine Berrut, and Yves Chiaramella
Laboratoire de Génie Informatique-IMAG,
BP 53, 38041 Grenoble cedex 9
France
E-mail: {Mourad.Mechkour, Catherine.Berrut, Yves.Chiaramella}@imag.fr

ABSTRACT

This paper presents an experience of implementing an image retrieval system using a conceptual graph framework. We first present the image model used (EMIR^2), which is expressed in a mathematical formalism. This model combines different interpretations of an image to build a complete description of it, each interpretation being represented by a particular **view**. This model provides also a basic query language, and the selection criteria to evaluate the query-image similarity. The conceptual graph (CG) framework, developed on top of an object oriented DBMS (o$_2$), is briefly presented after. A complete translation of EMIR^2 and its correspondence function in the CG formalism is given thereafter.

1. Introduction

The development of an image management system faces three major problems. The first two, storage and displaying of images, are finding satisfactory solutions with the great advances in hardware technologies. Optical disks, CD-ROM and WORM, for storage and high resolution display units for visualisation of high quality images, are the recommended solutions. The last problem and the hardest to solve is the difficulty of defining and interpreting image contents. This is a conceptual problem, and is due to the specificity of image data. A loss in information happens generally when replacing an image by a description of its content more suitable for computer handling, either it is textual or graphical, because the image is semantically richer than text or graphics. In addition, the existence of many plausible interpretations of the image contents makes the assignment of a description to an image very subjective, depending on the human perception of the application domain, background knowledge, specific needs, etc. These problems are more or less solved in developed systems, each one limiting the representation to the interpretation of the image relevant to the considered application[8].

The aim of this paper is to present our approach for an extended content based representation and retrieval of images (EMIR^2) and its implementation in a conceptual graph framework. EMIR^2 is a formal model of a general framework that integrates all aspects considered as relevant to image content description for effective information retrieval (IR)[12]. In this framework we combine different types of image representations to get the most precise and the most exhaustive image content description. These different representations are identified as particular views and an abstraction to combine them is defined. A general mathematical formalism has been used to state the model elements and operations.

This paper is organised in two parts: the first is devoted to the presentation of the formal image model and its query facility, and in the second part we present the representation of the model in the CG formalism.

2. The image model: EMIR^2

We will present here the basic elements behind the image model, the mathematical formalisation of the model, and thereafter the query language and the correspondence

---

[a] This work has been partially funded by the EEC under Basic Research Action FERMI, n° 8134.

128

function.

2.1. Basics of the image model

In EMIR^2 the basic description of an image is a particular interpretation of its content. An interpretation defines the semantics of the image objects considered as representative of the image topic in a particular context. To build the most exhaustive description of the image we combine a set of views, which correspond to partial descriptions of different natures of the image, and the image is said to be a multi-view object. The two principal views are the physical view and the logical view. The logical view groups all aspects of image contents and its general context. The logical view is an aggregation of different basic views, which are the spatial view, the structural view, the perceptive view, and the symbolic views.

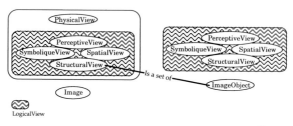

Fig. 1. Image and Image object representation in EMIR^2.

In our model an image is partitioned into a set of sub-images, each corresponding to some relevant object, which is designated by the term **image object**. An image object represents concrete objects that correspond to sub-image can be partitioned into other sub-images, which are represented by other image objects. The notion of complexity, inherent to images, is considered in EMIR^2 by representing the structural view of the image as the set of image objects corresponding to its sub-image partition. Here, an image object corresponds to the projection of the real word object of the scene in to the two-dimensional space of the image. The multi-view aspect of the image description is extended to the sub-images and their representation, the image objects. Figure 1 above shows the image and image object representation using a set of basic descriptive views. The principal views are described below.

2.2.1. The physical view

Since we consider in EMIR^2 only images in raster format, the physical view of an image is the corresponding pixel matrix. Four main image types are defined in our model: the bitmap images, where image pixels can be black or white; the grey scale images, where a pixel is one of the 256 grey levels; the palette colour images where a pixel has a colour among a set of 256 possible colours; and the true colour images, where a pixel can have a colour among a set of 2^{24} different colours.

2.2.2. The logical view

Each particular view describing the image content is partial, and the integration of a set of views in the same model leads to a more complete representation of the image. These different views are combined in a global view, the logical view, which integrates all aspects of the image content and can be used as a faithful representation of it. We identified four main complementary view types of the image.

❏ The structural view of an image defines the set of image objects that have been considered by the indexer as the most relevant to the image description. Each image object can be simple or complex, i.e. described by a structural view. The structural view is not a complete partition of the image, only relevant image objects are considered in the decomposition.

❏ The spatial view is concerned with the shape of the image objects (polygon, segment, ...) and the spatial relationships (far, north, overlap, ...) that indicate their relative positions inside the image. We define the spatial view of an image object as a combination of a set of four modelling spaces, generally used in the literature[3].

• The Euclidean space is used to describe the object shapes. We consider in EMIR[2] an approximation of the object shape using polygons, segments and points.

• The metric space is represented mainly by two spatial relation, far and close.

• The vector space considers the four direction relations North, South, East and West.

• The topological space includes a set of five basic topological relations[4], and these relations are Cross, Overlap, Disjoint, In, and Touch.

The Euclidean modelling space is a basic one, all other spaces can be inferred from it. We provide in EMIR[2] a set of procedures that determines the topological, metric, and vector space descriptions of an image given the Euclidean space description of the image objects that compose it. In order to compute the vector and metric spaces we substitute each spatial object by its equidistant barycentre.

❏ The perceptive view includes all the unbiased visual attributes of the image and/or image objects. It describes the appearance of the image components as perceived by an observer. For the moment, we consider in EMIR[2] mainly three basic visual attributes, the colour, the brightness, and the texture.

❏ The symbolic view associates a particular semantic interpretation of an image and/or an image object. An interpretation is generally done according to a particular context, which depends on the image domain and the image processing needs. Three general types of symbolic views are considered in EMIR[2]: Image object classification, Image and Image object properties, and events.

2.3. EMIR[2] formalisation

We present in this section the formalisation of the image model described above using a general mathematical formalism. This formal description considers all the elements presented above, plus some contextual elements necessary for the semantic interpretation of the image. Three main parts are used for image representation:

• The context that concerns the general image domain knowledge.

• The physical view of the image.

• The logical view of the image, which is decomposed in two parts. The first part is context free and groups the spatial view, and some elements of the image structural view. The second part is context sensitive and corresponds to the symbolic views, the perceptive views, and the image object structural views.

We list in the following the general description of these different parts of the image model and we refer the reader to the FERMI report[7] for the mathematical definition of the notions presented here.

2.3.1. Image content modelling

The image context definition groups the set of image object classes, the set of possible property and event definitions, and the general models of the possible perceptive views (colour space, textures, brightness values).

a. Image context model

The image context is defined as a tuple :

$$IC = (C, P, E, Tx, Br, Colour, \xrightarrow{C}, \xrightarrow{C\_P}),$$ which includes :

• The set of object classes (C), on which we defined two relations : the ISA relation $\xrightarrow{C} \subseteq C \times C$, and the composition relation $\xrightarrow{C\_P} \subseteq C \times C$. For example we consider the set C_1 and the relations $\xrightarrow{C}_1, \xrightarrow{C\_P}_1$:

$C_1 =$ {Person, Man, Woman, Animal, Dog, Trunk, Tree, Foliage, Door, House},

$\xrightarrow{C}_1 =$ (Person,Animal), (Man,Animal),(Woman,Person), (Dog,Animal),

$\xrightarrow{C\_P}_1 =$ (Trunk,Tree), (Foliage,Tree), (Door, House).

• The set of image and image object property definitions (P). For example in an image base representing photographs, an image is described by a set of attributes like the photographer name, the place where the image has been taken, etc. These attributes are defined in $EMIR^2$ using the property abstraction.

• The set of image object event definitions (E). For example actions implying persons (run after, hold, kiss, etc.) in an image are represented using event definition between object classes : kiss $\subseteq$ PERSON x PERSON, run_after $\subseteq$ PERSON x PERSON.

• The set of texture models (Tx),

• The set of possible brightness values (Br),

• The set of colour values representing the colour space (see 2.). We consider in $EMIR^2$, for the moment, the RGB colour space.

b. Physical view model

The physical view of image is defined by the pixel matrix with its colour table, the dimensions of the image (width, height), and its type.

$$\Phi IM = (\phi i, width, height, colour\_table, pixel, type)$$

c. Context free image description

The context free definition of an image associates with an image its physical view, its spatial view and the structural view of the image. It is defined by a tuple containing the image identifier (i), the physical view (ΦIM), the set of image object identifiers (IO), the composition relation between a sub-set of the image objects of the image ($\xrightarrow{IO\_P}$), the set of basic geometric objects identified in the image (SO), the set of spatial view identifiers used in the image (SV_{ID}), the relation that associates a spatial view the set of geometric objects that defines its contour (σ), the relation that associates an image object the spatial view that describes its shape (f_{sv}).

$$IM = (i, \Phi IM, IO, \xrightarrow{IO\_P}, SO, SV_{ID}, \sigma, f_{sv})$$

d. Context sensitive image description

The context sensitive image description corresponds to a semantic interpretation of the image content, according to a particular image context. It groups the symbolic views, the perceptive views and the image object structural views.

$$IR = (IC, IM, \xrightarrow{IO\_P}, \xrightarrow{O}, EP, EE, f_{tx}, f_{br}, f_{cl})$$

The IR tuple contains a valid image context definition (IC), a valid context free image representation (IM), the composition relation between the image objects, this relation represents the union of the structural views of the image objects ($\xrightarrow{IO\_P}$), the classification relation that associates each image object to its class ($\xrightarrow{O}$), a set of instantiated properties associated to the elements of IO (EP), a set of instantiated events linking the elements of IO (EE), a relation that associates to each image object its texture (f_{tx}), a relation that associates to each image object its colour (f_{cl}), a relation that associates to each image object its brightness value (f_{br}).

A set of constraints has defined to ensure the validity if the tuple definitions[7].

2.3.2. Image correspondence model and query language

We present in this section the elements of the correspondence model intended for EMIR^2. We will give the general guidelines for the query language, and the query definition, thereafter the list of selection criteria to be considered in comparing an EMIR^2 query and an EMIR^2 image.

a. The query language

A query q is a valid EMIR^2 image, defined relative to the context of an image base. This image definition is augmented by a set of relations and operations defined in EMIR^2, mainly the spatial relations, a set of generic image object and spatial view identifiers, and a set of fuzzy values for some perceptive views. We will describe each element in the following:

A query is defined by the context sensitive image and a context free image descriptions:

$$IR_q = (IC_b, IM_q, \xrightarrow{IO\_P} q, \xrightarrow{O} q, EP_q, EE_q, f_{txq}, f_{brq}, f_{clq})$$

$$IM_q = (i_q, \Phi_{iq}, IO_q, \xrightarrow{IO\_P} q, SO_q, SV_q, \sigma_q, f_{svq}, R_{sv})$$

such that,

• The image and physical image identifiers can be generic elements, represented by an asterisk, $i_q \in I \cup \{*\}$ and $\phi_{iq} \in \Phi I \cup \{*\}$.

• Only three constraints can be imposed on the physical view of the image in a query. These constraints correspond to the three simple attributes width, height, and type.

• We can use generic identifiers to define image objects or spatial views.

• Explicit spatial relations can be used in the query description :

$$R_{sv} \subseteq RelSpa \times SV_{idq} \times SV_{idq}$$

RelSpa = {North, South, West, East, Far, Close, Cross, In , Disjoint, Intersect, Overlap, Touch}

• Fuzzy values for the perceptive views Colour and Brightness can be used in a query. These fuzzy values correspond to a set of basic values from the domains Colour and Br defined in the image base context. This sub-set is denoted by the function dom. For example the colour Green, does not correspond to a single colour, but to a set of colours that can be perceived as green by a human being, dom(Green) = {$cc_1, cc_2, ..., cc_n$}. For the brightness, the fuzzy terms used represent sub-intervals of the possible brightness values, [0 , 1], this interval is denoted by the function dom. For example the term Dark corresponds to the interval dom(Dark) = [0 , 0.1], and the term bright corresponds to the interval dom(Bright) = [0.9 , 1].

b. Query evaluation

The image d is considered as answering the query q iff we can find an application, denoted I, from the set of image objects of the document (IO_d) in the set of image objects of the query (IO_q) that respects the following constraints: $I \subseteq IO_q \times IO_d$.

• The type, width, and height of the query are similar to image document physical view definition.

• $i_d = i_q$ xor $i_q = *$

• If a composition relation between two image objects from IO_q holds, then a composition relation must hold between their correspondent objects from IO_d, and considering the transitivity of the composition relation.

• The class, properties, and events of the query image objects should be generic of the correspondent document image object class, properties and events.

• The texture, brightness, and colour of a query image objet should be similar to the

texture, brightness, and colour of the correspondent document image object.
• The shape of corresponding image objects, represented by the spatial objects, should be similar and the spatial relations in the query defined in R_{SV} are respected in the document.
Important
        The function similar_to is used to estimate the similarity between two elements, its expression depends on the elements type (spatial objects, image width and height, property values, etc.). The simplest form for this function is the equality, that can be used to define a strict correspondence function for $EMIR^2$.

3. CG image representation

3.1. Introduction

        A wide range of knowledge representation formalisms from AI domain can be used as operational models for $EMIR^2$. The choice of a particular formalism depends mainly on its ability to model both the basic concepts of $EMIR^2$ and the similarity function between image descriptions. Other criteria may also be considered, like the expressiveness and the computation complexity. Different formalisms fulfil the first conditions, for example object oriented data models, first order logic, conceptual graph formalism, etc.
        In the first $EMIR^2$ implementation we chose Sowa's Conceptual Graph (CG) formalism[13], and its extension with notion of fuzziness[15]. Two principal reasons motivated this choice:
        ❏ An $EMIR^2$ description is based on a set of concepts (image objects, spatial objects, classes, ...) and a set of relationships (composition relation, spatial relations, events, ...) which are the basic component of a conceptual graph. The translation of an image description into the CG formalism will be straight to do.
        ❏ The CG formalism can represent all components of an IR system: the document and the query models can be represented using conceptual graphs, the context is represented using concept type and conceptual relation type lattices, and the correspondence function is implemented using the projection operator.
        We will review the principal definitions of CG formalism, before giving the translation of $EMIR^2$ formal description into this formalism, yielding $EMIR^2$-CG.

3.2. Conceptual graph framework

        A conceptual graph framework (CGF) has been developed on top of an object oriented DBMS (O_2)[8]. In CGF users can define knowledge bases (KB) combining a canon[13] and a set of fuzzy canonical graphs[15]. A fuzzy conceptual graph is a conceptual graph with weighted concepts and relations. A set of basic operations is provided for maintaining the KB: inserting and deleting concept and relation types, graphs form the canonical basis and from the canonical graphs collection. The basic operations, copy, join, restriction, simplification, and projection are also provided. CGF is accessible using an interface based on a linear form of conceptual graphs close to PEIRCE language[11].
        Note that the canon of an application is completely defined given the following elements:
        • A type hierarchy T (Concept Type Lattice, Conceptual Relation Type Lattice),
        • A set of individual markers I,
        • A conformity relation C that relates labels in T to markers in I,
        • A finite set of conceptual graphs B, called a canonical basis.
        The canonical graphs are obtained by the closure of B under the canonical formation

rules (copy, join, simplification, restriction).

The function δ defines for a weighted conceptual graph (w-graph) its truth value, δ(w-g) $\in [0,1]$. It is computed using a combination of the relation and concept weights in the w-graph.

3.3. The image model: EMIR^2-CG

The EMIR^2 model is now to be described using the operational model based on Sowa's conceptual graph formalism. Two principal elements of EMIR^2 are partially considered in this translation: the physical and the spatial views. This limitations are due to the formalism itself, since it did not provide basic data structures nor mathematical operations necessary for this particular goal. In this representation the spatial relationships can not be computed using Euclidean description of spatial objects, they have to be explicitly stored in the spatial view of the image description to be used later. So, we have to generalise the context free image description used for queries to all images. The spatial relations are now explicit in the image description and no more computed.

The description of an image in the formalism of CG is a canonical graph according to the canon defined for images, and each particular view defined in the model can be seen as a sub-graph of the image graph. In this graph all the concepts are specific, since they represent real objects found in the image and their descriptions. A complete definition of our image model in the formalism of conceptual graphs consists in providing a translation of the basic concepts of model (image, image object, views, ...) in this formalism and the definition of a canon that controls the canonical graphs describing the images.

An image is represented by a concept whose type is Image, and the referent is the image identifier, and the two image representations (context free and context sensitive) are represented by the entire conceptual graph.

The image representation in EMIR^2-CG is controlled by a canon, which consists of the concept type and conceptual relation lattices, and the canonical basis. The two first elements model all objects defined in EMIR^2 that are used in the representation of an image, and the third element is used to represent the general knowledge of the domain, which can be reduced to ontologies, with a set of constraints on graph generation.

We will present in the following a partial canon for each component of the image model (IC, IM, IR, ΦI) and make the union of these different partial canons to obtain the global EMIR^2-CG canon.

3.3.1. The image context representation

The corresponding representation of each component of IC in EMIR^2-CG is given below:
- Each class c from C is represented by concept type.
- The partial order between image object classes, $\xrightarrow{c}$, is represented by a lattice (CT$_{IC}$) of the corresponding concept types.
- The set of property definitions is represented by a set of graphs in the canonical basis (CB$_{IC}$) of the image context. An image object property (p_{io}, c, bt) $\in$ P, is represented by the generic graph: [c]->(p_{io})->[bt] $\in$ CB$_{IC}$, and an image property (p_i, Image, bt) $\in$ P is represented by the graph [Image]->(p_i)->[bt] $\in$ CB$_{IC}$, where p_{io}, p_i are conceptual relations corresponding to the properties, p_{io}, p_i $\in$ RT$_{IC}$.
- The set of event definitions is represented by graphs in the canonical basis CB$_{IC}$.

A binary event $(e_b, c_1, c_2) \in E_b$, is represented by the graph $[c_1]\text{->}(e_b)\text{->}[c_2] \in CB_{IC}$, where $e_b \in RT_{IC}$. A unary event $e_u(c_1) \in E$, is represented by the graph $[c_1]\text{->}(is)\text{->}[e_u]$, where is $\in RT_{IC}$ is a particular relation, and the event e_u is represented by a concept, $e_u \in CT_{IC}$.

• Tx is represented by a set of concept types each corresponding to particular texture model from Tx, $Id_{tx} \in CT_{IC}$.

• Br is represented by a set of concept types each corresponding to particular brightness value from Br, $Id_{br} \in CT_{IC}$, augmented by the set of fuzzy brightness values (see 3.4.1.), $\forall$ vb $\in Val_{br}$, vb $\in CT_{IC}$.

• Colour is represented by a set of concept types each corresponding to particular colour code from Colour, $c \in CT_{IC}$, augmented by the set of fuzzy colour values (see 3.4.1.), $\forall$ vc $\in Val_{cl}$, vc $\in CT_{IC}$. A colour value vc $\in Val_{cl}$ is a super-type of the basic colour codes of the set, dom(vc).

• The class composition relation ($\xrightarrow{C\_P}$) is represented by a conceptual relation (Comp), and each element $\xrightarrow{C\_P}(c_1 , c_2)$ is represented by a generic graph of the canonical basis, $[c_1]\text{->}(Comp)\text{->}[c_2] \in CB_{IC}$.

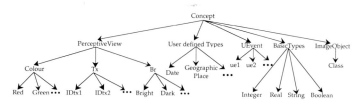

Fig. 2. Concept Type Lattice of the image context.

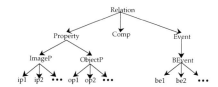

Fig. 3. Relation Type Lattice of the image context.

3.3.2. The physical image representation

The physical view representation in the CG formalism is limited to three simple attributes, the width, the height, and the type.

• The physical view is represented by a concept whose type is $\Phi Image \in CT_{\Phi IM}$, and the referent is the physical image identifier $\phi i \in \Phi I$, $[\Phi Image : \#\phi i]$.

• The width is represented by a conceptual relation (Width) that links an integer to the concept corresponding to the physical image. The following graph defines this link and is inserted into the canonical basis of the physical view, [ΦImage]->(width)->[Integer] ∈ CBΦIM.

• The height is represented by a conceptual relation (Height) that links an integer to the concept corresponding to the physical image. The following graph defines this link and is inserted into the canonical basis of the physical view, [ΦImage]->(height)->[Integer] ∈ CBΦIM.

• The type is represented by a conceptual relation (ΦType) that links a concept corresponding to the physical image to a concept from the set of image types, that are represented by concept types. The following graph controls the type of a physical view: [ΦImage]->(ΦType)->[ImageType] ∈ CBΦIM, with ImageType, BW, GS, CP, TC ∈ CTΦIM, and ΦType ∈ RTΦIM.

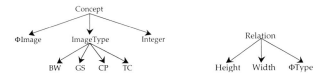

Fig. 4. Concept and Relation Type Lattices of the physical view.

3.3.3. The context free image representation

The context free image representation is defined by:

• The image is represented by a concept of type Image ∈ CTIM, and a referent represented by the image identifier ϕi, [Image : ϕi].

• The function ϕv that associate an image with its physical view is represented by a conceptual relation, ϕv ∈ RTIM, and a graph from the canonical basis, [Image]->(ϕv)->[ΦImage] ∈ CBIM.

• Each element of IO is represented by concept, whose type is ImageObject ∈ CTIM, and the referent is the image object identifier, [ImageObject : #io].

• The relation $\xrightarrow{\text{IO\_P}}$ is represented by the composition relation, Comp ∈ RTIM, defined by the following graph from the canonical basis, [Image]->(Comp)->[ImageObject] ∈ CBIM.

• The spatial aspect of an image object is represented by a single concept, whose type is a basic geometric type (polygon, segment, ...) and the referent is the spatial view identifier. In this representation, we consider simple spatial objects, and the concept Type SpatialView is a super-type of all spatial object types.

SpatialView, SpatialObject, {Polygon, Segment, Point, ...} ∈ CTIM, RelSpa ∪ {DirectionRelation, MetricRelation} ⊆ RTIM.

• The functions σ and f_{SV} are represented by the same conceptual relation, f_{SV} ∈ RTIM, that links an image object to its spatial view. This link is represented by the following graph of the canonical basis: [ImageObject]->(f_{SV})->[SpatialView] ∈ CBIM.

136

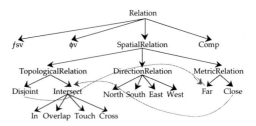

Fig. 5. Relation Type Lattice of the context free image representation.

- R_{SV} (see 3.4.1. for definition) is represented by a set of conceptual relations, corresponding to the spatial relations, linking spatial views. The graphs produced for R_{SV} are conform to the following graphs from the canonical basis, CB_{IM}.

[SpatialObject]->(DirectionRelation)->[SpatialObject],
[SpatialObject]->(MetricRelation)->[SpatialObject],

[SpatialObject]->(In)->[Polygon],   [Point]->(In)->[Segment],

[Segment]->(In)->[Segment],   [Segment]->(Cross)->[Segment],

[Polygon]->(Cross)->[Polygon],   [Polygon]->(Overlap)->[Polygon],

[Segment]->(Overlap)->[Segment],   [SpatialObject]->(Touch)->[Polygon],

[SpatialObject]->(Touch)->[Segment],   [Segment]->(Touch)->[Point],

[Polygon]->(Touch)->[Point],   [SpatialObject]->(Disjoint)->[SpatialObject].

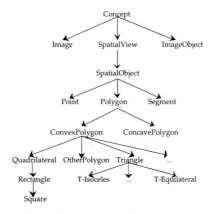

Fig. 6. Concept Type Lattice of the context free image representation.

3.3.4. The context sensitive image representation

The context sensitive image representation is defined by:

- $\xrightarrow{IO\_P}$ is represented by the composition relation Comp $\in$ CB_{IR}, that links image objects from IO. These composition relation is controlled by the composition relation defined in the context image definition (CB_{IC}).

- $\xrightarrow{O}$ (io_1, c_1) is represented in the concept corresponding to the image object io_1, the concept type is the class of the object and the referent is the image object identifier [c_1 : #io$_1$].

• An element of EP is an instance of a graph from CB$_{IC}$ corresponding to the property definition, where the referents of the concepts are all elements of IO.

• An element of EE is an instance of a graph from CB$_{IC}$ corresponding to the event definition, where the referents of the concepts are all elements of IO.

• An element of f_{tx}, f_{tx}(io$_1$,id$_{tx}$), is represented by a relation linking a concept, corresponding to the image object, to a concept representing a texture model, [c_1 : #io$_1$]->(f_{tx})->[id$_{tx}$]. The canonical basis CB$_{IR}$ contains a graph to control the texture description of an image or image object: [Image]->(f_{tx})->[Tx], [ImageObject]->(f_{tx})->[Tx].

• An element of f_{br}, f_{br}(io$_1$,b), is represented by a relation linking a concept, corresponding to the image object, to a concept representing a brightness value, [c_1 : #io$_1$]->(f_{br})->[b]. The canonical basis CB$_{IR}$ contains a graph to control the brightness value of an image or image object: [Image]->(f_{br})->[Br∪Val$_{br}$], [ImageObject]->(f_{br})->[Br∪Val$_{br}$].

• An element of f_{cl}, f_{cl}(io$_1$,c), is represented by a relation linking a concept, corresponding to the image object, to a concept representing the colour, [c_1 : #io$_1$]->(f_{cl})->[b]. The canonical basis CB$_{IR}$ contains a graph to control the colour description of an image or image object: [Image]->(f_{cl})->[Colour∪Val$_{cl}$], [ImageObject]->(f_{cl})->[Colour∪Val$_{cl}$].

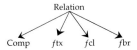

Fig. 7. Concept and Relation Type Lattices of the context sensitive image representation.

3.3.5. The EMIR^2 global canon

The global EMIR^2-CG canon is obtained by considering the union of the individual canons, its defined by the triplet, (CT$_g$, RT$_g$, CB$_g$).

CT$_g$ = CT$_{IC}$ ∪ CT$_{ΦIM}$ ∪ CT$_{IM}$ ∪ CT$_{IR}$

RT$_g$ = RT$_{IC}$ ∪ RT$_{ΦIM}$ ∪ RT$_{IM}$ ∪ RT$_{IR}$

CB$_g$ = CB$_{IC}$ ∪ CB$_{ΦIM}$ ∪ CB$_{IM}$ ∪ CB$_{IR}$

Example 1. An image containing a Man, named Jim, running after a girl named Mary, is represented in EMIR^2-CG using the following graph.

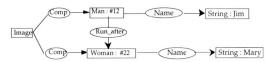

Fig. 9. Example of an image description using a binary event and image object properties.

Example 2. The following graph shows a partial description of a house image in which the term symbolic view is used to identify the image objects.

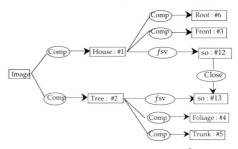

Fig. 8. Image description example in EMIR^2-CG.

3.4. Query expression in EMIR^2-CG

The queries in EMIR^2-CG are descriptions of hypothetical images, and the query language is identical to the image model used to represent the image collection. Depending on the views the user is interested in, the query can be classified in one of the different query types. All query type graphs contain at least basic structural elements of the image, which are the concepts Image and ImageObject and the relations Comp. The semantic content based queries defines constraints on the symbolic views of the image. The spatial queries express spatial descriptions of image content, represented by the shape of objects, and the relative positions of objects. The perceptive queries define constraints on the perceptive view of the image. The combined queries, structural-spatial, structural-symbolic, and symbolic-spatial combine concepts from two different views to get a more precise description of the hypothetical image. Finally, the general queries can combine all the elements used in the image model. For example we can ask questions about images containing a house with a window and a door, and a tree with a particular shape #shape, and the tree being close to and to the left of the tree. See [7] for a more complete presentation of EMIR^2-CG query categories.

Fig. 10. Example of a query in EMIR^2-CG.

3.5. Image correspondence in EMIR^2-CG

The correspondence model developed in EMIR^2-CG is based on an extension of the logical model of IR[14] defined by J. Nie[10]. In this model the basic operation is the comparison of a document and a query. The document and the query are considered as set of sentences which are interpreted in a predefined semantics; the query being usually reduced to a single sentence. For a document to be considered relevant to a query, it must "imply" the query. In IR this implication is always plausible rather than strict, so a certainty measure is associated to it. Estimating the relevance of a document D to a query Q, is reduced to the computation of the implication strength, that is $P(D{\rightarrow}Q)$. The symbol $\rightarrow$ does not correspond to the material implication in classical logic. VanRijsbergen proposed a conditional logical evaluation for this implication, in EMIR[2]-CG we will use Conceptual Graph specific operations.

According to Nie[10] the function $P(D{\rightarrow}Q)$ considers only the **exhaustivity** of the document to the query, i.e. which elements of the query are mentioned in the document; but not the **specificity** of the document to the query, i.e. in what details the element of the query are mentioned in the document. Expressed in notion of implication, $D{\rightarrow}Q$ corresponds to exhaustivity, and $Q{\rightarrow}D$ corresponds to specificity. If the document mentions all query elements, $D{\rightarrow}Q$ is estimated to 1, and if the document mentions only elements of the query $Q{\rightarrow}D$, is estimated to 1. Considering both exhaustivity and specificity in estimating the relevance of the document D to the query Q leads to the following function:

$$R(D,Q) = F[P(D{\rightarrow}Q),P'(Q{\rightarrow}D)] \qquad (1)$$

The definition of the correspondence function for EMIR[2]-CG consists in implementing the functions P, P' and F from the formulae (1), with D and Q being represented by weighted conceptual graphs.

3.5.1. The P function

The logical implication of VanRijsbergen $D{\rightarrow}Q$ is instantiated in EMIR[2]-CG using the projection operator, since this operator is equivalent to the material implication. Indeed, using the ϕ operator defined by Sowa, if a projection $\pi(Q,D)$ exists then $\phi(D) \subset \phi(Q)$. In other hand the projection $\pi(Q,D)$ exists if D is a specialisation of Q, which is the principle used in IR, the document is specific to the query.

In EMIR[2] we defined a set of selection criteria for an image to be relevant to a query. The projection operation respects most of these criteria, considering the function similar_to as the equality or the specific relation between concepts.

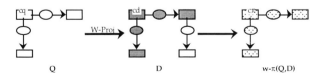

Fig. 10. The correspondence function of EMIR[2]-CG.

The function P is then instantiated using the function δ, that computes the truth value of the weighted conceptual graph resulting from the projection of Q on D:

$$P(D \rightarrow Q) = \delta(w - \pi(Q,D)) \qquad (2)$$

δ being the average of the concept and conceptual relation weights.

3.5.2. The P' function

The exhaustivity function P' estimates how much information in the document D are not present in the query. This difference is computed in terms of basic information elements. As a conceptual graph is composed by joins of a set of graphs of the canonical basis, we consider the graphs of the canonical basis as the basic information elements.

$$P'(Q \rightarrow D) = \Delta(Q,D) = \frac{\text{BasicGraphNumber}(D) - \text{BasicGraphNumber}(w - \pi(D,Q))}{\text{BasicGraphNumber}(D)} \quad (3)$$

3.5.3. The F function

The function F currently in use in EMIR^2 is defined as follows:
$$F(a,b) = a * (1 - b).$$
Finally the relevance function used in EMIR^2-CG is defined by,

$$R(Q,D) = \delta(w - \pi(Q,D)) * (1 - \Delta(D, w - \pi(Q,D))) \qquad (4)$$

4. Conclusion

We suggested in this paper the use of an extended model for image content representation suitable for information retrieval. This model is based on a multifaceted vision of the image, and integrate all aspects of image description in the same framework in an homogeneous way. Four major logical facets (views) have been identified and integrated in EMIR^2 for beast image modelling. These views are: the symbolic view, which models semantic interpretations of the image content; the spatial view, which represents the inherent bi-dimensional aspect of images; the structural view, which models the complexity of image content; and the perceptive view which represents the visual aspects of the objects in an image. This general model, has been formalised using a general mathematical formalism and a query language has been proposed to permit user queries expressions. A set of selection criteria has been stated to permit query-document similarity estimation, and can be used as a kernel for an image retrieval system.

An operational model based on the fuzzy conceptual graph formalism has been defined to implement the EMIR^2 model. A prototype of an IRS retrieval engine implementing this operational model has been developed on top of the object oriented database system O_2[5]. Queries can be posed using a linear form of conceptual graphs, and the result is presented as a set of images ordered by estimated relevance value.

Experimenting

When evaluating effectiveness of such semantic models in IR domain, it is essential to develop a test collection and an IRS based on this model. We are currently experimenting EMIR^2-CG using a collection of images of the old Paris areas. The test collection is composed of two main parts: the indexing of the images, which has been done by specialists, using a sophisticated concept based symbolic views, and the modelling of domain dependent knowledge which includes the concept type lattices corresponding to the different views, mainly the class type symbolic view (thesaurus of the domain), and a set of image properties[8].

Future work

EMIR^2 is open to integrate other media description in the same framework. The symbolic view associated to images was inspired from textual data representation, and according to that a text can be easily represented in EMIR^2 using a particular symbolic view, and then a comparison between an image and a text could be based on this symbolic description. On the other hand the spatial view of an image, which is based on a graphical description of the objects, can be extended to model graphics. We are currently working in the integration of graphic and modelling and image modelling[9].

Uncertainty and relevance are two central notions in Information Retrieval, and should be integrated in the document model and the correspondence model as well. A first step towards this integration has been done in [7] by using fuzzy relations, but we lack a general theory of uncertainty to formalise the problem correctly.

5. References

1. E. Aïmeur and J. G. Ganascia, *Elicitation of Taxonomies Based on the Use of Conceptual Graph Operators*, Proceedings of the First International Cobference on Conceptual Structures, ICCS'93, Quebec City, Canada, August 1993.
2. C. Berrut and M. Mechkour, *Representation of images for multimedia databases. A preliminary study*, IFIP WG 2.6, 2nd Working Conference on Visual Database Systems. Budapest, Hungary, September 30 - October 3, 1991.
3. L. Buisson, *Reasoning on space with object-centered knowledge representations*, Lecture notes in computer science. Design and implementation of large spatial databases. First Symposium SSD'89. Santa Barbara, California, July 1989, Proceedings. A. Buchmann, O. Günther, T.R. Smith and Y.-F. Wang (Eds), pp 325-344.
4. E. Clementini, P. Di Felice and P. Van Oostrom, *A small set of formal topological relationships suitable for end-user interaction*, Lecture Notes in computer science, 692. Advances in Spatial Databases. Proceedings of the third international symposium, SSD'93, Singapore, June 1993. pp, 277-295.
5. O. DEUX et al, *The O2 system*, Communications of the ACM, Vol. 34, N° 10, October 1991, pp 34-48.
6. G. Halin, M. Creange and P. Kerekes, *Machine learning and vectorial matching for an image retrieval model : EXPRIM and the system RIVAGE*, ACM-SIGIR, Brussels 1990, pp 99-114.
7. M. Mechkour, *EMIR^2. An Extended Model for Image Representation and Retrieval*, in WorkPart 3 Delivrable : A Model for the Semantic Content of Multimedia Data, ESPRIT BRA Project N° 8134 : FERMI, chapter 3, May 1995.
8. M. Mechkour, *EMIR^2. Un modèle étendu de représentation et de correspondance d'images pour la recherche d'informations. Application à un corpus d'images historiques*, PhD thesis, Grenoble University, 1995 (In french).
9. M. Mechkour, *A Conceptual Graphics Model for Information Retrieval*, in WorkPart 3 Delivrable : A Model for the Semantic Content of Multimedia Data, ESPRIT BRA Project N° 8134 : FERMI, chapter 3, May 1995.
10. J. Nie, *An Outline of a General Model for Information Retrieval Systems*, Proceedings of the 11th ACM SIGIR conference, Grenoble 1988, pp 495-506.
11. Proceedings of the second interbational workshop on PEIRCE : *A conceptual graphs workbench*. Robert Levinson, Gerard Ellis (Eds.), Laval university, Quebec, Canada, August 7, 1993.
12. G. Salton and M. J. McGill, *Introduction to modern information retrieval*, McGraw-Hill, New York, 1983.

13. J. F. Sowa, *Conceptual structures : information processing in mind and machine*, Addison-Wesley publishing company, 1984.
14. C. J. VanRijsbergen, *A non-classical logic for information retrieval*, Computer Journal, Vol. 29, No. 6, 1986.
15. V Wuwongse and M. Manzano,*Fuzzy conceptual graphs*, Proceedings of the First International Cobference on Conceptual Structures, ICCS'93. Quebec City, Canada, August 1993.

Chapter 4

Interactive Multimedia

ELEMENTS FOR MODELING AN INTERACTIVE ENVIRONMENT BASED ON A DISTRIBUTED AND REAL-TIME ARCHITECTURE

Gilbert PINOT

ESSAIM - Laboratoire LSI
Université de Haute-Alsace
12, rue des frères Lumière - 68093 Mulhouse Cedex - FRANCE
E-mail : G.Pinot@univ_mulhouse.fr

and

Gérard METZGER, Bernard THIRION

ESSAIM - Laboratoire LSI
Université de Haute-Alsace
12, rue des frères Lumière - 68093 Mulhouse Cedex - FRANCE
E-mail : G.Metzger@univ_mulhouse.fr - B.Thirion@univ_mulhouse.fr

ABSTRACT

Today's desktop Multimedia technology offers many ways of developing self-applications or interactive systems. However this technology is still expensive for wide development applications such as interactive information systems, model animations.The digital sounds and video data manipulation requiers powerful installations to obtain enough system reactivity. Distribution of this manipulation on different platforms is therefore a solution. This paper presents first a small critical description of usual solutions, nowadays interactive system performances and the interest in choosing a distributed solution. Then some elements for modeling a distributed multimedia architecture with sounds, images and video images, also able to control special actuators, is giving. The multimedia part is based on standards like Quicktime™ and the smart actuator part uses the distributed control-command possibilities of a field bus. Finaly, a typical   application of a reactive multimedia area for a technical museum is presented. Such an architecture leads to the development of an intelligent interactive environment.

KEYWORDS

Multimedia, distributed architecture, real-time, interactive environment, reactive area

1. Introduction

Easy manipulation of heterogeneous static and dynamic information such as sound, photograph and video-images is the main characteristic of multimedia with the aim of improving user/computer communication. This technology, which is acknowledged as the next revolution in computing (T. Yager 1991), tries to provide a seamless integration of dynamical data on personnal computers (or information terminals). Typical fields of application are education, decision making or entertainment. Theatres, conferences or exhibitions, as well as museums have virtually the same goals as multimedia, but they refer to larger audiences.This kind of group applications requires the integration and the control of standard multimedia equipment and more specific equipments such as spotlights, slide or video projectors, motorized mirrors, etc. They use more and more multisensorial presentations in order to compel more emotion or understanding. In this context, work is made easier by the hegemony of digital techniques over analog techniques, the digitalization of sound and image is then the only solution for an easy use of information. Unfortunately, the size of digital multimedia data is still considerable : large processing power and data flow are required, hence the study and use of specialized chips in numerical signal processing.

Our laboratory proposes a dedicated distributed architecture allowing to get advantages of the new multimedia techniques for this kind of wide interactive environment (especially museums and planetariums). In this study, we designed a real-time interactive information system which will develop into a real-time interactive area. We lay emphasis on user comfort, especially on the ability of the system to respond quickly to external solicitations.

2. Interactive System Environments

2.1. Usual solutions

Interactive terminals are one of the multimedia fields which most concern general public. Numerous examples of information or orientation systems are installed in public places (railway halls, exhibitions, general stores, etc). These systems allow the users to find his bearing, to look for one product, to help him to make a purchase. It is possible for him to explore his own option at his own step. These interactive systems are generaly fit out with touch screens, and deliver sound informations and graphical images for the most sophisticated.

In a generical way, an interactive system is an individual user controled automaton, integrated and multimodal, for audio-visual information delivering. Dynamics and expression of dialogue are essential. Such system must provide instantaneous information to user sollicitations, in ergonomical manner, whithout previous learning. Delivered information must be pertinent, even if the user's choices have bad formulation.

Inputs are typically keyboard, mouse, or touch screen menu selections. For outputs, sound is generally provided by synthesizers, restricting dialogue to small sentences, or in another way comes from large storage media such as videodisks. It is the same for still images and animations which are usually stored on the same analogue media or provide a poor quality and short duration. At this point, it is necessary to differentiate the presentation's running from it's creation, usually performed on a different plateform. These systems are still technically limited and are stated with synchronization and coordination problems (mechanical and temporal constraints).

2.2. Digital solutions

New technics of digital data processing (ex: compression) have much more advantages: digital data media have short access time ($\approx$20ms), completely controlable. All the information given to the developper has the same visible format and is administrated directly by the same system. Therefore, simultaneous data supply synchronisation (sound, video, etc.) is perfect and above all very easy to be done by a computer. In addition, scenario modification is much more simplified.

Numerical systems architecture has the same general features as usual ones. It is built around dialogue event sensors, global management and synchronization processors, presentation effectors and storage media (Fig. 1).

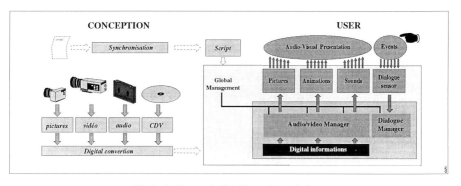

Fig. 1. Architecture of a digital interactive terminal

The main difference lies in the data support, hard disk in general, which allows a very short access time to information, compatible with an ergonomical utilisation.

3. Elements for Modeling an Interactive Distributed Environment: ENVI

3.1. Real time consideration

Present multimedia concepts suppose first digital solutions, so today's limits are relative to computer facilities to manipulate this dynamical information in suitable conditions. Required data flow is still important facing the size of the manipulated information. Some examples:
- 1 minute hifi sound (10 bits - 44,1 KHz) ≈ 5 Mbytes
- 10 sec. video (240x400 pixels -30 ips) ≈ 30 Mbytes

These constraints due to large data size and media flow have dictated the necessity to modify data format by using Digital Signal Processors. These expensive solutions are not usual on personal computers, reducing particularly their multimedia capabilities. For example, all the digital video demonstrations on general public middle scaled computers are restricted in size (320 x 240 pixels), in rate (12 ips) , in quality (256 colors), and above all, their utilization on interactive applications are not pleasant because of prohibitive response time.

In our point of view, it's the main lack of these interactive systems. There will always be a moment when the user will not be the dialogue master, even for a few seconds. Therefore, we introduce the "real-time interactive system " concept. The real-time requirement in our case is that the interactive system reacts immediatly to user sollicitation. This one must always keep the dialogue control and never be waiting for data loading from their media.

3.2. ENVI Basic Model Objects

The solution we offer with ENVI is to distribute all the activity of an interactive multimedia system on several low scale computers connected by a hierarchy of networks. Each kind of activity is instantaneously handled by one processor, according to orders sent by the host processor (Fig. 2).

We introduce here the concept of "station", that is to say each computer is a specific unit of the interactive multimedia presentation, for example the "sound station", the "touch-screen station", etc. On this architecture could be add some specific stations controling physical effectors, just like "spot-light station" or "stepping motor station". Stations activity could be completely concurrent. The whole is remotely controled by a supervisor called "director". ENVI is built on an hierarchical software structure. Host management is made by Hypercard™ software around which were installed external commands for communication control with lower layers (Fig. 3). Low management is realised with a self-made software called MultimediaStation which controls user interface. This one is built on Apple standard for dynamical data manipulation, QuickTime™ (Walsh 1992). An homogeneous information encapsulation is easily obtained by this way .

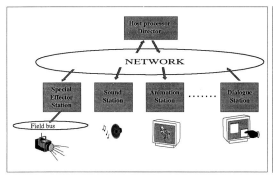

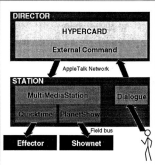

Fig. 2. Interactive and Distributed Environment: ENVI

Fig. 3. Global software structure of ENVI

The supervisor (director) makes the global management of the interactive system (Fig. 4). It is continuously waiting for external events (switch, touch-screen action, radar detection, etc). It receives external user solicitations through the event manager and sends, via the network hierarchy, the global control commands for the dedicated stations. Then the remote stations start and control the selected effects.

Exemple of global control command :

```
Sendtostation Station Id,Action Id, Effect Id
```

The interactive presentation scenario is scripted and so, easy to modify. Example :

```
on dialogue2
  Sendtostation sound, play, intro
  Wait 2
  Sendtostation moovie, stop, jingle
end dialogue2
```

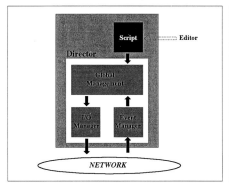

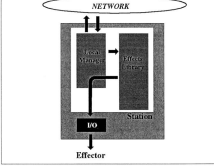

Fig. 4 . Director Architecture

Fig. 5. Station Architecture

Each station must be able to process immediately an order (sound emission, video playing, etc.) from the director processor. Data transfer time will be inevitably penalisant, therefore the adequate information is resident to the station. Multimedia information is stored in libraries on the local stations hard disk and is selected by the local manager for its execution (Fig. 5).

This data has usual multimedia type just like SOUND, MOOVIE and PICT. Each station is able to process one data type (or more in regards of its computing power) and could handle functions such as SELECT, PLAY, STOP, PAUSE, PREVIOUS, NEXT. Manipulation of multimedia information on each station is made by the MultimediaStation application. We wanted to favour execution time of a director command. In this way, even if the data size is large (ex: digital video ≈ few Mbytes), its loading must be instantaneous. For this, MultimediaStation could preload the largest data in memory and ensure a short access time.

Remote stations can also control power effectors, for instance spot-lights, stepping motor, or more general scenery. These theatrical-set effect controllers are built around a powerful hardware called Shownet™ (Schittly 1988). This architecture is based on the Bitbus™ field bus and interconnects 8044 processor-based slave modules. Each module runs the IDCX51 distributed multi-tasking kernel and, a master module interacts both with the slaves and with a Macintosh host. The slaves adapt the specific peripheral hardware to the network and run instantiations of generic control tasks. This architecture is under control of a specific software PlanetShow™ (Thirion 1988/1993) wich allow for setting-up of the network, definition of show hierarchy, interactive learning of an effect or description of more generic effects based on a scripting langage.

Example :

```
Define swithTheSlides with (switchOnList, swithOffList, switchTime) {
    for each projector in the swithOffList {
        change brightness of the projector to 0 in switchTime seconds
    }
    for each projector in the swithOnList {
        activate forward of the projector
        change brightness of the projector to 100 in switchTime seconds
    }
}
Define crossfade with (toTurnOn, toTurnOff, riseTime, holdTime, count)
{
    cycleTime = riseTime + holdTime
    repeat  count times, at cycleTime intervals {
        execute swithTheSlides (toTurnOn, toTurnOff, riseTime)
        temporary = toTurnOff
        toTurnOff = toTurnOn
        toTurnOn  = temporary
    }
}
```

4. Experimental Environment

We experimented our architecture in the realisation of an interactive area or environment for a scientific museum which has planned some interactive guide terminals or scientific informations terminals. The objective for this interactive environment is to offer an educational function. In this case, the dispached data gives complementary information on a technical object or on a cultural subject. This information machine needs multisensorial mechanisms to improve communication effectiveness.

The main point of interest is of course the ability of the interactive system to respond quickly to visitor's solicitation. A typical example of a museological object to present is a television. In this context, the system must explain to the museum's visitor how a TV set is working, how image is built on the screen, how color is constructed, what is the rule of an antenna, etc.

For a better evaluation, we installed successively two different terminals in the museum. First a classical monoprocessor solution using a usual touch-screen on which was displayed the object to explain for the visitors. This multimedia presentation was realised with standard software and calls for video and sound sequences stored on the hard-disk. Then we introduced the ENVI architecture. In this case, interaction is not realised on a touch screen on which is displayed the technical object to present but directly on the object itself, which is completely manipulable by the user. Visitor's entrance and motion in the reception area (radar, sensor, switch, etc.) and every object manipulation triggers events which start multimedia sequences. This build a complete reactive environment (Fig. 6).

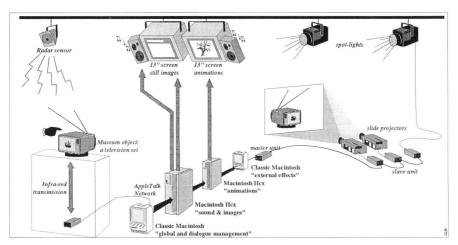

Fig. 6. Example of the ENVI architecture for a museum application

The multiprocessor solution is choosed naturally. Several slave processors are connected on a AppleTalk™ network to the master processor which controls the general synchronization.

For this system, the processor task repartition is (Fig. 7):

• global synchronization and dialogue management (external events)
• audio and still images sequences handling (13" color screen)
• video sequences handling (13" color screen)
• external effects handling (spot-lights, slide projectors)

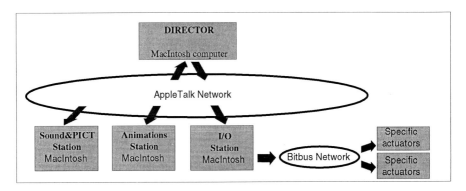

Fig. 7. Processor task repartition

The experimental application consists of several Macintosh computers, from Classic Macintosh for global and dialogue control up to Cx Macintosh for powerfull tasking. Every sequence is labeled and selectable by the director for a local processing.

4.1. Performances

In the museum, we observed visitor's attitude in both situations. With the standard solution set up with only one processor, user is rapidly confused. He lose patience during large data loading and don't stay in front of the terminal. At the opposite, with ENVI, visitor is much more interested. Each of his action activate immediately a short explanation sequence (sounds and video) with special effects in the demonstration area (lights, slides, etc.). With this prototype, we wanted to introduce the concept of reactive environment. Modelization of user's behaviour and observation of his actions featuring his point of interest allow to build a reactive multimedia presentation. Our main goal which was to obtain an immediate system reaction after a user solicitation was successful. Even with the largest video sequence (12Mo), response is immediate . The user is effectively surprised by some incisive sequence (ex: instantaneous loud sound and light) created to amaze him.

A significiant problem was to propose directly the object to explain (the TV set for example), with all the sensors without modifying its original function. For this, all the electronical equipment had to be hidden.

5. Conclusion

We have proposed a new kind of group application which tries to apply multimedia technologies to large environments such as museums or theatres. The application runs on a distributed real-time multimedia architecture including a field bus for the control of specific actuators. The system is operated by a complex set of distributed software modules which are synchronized by a hierarchical control system. This system was validated on a typical museum application where the innovating principles are: integration of a numerical and distributed system for interactive presentation which offers a direct and real-time interaction with the object to present.

In the future this environment will move toward an intelligent environment, more sensitive to user actions and reactions. The encouraging results allow to consider research on smart sensors field, to improve the adaptative characteristic of our system. For this last aim, different works on user behaviour modeling are jointly realised. This allow to consider the integration of an intelligent agent assisting the user (ACM 1994).

6. References

- ACM - *Special issue on Intelligent Agents* - Communication of the ACM , Vol 37 N°7 1994

- Morril, J. - *Sound and Image Processing* - Byte, 240-316 - December 1989

Nicolaou, C. - *An Architecture for Real-Time Multimedia Communication Systems* IEEE Journal on Selected Areas in Communication - April 1990

- Pinot, G. - *Concepts Multimédia et Technologies Associées. Applications: Consultation d'une Base de Données d'Images, Bornes Interactives* - Ph. D. Thesis, Mulhouse France - Mai 1993

- Schittly, S. and Perrin, M. - *Shownet™: Interconnection of auxiliary effects projectors* - Comptes-rendus du 2ème Colloque des Planétariums Européens, Paris, 1988

- Thirion, B. and Perrin, M. -*PlanetShow™: Un logiciel interactif pour la construction et l'exploitation des spectacles de planetariums* - Comptes-rendus du 2ème Colloque des Planétariums Européens, Paris, 1988

- Thirion, B -*Construction of an Interactive Programming Environment for Control of Theatrical-Set Effects via Object-Oriented Methods* - Software Practice and

Experience, Vol 23, N°6, 1993

- Thirion, B. -*Génie Logiciel : Thème et Variation* -   Habilitation à diriger des recherches, Mulhouse France - 1993

- Walsh, A. - *Programming Quicktime* - Dr Doobs Journal - July 1992

- Yager, T. - *Multimédia, Solutions Anticipating a Market* - Byte, 151-202 , December 1991

ON MAKING A BETTER INTERACTIVE MULTIMEDIA PRESENTATION

Timothy K. Shih
Department of Computer Science and Information Engineering
Tamkang University
Tamsui, Taiwan
R.O.C.
fax: Intl. 02-623-8212
email: TSHIH@CS.TKU.EDU.TW

Abstract

Multimedia technologies change the ways human interact with computers. Especially on hardware designs, the quality of digitized sound and video became better and better. However, even multimedia software systems provide friendly environments for the presentation authors to use multimedia hardware facilities easily, most of the interactive presentations generated by these systems does not allow the audiences to interact with their computer differently. In this paper, we introduce an interactive presentation design system that allows a presenter to plan the audience's reaction in advance. While the audience is watching a presentation, the underlying inference system is learning from his/her response. This mechanism makes a presentation to be proceed again act according to the audience's background and knowledge. Thus, the resulting presentation is more diversified. A model of presentation is defined. Based on this model, we design a graphical user interface and a language facilitate the presentation design.

Key words: Interactive Multimedia Presentation, Intelligent Multimedia

1 Introduction

As multimedia technologies largely increase communication effectiveness between human and computers, the importance of efficient multimedia authoring tools brings the attention to both researchers and software venders. Many presentation or authoring tools were developed for presenters or artists in various fields. However, presentations created by these tools were either communicating with its addressees in a single direction, or providing limited navigation controls for the audiences via push buttons or menus. These presentations can not incorporate addressees' responses. Thus, an audience watches the same demonstration over and over again even he/she has told the computer one understands the topic. As the communication efficiency became better and better between multimedia computers and human, an intelligent multimedia presentation design system will further make computers speak, show, and interact with human better.

This research is to investigate presentation design techniques and to develop a system that helps multimedia presentation designers to deliver intelligent multimedia applications as CD ROM titles. The system focuses on the following criteria:

- Intelligent presentation specification language

- Addressee characteristics specification and learning

- Canonical representation of knowledge

- Multimedia resources DBMS supporting intelligent queries

- Reuse of presentations

Presentation intelligence is represented in a canonical rule-based format. These knowledge not only include the addressee's background (i.e., common sense of the person who watches the presentation), but allow human reactions to be learned by the presentation program. A database management system is also designed for the CD ROM title designers to organize and store multimedia resource information. This database can be integrated to the presentation reuse model thus the system performs as a configuration management system for multimedia presentation development. An intelligent specification language is designed. The language provides facilities for hypermedia access and rule-based statements for knowledge representation. The system supports personalization. Not only the graphical user interface of the generated presentation can be fully customized, but the underlying knowledge of the addressee can be easily updated. The system also provides a learning subsystem to be included in the generated title which allows an addressee's interaction be asserted into the knowledge base. This learning environment, the presentation inference engine, and components marked with a "*" in Figure 1 will be provided as the runtime environment of a CD ROM title. Figure 1 illustrates the overall architecture of our proposed system.

Section 2 discuss authoring or presentation systems and issues related to intelligent presentations in order to compare our approach to others. In section 3, we proposed a model for the representation, navigation, and inheritance of presentation frames (to be discussed). We then address the language designing issues in section 4. A short section (section 5) is given to highlight our contributions and point our our further directions.

2   Related Works

A number of researchers developed domain specific presentations using artificial intelligence techniques. For example, COMET (COordinated Multimedia Explanation Testbed) [13, 14] uses a knowledge base and AI techniques to generate coordinated, interactive explanations with text and graphics that illustrates how to repair a military radio receiver-transmitter. WIP [1, 2] is able to generate knowledge-based presentations that explain to a user how to use an espresso machine. The work described in [4] integrates knowledge representation systems and a propositional logic theorem prover to create text and map based illustrations showing the situations and plans of a Navy's fleet. APT (A Presentation Tool) [17, 18] automatically generates graphical presentations of relational information. A Piano tutor described in [10, 11] is able to use coordinated media, video, voice, and graphics display, to teach beginners how to play the piano.

Other articles [20, 5] address relations between multimedia and multiple modalities. A modal is the way information is presented, such as a natural language statement, one piece of picture, or

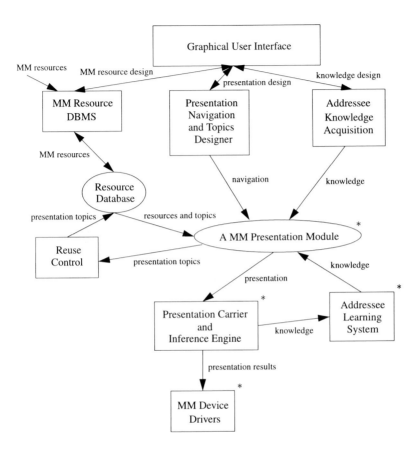

Figure 1: A system for intelligent multimedia presentation designs

a table. A medium is the device which presentation is delivered, such as sound, text, or video. The approach described in [5] suggests that the mapping should be construted between characteristics of media and characteristics of information. The research discussed in [5] also proposes that presentation knowledge can be classify naturally into four major groups: characteristics of media, characteristics of information, goal of the presenter, and the background of addressees. Issues related to solving the synchronization problems of temporal multimedia resources can be found in [21, 7]. A multimedia collaborative design environment for scientific and engineering applications can be found in [3]. The work described in [15] is a learning environment for the second year French students to learn about French culture. This multimedia application uses maps and visual icons as well as video files to show locations that can be visited in a city.

3 A Model of Presentation

Most presentations produced by multimedia authoring tools are designed as a hypermedia document. Unlike traditional presentations using slides, multimedia presentations are proceed in a nonlinear manner in that push buttons are provided for the presenter to navigate among different related issues in a presentation. These presentation issues are not totally independent for two reasons. Firstly, two issues closely related to each other should be linked such that an addressee watches the presentation can refer to related issues easier by following the links. For instance, a presentation touring Paris may links a picture of the Paris Tower with a description, either by audio or text, of its history. Secondly, two issues presented in a presentation may share common information. There is no reason of storing duplicated data in one presentation which makes a consistent update becomes tiresome. For instance, the addressee's name and background can be used in an interactive presentation should be stored only once in the presentation. While updated, the addressee's name will be changed consistently. We suggest that a presentation can be designed from two different point of view: the *navigation view* and the *representation view*. Figure 2 shows a presentation navigation and a knowledge inference subsystem facilitate these two views. A Windows I/O Control subsystem is also used to collect addressee navigation messages and to accept media operation messages from the navigation subsystem. The navigation subsystem communicates with the inference subsystem via messages that assert or retract knowledge rules such that addressee's behaviors will be learned by the computer. The knowledge inference result can also produce a side effect that sends a message to the navigation subsystem for an action.

From the navigation view, a presentation is a graph with nodes as issues in the presentation and edges as relations between issues. From the representation view of a presentation, information that can be shared among issues are background of the addressee (e.g., the addressee's name or knowledge to the presentation topic), multimedia resources (e.g., a text file of description or a video file showing a mechanical operation), or other knowledge useful in the presentation. A property inheritance structure such as a tree or a DAG (directed acyclic graph) is suitable for our knowledge representation architecture. In this section, we propose a presentation model meets the above two criteria.

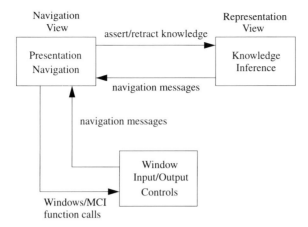

Figure 2: A presentation from different point of view

3.1 Presentation Navigation Via Message Passing

Before we discuss the presentation model, some terminologies are addressed. A multimedia *resource* is a picture, a description, a vedio, or other materials that can be used in a multimedia computer. A *topic* is a resource carrier that presents the resource to the addressee. A *frame* is a composed object which represents related issues that a presenter wants to illustrate. A frame may contain push buttons, one or more topics to be presented, and a number of knowledge rules. A *message* with optional parameters is passed between two frames (or back to the same frame). An *object* in our presentation model could be an atomic object (e.g., a button, or a message), or one composed by the following composition operation:

$$object = \langle comp_1, comp_2, ..., comp_n \rangle$$

where $comp_k, \forall 1 \leq k \leq n$, are *components* of *object*. A *component selector*, $\downarrow$, selects a component from an object if the component exists within the object; otherwise, the selection reslut is undefined (represented by $\perp$):

$$object \downarrow comp_k = comp_k, \forall 1 \leq k \leq n \text{ or}$$
$$object \downarrow comp_k = \perp, \forall k < 1, or \ k > n.$$

Using the above notations, the model of presentation is defined as the following.

Let $\mathcal{P}$ be the domain of presentations, $\mathcal{F}$ be the domain of frames, and $\mathcal{M}$ be the domain of messages, we have

$$\mathcal{P} = \mathcal{G}(\mathcal{F}, \mathcal{M})$$

where $\mathcal{G}$, with signature $\mathcal{F} \times \mathcal{M} \rightarrow \mathcal{P}$, is a multi-digraph with possible loops. That is, a graph with multiple edges between two nodes and an edge starts and ends with the same node is possible. A frame is a node while a message is an edge in G. Figure 3 shows a presentation with five frames.

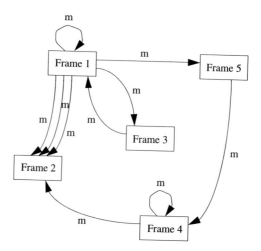

Figure 3: The navigation view: a presentation as a multi-digraph with loops

In our discussion, domains of primitive objects, such as message names or parameters, are omitted. The domain of message is defined as:

$$\mathcal{M} = \mathcal{F} \times \mathcal{F} \times \mathcal{N} \times \mathcal{PAR}$$

where $\mathcal{N}$ and $\mathcal{PAR}$ are domains of message names (represented by regular strings) and message parameters (strings or numbers), respectively. For each pair of frames, there exists no messages passed in between of the same name. If

$$m1 = \langle sf_{m1}, df_{m1}, n_{m1}, par_{m1} \rangle \text{ and}$$
$$m2 = \langle sf_{m2}, df_{m2}, n_{m2}, par_{m2} \rangle, \text{ where } m1, m2 \in \mathcal{M}$$

then

$$(sf_{m1} = sf_{m2}) \wedge (df_{m1} = df_{m2}) \rightarrow (n_{m1} \neq n_{m2}).$$

The domain of frames can be defined similarly:

$$\mathcal{F} = \mathcal{FN} \times \mathcal{B} \times \mathcal{T} \times \mathcal{M} \times \mathcal{M} \times \mathcal{K} \times \mathcal{D}$$

where $\mathcal{FN}$ is the domain of frame names (represented by regular strings), $\mathcal{B}$ is the domain of buttons, $\mathcal{T}$ is the domain of topics, $\mathcal{K}$ is the domain of presentation knowledge, and $\mathcal{D}$ is the domain of message distribution functions. Note that the first $\mathcal{M}$ in the above signature of $\mathcal{F}$ is the domain of incoming messages while the second $\mathcal{M}$ is the domain of outgoing messages.

A button, in addition to being defined by its appearance properties, receives a message with name **enable** or **disable** for setting its button status. Also, a button can send out a message while pushed:

$$\mathcal{B} = \mathcal{BD} \times \mathcal{M} \times \mathcal{M}.$$

where the first $\mathcal{M}$ is for setting buttons while the second $\mathcal{M}$ is for messages sent out. If $b \in \mathcal{B}$, and $b = \langle def, m_i, m_o \rangle$, where $def \in \mathcal{BD}$ contains appearance properties of the button, and $m_i, m_o \in \mathcal{M}$ are incoming and outgoing messages, then $m_i \downarrow n$ (i.e., the message name) is restricted such that $m_i \downarrow n \in \{$ enable , disable $\}$.

A topic, in addition to being defined by its appearance properties, can carry out a multimedia resource and receive messages to perform appropriate operations:

$$\mathcal{T} = \mathcal{TD} \times \mathcal{RES} \times \mathcal{M}.$$

where $\mathcal{TD}$ is the domain of topic appearance properties (e.g., size and location of the topic window, what type of medium it can carry), $\mathcal{RES}$ is the domain of resources (r.g., text, video, sound, etc.), and $\mathcal{M}$ is the domain of all incoming messages.

The domain of presentation knowledge, $\mathcal{K}$, will be discussed in the next subsection. The domain of message distribution functions, $\mathcal{D}$, is defined as

$$\mathcal{D} = \mathcal{N} \times \mathcal{PAR} \rightarrow \mathcal{MD}.$$

where $\mathcal{MD}$ is the domain of methods. Every frame is associated with its own message distributor. Upon receiving a message $\langle n, par \rangle \in (\mathcal{N} \times \mathcal{PAR})$, the message distributor searches for a method md, $md \in \mathcal{MD}$, and applies md to par. A message distributor only processes messages whose destination is the frame the distributor belongs to. If a message is sent to a frame doesn't exist in the presentation, an error message is shown by the presentation navigation subsystem. The above phenomenon can be described as the following. Suppose $f \in \mathcal{F}$ is the current frame:

$$f = \langle n, b, t, m_i, m_o, k, d \rangle,$$

we have

$$f \downarrow m_i \downarrow df \downarrow n = f \downarrow n \wedge f \downarrow m_o \downarrow sf \downarrow n = f \downarrow n.$$

where df and sf are destination frame and source frame of messages m_i and m_o, respectively.

A method can be a call to a C function which in turn plays a video file or disable a button, an assert or retract command which adds/deletes a knowledge rule to/from the knowledge set of a frame, or send out a message to a destination frame. Table 1 illustrates some methods used in our system.

For each message distributor, $d \in \mathcal{D}$, of a particular frame, $f \in \mathcal{F}$, each incoming message is taken care by one method. That is

$$\bigcup \langle f \downarrow m_i \downarrow n, f \downarrow m_i \downarrow par \rangle \subseteq \text{dom } f \downarrow d$$

where dom $f \downarrow d$ represents the preimage of the mapping.

All messages of a frame f are sent out by a button, or by a knowledge inference side effect:

$$f \downarrow m_o = (f \downarrow b \downarrow m_o) \cup (f \downarrow k \downarrow m_o)$$

Figure 4 shows a typical frame in our system.

Table 1: Example of Distributor Methods

$\mathcal{N}$	$\mathcal{PAR}$	$\mathcal{MD}$
open	-	proc_call(open_frame(FrameName))
close	-	proc_call(close_frame(FrameName))
play	Resource	proc_call(play_resource(Resource))
enable	Frame, Button	set_btn(Frame, Button, "enable")
disable	Frame, Button	set_btn(Frame, Button, "disable")
send	SrcFrame, DstFrame, Msg, Parms	send Msg(SrcFrame, DstFrame, Parms)
assert	KnowledgeRule	assert(KnowledgeRule)
retract	KnowledgeRule	retract(KnowledgeRule)
etc.	...	...

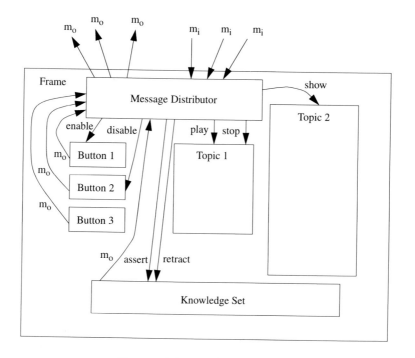

Figure 4: A frame and its components

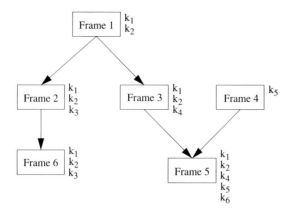

Figure 5: The representation view: a presentation as a DAG

3.2 Knowledge Inheritance in a Presentation

As mentioned at the beginning of this section, common knowledge and information regarding the addressee's background can be shared through a presentation. We are considering three types of knowledge in our knowledge domain, $\mathcal{K}$. *Knowledge rules* are logical implications[1]. *Knowledge facts* are conclusions hold in a frame. In order to start the knowledge inference, the third type of knowledge is a *query* associated with each frame that, when the frame receives an **open** message, starts the inference. These three types of knowledge are $\mathcal{KR}$, $\mathcal{KF}$, and $\mathcal{KQ}$ for rules, facts, and the query, respectively. The knowledge domain $\mathcal{K}$ thus can be defined as:

$$\mathcal{K} = \mathcal{KR} \cup \mathcal{KF} \cup \mathcal{KQ}.$$

From the knowledge (or representation) point of view, a presentation is a directed acyclic graph (i.e., DAG) with frames as nodes and inheritance relations as edges (as shown in Figure 5). Before the inheritance strategy can be defined, we need to introduce some notations.

Let σ be a knowledge inheritance operator, while applied to the knowledge set of a frame, yields the knowledge set of a subframe. We have the following restrictions in the system:

$\sigma(f \downarrow k) \supseteq (f \downarrow k)$, and
$((f_{s1} \downarrow k = \sigma(f \downarrow k) \cup k') \wedge (f_{s2} \downarrow k = \sigma(f \downarrow k) \cup k'')) \rightarrow (f_{s1} \downarrow k \cap f_{s2} \downarrow k = f \downarrow k)$

where k' and k'' are additional knowledge defined in the two subframes, f_{s1} and f_{s2}. The first expression indicates that a subframe inherits all knowledge from its super frame, with possible extra knowledge defined in the subframe. The second expression indicates that knowledge in the super frame is shared by two of its subframes. And if there exists a rule that is used in both subframes derived from a super frame, that rule should be defined in the super frame. Otherwise, the equality sign in the conclusion part of the above logical implication would be replaced by

---

[1]We have also defined language constructs that allow rules to be expressed easier in addition to using implications.

a "$\supseteq$". When a new knowledge set is instantiated from more than one super frame, multiple inheritance occurs. In this situation, the σ operator is applied to a set union of two or more knowlege sets. The only exception in knowledge inheritance is the query. Since our system only allows a query for each frame, the query of a subframe is defined to override one of its super frame. Thus, query of the super frame is undefined:

$$\sigma(f \downarrow k) \searrow \mathcal{K}\mathcal{Q} = \perp$$

where $\searrow$ is an infix projection operator, while applying to a value set (e.g., k) and a domain (e.g., $\mathcal{K}\mathcal{Q}$), restricts values in the set k to the domain $\mathcal{K}\mathcal{Q}$.

When a frame receives an **open** message, its query is passed to a knowledge inference engine. A number of knowledge rules or facts are collected for the frame before the inference proceeds. Let Θ denote a super frame operator. We have

$$(f_s \downarrow k = \sigma(f \downarrow k) \cup k') \leftrightarrow (f = \Theta f_s)$$

We further define the Θ^+ operator as the following:

$$(f = \Theta f_s) \rightarrow (f = \Theta^+ f_s), \text{ and}$$
$$(f = \Theta f_{s1}) \wedge (f_{s1} = \Theta^+ f_{s2}) \rightarrow (f = \Theta^+ f_{s2}).$$

When one looked at a presentation from the knowledge (or representation) point of view, we suggested that a presentation is a DAG of frame knowledge sets and inheritances. The acyclic property of a presentation can be specified as:

$$\forall f \in \mathcal{F}, f \neq \Theta^+ f$$

The knowledge of a subframe f_s is inherited from all of its super frames upto a finite number of levels, plus those defined explicitly in the subframe:

$$f_s \downarrow k = \bigcup ((\Theta^+ f_s) \downarrow k) \cup k'$$

Queries and facts are predicates similar to those defined in logic programs. Rules in our language are logic implications that can be represented in the following two forms:

$$q \rightarrow p_1 \wedge p_2 \wedge \dots \wedge p_n, \text{ or}$$
$$\neg q \rightarrow p_1 \wedge p_2 \wedge \dots \wedge p_n$$

where q and p_k, $1 \leq k \leq n$, are predicates. Suppose k is the knowledge set of a frame f, we can define the knowledge inference of frame f as the following. Let

$$\mathcal{K}\mathcal{N} = \mathcal{K}\mathcal{F} \cup \mathcal{K}\mathcal{R}$$

be the domain of facts and rules. And let

$$\mathcal{I} = \mathcal{K}\mathcal{Q} \times \mathcal{K}\mathcal{N} \rightarrow \{ true, false \}$$

be the signature of a knowledge inference function. And

$$k_q = k \searrow \mathcal{K}\mathcal{Q}, \ k_f = k \searrow \mathcal{K}\mathcal{F}, \ k_r = k \searrow \mathcal{K}\mathcal{R}, \ k_n = k \searrow \mathcal{K}\mathcal{N}, \ k_q = \{ q \}.$$

where q is the unique query of frame f. We can find an inference function $ifun$, $ifun \in \mathcal{I}$, of frame f such that the following conditions hold:

$ifun(q, k_n) = true$, if $q \in k_f$

$ifun(q, k_n) = ifun(p_1, k_n) \wedge ifun(p_2, k_n) \wedge ... \wedge ifun(p_n, k_n)$,

if $\exists q' \in k_f, \exists r \in k_r$ such that $q' = q \wedge (r = (q' \rightarrow p_1 \wedge p_2 \wedge ... \wedge p_n))$

$ifun(q, k_n) = ifun(p_1, k_n) \wedge ifun(p_2, k_n) \wedge ... \wedge ifun(p_n, k_n)$,

if $\forall q' \in k_f$ such that $q' \neq q$, and

$\exists r \in k_r$ such that $r = (\neg q \rightarrow p_1 \wedge p_2 \wedge ... \wedge p_n)$

$ifun(q, k_n) = false$, otherwise.

The above conditions are the declarative semantics of $ifun$. If the query is equal to a fact exists in the knowledge set of frame f, the inference stops and returns $true$. Otherwise, the query must match the test part (or the negation of a test part) of a rule in the knowledge set. In this case, the inference proceeds from the conclusion part of the rule. If non of the above condition holds, the inference returns false indicates that the knowledge set k of frame f has a problem. The system will raise an exception in this case. However, each rule in our language can have a default case. The default case of rules should make sure the inference proceeds smoothly.

A presentation in our system starts while a special frame called root receives an open message from the system.

4 The Proposed Language

Our original goal was to design a specification language that allows a presenter to design a presentation as a collection of frames, with messages and inheritance relations defined in these frames. However, since the system will be used by a non-programmer eventually, a language is not superior than a friendly user interface that guides a presenter to accomplish his/her presentation design. Thus, we refined the language and designed a graphical user interface. The system will collect pieces of statements specified by the designer in different windows of our interface and compose an internal specification program for each presentation designed. The formal syntax of the internal language is given in appendix A.

To create an intelligent presentation, a presenter needs to provide the following information:

- Presentation Resources

- Presentation Knowledge

- Navigation Rules

- Frame layouts

Presentation resources are standard multimedia files, such as a Windows AVI file, created by the designer using commercial tools. Our current system does not yet support the multimedia resource DBMS and the presentation reuse control subsystem. Thus, the designer will create these external resource files via other multimedia tools (e.g., a bitmap editor, a wave editor, or a video editor) and store them in some directory structures. The user interface allows a presentation designer to specify resource files in different list windows.

Presentation knowledge is a set of rule-based representation of the addressee's background, such as the addressee's familiarity with a special keyword, the presentation designer must consider in the presentation. Also, as the presentation proceeds, the user's knowledge may be incorporated into the presentation knowledge base. A presentation intelligence window allows the designer to specify a query, facts, and rules for each frame. The query and knowledge facts have the following syntax:

```
query Predicate.
known Predicate.
```

where `Predicate` is a Prolog term. A knowledge rule can be specified in one of the following formats:

```
    if Predicate then Predicates.
or
    if Predicate then Predicates
                else Predicates.
or
    case Predicate -> Predicates $
         Predicate -> Predicates $
         ...
         Predicate -> Predicates $
         true -> Predicates.
```

where `Predicates` is a list of one or more `Predicates` separated by commas. The first rule above indicates that if the predicate in the test part of the `if-then` rule satisfies, the conclusion predicates follow. The second rule specifies that if the testing predicate succeeds, the predicates after the `then` keyword hold; otherwise, the predicates after the `else` keyword hold. The `case` rule is an extension of the `if-then` rule. If any of the testing predicate holds, the corresponding predicates after the `->` keyword also hold. The last branch `true -> Predicates` is optional, which allows a default case to be declared. Knowledge inheritance relations are declared by specifying the super frame of each frame. A special frame named `root` is a place holder. When a frame declares `root` as its super frame, the frame must be the first to be invoked in a presentation.

We allows the designer to take a hypermedia traversal approach in the design of their presentation navigation. Three types of objects need to be defined for each frame. They are button definitions, topic definitions, and message definitions. The appearance of a button is drawn in the design area of a frame. This button appearance will be converted to a list of property-pair items as the property list of the button. Moreover, each button is associated with one or more actions separated by commas. These actions will be applied while the button is pushed. The kinds of actions used in our system could be:

```
send Msg(SrcFrame, DstFrame, [ Parms ])
set_btn(Frame, Button, "enable")
set_btn(Frame, Button, "disable")
assert(Predicate)
retract(Predicate)
proc_call("C_procedure_call")
```

The `send` action sends a message `Msg` from `SrcFrame` to `DstFrame` with optional parameters `Parms`. It is necessary to keep the source frame of a message in the internal representation of a presentation since, in some cases, frames are designed with a "back" button that allows the addressee to backtrack to a previously worked frame. The `set_btn` action will enable or disable a button in a particular frame. The `assert` and the `retract` actions apply only to the current frame. We only allow the knowledge set of a frame to be changed while the addressee is visiting the frame. This makes the knowledge assertion or retraction local to a particular user interaction and simplifies the knowledge collection process. The `proc_call` action calls an external C procedure which in turn makes an MCI (i.e., Media Control Interface by Microsoft) call to the underlying MS Windows multimedia drivers.

A topic definition is similar to a button definition, excepts that a topic does not send out a message. However, a topic can receive a message (e.g., `play`, `stop`, `forward`) from the message distributor and response with an appropriate action.

A message definition is a collection of message-action pairs. Each pair has the following format:

```
on_message: Message_name( Parms ) do [ Actions ]
```

`Message_name` is the name of the message received by the current frame. `Parms` and `Actions` are lists of terms with possible sharing of variables. For instance a message-action pair can be defined as:

```
on_message: play(AVI_file_name) do [proc_call("play_resource(AVI_file_name)")]
```

where `AVI_file_name` is the name of a video file. When `AVI_file_name` is instantiated to its value, the file name is passed to a C function for playing a video.

The definition of frame layouts is omitted in our discussion. A presentation can be designed using our internal language, or using a graphical user interface of the system which generates the presentation program. After the presentation program is generated, it is run under the presentation carrier and inference engine subsystem.

5 Conclusions

In this paper, we introduced an intelligent multimedia presentation system allowing a presenter to design intelligent presentations. The presentations designed allow addressees' response to be learned via knowledge assertions as knowledge inference side effects of some pre-planned knowledge rules. Our new proposed model, by using an object-oriented approach, allows a presenter to design his/her presentation as a hypermedia document with navigation specified as messages among frames. This model, by allowing knowledge inheritance, also facilitates data sharing and ensures a consistent updating of knowledge. A presentation design is entered via our graphical user interface. Different components of a frame are given in different windows. A program generator takes these components and produces a presentation which is run by our presentation carrier and inference engine subsystem. We have a prototype environment designed under Microsoft

Windows. The implementation language is C and Prolog. A sample application is also designed to show the usage of our system.

However, we are still seeking for solutions to improve our system. For instance, the TMS (Truth Maintenance System) technique could be used to check the consistency of knowledge rules in a presenter's design. And, we are designing the second version of our graphical user interface which is more friendly and powerful. Also, we are analysing presentation rules used commonly by people. Some system wide rules address mappings between multimodal and multimedia need to be defined in our system in order to help the presenters to make better presentations.

Our contributions in this paper are, firstly, we use object-oriented techniques to design a model for presentations by specifying relations between frames. Secondly, a language and a user interface are defined and its supporting environment is implemented. This system can be used for general purpose presentations or demonstrations in different fields such as education, training, product demonstration, and others. Finally, a sample application is designed showing our research results.

References

[1] E. Andre, et. al., "WIP: The Automatic Synthesis of Multimodal Presentations," In Intelligent Multimedia Interfaces, edited by Mark T. Maybury, American Association for Artificial Intelligence, pp 75–93, 1993.

[2] E. Andre and T. Rist, "The Design of Illustrated Documents as a Planning Task," In Intelligent Multimedia Interfaces, edited by Mark T. Maybury, American Association for Artificial Intelligence, pp 94–116, 1993.

[3] V. Anupam and C. L. Bajaj, "Shastra: Multimedia Collaborative Design Environment," IEEE Multimedia, summer, 1994.

[4] Y. Arens, et. al., "Presentation Design Using an Integrated Knowledge Base," In Intelligent User Interfaces, edited by J. W. Sullivan and S. W. Tyler, ACM Press, pp 241–258, 1991.

[5] Y. Arens, et. al., "On the Knowledge Underlying Multimedia Presentations," In Intelligent Multimedia Interfaces, edited by Mark T. Maybury, American Association for Artificial Intelligence, pp 280–306, 1993.

[6] D. S. Backer, "Multimedia Presentation and Authoring," In Multimedia Systems, edited by J. F. K. Buford, ACM Press, pp 285–303, 1994.

[7] Herng-Yow Chen, et. al., "A Novel Audio/Video Synchronization Model and Its Application in Multimedia Authoring System," In Proceeding of the 1994 HD-MEDIA Technical and Applications Workshop, October 6-8, Taipei, Taiwan, 1994.

[8] Chih-Wen Cheng, et. al., "Networked Hypermedia Systems," In Proceeding of the 1994 HD-MEDIA Technical and Applications Workshop, October 6-8, Taipei, Taiwan, 1994.

[9] D. N. Chin, "Intelligent Interfaces as Agents," In Intelligent User Interfaces, edited by J. W. Sullivan and S. W. Tyler, ACM Press, pp 177–206, 1991.

[10] R. B. Dannenberg, et. al., "A Computer Based Multimedia Tutor for Beginning Piano Students," In Interface 19(2-3), pp 155–173, 1990.

[11] R. B. Dannenberg and R. L. Joseph, "Human Computer Interaction in the Piano Tutor," In Multimedia Interface Design, edited by M. M. Blattner and R. B. Dannenberg, ACM Press, pp 65–78, 1992.

[12] S. Feiner, "An Architecture for Knowledge Based Graphical Interfaces," In Intelligent User Interfaces, edited by J. W. Sullivan and S. W. Tyler, ACM Press, pp 259–279, 1991.

[13] S. K. Feiner and K. R. McKeown, "Automating the Generation of Coordinated Multimedia Explanations," In Intelligent Multimedia Interfaces, edited by Mark T. Maybury, American Association for Artificial Intelligence, pp 117–138, 1993.

[14] S. K. Feiner, et. al., "Towards Coordinated Temporal Multimedia Presentations," In Intelligent Multimedia Interfaces, edited by Mark T. Maybury, American Association for Artificial Intelligence, pp 139–147, 1993.

[15] E. Schlusselberg, "Dans le Quartier St. Gervais: An Exploratory Learning Environment," In Multimedia Computing: Case Studies from MIT Project Athena, eited by M. E. Hodges, and R. M. Sasnett, Addison-Wesley, pp 103– 115, 1993.

[16] B. Laurel, et. al., "Issues in Multimedia Interface Design: Media Integration and Interface Agents," In Multimedia Interface Design, edited by M. M. Blattner and R. B. Dannenberg, ACM Press, pp 53–64, 1992.

[17] J. D. Mackinlay, "Automatic Design of Graphical Presentations," Ph. D. thesis, Stanford University, 1987.

[18] J. D. Mackinlay, "Search Architectures for the Automatic Design of Graphical Presentations," In Intelligent User Interfaces, edited by J. W. Sullivan and S. W. Tyler, ACM Press, pp 281–292, 1991.

[19] M. J. Muller, et. al., "Issues in the Usability of Time-varying Multimedia," In Multimedia Interface Design, edited by M. M. Blattner and R. B. Dannenberg, ACM Press, pp 7–38, 1992.

[20] J. G. Neal and S. C. Shapiro, "Knowledge Based Multimedia Systems," In Multimedia Systems, edited by J. F. K. Buford, ACM Press, pp 403–438, 1994.

[21] B. Prabhakaran and S. V. Raghavan, "Synchronization models for multimedia presentation with user participation," Multimedia Systems, Vol. 2, pp 53–62, Springer-Verlag, 1994.

Managing Complex Object Information for Interactive Movie Systems

Fumiyuki Tanemo, Tadashiro Yoshida, and Ryoji Kataoka

NTT Information and Communication Systems Laboratories
1-2356 Take Yokosuka Kanagawa 238-03 Japan
E-mail: {tanemo,yosh,kataoka}@syrinx.dq.isl.ntt.jp

Abstract

When people watch such motion pictures as documentaries or educational-type films, it is very natural for them to be interested in moving objects in the movies and be eager to know the detailed information related to these object. Therefore, a mechanism that enables users to pick up object information directly from motion pictures is necessary to make a movie system feasible. For this reason, we are researching techniques on using objects in motion pictures as hypermedia anchors. We call a movie system that provides the above mechanism *a video hypermedia system*.

An object in a motion picture can generally be considered as a complex object which includes many parts. To allow users to obtain information related to each part, a system must be able to provide anchors corresponding to each part in each complex object. For this, authors cannot help defining all anchors in all frames, since the visual status of each part varies from moment to moment. This paper presents our approach for managing objects in motion pictures for video hypermedia systems. The main feature of the proposed method is to apply computer graphic techniques to the defining of anchors for a complex object.

1. Introduction

A number of interactive movie systems have been recently developed. These include video-on-demand or VOD systems, which enable users to select any part of any video program at any time. Also included are video database systems, which enable users to retrieve desired movie scenes by specifying the conditions for the scene properties. These traditional systems are generally designed for retrieving the motion pictures themselves and cannot support such interaction as directly obtaining information from motion pictures.

When people watch such motion pictures as documentaries or educational-type films, it is very natural for them to be interested in the objects moving in these pictures and be eager to know the detailed information pertaining to those objects. For example, when watching a documentary program of a car race, the user may want to know who is driving a specific car, or what type of engine is in that car. Also, when watching a video program of an aquarium, some people may want to inquire about the names of fishes or other detailed information. Therefore, a mechanism that enables users to select object information directly from motion pictures is necessary in order to make a movie system feasible.

For this reason, we are researching techniques on using objects in motion pictures as hypermedia anchors. In general, hypermedia consists of various types of information, called nodes, which are inter-associated through links. In each node, links are explicitly shown as anchors, and users can navigate through a network of nodes by repeatedly pointing to these anchors. In a system which can treat a motion picture as a node and the objects contained in them as anchors, users can obtain information by directly selecting desired objects in the motion pictures. We call a movie system that provides the above feature *a video hypermedia system.*

An object in a motion picture can be generally considered as a complex object which includes many parts. For example, a car in a motion picture consists of a variety of parts such as an engine, tires, and headlights. To allow users to obtain information related to each of these parts, a system must be able to provide anchors corresponding to each part of the object.

The same requirement holds true when still images are used for hypermedia. This requirement is satisfied by forcing authors to define anchor positions for each part of a complex object. It is, however, difficult to treat motion pictures in the same manner as still images because authors must define all the anchors in all frames. This is because the visual status of each object varies from moment to moment. Furthermore, the author's difficulty in defining anchors increases as the number of parts in each object increases. Therefore, to use parts as anchors, an efficient method is needed which can manage the temporal variance of these complex objects.

This paper presents our approach for managing objects in motion pictures for video hypermedia systems. The main feature of the proposed method is to apply computer graphic techniques to define anchors for a complex object. This method does not increase the author's work for defining anchors even if the number of parts in each object increases.

The rest of the paper is organized as follows. Technical requirements and our approach are summarized is Section 2. A method for managing the three-dimensional structure and the visual status of a complex object in motion pictures are proposed in Section 3. In Section 4, the capability for implementing the proposed method is confirmed through construction of a prototype system. Finally, concluding remarks appear in Section 5.

2. Video Hypermedia

2.1. Related Work

Many methods for structuring movies have been previously proposed. Most of them are based on the concept that movies consist of logical time intervals, i.e., cuts or

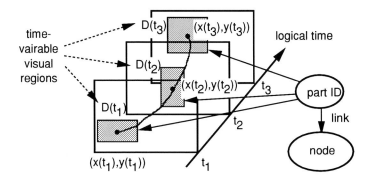

Figure 1: Video hypermedia model

scenes. By extracting these cuts or scenes from the movie and assigning some attributes such as a scene description to them, the system can support interactive retrieval of the user's desired scenes.

For a video hypermedia system, however, the general method mentioned above cannot sufficiently handle the visual status of moving objects in movies which is needed for directly selecting objects in movie windows to retrieve information.

In [3], we proposed a method for implementing such a functionality, which manages the visual status of moving objects using time-variable position (x, y, t) where t is the logical time of the movie and indicates a specified frame. The position (x, y) is a two-dimensional position of the object in a frame. Also, Hirata et al. proposed a structuring method called the MOL model [1],[2]. This model can manage the visual status of objects using not only (x, y, t) but also the visual region D of each of these objects represented as rectangles surrounding them. Therefore, the MOL model can describe more detailed object movements than our previous method. These two methods for a video hypermedia system also differ in the visibility of anchors to users: anchors in our method are invisible, whereas those in the MOL model are presented by rectangles equal to the visual region D of each object.

To sum up, video hypermedia systems must manage the visual status of objects using time-variable parameters (x, y, D, t), where each D is the visual region of each object in a frame. Figure 1 illustrates this method for managing the visual status of moving objects. Authors can construct video hypermedia systems for each part of an object by repeating the following steps:

1. Preparing attribute information for the part.

2. Adding an identification number (ID) to the part, and creating links between

the ID and the attribute information of the part.

3. Identifying each position (x, y) and visual region D of the part for each frame.

2.2 Technical Requirements

The system must store information relevant to each part in a database and must manage the motions of each part. When using the above method, the work of preparing the visual status of each complex object causes problems. These problems includes:

Creating anchors: Complex objects generally have many parts. Therefore, anchors must be created to correspond to their respective parts by extracting regions of parts from all frames.

Creating links: Complex objects have many levels of parts. Therefore, the system must determine which information related to the part should be presented.

A method that avoids these problems is necessary for the video hypermedia system that manages complex objects.

2.3. Proposed Method

To prepare such a method, we focus on the fact the relative 3-dimensional locations of parts in an object may rarely vary in the real world. For example, when an automobile is moving, the amount of mutation of the relative locations of its body and its wheels is far smaller than that for the movement of the automobile itself. This paper will concentrate only on objects whose parts move relatively little, such as for automobiles, and ignore the amount of relative mutation for that part.

In the proposed method, the visual status of parts in a complex object is managed using two elements of the object: 3-dimensional structure and 3-dimensional motion. The 3-dimensional structure of an object includes not only a figure of its surface, but also the information for the relative position of each of its parts. In each movie frame, for determining the position and the region of a part of an object, the system must be able to place the 3-dimensional structure into a 3-dimensional space and project the space in order to display the window using parameters corresponding to its visual status in the frame. The 3-dimensional motion is the sequence of such parameters projected frame by frame.

The computer graphics (CG) techniques contribute to these two object elements. These techniques can treat a variety of surface models, e.g., polygon models, project a graphics world including the models onto 2-axis coordinates, and can render it in a display window. When rendering, CG systems need a virtual viewpoint which is considered to exist in the space, and can project the model to a window using attributes of the viewpoint, e.g., position and direction. Therefore, 3-dimensional

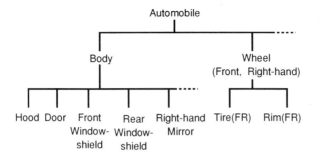

Figure 2: An example of a parts tree

motion is constructed from viewpoints corresponding to the visual status of each frame.

As discussed above, the proposed method makes it possible to independently manage 3-dimensional structures and 3-dimensional movements of each complex object. Therefore, it does not increase the author's work for defining anchors even if the number of parts in each object increases, since authors can consider the visual status not by part, but by object. Also, we present a dynamic link method which selects the desired part according to the visual status of movies. This method is expected to facilitate the defining of links in the video hypermedia system.

3. Moving Objects as Anchors

3.1. Three-Dimensional Structures

Movies include moving objects and each part of each object has its own specific information stored in a database. Each part of the object is positioned as a node in a hierarchy (called a *parts tree*, as shown in Figure 2) where *root* is a moving object. By using this hierarchy, we term a moving object, its bottom-level parts, and other parts as *a root object, leaf objects, branch objects,* respectively.

Our method manages solid figures from each object as a *polygon model*, which is a 3-dimensional model. In this polygon model, the surface of a solid is represented by a set of polygons. A root object is represented by a set of polygons $P = \{p_1, \ldots, p_k\}$ (p_i is a polygon).

All objects $(o_1, \ldots, o_l \in O)$ in a parts tree are related to a subset of the polygon set P. The object set O includes m leaf objects, n branch objects, and a root ($l = m+n+1$). In particular, a set of leaf objects $(lo_1, \ldots, lo_m \in O)$ represents completely exclusive subsets of P ($lo_i \cap lo_j = \phi, \bigcup_i lo_i = P$). A branch object $(bo_1, \ldots, bo_n \in O)$ includes the polygons in all nodes in a sub-tree of the parts tree whose root is

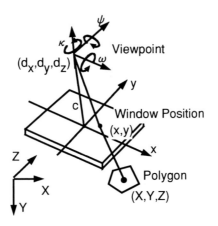

Figure 3: Perspective Projection

itself. For example in Figure 2, if "Rim" includes polygons $p_{s+1}, \ldots, p_{s+i}$, and "Tire" includes $p_{t+1}, \ldots, p_{t+j}$, then "Wheel" includes $p_{s+1}, \ldots, p_{s+i}, p_{t+1}, \ldots, p_{t+j}$.

Now, a solid figure of a moving object can be defined as the fragment of a movie structure. A solid figure of a moving object is defined as a quartet consisting of polygon set P, object set O, leaf-object associations (of polygons), and a parts tree.

Finally, we call the name of an object o_i, $Name(o_i)$. A database stores the information relevant to the object o_i with $Name(o_i)$.

3.2. Three-Dimensional Motion

Our goal is to project, using video cameras, a real world onto movie pictures which consist of a sequence of two-dimensional frames. This projection is called a *perspective projection* or *central projection*. The visual status of objects in a specified frame is dependent on the relative positions and relative directions between objects and the video camera.

In a three-dimensional cartesian coordinate centered on a specified object, the video camera lies in position $D = (d_x, d_y, d_z)$ and has an attitude denoted by euler angle $R = (\omega, \psi, \kappa)$. Figure 3 illustrates these parameters. Then, using a principle of perspective projection, the relationship between positions in the real world (X, Y, Z) and the two-dimensional position in a frame (x, y) is calculated by the following formula:

$$\begin{bmatrix} X' \\ Y' \\ Z' \end{bmatrix} = \begin{bmatrix} 1 & 0 & 0 \\ 0 & cos(\omega) & -sin(\omega) \\ 0 & sin(\omega) & cos(\omega) \end{bmatrix} \begin{bmatrix} cos(\psi) & 0 & sin(\psi) \\ 0 & 1 & 0 \\ -sin(\psi) & 0 & cos(\psi) \end{bmatrix}$$
$$\begin{bmatrix} cos(\kappa) & -sin(\kappa) & 0 \\ sin(\kappa) & cos(\kappa) & 0 \\ 0 & 0 & 1 \end{bmatrix} \begin{bmatrix} X - d_x \\ Y - d_y \\ Z - d_z \end{bmatrix} \tag{1}$$

$$x = -c\frac{X'}{Z'} \tag{2}$$

$$y = -c\frac{Y'}{Z'} \tag{3}$$

where c is the distance from the viewpoint to the frame.

Positions P and Directions D are parameters which vary with the movement of the video camera and objects. Parameters P and D must be determined frame by frame to describe the transitions of the visual status of objects in movie pictures [a].

These parameters describing the relationship between a real world and movie frames also can be used for mapping polygon models to these frames because these polygon models are accurate miniatures of objects in the real world. A polygon in a polygon model has a centering position (X, Y, Z). Therefore, using the above formula (1) – (3), we can calculate the position in each frame where the polygon lies. Since this calculation is common in the computer graphics area, we can simply use the existing graphics libraries for accomplishing this.

The method to extract these parameters expressing the visual status of objects from each frame in the movie is very important. Ullmann presents a method to automatically obtain object motion from motion pictures, using 3-dimensional object models [5]. We, however, cannot use this method since he assumes parallel projection rather than perspective projection. We use a manually interactive mapping method which will be discussed in section 4.

3.3. Using Computer Graphic Techniques

Computer graphic (real-time graphics) techniques have two major characteristics: rendering and picking. Rendering is the ability to project a graphics world to 2-axis coordinates and rendering it in a display window. Picking is the ability to select polygons or objects lying in specified positions in the window.

---

[a] A projective distance, c, is relative to the zooming volume of the video camera. In general, a movie creator may change the zooming volume in a movie. Therefore, c is a dynamic parameter. However for simplity, we treat movies whose zooming volume is seldomly changed and we regard c as a static parameter.

We can create a real-time graphics sequence using movie structures, i.e., polygon models, positions, directions, and view angles of 3-axis coordinates. If the video status of a specified video frame has parameters such as position and direction, a relative frame in the real-time graphics sequence is made by projecting the graphics world which includes the polygon model using these parameters. Then, objects can be managed as anchors in the following way:

1. Create a real-time graphics sequence using movie structures.

2. Run the sequence synchronized with movie pictures.

3. When a user specifies a position in a movie window, transmit the position from a movie system to a real-time graphics system, and select a polygon lying in the transmitted position (if there are several polygons lying in the position, the one closest to the viewpoint is selected).

4. Identify a leaf object including the selected polygon using leaf-object associations.

For the sake of simplicity, we suppose in the process of transmitting window positions that a video window and a real-time graphics window share the same coordinates. For example, centering point $(0, 0)$ of these windows is the center of the window and the center of the x-axis and y-axis. We also suppose that the two windows share the same width. That is, if the width of the video window is (h_x, h_y), and the width of the graphics window is (g_x, g_y), then $h_x = g_x$ and $h_y = g_y$. If the two windows have differing orthogonal coordinates or widths, only a linear function is needed to transmit positions from one window to another.

3.4. Identification Method

Information related to not only leaf objects but also a root object and branch objects are stored in a database. When a user clicks a position in the window, the system can determine a polygon lying in the position, and can determine a leaf object including the polygon. However, the system cannot determine information to be retrieved because the polygon is included by a leaf object, a root object, and several other parts.

We propose a mechanism for selecting the user's picked object from alternative objects by using the visual magnitude of each object. This method regards the object which has an adaptive size in the window as the user's picked one. An object has an adaptive size when it occupies a particular percentage of the window.

More concretely, the identification method has two phases as follows:

1. Calculates the size of all objects in a specified frame which includes the specified polygon.

2. Evaluates the calculated size using a predefined evaluation function and selects the best part.

The predefined evaluation function has an object-magnitude value, called *adaptive visual size*, and the system selects an object having the closest visual magnitude to the adaptive visual size, from all alternative objects.

We present a detailed explanation of this identification method in the following subsections.

3.4.1. The Visual Magnitudes of Objects

The size of object o in the 3-dimensional model (denoted by $Ext(o)$), is defined by a radius of a circumscribed sphere of a set of polygons included in object o. Then, the visual magnitude of object $Mag(o)$ in a specified frame is calculated using the following formula:

$$Mag(o) = Ext(o)/(d_z * tan\alpha) \tag{4}$$

where α is a view angle.

The right-hand formula $p_z * tan\alpha$ is related to the window edge. If $d_x = d_z * tan\alpha$, positions $(d_x, 0, d_z)$ lie on the right-hand edge line on the x-z plane.

The relationship of visual magnitudes of objects and a parts tree is described. Suppose a user-picked polygon p, objects $\{o_1, \ldots, o_n\}$ which include polygon p, and object relationship in the parts tree are represented as

$$o_1 \succ \ldots \succ o_i \succ \ldots \succ o_n$$

($o_i \succ o_j$ means that o_i is the upper object of o_j). Object o_1 is the root object. Then, the relationship among visual magnitudes of objects is as follows:

$$Mag(o_1) > \ldots > Mag(o_n)$$

3.4.2. Evaluation Function

Evaluation function evaluates the visual magnitude of an object and returns its value. When object o occupies a $Mag(o)$ percentage of the movie window, the evaluation function having an adaptive visual volume $s(0 < s < 1)$ is defined as follows:

$$E(o_i) = e^{-(Mag(o_i)-s)^2} \tag{5}$$

The constant, s, is an occupied rate in the whole window size. The evaluation function $E(o_i)$ returns the max value when $Mag(o_i)$ equals s and it returns the bigger value as $Mag(o_i)$ is closer to s.

When the user picks polygon p, the system identifies object o_i and searches the related information including $Name(o_i)$ in the database.

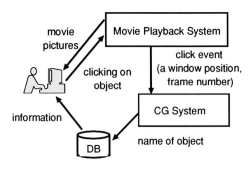

Figure 4: Prototype system

4. Prototype and Performance

To verify our proposed method, we have developed a movie system. We present the details of the prototype and briefly introduce the applied movie and the moving object in it. We also compare our proposed method to existing hypermedia methods.

4.1. Prototype

The prototype is implemented on a graphics workstation capable of making up polygon models and operating them in 3-dimensional coordinates. As shown in Figure 4, the movie system consists of two subsystems: a movie playback system and a computer graphics (CG) system. These two subsystems each have a process, and these two processes communicate with each other by passing messages.

To synchronize the CG process and the playback process, the following two methods can be used: full synchronizing and event-driven methods.

Full synchronizing: This method completely synchronizes the CG to the movie. Rendering using a new visual status is done as one frame passes to the next.

Event-driven: Only if a user clicks in the movie window, does the rendering using a visual status relative to the clicking-time frame occur.

The two methods have the same capacity because the system only needs a visual status corresponding to the picking-time movie frames to obtain information related to the part. The prototype selects the event-driven method for easy implementation.

The roles of the two subsystems in the movie system are described below. The movie playback system is responsible for:

- Playing back the movie into a movie window in a display and supervising the user picking events in the window.

- Casting the event into the CG system with a picked window position and a picking-time rendering movie frame, when a user picking event occurs.

Cast messages do not only need picked window positions but also picking-time frame numbers because the event-driven synchronizing method works.

The CG system is responsible for picking, identifying a part, and retrieving a database. In the identification method, the CG system proceeds as follows:

- Determining all objects including the polygon using the leaf-object associations and a parts tree.

- Calculating the visual magnitude, evaluating the value of each object, and identifying a picked object.

4.2. Example Application

We examined our method by making up an example application. In the example application, the contents of the movie is an automobile travelling on a road. In the movie, the automobile changes its visual size frame by frame, and its attitude in all the frames is different. For example, the automobile's view changes from front to right, etc. and the camera zooms in and out.

The movie is about 3 minutes long, captured in 8 frames per second, and digitized and stored on a computer hard disk. That is, the movie is a sequence of about 1,400 frames in all.

We prepared a polygon model which consists of 3,000 polygons for the automobile in the movie. We also prepared 20 object names and their related information corresponding to the parts of the automobile such as tires, wheels, the body, and the hood. In these objects, there is a root object which is the automobile itself. We regard 12 objects as leaf objects which are the hood, door, and so on. These objects including the root, branches, and leafs are related to each others through the defining of the parts tree, the same as the one shown in Figure 2.

The interface of the example application is shown in Figure 5. The upper window in the figure is the movie playback window, where the movie is played and a user can select parts of the object *car* by picking its positions. The lower left window is the CG window, where the polygon model of the *car* is rendered. For example, when a user clicks on the position of the left headlight of the car, the movie playback system transmits the clicked position to the CG system. Then, the part *headlight* is selected and its information is displayed in the lower right window shown in the figure.

In Section 3, we described the manual mapping method as our choice. Our manual mapping method in the example application uses a tool which can indicate the polygon

Figure 5: The prototype interface

model in the movie, and can handle the position and attitude of the model and store them. Using the tool which has the window where the movie plays, an author stops at each frame and indicates the model on the window. Then, the author interactively minimizes the visual position between moving objects and the models. The final position and attribute of the model is stored in the system. The tool was easily implemented using existing computer graphics libraries running on X window systems, and is not discussed in detail here.

4.3. Performance Analysis

In the example application presented above, we try to compare the performance between our methods and existing hypermedia methods.

As mentioned in Section 2, our method is expected to provide two kinds of contribution to authors: easy creation of anchors and easy creation of links. Our method makes it easy to create links because it is difficult for authors to define anchors that correspond to the parts that users are supposed to want, at the same time watching objects in each movie frame. However, quantitative comparison on this point is considered to be difficult to analyze, unless another example application is created with the same movie and related information using existing methods. Therefore, this paper presents the performance comparison from the viewpoint of the ease in creating anchors.

The first example is the case in which an author creates a new application with a limited number of parts for a moving object. In the example application, an automobile is considered to provide leaf objects. In general existing methods, the number of anchors that the author needs to prepare is $12\ points/flame \times 1400\ flames = 16800\ points$

In our proposed method, the author needs to prepare polygon models and leaf object relationships. The number of polygons needed is $3,600\ polygons$. The number of parts identified in the defined polygon models is $12\ points$, and the number of anchors needed is $1\ points/flame \times 1,400\ flames = 1,400\ points$.

In the above discussion, if the work of creating polygon models is simple enough, it is clear that our method provides an easy way of creating anchors.

Another example is the case in which the author adds new related information, and needs to identify a new part of the automobile for retrieval. In existing methods, the author needs to extract the region of the new parts for every frame just as for other parts. That is, the newly created number of anchors needed is $1\ point/frame \times 1,400\ frames = 1,400\ points$

On the other hand, in our proposed method, the author needs to extract only one part of the polygon model.

5. Concluding Remarks

We present our approach to manage complex objects in motion pictures for video hypermedia systems. The main feature of the proposed method is to apply these computer graphic techniques to defining anchors for a complex object. The proposed method makes it possible to independently manage 3-dimensional structures and 3-dimensional motion of each complex object. Therefore, it does not increase the author's work for defining anchors even if the number of parts in each object increases, since authors can consider the visual status not by part, by object.

Acknowledgement

We would like to thank my colleagues, especially, Ushio Inoue, Hideaki Takeda, Shinji Morishita for their helpful comments. Also, we would like to thank the referees for their valuable comments.

References

[1] K. Hirata, et.al, *Media-based Navigation for Hypermedia Systems*, ACM Hypertext'93 (Nov. 1993).

[2] K. Hirata and Y. Hara, *Implementation of a Distributed Video Hypermedia System*, Proc. of Advanced Database System Symp. '94, pp. 165–173, Tokyo, Japan (Dec. 1994).

[3] R. Kataoka, T. Satoh and U. Inoue, *VideoReality: A Multimedia Information System Based on a Visual Conducting Model*, Proc. of Int. Symp. on Advanced Database Technologies and Their Integration, pp. 207–214, Nara, Japan (Oct. 1994).

[4] J. Nielsen, *HyperText & HyperMedia*, Academic Press (1990).

[5] S. Ullmann, *The Interpretation of Visual Motion*, MIT Press (1979).

[6] V. Mey and S. Gibbs, *A Multimedia Component Kit : Experiences with Visual Composition of Application*, ACM Multimedia, pp. 291–299 (June 1993).

[7] K. Gronbaek, *The Amsterdam Hypermedia Model*, Comm. of ACM, pp. 50-62 (Feb. 1994).

Chapter 5

Multimedia Synchronization

A TOOLKIT FOR THE MODELLING OF MULTIMEDIA SYNCHRONIZATION SCENARIOS

François FABRE, Patrick SENAC
ENSICA
49, avenue Léon Blum
31056 Toulouse Cedex France
e-mail: fabre@ensica.fr

and

Michel DIAZ
LAAS du CNRS
7, avenue du colonel Roche
31077 Toulouse Cedex France

ABSTRACT

Multimedia documents design, within distributed asynchronous systems, requires methods allowing a complete and precise specification of temporal constraints to keep up with an accurate presentation of multimedia objects. This paper introduces a toolkit for the prototyping of multimedia synchronization scenarios combining the modelling power of a digital video production studio with the expressive power of a formal specification technique. This toolkit ensures the complete line of synchronization scenario prototyping with the help of a graphic editor, a static checker, a simulator, a validation tool and a presentation kernel.

Introduction

Processing and storage power of workstations and personal computers has allowed multimedia technologies to be introduced into computer tools in a significant way. Texts, graphs, vocal annotations and all kinds of stereophonic sound effects, synthesis images and video sequences represent new information vectors a computer can use in a transparent way for the user.

The promise of increasingly developing networked multimedia applications has stimulated the creation of *CESAME*, a french national research which covers the design of high-speed cooperative multimedia systems over *ATM* networks, putting particular emphasis on the use of formal methods for specifying and verifying multimedia and hypermedia synchronization scenarios in weakly synchronous distributed systems. The model created and used in the framework of this project for the specification of multimedia and hypermedia synchronization is called *Time Stream Petri Net* (*TSPN*) [1].

Based on this model, this paper introduces a toolkit for the prototyping of multimedia synchronization scenarios which allows the author to construct and to handle a multimedia document in a formal way using the *TSPN* model. This toolkit allows the author to quickly specify and verify multimedia synchronization scenarios. It is composed of five units that allow the prototyping and analysis of multimedia synchronization scenarios : edition, static checking, simulation, validation and execution.

The first part of this paper is dedicated to an overview of the existing multimedia authoring tools. The second part motivates the use of the *TSPN* model. The third part introduces the prototyping toolkit of multimedia scenarios and illustrates our methodology for prototyping synchronization scenarios.

1. Multimedia authoring

As for a traditional textual document, a multimedia document needs tools that allow its creation, edition and visualization. This part reviews the common approaches for multimedia modelling. The sphere of application of these new kinds of documents is very huge. It covers a wide range of applications such as slide shows bringing into play a variety of medias (text, picture, audio and video), or applications of computer aided training, or hypermedia data bases particularly thanks to the emergence of services like *WWW* over the *Internet*, or virtual reality applications, or multimedia collaborative environments.

Our approach lies within the scope of a software engineering process. Indeed, the specification and the design of distributed multimedia scenario is a complex task which benefits from modelling techniques and tools. Therefore, formal approaches are of the greatest relevance in order to depict this kind of specification with the help of simulation and analysis techniques of synchronization scenario. So, we suggest a multimedia authoring methodology based on the *TSPN* model coupled with a prototyping software toolkit providing a formal support for the specification, simulation and analysis of synchronization constraints within multimedia systems.

1.1. Authoring life cycle

The conception of multimedia documents is usually based on the use of two tools : an *authoring unit* and a *presentation unit*. The presentation unit aims to visualize the scenario for the user according to the spatial and temporal layouts defined by the authoring software. As for the authoring unit, it is a creation support for multimedia documents. It allows the author to construct the story-board, that is the scenario, which specifies the scheduling of medias brought into play. Three scheduling classes must be implemented :

- a *spatial scheduling* allowing to specify the presentation geometrical constraints in order to judiciously lay the windows on the screen, and to manage the critical resources access conflicts (audio device for example).
- a *temporal scheduling* allowing to specify synchronization and temporal constraints within multimedia scenario.
- a *logical scheduling* in the framework of hypermedia applications allowing to manage interactions with the user and to direct the presentation according to his choices.

In this paper, we only address temporal synchronization. Indeed, many researches have been carried out in context of textual presentation standards [2]. This paper focuses on multimedia documents[1] which do not consider user interactions.

Multimedia documents design is usually based on a combined use of the authoring unit and the presentation unit through a spiral life cycle shown on *figure 1*. The authoring tool allows to specify the whole presentation constraints. But these constraints and the user personal perception are strongly coupled together. At the construction stage, the presentation unit job consists in verifying if the specifications imposed by the author do have a behaviour closely related to what he wants to deliver to end-users. Therefore, this unit plays the part of a debugger which can be extended through step by step or with breakpoints execution functionalities and sub-part visualization capabilities. This interactive cycle between both units allows the author to conceive multimedia documents by gaining a visual experience of his work. Thus, the construction evolves in a spiral life cycle by successive refinements of the specification according to the result perceived by the author.

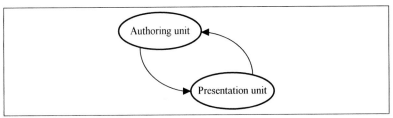

Fig. 1. Multimedia temporal synchronization life cycle

1.2. Multimedia synchronization issues

In order to illustrate the different levels of synchronization potentially involved in a multimedia document, we rely on a small multimedia scenario described on *figure 2* using a time-line paradigm. This scenario is composed of three streams : a video sequence, an audio sequence and a text. Both first streams can be broken down into a sequence of video frames (VU_N) and audio samples (AU_N). Three synchronization levels appear on this synchronization scenario :

- The first level is in charge of *discrete inter-media synchronization*. It is dedicated to coarse synchronization relationships between the beginning and the end of various streams. For instance, the τ_6 date corresponds to this synchronization level and specifies that the text stream presentation must begin at the end of the video and audio streams.

- The second level is dedicated to *continuous inter-media synchronization*. It ensures fine synchronization relationships periodically applied between the synchronization units of several continuous streams. In our example, it allows to synchronize the video and the sound track which goes with it in order to avoid temporal drifts between both medias. For instance, τ_2, τ_4 and τ_6 dates provide synchronization points between each video frame presentation (VU) and the two related audio samples (AU).

---

[1] An extension of our works to the hypermedia documents is presented in [3].

- The third level ensures the *continuous intra-media synchronization*. It specifies the synchronization constraints of information units which are internal to each stream regardless of other streams. For example, each video frame (VU) must be presented at a given instant and for a given duration.

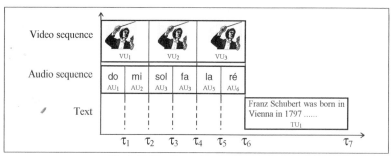

Fig. 2. Multimedia synchronization moments

Moreover, currently used universal distributed systems are weakly synchronous. That means that they are not able to ensure strict temporal determinism for synchronization schemes. In particular, multimedia processings are submitted to temporal jitter in these systems. Fortunately, multimedia processings are soft real time ones. Therefore, they can accept a certain degree of temporal undeterminism [4]. However, the admissible temporal variability of multimedia processings can induce temporal drifts between the various streams of a multimedia scenario. This temporal drift can modify deeply the synchronization relationships within a multimedia scenario. Therefore, in order to ensure deterministic synchronization behaviour within multimedia applications, a semantic of synchronization within weakly synchronous systems must be defined and used by a multimedia authoring or prototyping tool.

1.3. Overview of existing authoring tools

The generalization of computer at home and the popular success achieved by *Microsoft Windows* have promoted the arrival of multimedia authoring softwares driven by visual programming techniques [5]. Several products, directed to end-users who can thus easily construct multimedia documents, exist in the *Windows* world like the well-known *IconAuthor* [6] or *Adobe Premiere* [7].

IconAuthor makes a multimedia document with the help of icons-based flowcharting approach allowing the document outline to be visualized in a multi-dimensional graphic view and to specify one element just by clicking on it. Each icon is drawn from a library holding a wide range of presentation icons (medias or animations), of flow control icons (if, while ...) and of interactions control icons (menus drivers, buttons ...). The specification is carried out through dialogue-boxes appropriate for the selected icon type. This software overlooks some serious deficiencies as regards the parallel presentation of numerous medias by totally skipping over inter-media temporal synchronization. So, it does not allow to synchronize several medias together.

As for *Adobe Premiere*, it offers a complete environment of digital video production studio : audio and video digitizers, editing, special effects, titling ... This software offers a time-line paradigm for the scenario design allowing the whole synchronization levels to be specified : discrete inter-media, continuous inter-media and intra-media.

These commercial tools greatly favour the easy use in relation to specification power. They do not tackle the problematic of weakly synchronous distributed systems. Therefore, some toolkits, which are research prototypes, have been implemented to compensate for these lacks by using a more formal approach in order to specify synchronization.

Koegel suggests an authoring tool called *Eyes MM* using icons combined in a flowchart equivalent to a *Timed Petri Net*[2] [8]. Three kinds of icons exist : medias icons which manage the presentation, input icons which provide the user interactions and connector icons which allow to manage synchronization points. There are two types of connector icons meaning two strategies : AND and OR. The AND connector icon waits until the whole flows reach the synchronization point. While the OR connector icon waits until any flow reaches the synchronization point ; when the others flows reach the icon, they are ignored, what is in contradiction to the *Timed Petri Net* synchronization semantics which makes it clear that a transition can only by fired when it is totally enabled and when its fire leads to the removal of the upstream places token (*i.e.* the presentation stop). This tool does not fit much to the distributed context because it does not allow any dynamic elasticity (jitter) in the inter-media synchronization.

In the *MODE*[3] project, Blakowski [9] proposes tools for the edition and the presentation of synchronized multimedia objects in the framework of distributed systems. This toolkit relies on the *OCPN*[4] model [10] and ensures synchronization by means of reference points. Exception mechanisms can be performed for reference points (waiting, acceleration or skipping actions) and for medias (alternative presentation) but must be individually specified by the author.

All these tools have at last two main drawbacks. Firstly, they do not take into account the weakly synchronous feature of distributed multimedia systems. Secondly, they do not allow the temporal and logical properties of multimedia scenario to be analysed.

Therefore, we intend to present a new authoring tool based on the *TSPN* model which introduces a formal semantic of synchronization within weakly synchronous systems and allows temporal and logical properties of multimedia systems to be verified and analysed.

---

[2] Petri nets with duration on transitions.
[3] Multimedia Objects in a Distributed Environment
[4] Temporal structures built over *Timed Petri Net*

2. The *TSPN* model

The *TSPN* model[5] has been initially used for the modeling of multimedia synchronization scenarios within distributed weakly synchronous systems. This extended Petri Net model uses timed arcs for the modeling of multimedia processings (access, communication or presentation of multimedia data). Associating temporal intervals to output arcs from places (*Figure 3-a*), the *TSPN* model allows both the temporal non-determinism of weakly synchronous distributed systems and the admissible temporal variability of tasks to be taken into account. Moreover, from a software engineering point of view, temporal validity intervals are a good support for expressing the specifications undeterminism in the early stage of software life cycle. In *TSPN*, arc temporal intervals are 3-uples (x,n,y), called static temporal validity intervals, such as x, n and y are respectively, the minimum, nominal and maximum admissible durations of the related processing. Thus, *TSPN* allows temporal jitter and skew inside weakly synchronous systems to be modeled [11]. Moreover, such a modeling allows an easy specification of intermedia or inter-stream synchronization by merging transitions, according to a « digital production studio » composition paradigm [12].

Synchronization schemes between tasks can be accurately and fully controlled with the help of nine different synchronization semantics. From a runtime point of view these synchronization semantics are defined as precise synchronization instants taking into account real process durations. From a modeling point of view the firing rules define firing intervals covering all the possible synchronization instants. These synchronization intervals are obtained from a complete and consistent combination of absolute dynamic temporal validity intervals of the related arcs. For instance, using these firing rules, we can specify synchronization schemes driven by the earliest processing (*i.e.* the *strong-or* firing rule), the latest processing (*i.e.* the *weak-and* firing rule) or a given processing (*i.e.* the *master* firing rule). Thus, these synchronization semantics allow the synchronization instant to be defined by a dynamically or statically selected arc (*i.e.* a task). These nine synchronization semantics and their related firing intervals are illustrated on *Figure 3-b*, where, if τ_i is the enabling date of arc (p_i,t), with (x_i,n_i,y_i) the arc static temporal validity interval, then τ_i^{min} and τ_i^{max} are nicknames for τ_i+x_i and τ_i+y_i respectively.

The notion of *TSPN* state [11] associated to formal rules for the evolution between states allows formal simulation of the dynamic behaviour of a *TSPN* to be done. A reduction algorithm applied to synchronization structures and coupled with a worst case analysis of the reduced synchronization structures allows the temporal consistency of synchronization schemes to be verified. Moreover, this reduction allows to transform every structured *TSPN* (*i.e.* a *TSPN* made up only with sequential and parallel synchronization structures) into a temporally equivalent timed arc. The reduction entails for *TSPN* hierachical capabilities by allowing to associate both temporally and structurally equivalent *TSPN* subnets to abstract places [12]. The verification of both temporal and logical properties of *TSPN* can be done through an enumerative approach that allows to build the accessibility graph of bounded *TSPN*.

---

[5] A deeper introduction of this model and its motivation may be found in [11]

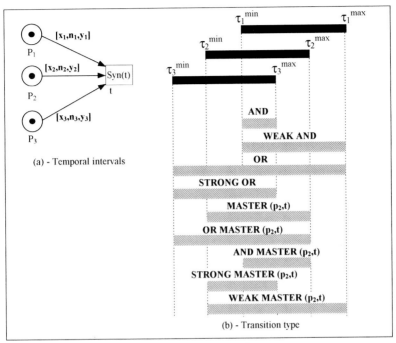

Fig. 3. The *TSPN* firing rules

3. The *TSPN* Toolkit

The toolkit allows the author to construct and to handle a multimedia document in a formal way thanks to the *TSPN* model, and in a natural way by means of a graphic interface based on the digital video production studio paradigm allowing the author to quickly specify synchronization scenarios through a visual formalism. It emphasizes the assistance given to the author by combining the use of four authoring units and a presentation unit which lead him through his specification processes and ensure the complete line of synchronization scenario prototyping. The toolkit authoring units are presented below :

- an *editor* allowing the user to construct the multimedia document.
- a *static checker* allowing the temporal analysis of the *TSPN* in order to detect the network risks of desynchronization and to warn the user.
- a *simulator* allowing to dynamically and interactively simulate the temporal evolution of the specification displayed through the tokens moving.
- a *validation tool* allowing to obtain the *TSPN* accessibility graph.

The life cycle can be compared to a two-dimensional spiral described on *figure 4*. Indeed on the one hand, a first traditional spiral cycle is obtained between authoring units and the presentation unit. It evolves by successive refinings according to the result detected by the author. On the other hand, a second spiral cycle can be noticed between the various authoring units which bring up to date desynchronization risks and suggest solutions to the author so that he could correct his specification.

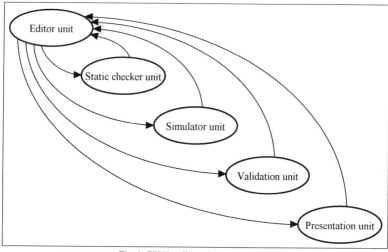

Fig. 4. *TSPN* toolkit units and life cycle

3.1. Editor unit

The author of a multimedia scenario is helped by a graphic interface which allows him to quickly construct a *TSPN* specification describing the synchronization constraints. The construction is easy given that all the operations are accessible just by mouse-clicking on an object which proposes to the user the whole actions which can be applied. The specification takes three stages. Firstly, the author must construct the scenario frame by freely handling places, arcs, transitions or using exclusively, according to a structurally constrained approach, the thirteen synchronization structures defined by Allen [14]. Then, the author must link media data with the places, and finally, he must specify the temporal constraints of media processings, and inter-media synchronization semantics associated to transitions in the resulting *TSPN*. According to a digital video production studio composition paradigm of multimedia streams, the various synchronization structures specified during the edition step can be composed through arcs connections and serial or parallel transitions mergings.

Moreover, the *TSPN* model allows to hierarchically specify temporal synchronization by linking various granularity levels with places in terms of information units size. For example, a place which models a video sequence processing can be broken down into a sequence of several places, each one representing the processing of one or several video frames. Three different synchronization layers are distinguishable and are described on *figure 5*.

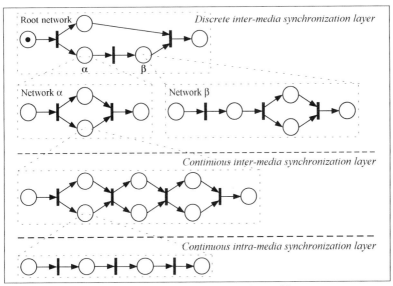

Figure 5 - Synchronization layers in *TSPN* toolkit

Firstly, a *discrete inter-media synchronization layer* which allows discrete inter-media synchronization schemes. In this layer, a place models a media processing (*atomic place*), or a finer multimedia synchronization schemes (*composite place*). The recursive use of composite places allows the author to hierarchically build *TSPN* modules. Then, a *continuous inter-media synchronization layer* which allows to specify accurately continuous synchronization schemes between several continuous medias. Finally, a *continuous intra-media synchronization layer* which describes the synchronization constraints of the smallest synchronization units within streams of multimedia processings.

Given *TSPN* hierarchical capabilities, the author can compose his synchronization scenario according three ways :

- *bottom-up way* : The author builds in ascending way his specification by referencing previously specified and validated *TSPN* with the help of composite places.
- *top-down way* : First, the author puts his effort on high level synchronization considerations. Lower level synchronization issues are delayed by using composite places which will be refined afterwards in an incremental way. Some complex scenarios can

generate *TSPN* which are hard to manage in a monolithic way. So, the scenario construction benefits from the modular structuration mechanisms offered by composite places and their related sub-networks. The recursive use of composite places allows to define several abstraction levels for a specification.

- *mixed way* by using bottom-up and top-down approaches.

A lot of information is associated to a *TSPN* synchronization scenario (validity intervals, firing strategies, master arcs ...). In order to avoid overloading the scenario display while keeping the maximum of information on the screen, we have adopted a color code approach making graphically explicit each object semantics. For example, the color of a transition refers to the selected firing strategy, the line style allows to distinguish both types of places : dotted lines are used in order to represent delays whereas unbroken lines symbolize a processing place.

3.2. Static checker unit

Once the scenario has been built and specified, the author can check the consistency of the synchronization schemes he has specified. Note that the checking procedure evoked in this section can only be applied, with a polynomial complexity, on *Structured TSPN*[6] (*STSPN*). Static checking constitutes a major unit of the toolkit. Indeed, it guarantees to other units (simulation, validation, and presentation) that a *STSPN* does not contain synchronization schemes potentially submitted to important risks of desynchronization. *Figure 6* describes the general synopsis of the static checking unit.

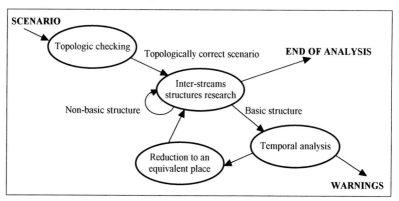

Fig. 6. General synopsis of static temporal checking

Before any static temporal analysis, a topologic checking allows to free from scenario construction mistakes. Then, static temporal checking allows to detect inter-streams

---

[6] A *STSPN* is built using exclusively parallel and sequential synchronization structures.

desynchronization risks. In order to detect inter-streams desynchronization risks, we adopted the following two steps procedure :

- First, let us note that, given the synchronization structures recursively used for building *STSPN*, transitions are paired. That is, each synchronization structure has an input transition and an output transition. For checking risk of desynchronization related to a transition, we consider the sub-network between the related transition and its «input» transition. This *STSPN* is reduced in a canonical form as the one illustrated on *figure 7*. This form results from applying the reduction algorithm evoked in [13] to upstream synchronization structures related to each synchronization unit involved in the considered synchronization point. These upstream synchronization structures are reduced into timed arcs which synthesize the temporal behaviour of upstream synchronization units.

- Then, a worst-case temporal analysis is applied on the canonical *STSPN* resulting from the first step. This analysis allows risks of important drift between multimedia streams to be detected. Note that *TSPN* uses a best-effort synchronization semantic. That is, *TSPN* firing rules try to preserve for the best the temporal constraints of the synchronization unit dynamically or statically privileged by the synchronization semantics associated to the considered transition. However, because of temporal drifts between multimedia streams, the temporal constraints of this elected synchronization unit can not be ever satisfied. Therefore, this second step aims to check wether the firing of the transition is always done inside the temporal validity interval of the dynamically or statically defined synchronization unit. This step is illustrated on the following example :

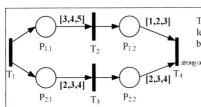

The *strong-or* strategy covers a synchronization lead by the earliest stream. So, transition T_4 will be fired :
- at the earliest when any arc reaches the lower bound of its temporal validity interval and when T_4 is entirely enabled.
- at the latest when any arc reaches the upper bound of its temporal validity interval.

For a place P_α, we define the following instants :

$[x_\alpha, n_\alpha, y_\alpha]$ is the temporal interval related to arc outgoing from the place

τ_α^{tok} is the marking date of the place

τ_α^{min} is the date when the age of the token reaches the lower temporal bound ($\tau_\alpha^{min} = \tau_\alpha^{tok} + x_\alpha$)

τ_α^{max} is the date when the age of the token reaches the upper temporal bound ($\tau_\alpha^{min} = \tau_\alpha^{tok} + y_\alpha$)

$\Rightarrow$ The worst-case analysis consists in making sure that the transition is always entirely enabled when any arc reaches the lower bound of its validity interval in order to be sure that the considered arc is not delayed.

$\Rightarrow \tau_{i2}^{min} \geq \tau_{j2}^{tok} \ \forall \ i \neq j$

$\Rightarrow \min(\tau_{i2}^{min}) \geq \max(\tau_{j2}^{tok}) \ \forall \ i \neq j$ in worst case approach

$$\min(\tau_{i2}^{tok} + x_{i2}) \geq \max(\tau_{j2}^{tok}) \ \forall \ i \neq j$$
$$\min(\tau_{i2}^{tok}) + x_{i2} \geq \max(\tau_{j2}^{tok}) \ \forall \ i \neq j$$
$$\tau_{i1}^{min} + x_{i2} \geq \tau_{j1}^{max} \ \forall \ i \neq j$$
$$\tau_{i1}^{tok} + x_{i1} + x_{i2} \geq \tau_{j1}^{tok} + y_{j1} \ \forall \ i \neq j$$
$$x_{i1} + x_{i2} \geq y_{j1} \ \forall \ i \neq j \text{ given that } \tau_{i1}^{tok} = \tau_{j1}^{tok}$$

$$\Rightarrow x_{i1} + x_{i2} \geq y_{j1} \ \forall \ i \neq j$$

Let's apply this analysis to our beam :

- $x_{11} + x_{12} \geq y_{21}$
  $3 + 1 \geq 4 \ \Rightarrow$ The fire of T_4 will never be delayed by the stream $(P_{11} \rightarrow T_4)$
- $x_{21} + x_{22} \geq y_{11}$
  $2 + 2 \geq 5 \ \Rightarrow$ The fire of T_4 may be delayed by the stream $(P_{21} \rightarrow T_4)$

Fig. 7. Example of static checking

3.3. Simulation unit

Then, the author can carry out a dynamic and interactive simulation of his specification in order to study the scenario behaviour by integrating the indeterminism of processing duration (CPU load, network overcrowding ...) typical of weakly synchronous distributed systems. Interactive simulation can help to get additional understanding of the modelled systems. This step can be used for the purpose of debugging and performances evaluation of synchronization scenario. Moreover, an automatic simulation can detect failures in specification. Indeed, the statistic exploitation of results stemming from simulation samples can reveal itself a powerful tool able to assist the author. This simulation relies on the notion of a *TSPN* states as introduced by [11]. *Figure 8* describes the general synopsis of the simulation unit.

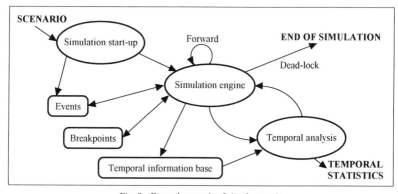

Fig. 8. General synopsis of simulator unit

The staple principle of the simulation is that it is driven by the *TSPN* events. Eight kinds of events are taken into account :

- P_ENABLE linked with a place enabling.
- P_END linked with a place processing end. The duration of the latter is randomly determined with the help of a deterministic distribution over the place temporal interval.
- P_LOW_BOUND, P_NOM_BOUND and P_UP_BOUND linked with the overstepping dates of lower, nominal and upper bounds of the validity interval. These events are secondary because they express no stage in a scenario execution but they are used here in a statistic aim.
- T_ENABLE linked with a transition enabling. This event is post-conditioned by the enabling of the whole ingoing places.
- T_FIRE linked with a transition fire. The firing date is randomly determined by associating a probabilistic or deterministic distribution with the firing interval.
- DEAD_LOCK linked with the token death. This state is reached when a token gets at the final place.

So, before starting the simulation, a start-up unit initializes the simulation engine by generating and dating the whole events brought into play in the synchronization scenario. The events initialization is based on a waterfall technique which generates the post-conditioned events from the P_ENABLE event related to the beginning place at the initial time. The used method is illustrated on *figure 9*.

The simulation engine manages the evolution of the scenario execution symbolized by the tokens progress. In order to make easier the visualization of the tokens progress, a color code characterizes the temporal state (early, on time or late) whereas a shape code allows to know the processing state (running or ended). All dynamic temporal informations (enabling dates, processing durations, transition firing dates) are stored in order to analyse them later on. At any time, the author can interact on the simulation. First of all, he can modify or suppress random events (P_END and T_FIRE) in order to see how the specification reacts in case of failure. He can also put breakpoints in order to set the granularity level of the simulation and increase time step by step, or up to the next breakpoint.

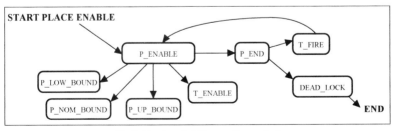

Fig. 9. Events waterfall generation method

At any time, a temporal analysis unit allows the author to exploit temporal information (jitter, drift ...) of the places outgoing arcs and of the whole streams through automatic composition. By focusing on temporal information relative to P_END events happened late typical of a desynchronization, this unit shows the author the various points of the specification he has to correct.

3.4. Validation unit

The validation unit aims at the analysis of the temporal properties of the synchronization scenario. It consists in generating the underlying timed state graph of the considered *TSPN*. Theoretical bases are acquired and consist in an extension of the validation method proposed by [15] for *Time Petri Net*. The analysis technique we have developed allows exhaustive analysis of both temporal and logical properties of bounded *TSPN* to be done. This unit is under development.

4. Conclusions and perspectives

The *TSPN* model allows to formally represent the behaviour of complex real multimedia streams, taking into account the temporal non-determinism of weakly synchronous distributed systems and the admissible temporal variability of multimedia objects. *TSPN* introduces a formal semantic of synchronization which ensure selectively for the best the satisfaction of temporal constraints of multimedia processings and their continuity.

This paper has introduced a multimedia synchronization prototyping toolkit based on the *TSPN* model and which covers all the multimedia document life cycle, that is :

- graphic construction of a scenario and formal specifications of temporal constraints.
- temporal checking in order to detect possible desynchronization risks.
- interactive simulation for debugging and performances studies.
- validation in order to obtain an accessibility graph.

The toolkit entails a prototyping method based on a scenario spiral life cycle. Indeed, the author can specify his scenario by successive attempts taking into account results of verification, simulation and analysis steps. Several authoring units lead the author in his specification proceeding by making deynchronization risks in the limelight. At any time during the prototyping cycle, the author can modify the specification by changing temporal validity intervals, types of transition or synchronization granularity of inter and intra-stream schemes.

Currently, the toolkit is operational and is used for the prototyping of a computer aided teaching environment for *Airbus Training*.

Numerous extensions are also under consideration. Given the emergence of hypermedia and multimedia documents standards of structures like *MHEG* or *Hytime* which normalize synchronization schemes between numerous multimedia objects presentations, an automatic conversion unit from *TSPN* form into *MHEG* form is in the process of being developed. The validation unit whose theoretical bases are acquired, is also in the process of being developed. Moreover, the *TSPN* model has still some intrinsic limitations. In its current form, the model only allows the specification of synchronization scenarios and does not taking into account user interactions. Therefore, *TSPN* does not allow hypermedia systems to be modelled. The *Hierarchical TSPN* (*HTSPN*) model extends *TSPN* and allows hypermedia systems to be easily and fully modelled [12]. Therefore, toolkit units will have to be modified in order to take into account the hypermedia documents.

5. References

[1] P. Sénac, M. Diaz, P. De Saqui Sannes, *Time Stream Petri Net, a model for timed multimedia informations*, Proc. of the 15th International Conference on Application and Theory of Petri Nets, Zaragoza, Spain, June 94

[2] U. Bormann, C. Bormann, *Standards for open document processing : current state and future developments*, Computer Networks and ISDN systems, n° 21, 91

[3] P. Sénac, F. Fabre, E. Chaput, M. Diaz, *A model and a toolkit for the formal specification of weakly synchronous systems*, to be published in IEEE International Conference on Systems, Man and Cybernetics, October 95

[4] R. Steinmetz, *Synchronization properties in multimedia systems*, IEEE Journal on Selected Areas in Telecommunications, vol 8, n°3, April 90.

[5] J.F. Koegel, J.M. Heines, *Improving visual programming languages for multimedia authoring*, Proc. Of ED-MEDIA 93, Assoc. For the Advancement of Computing in Education, June 93

[6] AimTech Corporation, *Icon Author user manual*, 91

[7] S. Pallix, *Premiere 4.0 for Windows*, Multimédia solutions, n° 29, April 95

[8] J.F. Koegel, J.L. Rutledge, J.M. Heines, *Toolkits for multimedia interface design*, Proc. of Xhibition 92, San Jose, USA, June 92

[9] G. Blakowski, J. Hübel, U. Langrehr, M. Mühlhauser, *Tool support for the synchronization and presentation of distributed multimedia*, Computer Communications, vol 15, n° 10, December 92

[10] T. Little, A. Ghafoor, *Synchronization and storage models for multimedia objects*, IEEE Journal on Selected Areas in Communications, April 1990.

[11] P. Sénac, M. Diaz, P. de Saqui Sannes, *Toward a formal specification of multimedia synchronization scenarios*, Annals of Telecommunications, vol 49, n° 5-6, June 94

[12] P. Sénac, M. Diaz, A. Léger, P. de Saqui-Sannes, *Modelling logical and temporal synchronization in hypermedia systems*, to be published in IEEE Journal on Selected Areas in Telecommunications, 95.

[13] P. Sénac, P. de Saqui-Sannes, R. Willrich, *Hierarchical Time Stream Petri Net : a model for hypermedia systems*, to be published in 16th International Conference on Applications and Theory of Petri Nets, Turin, June 95.

[14] J.F. Allen, *Maintaining knowledge about Temporal Interval*, Comm. of the ACM, November 83

[15] B. Berthomieu, M. Diaz, *Modelling and verification of time dependant systems using time Petri nets*, IEEE Transaction on Software Engineering, March 91.

FIDELITY AND DISTORTION IN MULTIMEDIA SYNCHRONIZATION MODELING

JIANHUA MA

Computer Architecture Lab., Department of Computer Hardware
The University of Aizu, Aizu-Wakamatsu City, 965-80 Japan
E-mail: jianhua@u-aizu.ac.jp

RUNHE HUANG

Computer Science and Eng. Lab., Department of Computer Software
The University of Aizu, Aizu-Wakamatsu City, 965-80 Japan
E-mail: r-huang@u-aizu.ac.jp

TOSIYASU L. KUNII

Computer Science and Eng. Lab., Department of Computer Software
The University of Aizu, Aizu-Wakamatsu City, 965-80 Japan
E-mail: kunii@u-aizu.ac.jp

Abstract

Both good measures and essential models are the important premises of evaluating models and mechanisms of distributed multimedia synchronization. Multimedia distortion and fidelity are introduced as the bases of measuring the performance of a reproduced or synthetic multimedia object. Time fidelity, as one kind of important construction information fidelity, is classified into intra-media, inter-media and inter-destination fidelity. The essential model of distributed multimedia synchronization is proposed, and many other models may be regarded as special cases of the essential model. Transmission error and transformation distortion as two new sources of time distortion, are addressed in this paper, and the detailed forms of time distortion are presented and discussed from different viewpoints.

1. Introduction

Multimedia has become one of the hottest research topics and application areas in the information era. A variety of multimedia products have been available on the market. However, in view of academic research, there are still many unsolved problems. One of the most important and urgent tasks is multimedia modeling, such as, representation and modeling of multimedia information, multimedia database modeling, speech and music modeling, and multimedia synchronization modeling. Multimedia is still a young discipline intersected with many other disciplines. The researchers are from a variety of backgrounds and fields. Partially because of such a situation, varieties of models and mechanisms have been proposed on any modeling topic.

Let us focus on multimedia synchronizations modeling. From a viewpoint of hierarchical layering, they can be classified into synchronization in the application layer, the language layer, the transportation layer and the operating system layer. From a viewpoint of synchronization function location, they can be classified into synchronization at source end, transmission path, and destination end. From a viewpoint of control manner, they can be classified into steady and dynamic synchronization. It is expected there will be more and more different models and mechanisms which may be proposed in next few years. Facing to so many various models and mechanisms which were proposed [1,2,9~12,14,15,17] and will be proposed, natural and basic questions to ask are: whether those proposed models and mechanisms are good or not, how to not only qualitatively but also quantitatively evaluate them, and how to construct better or optimum models and mechanisms.

It is very helpful to look at Kunii's three-step model for creation [6,7]. Kunii divided the creative process in engineering field into three steps: *the derivation process* from an artificial world to a set of requirements; *the construction process* from the set of requirements to engineering model; and *the test process*. He further elaborated the first step and gave the three-stage model of derivation process as construction of a prototype *object model*, construction of a prototype *typical object model*, and construction of a prototype *essential object model*. It can be seen from the three steps that the derivation process is the basic premise of designing and constructing models, and test process is the key of constructing a successful model. That is to say, a constructed model, whether it is good ot not, has to be evaluated by the test process and the results of the evaluation are feedbacked to construct a better model. This convinces us that the good measures for evaluating proposed synchronization models and mechanisms are very important to design better models and mechanisms of multimedia synchronizations. It is also clear from the three stages that construction of essential object models is important in requirement formation. This gives us a heuristics that it is very necessary to construct essential models for multimedia synchronization from various typical models. In conclusion, both good measures and essential models are important for researches on multimedia synchronizations. It seems that these two tasks have not being carried out yet.

However, it is not easy to give a measure which can qualitatively and quantitatively evaluate multimedia synchronization models and mechanisms, since this area is intersected with many other disciplines. Moreover, a good measure, in multimedia context, should consider both the subjective perception of users and the objective measures of engineering. With consideration of both the subjective and objective factors, this paper proposes a reasonable measure on basis of the concepts of multimedia fidelity and distortion. Based on general principles of information processing and special features of time information, in conjunction with multimedia distortion and fidelity, an essential model is constructed. Given fidelity and an essential model, the question followed is what factors will affect time information fidelity. Thus, various sources and forms of time information distortion are discussed.

The rest of this paper is organized as follows: Section 2 introduces the concept of multimedia fidelity and focuses on forms and classification of multimedia time information fidelity. The essential model of multimedia synchronizations is given in Section 3. In section 4, the sources and forms of distortion are discussed. Finally, we conclude this paper in Section 5.

2. The Concept of Multimedia Fidelity and Its Classification

2.1. A Reasonable Measure

To work out proper and complete measures of multimedia synchronization models and mechanisms, we have to take into account both the subjective needs and effective perception of users and the objective measures of engineering. Regarding the measures of virtual presence in virtual environments, Sheridan states that "Presence is a subjective sensation and as such any subjective measures are likely to be multidimensional" [16]. And Ellis says that "A large part of our sense of physical reality is a consequence of internal processing rather than being something that is a developed only from the immediate sensory information we receive" [3]. As it can be seen that Sheridan emphasizes subjective factor of measures and what Ellis emphasizes is human internal processing effects on our sense. There is no doubt that these viewpoints are also suitable for the evaluation problem of multimedia synchronization models and mechanisms. That is to say, we have to have both objective and subjective measures of synchronization performance. However, so far we have neither objective measures nor subjective measures of multimedia synchronization models and mechanisms. And giving a complete both quantitatively objective and qualitatively subjective measure of synchronization models and mechanisms is not an easy task and requires various knowledge from many different disciplines, such as physiology, cognitive psychology, computer science, and communication. So an alternative reasonable approach is to look for some measures which consider more or less both subjective and objective factors and are relatively easy to be measured.

As we know, human understanding of the outside world is mainly a kind of subjective behavior, but precisely receiving the outside information is the premise of human understanding. Here, the concepts of distortion and fidelity are introduced to measure the objective accuracy and subjective perceptive behavior of reproduced or synthetic multimedia information respectively. The terms, fidelity and distortion, are widely used in image, video, speech and audio processing and communication. Mathematical definitions of them and their relationships with designs of communication systems were originally given by Shannon in his entropy theory [13] Multimedia is not a simple combination of various media, multimedia fidelity is thus not a simple extension of each single medium fidelity. Concretely speaking, multimedia object information does not only consist of object information or content information and also includes construction information, i.e. space, time, conditional relationships among objects. Therefore, multimedia fidelity is composed of both content information fidelity and construction information fidelity. In studying media fidelity and distortion, we have to have a reference object, which is used for comparison, so we should firstly distinguish perception of a real world from perception of a synthetic world.

2.2. Perception of Real World and Synthetic World

Human being conduct their communication with the outside real world by means of certain machines or systems so as to greatly improve the limits of human senses in space and time. Therefore, the machines or systems play an important role as communication media between human and a real world as shown in Figure 1.

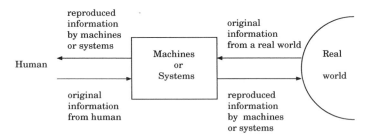

Figure 1. Information communication between human and a real world

As it can be seen from Figure 1, machines or systems in such a case are mainly implementing a reproduction function. Due to various limits, such as limits in the ratio of signal to noise, model completeness, process ability, and transmission bandwidth, reproduced information may not be always same as its original one. Thus, what basically concerned about the reproduced information is reproduction accuracy and real-timeness in view of perception. The question followed is how to measure reproduction accuracy and real-timeness. As far as in a real world, measures are relative direct since original information physically exists, and what we have to do is to compare the reproduced information with the original information.

However, with the advances in computer science and technology, especially new developments in visualization and multimedia, we can now perceive and create varieties of novel real worlds and synthetic worlds. Sometimes, such a synthetic world does not actually exist in physical worlds and it may even not have to satisfy various laws and constraints which should be followed in the real worlds. In such created synthetic worlds, the measures of synthetic information accuracy and real-timeness would be much more difficult and indirect. In Figure 2(a), the synthetic worlds are assumed to be generated or created by a computers based system. It is necessary to point out that computer systems including distributed computer systems have their own various limitations, such as model in completeness, algorithm in accuracy, computation power shortage, and transmission in ability. Thus, synthetic information from synthetic worlds cannot be what we exactly expect. Now, let us assume there is an ideal system which has no default and limit in its computation and transmission power, and so on. Thus, synthetic worlds created by such an ideal system would be what we expect. The outputs from such synthetic world are ideal synthetic information as shown in Figure 2(b). Naturally, the evaluation of the synthetic information from synthetic worlds can be now turned into the problem of the measurement of the similarity of the synthetic information with the *ideal synthetic information*. One of the basic perception requirements is to produce the synthetic information as similar as possible with the ideal ones. On the other hand, in the real worlds, if a reproduction machine or system is an ideal one, then the reproduced information should be the same with their original information, here the reproduced information is called as the *ideal reproduced information*. If we call both the ideal reproduced information and ideal synthetic information as the *ideal information*, and reproduced information and synthetic information as the *received information*, then irrespective of the perception in the real world or synthetic world, we have a common basic requirement which is to make received information as similar as possible with the ideal information.

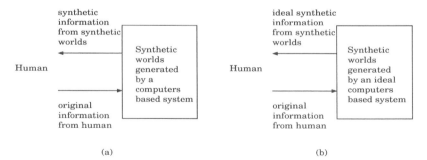

Figure 2. Information communication between human and synthetic worlds

2.3. The Concepts of Multimedia Fidelity and Distortion

Generally speaking, what we can perceive is received information but not the ideal information. In this context, both ideal and received information we consider are meant to be multimedia type information because human being are built to perceive things in multimedia. Let MMO(t) denote ideal multimedia object and MMO'(t) represent received multimedia object as shown in Figure 3. In the figure T is the latency of MMO'(t) relative to MMO(t). In the case of reproduction, T is the time difference between the time at which a machine starts to receive outside world information and the time at which the machine starts to output the information. In the case of syntheses, T is the time difference between the time at which computers based system receives commands of synthesizing information and the time at which the system starts to output synthesized information to human. For all the cases, there are two basic requirements for received MMO'(t), one is real-time requirement T_r, and the other is accuracy requirement A_r. So called real-time requirement means that latency T is not greater than the given T_r, that is, $T \leq T_r$. And so called accuracy is the difference of MMO'(t) and MMO(t) within a certain allowed range. As we know, the concepts of fidelity and distortion are widely used in image, video, speech and audio processing and communication. However, we believe that fidelity and distortion are also important and useful for measures of perception difference between MMO'(t) and MMO(t) in multimedia context.

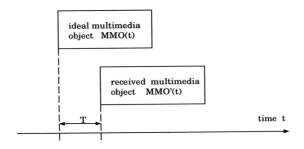

Figure 3. Ideal and received multimedia objects

Definition *(multimedia distortion and fidelity)*
D is assumed as a non-negative function of MMO(t) and MMO'(t), that is,

$$D = G(MMO(t), MMO'(t)) \geq 0 \qquad or \qquad D = G(MMO(t) - MMO'(t)) \geq 0$$

where, $G(\cdot)$ is a function relative to measure types, D is a sort of the measure of the difference of MMO'(t) and MMO(t), and we call D as distortion of MMO'(t) relative to MMO(t). Generally speaking, MMO(t) and MMO'(t) are vectors. F is a function of distortion D with the values in the normalized range of [0,1], that is,

$$0 \leq F = F(D) \leq 1$$

where, as it can be seen that F is a sort of the measure of the similarity of MMO'(t) and MMO(t), and hence we called F as fidelity of MMO'(t) relative to MMO(t).

When $D = 0$ and $F = 1$, that is an ideal case: MMO'(t) = MMO(t). Such ideal case is called as reproduction or syntheses *without distortion* versus reproduction or syntheses *with distortion*. However, such an ideal case is practically hardly realized in most applications because of the following two factors: (1) Multimedia system would have to possess too many resources to be practical for reproduction or syntheses without distortion if real-time requirement is maintained reasonably high; (2) A certain amount of distortion is allowed for most applications in view of perception aspects.

Distortion D is relatively easy get analyzed based on some observable parameters, such as ratio of signal to noise, position, speed, delay, and error rate. And it can be calculated by exploiting linear distance, the Hamming distance, the Euclidean distance and other mathematical formulae. That is to say, distortion is of objective bias difference measure of MMO'(t) and MMO(t). While fidelity F considers not only objective difference but also influence of such objective difference on human subjective perception. For example, in video-phone communication, speech communication plays a main role. Relative large amount of image distortion may not affect information perception greatly while relative small amount of speech distortion may seriously affect quality of this communication. To some extent, fidelity F reflects the nature of subjective perception. As we have mentioned above, the measures of subjective perception is a rather difficult task. Now a problem we face is how to define fidelity function. In order to solve this problem, we have to firstly discuss about multimedia fidelity and distortion features and classifications. Meanwhile, it is necessary to point out the differences of the concepts between fidelity and QoS(quality of service). QoS is a set of qualities related to the collective behavior of one or more objects from the viewpoint of ODP (Open Distributed Processing), or is a set of qualities related to the provision of an (N)-service, as perceived by an(N)-service user from the viewpoint of OSI reference model [5]. QoS emphasizes functions and performances provided by a system or a sub-system. While fidelity emphasizes perception and distortion of a reproduced or synthetic information media.

2.4. Fidelity and Distortion of Content and Construction Information

Assume multimedia object MMO is composed of a set objects which is represented as $O = (o_1, o_2, ..., o_m)$. The set O is called *content information* or *object information*. In order to represent a meaningful multimedia object from viewpoint of human perception, the *construction information* of object elements $o_1, o_2,..., o_m$ is necessarily to be defined. There is various construction information, such as information related to time, space, and attributes. Thus, construction information C is composed of space information S, time information V and attribute information A. And a multimedia object can be represented as

$$MMO = (O, C) = (O, S, V, A)$$

A basic objective of multimedia communications is to reproduce or synthesize not only content information but also construction information. There have been a lot of theories and techniques to reproduce or synthesize the content information of a multimedia object. The more challenging problem is to reproduce or synthesize both content information and construction information of multimedia in heterogeneous networks. Like reproduction or syntheses of content information, the reproduction or syntheses of construction information has to satisfy its associated fidelity and distortion requirements. A classification of fidelity and distortion is shown in Figure 4.

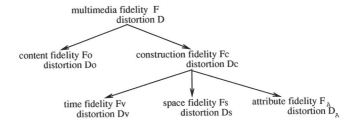

Figure 4. Fidelity and distortion of content and construction information

The existence of construction information is one of the important symbols that multimedia objects distinguish them from single medium objects. Therefore, study on fidelity and distortion of multimedia construction information becomes extremely important. As we know, there have been few researchers [8] who have started to study on space perception and distortion although they have considered only few kind of media. There have been the lack of systematic study on perception fidelity and distortion of time information for multimedia objects. Since multimedia synchronizations have close relationships with time information fidelity and distortion, we will focus on discussing time information fidelity and distortion.

2.5. Fidelity and Distortion of Time Information

When studying multimedia synchronizations, the composition of a multimedia object can be simplified as

$$MMO = (O, V).$$

Corresponding to time information V, content information sometimes is also called non-time information. The fidelity and distortion of the time information are classified into the following three kinds: (1) *intra-media time* fidelity $F_{v_{intra}}$ and distortion $D_{v_{intra}}$, (2) *inter-media time* fidelity $F_{v_{inter}}$ and distortion $D_{v_{inter}}$, and (3) *inter-destination time* fidelity $F_{v_{desti}}$ and distortion $D_{v_{desti}}$. Apart from the above three kinds of requirements, multimedia time management also has to consider following two important requirements: real-timeness requirement and dynamic management requirement. In conclusion, management of multimedia time fidelity and distortion may be summarized in the following architecture:

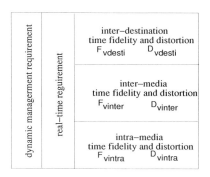

Figure 5. An architecture of time fidelity and distortion

In order to compare and improve existing multimedia synchronization models and mechanisms, it is necessary to give an essential but general synchronization model. Also we should be clear about the various distortion resources and forms which affect fidelity. So, in the next two sections, we are going to present an essential model and discuss distortion resources and forms.

3. An Essential Model of Multimedia Synchronization

A layering architecture given in Figure 6(a) is often adopted by many synchronization mechanisms [1,9,11]. Although the debate on relations between the layering architecture and the seven layer OSI reference model is not over yet, there is no dispute about the basic idea of a layering architecture as used in multimedia synchronizations. Considering time information fidelity and distortion construction as shown in Figure 5, an improved layering architecture of distributed multimedia synchronizations is proposed in Figure 6(b).

Based on the idea of layering architecture, in conjunction with detailed logic con-

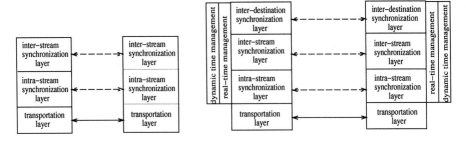

Figure 6(a). A conventional layering architecture of distributed multimedia synchronization

Figure 6(b). An improved layering architecture of distributed multimedia synchronization

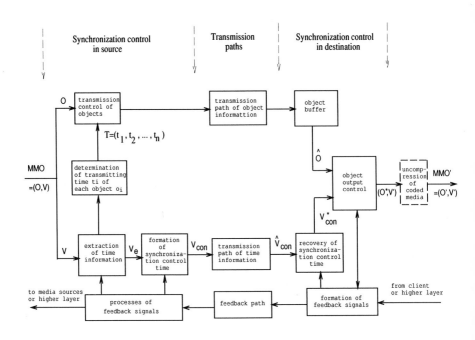

Figure 7 An essential model of distributed multimedia synchronizations

nections between two entities in the same layer, a complete model of multimedia synchronizations results. In other words, a complete model should include not only the layering architecture but also the detailed logic connections which describe how synchronizations in a stream or multiple stream layers at the source and at the destination are carried out logically. Different connection manner result in many different models as proposed in reference [2]. It seems that none of the proposed models so far can be chosen to model multimedia synchronizations of all applications. One of the reasons may be that the model proposed originally came from some specific application background and system environment. In order to obtain an essential model which is not limited to a specific application, a different approach is required.

One of basic ideas of this approach is that the information of a multimedia object consists of non-time information (or content information) and time information, and multimedia synchronizations are related to the processing of time information. For any kind of information process, there exist several common function modules, which perform information extraction, representation, transmission and transformation. There exist also some special features for time information. For example, time information may not be perceived independently, and it may be perceived only by combining it with non-time information. An essential model of multimedia synchronizations, therefore, naturally contains these common function modules of information processes and special features of time information. Based on these considerations, in conjunction with the considerations of application backgrounds and system environments, an essential model of multimedia synchronization is proposed in Figure 7.

3.1. Illustrations of The Essential Model

1). The essential model consists of three main parts: synchronization controls at the source end, transmission paths, and synchronization controls at the destination end. Although it may be reasonable for some kinds of multimedia communications to position synchronization only at the source, at the network or at the destination [2], this may not be sufficient for some other kinds of multimedia communications to solve various synchronization problems by only positioning synchronization at the source, the network or the destination. Therefore, the transmission and synchronization controls both at the source and destination should be coordinated to deal with various synchronization problems as shown in the essential model.

2). The uncompressing process, shown in the dotted lines box in Figure 7, is not a part of multimedia synchronizations, but it appears in the essential model of multimedia synchronizations. The reason is that we believe it is necessary somehow to illustrate the relations between synchronization controls and uncompressing process in the essential model since some synchronization control techniques, such as pausing and skipping audio or video frames, will in fact change the time order of the frames. Sometimes this change may introduce a sequence of errors if the uncompressing process is placed at the output of a synchronization control and an inter-frame source coding scheme is used.

3). Synchronization controls at the source end contain the process of extracting time information from multimedia object sources, determination of transmitting time t_i of each object o_i, and formation of synchronization control time. The determination of transmitting time is used to control extraction and transmission of objects. The multimedia object sources have no limitations on media types, local clocks of objects and geographical distribution of objects. In contrast to time information, synchronization control time is a different kind of time representation, to which it is easy to directly apply synchronization controls. One example is the time stamp which is widely used in computer communications. Another example is the synchronization mark which is firstly introduced by Nicolaou [10] and Shepherd [14].

4). Synchronization controls at the destination end contain a buffer, which is used to store partial objects dynamically, recovery of synchronization control time and object output control. Similarly, there are no limitations on local clocks and geographical distribution of objects at the destination end.

5). In the model there is feedback control. Its main functions are as follows: *(1)* reliable transmission of time information; *(2)* clock synchronization between the source and the destination; *(3)* coordinating of work between the synchronization controls at the source and the destination; *(4)* interactive control which is very important for interactive multimedia applications.

6). Transmission paths contain three kinds of paths: object (or non-time information), time information and feedback transmission paths. The logic partitioning of the transmission of non-time and time information does not mean that practical transmissions of non-time and time information should be realized by separate physical channels in communication networks. The transmission of non-time and time information can be accomplished by either the same physical channels such as with time stamp transmission or separate physical channels such as with the synchronization channel defined by Shepherd [15].

3.2. Relation of The Essential Model With Other Models

Since the essential model shown in Figure 3 is based not only on various multimedia applications and environments but also on general principles of information processing and perception, it forms a general synchronization framework and can be used by different applications. Many other models may be regarded as specific cases of the essential model. Let us list some typical examples. Little's work [9] was focused on providing synchronization control time with an Object Composition Petri Net (OCPN) and by determining transmitting time t_i of each object o_i. Since time information is known in advance, extraction and recovery of the time information is easy and no feedback control is necessary. Ferrari [4] gave a mechanism to reduce jitter of the object transmission path which would make media synchronization become easy. Nicolaou's LSF/PSF (Logic/Physical Synchronization Frame) [10] and Shepherd's synchronization mark [15] may be seen as inserting some time symbols to form synchronization control times. Shepherd's synchronization channel is a pure central time structure and is transmitted by independent channels [14]. Ramanathan and Rangan's scheme [11] is focused on synchronization based on feedback control to solve problems introduced by delay, jitter and different local clocks. Although particular synchronization mechanisms are not given in the essential model, the given architecture and function modules lays a foundation on which different synchronization mechanisms can be easily analyzed and compared so as to make innovations with respect to the synchronization mechanism possible.

4. Sources and Forms of Time Distortion

Almost every model or mechanism of multimedia synchronization proposed up to now has considered only the following two sources of time distortion: different local clocks, and delay and jitter of the transmission and process. Besides above sources we have found that there exist other two sources of time distortion which should be considered but have not yet been addressed in the literature on multimedia synchronizations. (1) Time information transmission error. As shown in Figure 7, a multimedia object is composed of non-time information and time information. Time information is also sent to destinations from some sources through a network in most of cases. (2) Transformation distortion. As shown in Figure 7, the essential model of multimedia synchronization contains many concatenated function modules, such as the extraction of time information, and the formation of synchronization, transmission, recovery and object output controls. Any of these modules may introduce time distortion because of the above three factors and those distortions may be passed through to other modules before multimedia output. This means that degrees and forms of distortion may be changed when it passes a module. This kind of distortion is called as transformation distortion. It is necessary to attend to transformation distortion since it has a great influence on the overall distortion of the output multimedia objects and, therefore, it should be considered in designs of synchronization mechanisms. We believe that the above four kinds of sources of time distortion should be considered integratively in future research on more complete multimedia synchronization mechanisms.

Some kinds of time distortion in multimedia communications have been recognized. Continuous distortion, time skew and deadline missing have been mentioned as three forms of time distortion in many research papers. The above classification of time distortion is very important indeed, but the classification is too coarse to allow deeper study and to realize more practical multimedia synchronizations. We believe a finer classification is required. In fact each form of distortion stated above may be further divided into more detailed forms which are related more directly to the various sources of distortion and perception of multimedia objects. Obviously studies of multimedia synchronizations with respect to the detailed behavior of time distortion are quite difficult. However, the study is inevitable because of the higher and higher fidelity requirements of multimedia communications with limited sources and costs. Some distortion forms are: (1) deterministic bounds distortion, (2) statistic bounds distortion, (3) non-correlated and correlated distortion, (4) diffused and non-diffused distortion and (5) non-accumulative and accumulative distortion.

5. Conclusions

Facing to so many various models and mechanisms of multimedia synchronizations which have been proposed and will be proposed, two the basic problems are how to evaluate them quantitatively and qualitatively and how to construct better or even optimum models and mechanisms. This paper presents our original research on the above problems. We are convinced that both good measures and essential models are important premises for evaluating models and mechanisms of multimedia synchronization and constructing better or optimum ones. Multimedia distortion and fidelity are introduced as bases of measuring the performance of a reproduced or synthetic multimedia object. Time fidelity, as one important form of information fidelity in multimedia synchronizations, is emphasized and classified into intra-media, inter-media and inter-destination fidelity. An essential model is constructed based on general principles of information processing and special features of time information, in conjunction with multimedia distortion and fidelity. Many other models may be considered as special cases of the essential model. Time information distortion is one factor which affects time information fidelity, so various sources and forms of distortion are presented and discussed from different viewpoints, in which transmission error and transformation distortion are found to be two new sources of time distortion.

This paper has presented, however, only our preliminary effort at systematic study of the above problems, and many aspects are left and further research is necessary.

Acknowledgement
We would like to thank Professor Steven D. Tripp for revising the paper.

Reference

1. C. Coulson, *Multimedia application support in open distributed systems*, a PhD dissertation, Computing Department, Lancaster University, UK, 1993.
2. L. Ehley, B. Furth and M. Ilyas, *Evaluation of multimedia synchronization techniques*, in the Proceedings of International Conference on Multimedia Computing and Systems, Boston, USA, May 1994, pp514-519.

3. S. R. Ellis, *Representation in Pictorial and Virtual Environments*, in "Pictorial communication in virtual and real environments", London: Taylor and Francis, ISBN 0-74840-008-7, 1991.

4. D. Ferrari, *Design and application of a delay jitter control scheme for packet-switching internetworking*, Proc. Forth International Workshop on NOSSDAV, Springer-Verlag, Heidelberg, Germany, November 1991, pp72-83.

5. ISO, *Quality of service framework - and work draft*, ISO/IEC JTC1/SC21 N7993, 1993.

6. T. L. Kunii, *Computing as Creative Science* (in Japanese), bit, Vol.22, No.5, Kyoritsu Shuppan Co. Ltd. ,May 1990, Tokyo.

7. T. L. Kunii and Y. Shinagawa, *Visualization Modeling: Making Visualization a Creative Discipline*, in "New Trends in Animation and Visualization", edited by N. M. Thalmann and D. Thalmann, pp117-133, 1991.

8. G. E. Legge, *Efficiency of graphical perception*, in "Pictural communication in virtual and real environments", London: Taylor and Francis, ISBN 0-74840-008-7, 1991.

9. T. D. C. Little and A. Ghafoor, *Interval-based conceptual models for time-dependent multimedia data*, IEEE Trans. on Knowledge and Data Eng., vol.5, no.4, August 1993, pp551-563.

10. C. Nicolaou, *An architecture for real-time multimedia communication systems*, IEEE JSAC, vol.8, no.3, April 1990.

11. S. Ramanathan and P. V. Rangan, *Feedback Techniques for intra-media continuity and inter-media synchronization in distributed multimedia systems*, Computer Journal, vol.36, no.1, 1993, pp4-18.

12. K. Ravindran and V. Bansal, *Delay compensation protocols for synchronization of multimedia data streams*, IEEE Trans. on Knowledge and Data Eng., vol.5, no.4, August 1993, pp574-589.

13. C. E. Shannon, *Coding theorems for discrete source with a fidelity criterion*, IRE Nat. Conv. Rec. part 4, 1959, pp142-163.

14. D. Shepherd and M. Salmony, *Extending OSI to support synchronization required by multimedia application*, Computer Communications, vol.13, no.7, September 1990.

15. D. Shepherd, D. Hutchinson, F. Garcia and G. Coulson, *Protocol support for distributed multimedia applications*, Computer Communications,vol.15, no.6, July/August 1992.

16. T. B. Sheridan, *Musings on Telepresence and Virtual Presence*, Presence, 1(1), pp120-125, 1992.

17. R. Steinmetz, *Synchronization properties in multimedia systems*, IEEE JSAC, vol.8, no.3, April, 1990, pp.401-412.

Chapter 6

Networked Multimedia

Performance Comparison of a New Traffic Shaper and Leaky Bucket for Bursty Real-Time Traffic

S. Radhakrishnan   S. V. Raghavan*

Department of Computer Science & Engineering,

Indian Institute of Technology, Madras 600 036, India

Email:radha,svr@iitm.ernet.in

Ashok K. Agrawala

Department of Computer Science,

University of Maryland,

College Park, MD, USA

Email:agrawala@cs.umd.edu

Abstract

The need to provide Quality of Service (QoS) guarantees for multimedia applications in current day networks calls for effective congestion control schemes. Admission control and traffic shaping are two such schemes to prevent losses and delays in intermediate switching nodes. The stress in this paper is on traffic shaping. Of the many traffic shapers hitherto proposed [20], the Leaky Bucket (LB) is the most popular traffic enforcement scheme currently in vogue. Much of the research on auxiliary schemes like scheduling and admission control have been based on LB-shaped traffic.

This paper attempts a second look at the LB policing. LB, in its attempt to enforce smoothness often introduces excessive access delays thereby making it incapable of regulating real-time traffic. We argue for a policy which permits more short term burstiness than what is permitted by the LB. The need for peak rate control has also been recently addressed. LB being an average rate policer, peak rate control is performed using a separate stage.

We present a shaping policy which permits short term burstiness, bounds the maximum burst size and long term behavior, and is inherently peak rate controlled. The resultant advantage, in terms of violation probability and access delay is demonstrated through simulation.

---

*Further correspondence may be addressed to Professor S. V. Raghavan

1   Introduction

Supporting distributed multimedia on high speed networks is a challenging task due to the heterogeneity of the multimedia sources and their diverse QoS requirements. Effective congestion control schemes like admission control at the time of connection request, traffic control at the entry points and multiclass scheduling at the intermediate switches, need to work in unison to guarantee the service requirements. Some of the admission control, resource reservation and scheduling schemes proposed for integrated broadband networks in the recent past and the related issues are surveyed in [19]. The role of admission control is straightforward. A new connection should be admitted only if the network can support the QoS of the new connection without affecting the guarantees provided to the existing connections; else the request is rejected. A precise determination of the admission control function may be highly computing-intensive [12]. Many heuristic algorithms based on simple tests have been proposed for the admission control problem [9, 14]. Each admission control algorithm expects that the user abides by the negotiated parameters. To ensure this, traffic policing is mandatory at each user-network access point. Control parameters of the policer will be set by the network service provider based on the characteristics and the service requirements of the source. Several ways of characterizing the source traffic have been proposed [9, 10, 13].

In general data, voice and video streams may need different characteristic parameters to specify their behavior. In this paper, however, we assume the source to be bursty and characterized by the ON-OFF bursty model [2, 7, 22]. The traffic control parameters have to be derived from these as well as the type of guarantees requested (delay/loss, deterministic/statistical etc.). Traffic policers proposed in the literature include mainly Leaky Bucket (LB), Jumping Window (JW), Moving Window (MW), Exponential Weighted Moving Average (EWMA) and associated variations. A performance comparison among these schemes from the point of view of violation probability, sensitivity to overloads, dynamic reaction time and worst case traffic admitted into the network can be found in [20]. It has been shown that the LB and the EWMA are the most promising mechanisms to cope with short-term fluctuations and hence suited for policing bursty traffic. Several improvements of the LB has been proposed for increasing utilization in an ATM environment [3, 8, 21]. Of late, research on many auxiliary congestion control schemes like admission control, scheduling etc. have assumed the traffic injected into the network to be LB-policed [5, 6, 4, 16, 17]. Due to these reasons, LB can be considered as the de facto policer for studying and comparing the performance of new schemes.

This paper attempts a second look at the LB policing. LB, in its attempt to enforce smoothness often introduces excessive access delays thereby making it incapable of regulating real-time traffic [18]. We argue for a policy which permits more short term burstiness than what is permitted by the LB. The need for peak rate control has also been recently addressed. LB being an average rate policer, peak rate control is performed using a separate stage.

We present a window based shaping policy which captures the advantage of the LB scheme, permits short term burstiness in a more flexible manner and is inherently peak rate controlled. The new scheme reduces the access delay while providing LB-bounds. The scheme which uses a shift register (and hence referred to as SRTS:Shift Register Traffic Shaper) for remembering the temporal profile of the past is compared with an equivalent LB scheme through simulation. The rest of the paper is organized as follows..

Section 2 presents a general model for traffic shaping. The output of the LB with a Peak rate policer(LBP) is characterized. The relationship between policing, bandwidth allocation and performance parameters is brought out in Section 3. Section 4 presents the SRTS scheme and provides the framework for comparing the performance between SRTS and the LBP. The simulation experiments, results and inferences are presented in Section 5. Section 6 concludes the paper.

2   General Model for Traffic Shaping

A general framework for studying the performance of a traffic shaper is presented in this section. Source is characterized by a peak rate λ_p, an average rate λ_a and mean ON duration T_{ON}. We assume that the network access link at the output of the traffic shaper has a capacity equal to the peak rate of the source stream. Thus any burst arrival is serviced fastest at the peak rate. A traffic shaper which closely fits the model above is the Leaky Bucket with a Peak rate Policer(LBP). In the following sections, we first describe the characteristics of a LBP and then state how possible modifications of the characteristics motivated the development of our scheme.

2.1   *Leaky Bucket scheme*

Leaky Bucket [23] and its variant schemes are described in [21, 8, 3, 20]. In a generalized model of the leaky bucket shown in Figure 1, tokens are generated at a fixed rate as long as the token buffer of size b is not full.

When a packet arrives from the source, it is released into the network only if there is at least one token in the token buffer. This scheme enforces the token arrival rate λ_t on the input stream. Clearly, λ_t should be greater than the average arrival rate λ_a for stability/controlling losses and less than the peak arrival rate λ_p for achieving bandwidth utilization. An input data buffer of size "d" permits statistical variations. An arriving packet finding the input buffer full is said to be a violating packet and can be dropped or tagged for a preferential treatment at the switching nodes.

In this paper, we assume that a peak-rate limiting spacer is an integral part of the leaky bucket mechanism. When a burst of data arrives at the input, even if enough tokens are present, the packets are not instantaneously released into the network. Instead successive packets are delayed by τ, the transmission time at peak rate λ_p,

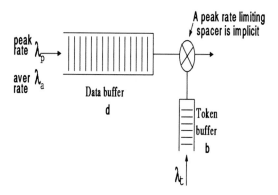

Figure 1: Leaky Bucket with Peak Rate Policer(LBP)

where $\tau = 1/\lambda_p$.

The output of the leaky bucket is characterized as follows:

1. **maximum burst size**: For the LBP, maximum burst size at the output is $b' = b/(1 - \lambda_t/\lambda_p)$, obtained as follows. If we assume the largest burst starts at t_1, the token buffer should be full at t_1. This would be possible only if the source generated an input burst after a prolonged OFF period of b/λ_t, where b is the token buffer size. Since the burst service is not instantaneous due to peak rate policer, more tokens may arrive during the consumption of the existing tokens. Since tokens are removed at λ_p and arrive at λ_t, the instantaneous token count in TB will be $b(t) = b + (\lambda_t - \lambda_p) \cdot t$ and hence TB empties at time $b/(\lambda_p - \lambda_t)$. The maximum burst size b' hence becomes $b/(1 - \lambda_t/\lambda_p)$.

2. **long term output smoothness**: over a large time duration T, no: of packets sent out by the leaky bucket,
   N(T) is $\leq \lambda_t \cdot T = n_t$.

   This relationship is also true for any time duration *T′ starting from zero*, if the token buffer is assumed to be empty at $t = 0$.

3. **short term burstiness**: Over durations smaller than T mentioned in the previous item and exceeding the burst size, leaky bucket output can be modeled as a Linear Bounded Arrival Process(LBAP) with parameters (σ, ρ) [5]. Here, σ represents the maximum burst size b' and ρ represents the token rate λ_t.

3 Shaping and BW Allocation

The bandwidth that needs to be allocated to the shaped stream depends on the shaper parameters. For instance, a LB produces a stream which requires, at a minimum, bandwidth equal to the token arrival rate, to be allocated at the access multiplexer. A larger token arrival rate reduces the access delay at the policer but needs a larger bandwidth allocation. For a source characterized by a peak rate λ_p and burstiness r(defined as peak rate to average rate ratio), bandwidth allocation λ_{bw} is such that $\lambda_p/r \leq \lambda_t \leq \lambda_{bw} \leq \lambda_p$. At the access multiplexer, the capacity of the output link $\lambda_o = \sum_{i=1}^{m} \lambda_{bw}(i)$ for m streams multiplexed to the same output. Since most multimedia traffic is bursty in nature, a large statistical multiplexing gain is possible only if λ_t is near the average arrival rate $\lambda_a = \lambda_p/r$. On the other hand, smaller the λ_t, larger the access delay and/or violation probability incurred by the source. A lenient enforcement policy can increase the delay at the multiplexing/switching nodes due to buffer overflows. Thus there is a trade off between the access delay introduced by the policer and the network delay at the switches. From the end user's point of view, the delay incurred by the application includes the access delay and the network delay.

For a constant bandwidth allocation, the effect of input rate control can be summarized by the following observations [18, 15].

1. The total delay experienced by a cell is the sum of the access delay due to queuing at the shaper and the network delay at the switch. The policer simply transfers the network delay on to the input side thereby avoiding overflow losses/delays within the network. Thus unless the source has a large buffer and can tolerate excess delay, the input rate control as performed by the LB can hardly improve the network performance [18]. For many real time applications, this access delay could be prohibitive.

2. A stringent input rate control may unnecessarily increase the user end-to-end delay by a significant amount [18].

3. The minimum total delay average delay is achieved when no traffic enforcement is invoked [15, 18]. This observation is applicable when the network bandwidth is considerably greater than the source transmission rate, in which case the effect of individual streams is smoothed by statistical multiplexing. Nevertheless, to check excessive burstiness and prolonged rate violations, input policer is practically needed.

It is evident from the aforementioned points that the access delay introduced by the traffic policer can be significant. One way of reducing the access delay would be to permit more short term burstiness subject to:

- the maximum burst size should be bounded and burst arrivals must be peak rate enforced.

- the number of arrivals over a larger time durations can be bounded at the average policing rate.

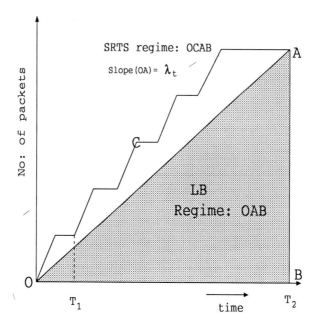

Figure 2: Permitted no: of packets vs time

The short term burstiness permitted by the LB is decided by the size of the token buffer b. As explained earlier, over any time duration T starting from 0 (or any epoch when the token buffer becomes empty), the number of packets admitted into the network are bounded by $\lambda_t * T$. With reference to Figure 2 which shows the number of admitted packets versus time, the operating region for LB operation is below the line OA corresponding to the average policing rate. A source is permitted to send a burst only if it remains inactive for a sufficient amount of time to gather enough number of tokens in the token buffer. Thus the operating point is always below the line OA. A well behaved source transmitting uniformly at the token arrival rate will operate along OA.

We describe in the next section a traffic shaper which has the following features:

1. permits short term burstiness but bounds long term behavior so that the number of packets admitted over a long time is same as that admitted by an equivalent leaky bucket.

2. it is inherently peak rate enforced.

3. it is a window based shaper consisting of two windows and the shaper behavior can be more flexibly set unlike the EWMA which has only one control parameter γ.

4. it is designed using a shift register and two counters and hence can easily be implemented in hardware.

4 Shift Register Traffic Shaper (SRTS)

4.1 *Introduction*

In Figure 2, the operating region of the LB was depicted. Previous section described how LB introduces access delays which can become prohibitive for real-time applications. With an aim to reduce the access delays, what we need is a traffic shaper which performs like the LB over longer durations, but allows short-term burstiness in a more liberal sense than is permitted by the LB. With reference to Figure 2, we attempt to operate above line OA over short durations while confining to the LB bound over a large interval (say OB). As mentioned in the previous section, OA is the upper boundary for LB operation. A typical upper boundary for the proposed shaper can be the piecewise linear line OCA. Thus by virtue of its short term operation above line OA, short term burstiness is more flexibly permitted by the proposed shaper. In the case of LB, a stream has to gather enough number of tokens by remaining inactive before it can afford to drive in a burst of data. On the contrary, a larger operating region of SRTS permits the source to have short term overdrafts as long as it confines within the operating region. A simple implementation of the scheme using 2 windows is outlined in the following section.

4.2 *SRTS Description*

The Shift Register Traffic Shaper (SRTS) makes use of the temporal profile [1] of the packet stream admitted by the shaper over the immediate past N time slots, where a time slot τ refers to the reciprocal of the peak rate. This temporal history can be maintained by a shift register with 1 bit corresponding to every packet sent. The shift register is shifted right every time slot τ. The entry of the bits into the shift register is decided as follows;

Let $f_d = 1$ if data buffer is not empty and 0 otherwise;
Also $n(T_i)$ denotes the number of packets within any time window of duration T_i. Similarly, let f_a denote the admit control function defined as
$f_a = (n(T_1) < n_1)$ and $(n(T_2) < n_2)$ and $(n(T_3) < n_3) \cdots$ depending on the number of windows, where n_1, n_2, n_3 etc denote the maximum number permitted within the respective window.

The data bit shifted in is 1 if $f_d = 1; f_a = 1$
$\qquad\qquad\qquad 0 \quad$ otherwise

Thus the bit contents of the shift register at any instant, provides an image of the history of the packets sent. All the time durations mentioned with reference to the

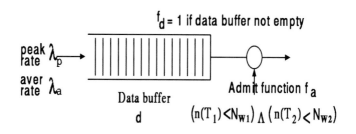

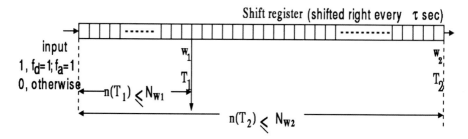

Figure 3: Shift Register Traffic Shaper(SRTS)

shift register start from the time point corresponding to the entry point of the shift register. To determine the number of packets in any time duration, a counter is used. It increments whenever a '1' enters the shift register and decrements when a '1' shifts out of the right edge of the corresponding window monitored by the counter.

Figure 3 describes an enforcement scheme using two windows. This scheme generates an $(n_1, T_1; n_2, T_2)$ smooth traffic, which means that over any period of duration T_1,
the number of packets $n(T_1) \leq n_1$
and over any period of duration T_2,
the number of packets $n(T_2) \leq n_2$.

Though we have described the scheme with two windows, further flexibility in moulding the burstiness is possible using the appropriate number of windows. Since the restriction on the number of packets permitted in a time window is enforced at the entry point of the shift register and the window shifts to the right every τ seconds, the smoothness is guaranteed over *any time window over the entire duration of the connection*.

One limitation that arises in the above arrangement is due to the discretization of time into slots of τ. A slot is termed active if a cell is transmitted during that slot and idle, otherwise. Since the cell arrival instant need not synchronize with the

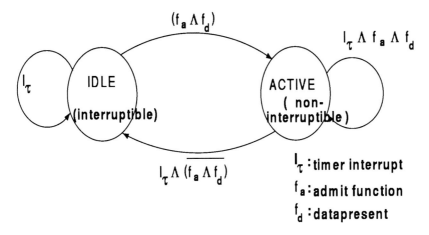

Figure 4: FSM describing the transitions between idle and active states

output slots, a cell arriving during an idle slot will have to wait till the end of that slot for transmission. *This limitation is removed* in our current scheme by using "soft" discretization. If a cell arrives during an idle slot, say after τ' elapses (out of τ), idle slot is frozen and an active slot is initiated immediately. At the termination of this active slot, if either data is absent or the admit function is false, the residual idle slot of duration $(\tau - \tau')$ commences. The end of a slot is indicated by the timer interrupt in Figure 4. The shift register is shifted right at the end of every slot, active or passive. The essence of the above arrangement is that an idle slot is interruptible whereas an active slot is not. Every time an idle slot is interrupted, the residual idle time is saved for future use up.

The modification described above is illustrated as an FSM in Figure 4.

The key features are:

- Idle to Active state transition is fired by the event $(f_a \wedge f_d)$ where f_a: admit function and f_d : data present flag.
  The following actions ensue:

  1. save residual time by freezing the counter.
  2. initiate transmission and go to active state.
  3. every slot timer interrupt in idle state will cause transition to itself after resetting the counter.

- Active to Idle state transition is fired by the timer interrupt.

  1. if $((f_a \wedge f_d) = 1$, initiate another active slot.
  2. else initiate an idle slot and go to idle state.

4.3 Choice of Windows

For comparing the performance of SRTS with the LBP scheme, the parameters of the two schemes have to be chosen to establish a functional equivalence. In this paper, we use a SRTS with two windows. Thus the shaping parameters are the window sizes W_1, W_2 and the maximum number of packets permitted in each window N_{W1}, N_{W2}. The window parameters can be derived from the key observations made earlier regarding the LBP scheme.

The maximum burst size b' for the LBP is $b' = b/(1 - \lambda_t/\lambda_p)$. If we observe the number of packets within a window of size W(say), the maximum number of packets allowed N_W within W is:

$$\text{for } W \leq b, N_W = W; \qquad (a)$$
$$\text{for } W > b, N_W = b' + \lambda_t \cdot (W - b) \cdot \tau; \qquad (b)$$
$$\text{for } W \gg b, N_W \cong W \cdot \tau \lambda_t; \qquad (c)$$

The values assumed for the LBP in the current simulation are $b = 18$; $\lambda_p = 100$ and $\lambda_t = 40$. Then max burst size $b' = b/(1 - \lambda_t/\lambda_p) = 30$. The first window W_1 is chosen as 50 to satisfy (b). Thus to admit more short term burstiness than what is permitted by the LBP, $N_{W1} should be \geq 30 + 20 \cdot 40/100 = 38$. For the LBP, the distribution of these packets within W_1 should be subject to operation within the shaded region in Figure 2. Whereas, for the SRTS, they can be more flexibly distributed since the SRTS operating regime is bigger than that of LBP. Window-2 parameters can enforce the average policing characteristics exhibited by the LBP over large time durations. Hence the window size, in this case, follows (c). Consequently, the number of packets policed over a time duration $T_2(= W_2 \cdot \tau)$ for the LBP and the SRTS are identical. For the current study, we have chosen $W_2 = 500$ and $N_{W2} = 500 \cdot \tau \lambda_t = 200$.

The exact choice of W_1 and W_2 is currently arbitrary and can be tailored to suit the application stream. The only criteria is that over W_1, we assume the "equivalent" LBP to generate a LBAP stream whereas over the larger window W_3, an averaging property is expected.

5 Performance Study: SRTS and LBP

Performance of the SRTS and its "equivalent" LBP is studied in this section . We use an ON-OFF bursty model for the source. The ON-OFF bursty model can be justifiably used in modeling many of the sources, currently of interest in multimedia networks. For example, voice sources using talkspurt and video sources after compression and coding, generate bursty streams. Since voice and video sources are *basically* of the CBR type, cell generation during ON period is periodic in nature. To model a generalized data source, as in the case of a large data file transfer application, the ON-OFF model can be modified to make the ON period intercell times exponentially distributed. This assumption will result in an Interrupted Poisson Process(IPP). Further generalizations will lead to 2-state and n-state Markov

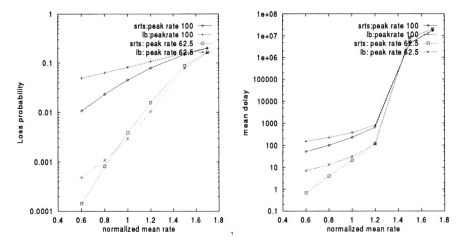

Figure 5: Loss and delay characteristics vs normalized mean rate

Modulated Poisson Process(MMPP) models [11] The two performance parameters studied through simulation are

1. Violation probability for a finite data buffer case

2. Access delay for an infinite buffer case

5.1 Simulation Experiments

Two simulation experiments are performed. The bursty source is characterized by average ON, average OFF time and the interarrival time of packets during the ON period. The ON and OFF times are exponentially distributed and the arrival of packets during the ON period is periodic at the peak rate λ_p. The interpacket arrival time $\tau_p \doteq 1/\lambda_p$. This model is derived from the voice model for which the ON and OFF times are exponential with mean 352msec and 650 msec and the peak rate τ_p is 16msec. Since we intend to vary the burstiness of the source, the mean ON time is kept 200msec. The OFF times and τ_p are appropriately adjusted to obtain the required mean rate.

SRTS is a peak as well as a mean rate policer. The two experiments study each of these characteristics. In both cases, we assume an overdimensioning factor $C = 1.5$ relating the policed rate and the mean rate of the source (as in [20]). The peak enforced rate is 100 and hence the minimum delay between consecutive packets at the output of the shaper τ is 10 ms.

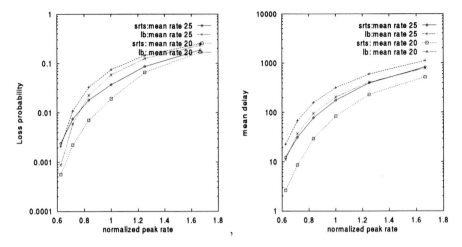

Figure 6: Loss and delay characteristics vs normalized peak rate

Experiment 1 In this experiment, we study the loss and delay characteristics for different source mean rates. The mean rate variation is achieved by varying the OFF time keeping mean ON time = 200 and mean policed rate, $\lambda_t = 40$. With the overdimensioning factor of 1.5, the negotiated mean rate = 26.67
The OFF time is varied as follows; $\lambda_p/(1 + \frac{(T_{OFF})}{(200)}) \leq 26.67$. Thus $T_{OFF} > 550$ for a well behaved source. X axis shows the normalized mean rate. For the first part which estimates the violation probability, a data buffer of 20 is assumed. In a practical case, the size can be based on the maximum access delay that can be tolerated by a particular application. For the second part of the experiment which studies the access delay, size of the data buffer is kept very large to keep losses close to zero. The experiment is performed for two values of the peak rate, $100(\tau_p = 10)$ and $62.5(\tau_p = 16)$. The results are shown in Figure 5.

The number of simulation runs are such that the results are accurate to within 5% with 95% confidence level.

Experiment 2 In this experiment, we study the loss and delay characteristics for different source peak rates. Thus we compare the peak rate enforcement provided by the SRTS and the LBP. For each run, the peak rate and the OFF duration are adjusted to keep the mean rate constant. X axis plots the normalized peak rates. The experiment is repeated for two values of the mean rate, 25 and 20. Both these values are within the negotiated rate of 26.67. Other parameters are as in the previous experiment. The results are shown in Figure 6.

5.2   *Observations & Inference*

Results of the simulation and inferences drawn, thereof, are as follows.

With reference to Figure 5, for an input stream with peak rate 100 (corresponding to the peak rate limit built in the shaper, SRTS has much lesser loss probability for mean rates up to the policed rate (1.5 * source mean). Beyond this, both the curves converge quickly. At the lower peak rate of 62.5, SRTS exhibits a steeper gradient than the LBP. The flexible admission of short term burstiness results in a lower access delay for the SRTS. This fact is evident from Figure 5. For well behaved sources with mean rate below the negotiated value, lower the mean rate, better the performance of the SRTS. At 0.6 times the mean rate, the access delay introduced by the SRTS is one order less than that introduced by the equivalent LBP.

Figure 6 depict the response of the shapers to peak rate violation. For the loss curves, violation is more gradual than in the mean rate case. For our simulation which assumed a data buffer of size 20, SRTS yields lower values of violation probability than the LBP for traffic conforming to the negotiated rate. This is due to the more liberal admission policy for burstiness existing over short durations. The access delay curves for the two shapers are almost parallel to each other. as in the previous case, SRTS shaped streams have a consistently smaller access delay compared to the LBP case.

The advantages of the SRTS policy in terms of lower violation probability and access delay for traffic *within the negotiated rates* is due to the the larger operating regime shown in Figure 2. This is due to the more liberal admission policy compared to that provided by the LB.

The above advantage of the SRTS however comes at a cost. The SRTS output is burstier than its LB counterpart. This would necessitate a more careful buffering and scheduling design at the switches to prevent congestion at the intermediate nodes. Since the network link transmission rate is generally much higher than the maximum source transmission rate, we expect that the fluctuations at the SRTS output will be effectively smoothed by the statistical multiplexing effect. Since the maximum burst size is limited and the long term behavior is bounded, the buffers and the schedulers can be dimensioned appropriately at the switches to provide the required degree of loss and delay guarantees.

From the point of view of minimizing congestion within the network, the policy adopted by the LB is quite effective. LB reduces the delays within the network by transferring them on to the input side. However, the stringent enforcement increases the access delay and hence raises questions regarding the suitability of LB for real time traffic. We show through this study that as an enforcement policy for real-time traffic, the access delays can be reduced by adopting a more liberal attitude over shorter durations while maintaining the LB bounds over larger durations. For the same bandwidth allocation at the switches, such a policy is shown to perform better for real time source traffic.

6 Conclusion

This paper studies the loss and delay performance of a new traffic shaper SRTS and compares with that of a Leaky bucket using a peak rate policer. LB is a stringent policer which enforces the mean rate of the source traffic. SRTS while enforcing the same mean rate as that of LB over larger durations permits more short term burstiness. This is done with an intention to reduce the violation probability and the access delay for traffic conforming to the negotiated values. The performance results substantiate our views. The advantage of the SRTS scheme, however, comes at a cost. The higher burstiness allowed into the network would oblige a judicious approach to buffer and bandwidth management at the intermediate nodes. We expect that adopting a more liberal attitude over short durations would result in a lower overall end to end delay compared to the rather stringent LB approach. With that advantage, this approach would be more suitable for shaping real-time traffic. A composite study involving the shaper and the scheduler is necessary to validate our assumptions. Such a study will constitute our future research.

7 References

[1] Ashok K. Agrawala. Temporal Profile Capture, 1994. Personal Communication.

[2] Jaime Jungok Bae and Tatsuya Suda. Survey of Traffic Control Schemes and Protocols in ATM Networks. *Proceedings of the IEEE*, 79(2):170 – 189, February 1991.

[3] Krishna Bala, Israel Cidon, and K.Sohraby. Congestion Control for High Speed Packet Switched Networks. In *IEEE INFOCOM*, pages 520–526, 1990.

[4] David Clark, Scott Shenker, and Lixia Zhang. Supporting Real-Time Applications in an Integrated Services Packet Network: Architecture and Mechanism. In *Proceedings of ACM SIG-COMM'92*, pages 14–26, Baltimore, Maryland, August 1992.

[5] R. L. Cruz. A Calculus for Network Delay, Part I: Network Elements in Isolation. *IEEE Transactions on Information Theory*, 37(1):114–131, January 1991.

[6] R. L. Cruz. A Calculus for Network Delay, Part II: Network Analysis. *IEEE Transactions on Information Theory*, 37(1):132–141, January 1991.

[7] Don Towsley David Yates, James Kurose and Michael G. Hluchyj. On per-session end-to-end delay distributions and the call admission problem for real-time applications with QoS requirements. In *Proceedings of ACM SIGCOMM'93*, pages 2–12, Ithaca,N.Y, USA, September 1993.

[8] A.E. Eckberg, D.T. Luan, and D.M. Lucantoni. Bandwidth Management: A Congestion Control Strategy for Broadband Packet Networks-Characterizing the Throughput-burstiness Filter. *Computer Networks and ISDN systems*, 20:415–423, 1990.

[9] Domenico Ferrari and Dinesh C. Verma. A Scheme for Real-Time Channel Establishment in Wide-Area Networks. *IEEE Journal on Selected Areas in Communications*, 8(3):368–379, April 1990.

[10] R. Guerin, H. Ahmadi, and M. Naghshineh. Equivalent Capacity and its Application to Bandwidth Allocation in High Speed Networks. *IEEE Journal on Selected Areas in Communications*, 9(7):968–981, September 1991.

[11] H. Heffes and D. M. Lucantoni. A Markov Modulated Characterization of Packetized Voice and Data Traffic and Related Statistical Multiplexer Performance. *IEEE Journal on Selected Areas in Communications*, 4(6):856–868, September 1986.

[12] Jay Hyman, Aurel A. Lazar, and Giovanni Pacifici. Joint Scheduling and Admission Control for ATS-based Switching Nodes. In *Proceedings of ACM SIGCOMM'92*, Baltimore, Maryland, August 1992.

[13] CCITT Recommendation I.311. B-ISDN General Network Aspects, May 1990.

[14] Sugih Jamin, Scott Shenker, Lixia Zhang, and D. D. Clark. An Admission Control Algorithm for Predictive Real-Time Service(Extended Abstract). In *Proceedings of Third International Workshop on Network and Operating System Support for Digital Audio & Video*, pages 349–356. Springer-Verlag, November 1992.

[15] Masayuki Murata, Yoshihiro Ohba, and Hideo Miyahara. Analysis of Flow Enforcement Algorithm for Bursty Traffic in ATM Networks. In *Proceedings of IEEE INFOCOM'92*, pages 2453–2462, Firenze, Italy, May 1992.

[16] A. K. Parekh and R. G. Gallager. A Generalized Processor Sharing Approach to Flow Control in Integrated Services Networks: The Single Node Case. In *Proceedings of IEEE INFOCOM'92*, Firenze, Italy, May 1992.

[17] A. K. Parekh and R. G. Gallager. A Generalized Processor Sharing Approach to Flow Control in Integrated Services Networks: The Multiple Node Case. In *Proceedings of IEEE INFOCOM'93*, pages 521–530, San Francisco, California, March 1993.

[18] San qi Li and Song Chong. Fundamental Limits of Input Rate Control in High Speed Network. In *Proceedings of IEEE INFOCOM'93*, pages 662–671, San Francisco, California, March 1993.

[19] S. Radhakrishnan and S. V. Raghavan. Network Support for Distributed Multimedia - Issues and Trends. In *Proceedings of SEACOMM'94, International Conference on Communications and Computer Networks*, Kuala Lumpur, Malaysia, October 1994.

[20] Erwin P. Rathgeb. Modelling and Performance Comparison Of Policing Mechanisms for ATM Networks. *IEEE Journal on Selected Areas in Communications*, 9(3):325–334, April 1991.

[21] M. Sidi, W. Liu, I. Cidon, and I. Gopal. Congestion Control through Input Rate Regulation. In *Proceedings of GLOBECOM'89*, pages 1764–1768, Dallas, Texas, November 1989.

[22] G. D. Stamoulis, M . E. Anagnoustou, and A. D. Georgantas. Traffic Source Models for ATM Networks: A Survey. *Computer Communications*, 17(6):428–438, June 1994.

[23] J. S. Turner. New Directions in Communications (or Which way to the Information Age? *IEEE Communications*, 24(10):8–15, October 1986.

A SURVEY OF MULTICAST PROTOCOLS FOR MULTIMEDIA COMMUNICATION

LI Hongyi, PUNG Hung Keng
Dept. of Information Systems and Computer Science
National University of Singapore, Singapore 0511
E-mail: lihy@iscs.nus.sg

and

NGOH Lek Heng
Institute of Systems Science
National University of Singapore, Singapore 0511

ABSTRACT

Multicast is the transmission of information to a specified group of hosts or processes in the network. Supporting multicast communication becomes more and more important in today's multimedia applications such as video conferencing, stock information distribution. This paper surveys the current state of the art multicast techniques by reviewing various important multicast protocols reported in the literature. It identifies and discusses the important issues of multicast communication in respect of multicast routing, group management and guarantee quality of services. These issues are closely related with each other and the existing techniques that deal with these issues are reviewed. The future research areas of multicasting are also suggested in this paper.

I. Introduction

In recent years, considerable research and development effort has focused on the development of high capacity and reliable B-ISDN transfer technology, network architecture and different service models. ATM (Asynchronous Transfer Mode) is often considered as the technology that allows total flexibility and efficiency to be achieved in future's high-speed multi-service multimedia networks[9]. Some important multimedia applications such as high quality video-conferencing, video-on-demand service and tele-shopping are becoming realistic over ATM networks. Sophisticated multicast support from the underlying network protocols is essential for these applications. Therefore, multicast is becoming an active research topic.

Multicast refers to the transmission of messages to a group of hosts or processes in a computer network. An efficient multicast protocol should provide data delivery to group of hosts at a lower network and host overhead than broadcasting to all hosts or unicasting to hosts in that group[21]. According to the nature of data flow, there are three types of multicast services, namely one-way multicast, two-way multicast, and N-way multicast. The one-way multicast service requires point to multipoint routes that start from sender to all the members in the group. In the two-way multicast, a sender sends messages to all the members of the multicast group and may also receive replying messages from the group members. In N-way multicast, any message sent by a member is multicasted to every other member of the same multicast group.

This paper surveys the current state of the art multicast techniques by reviewing various important multicast protocols reported and identifying the key research issues. A multicast protocol for group communication provides a set of multicast primitives that is capable of adapting to different application requirements and guarantees the performance of multicast communication. Functionally, a multicast protocol should at least perform *multicast routing*, *group management*, and *guarantee quality of service*. The multicast routing is to establish the data delivery paths from senders to all the active group members in the network. The multicast group management is an important function that manages the membership status and member joining or member leaving activities. The reliability and ordering issues are considered as the QoS (Quality of Service) guarantee that should be supported by the multicast protocols. Research issues of existing techniques for these three functions are reviewed in this paper.

The structure of this paper is organized as follows: In section II, the important multicast protocols are reviewed. In section III, various multicast routing topologies and implementation algorithms are surveyed. In section IV, various methods for implementing the multicast group management are examined. In section V, different QoS requirements are defined and their implementation methods are examined. Finally, a summary of the paper is given and further research topics are identified.

II. Overview of Existing Multicasting Protocols

Tracing back a decade, the earliest multicast protocol was reported in Cheriton's work of the V system extension which implemented the multicast communication among logical groups of processes[17]. By 90's, several multicast protocols were developed for better supporting of wide-area groupware. Among them, the most distinguished multicast protocol should be attributed to the IP multicast[20] which implemented group communication over the Internet with best effort delivery of data (i.e. the message is delivered zero, one, or more times). In IP multicast, group addresses are assigned by each application. The sender simply transmits packets to that address with routers determining the paths for multicast data delivery. Deering's work has been used as the main driving force behind the formation of the multicast backbone (MBONE) across Internet.

Recently, multicast protocols have received increasing attention by multimedia communication research communities because of the need to support emerging multiparty interactive applications, such as videoconference and video-on-demand. These applications require guarantee of higher level QoS and real-time information delivery[15]. To support these types of applications, Ngoh and Hopkins have identified varieties of QoS's (Quality of Services) that are important for a multicast protocol[40]. In early 90's, many multicast protocols were developed which guarantee certain levels of QoS. These protocols and their features are listed in Table 1. The significance of these multicast protocols are discussed in following paragraphs.

The Protocol Independent Multicast (PIM)[22] is an extension of the IP multicast. It allows the coexistence of two different multicast routing schemes, namely Source Based Tree (SBT) and Core Based Tree (CBT). PIM is the first protocol that allows the selection between dense or sparse mode routing based on the group member distribution in the network. The multicast of Xpress Transfer Protocol (XTP)[45] is similar to IP multicast but goes one step further by supporting limited reliability, called semi-reliable, which is defined as providing high probability of success in delivery of multicast data[27]. It uses a go-back-n approach for error correction. ISIS[12] is one of the pioneer protocol that provides high level QoS such as causal ordering and total ordering of data delivery. It was developed on top of a reliable multicast protocol. The Multicast Transport Protocol (MTP)[6] is based on the multicast master concept which controls all the activities of group communication. It supports total ordering and the flow control by using the master that issues tokens to the senders in the group which allows data to be sent in a specified rate and be received in order. MTP uses negative acknowledgment for error corrections. The Reliable Multicast Protocol (RMP)[5] is a promising multicast protocol that supports a wide range of QoS guarantees from best effort to total ordered data delivery. It is a transport level protocol implemented on top of IP multicast. RMP uses a rotating master approach to guarantee the reliability and ordering. ST-II[46] is one of the pioneer protocols that guarantee; end-to-end bandwidth and delay in multicast communication. It requires bandwidth reservations for all links before setting up and guarantees that the requested bandwidth is available through the lifetime of the link. RSVP[14,51] is a newly developed resource reservation protocol for supporting real-time multicast applications over Internet. It enables a receiver to reserve resources and the reservation is repeated at regular intervals for adapting changes of routes. We observe that the development of multicast protocols evolves from supporting simple service (i.e. best effort) to enhanced high level services that guarantee data reliability, ordering, delay, and end-to-end bandwidth. The idea is to develop reliable multicast protocols on top of a best effort multicast data delivery protocol (e.g., IP multicast) to support higher level of QoS's,

Table 1. Important Multicast Protocols in History

1984-	1990-1995	Future
V system (Cheriton et. al. 1984) - best effort 1988- IP multicast (Deering, et. al. 1988) - best effort - flexible address	PIM (Protocol Independent Multicast, Deering, 1993 - network level protocol, best effort - support two routing topologies (CBT, SBT) - selection of sparse and dense modes XTP (Xpress Transfer Protocol, PEI, 1992) - network & transport level protocol - best effort, semi-reliable - go-back-n error correction ISIS (Birman, et. al. 1991) - transport level protocol on reliable multicast - causal ordering, total ordering - separate acknowledgment from receivers MTP (Multicast Transport Protocol, Armstrong, 1992) - transport level protocol on top of IP multicast. - best effort, reliable, ordering - multicast master control joining / leaving - master issues token for flow control / ordering - NACK for error correction RMP (Reliable Multicast Protocol, Whetten, 1995) - transport level protocol on top of IP multicast - from best effort to total ordering - use a rotate master approach ST-II (Experimental Internet Stream Protocol, Topolcic, 1990) - network level protocol - guarantee end-to-end bandwidth, delay - sender and receiver negotiate for joining	Trend - develop multicast protocols on ATM network. - IP multicast over ATM - ATM specific approaches New topics - guarantee different QoS's, best effort, reliable, ordering, etc. - Support real-time traffic. - support selective transmission of partial streams. - support N-way multicast.

As ATM is becoming the major link layer protocol in the new generation of B-ISDN to support multimedia communication, many researchers have focused on implementing multicast protocols over ATM. The current standard for ATM UNI is a extension to Q.2931, a public network signaling protocol developed by ITU-T. It adds support for point-to-multipoint connection set up which also allows any leaf node to leave such a connection subsequently. The ATM Forum is currently working on new signaling capabilities UNI 4.0. It will add support for leaf-initiated joining to an existing multicast connection. It should be noted that signalling support for such connections does not imply the existence of a suitable mechanism for multipoint-to-multipoint connections[3,33]. Basically, there are two strategies of implementing multicast over ATM - *extension* of existing multicast protocols or development of *new protocols* from the scratch. The *extension* strategy is to implement existing multicast protocols (e.g., IP multicast) over ATM, then all the existing higher level protocols can be used directly. The *new protocol* strategy follows the development path of existing multicast protocols. It starts from implementing best effort multicast specifically for ATM for construction of higher level protocols that guarantee various QoS's. The *extension* strategy is easy to fit in the existing protocol stack while the *new protocols* strategy has more scope in exploring the potential capabilities of ATM technology. Currently, the extension of IP multicast over ATM becomes an active research area. The Internet draft for IP multicast over ATM proposed by Armitage[5] is under intensive discussion by IETF. In his draft, a Multicast Address Resolution Server (MARS) is used to manage the group membership. The protocol supports two types of routing topologies, namely multicast meshes and multicast servers. There are also ATM specific approaches that use the flexibility of ATM virtual channels to construct various multicast routing topologies[18].

In summary, multicast over ATM is a new research area at its infant stage. Some important issues have to be investigated further. The issues include: (i) How to guarantee different levels of QoS; (ii) How to ensure the bandwidth and delay of multicast links which consequently support the selective transmission of multicast data; and (iii) How to support N-way multicast. The last two issues are also the topics that should be investigated for non-ATM based multicast protocols.

III. Multicast Routing

The main objective of multicast communication is to supply various group communication services with required QoS while reducing the cost of data transfer (i.e. minimizing number of data copies are sent for a group). Multicast routing is inherited in some LANs such as the Ethernet that provides efficient broadcast delivery and a large space of multicast addresses[21]. However, two problems have to be solved when implementing multicast over multiple networks: Firstly, an efficient routing mechanism has to be developed; Secondly, the cost of maintaining multicast routing has to be reduced in supporting the scalability of the multicast services. To tackle these issues, several routing topologies and implementation algorithms have been developed. Among them the Source Based Tree (SBT)[1,20,38,42,47] and Core Based Tree (CBT) have received much attention from the researchers[8,22,49]. Recent developments in the Internet multicast have further emphasized the importance of support for both tree types[22]. Other types of multicast routing schemes are also being investigated such as the Steiner tree [29,31,32,49,50]. Another interesting routing topology is the matrix based multicast routing that is used in distributed or parallel systems[25,28,37]. Each of the above mentioned multicast routing schemes has their merits in specific network environments. Therefore, following paragraphs describe briefly the concepts of different routing topologies and the algorithms to implement them, and analyze the pros and cons of these approaches.

3.1. Source Based Tree

The source based tree is a popular multicasting routing topology which uses source as root, receivers as leaves, and routers or switches as intermediate nodes of the tree, as shown in Fig. 1. Multicast data packets are therefore delivered to receivers along the paths from source to receivers. To construct a SBT, several algorithms have been developed. Among them, DVMRP (Distance-Vector Multicast Routing Protocol) and MOSPF (Multicast Open Shortest Path First) have received more attention.

The distance-vector routing has been used in many networks as an unicast routing algorithm[19]. Routers that use the distance-vector routing algorithm maintain a routing table containing an entry for every reachable destination in the network. Each router sends a routing packet periodically out of its incident links. On receiving a routing packet from a neighboring router, the receiving router may update its own table if the neighbor offers a new shorter route to a given destination, or if the neighbor has no longer offered the route that the receiving router used. In this way, the routers can maintain the shortest routes to all network destinations.

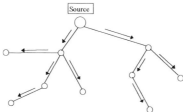

Fig. 1 Source based tree

Two simple multicast routing algorithms, based on the distance-vector routing, are Reverse Path Forwarding (RPF) and Reverse Path Broadcasting (RPB). These algorithms are implemented by broadcasting along the source based shortest-path broadcast tree and rely on the receivers to select the data packets that are destined for them. These algorithms are not efficient for multicasting in large extended networks. DVMRP is a more sophisticated approach which uses a modified RPF algorithm to provide on demand pruning of the shortest-path multicast tree. In DVMRP, the first multicast packet is sent by a broadcast along the shortest broadcast tree to all the links except the non-member leaves. When the package reaches a router for whom all of the child links are leaves and none of them has members in the destination group, a NMR (Non Membership Report) is generated and sent back to the router that is one hop toward the source. If the one-hop-back router receives NMRs from all of its child routers and if its child links have no members, it in-turn sends an NMR back to its predecessors. Eventually, information about the absence of members propagates up the tree along all branches that do not lead to members. In this way, a prune tree is created and subsequent multicast messages are blocked from traveling down the unnecessary branches by the NMRs sitting in the intermediate routers. The DVMRP is used by the MBONE routers[24], the MBONE is the Multicast Backbone, which is a virtual network on top of the Internet providing a multicast facility to the Internet.

Another major algorithm for constructing multicast tree is MOSPF (Multicast Extensions for Open Shortest Path First) based on the link-state routing. In the link-state routine, every router has a identical copy of link state database that is a dynamic map of the Internet, describing the Internet's components and their current interconnection. The synchronization of the databases over different routers is achieved through a flooding mechanism to broadcast Link State Advertisement (LSA) which ensures all routers shortly receive identical copies of new information of link state changes. Consequently, each router can compute the best paths to any destination using Dijkstra's shortest path algorithm. The link-state routing algorithm can easily be extended to support the MOSPF.

MOSPF routers use the IGMP to establish the location of group members and distribute the group location information throughout the network by flooding new type of LSA, namely the group membership LSA. With full information of which groups have members on which links, any router can compute the shortest path multicast tree from any source to any group member using the Dijkstra algorithm. The MOSPF routing calculation is performed in an "on-demand" fashion. The first time a multicast datagram having a given source and destination is received, the MOSPF router calculates a shortest path tree rooted at the packet's source. If the router doing the computation is on the multicast tree, it can determine which links it must use to forward copies of the packets. The results of these on-demand tree are cached for later use by subsequent matching packets.

The algorithms to implement SBT rely on the unicast algorithms which complicates the development of unicast algorithm and limits the flexibility of multicast routing. Another drawback of the SBT is its construction which has a poor scaling property. The DVMRP algorithm requires the routers to store membership information for each source. If the number of active sources is S and G is the multicast groups, it results in a scaling factor of O($S{\times}G$). In the link-state routing, the processing cost of Dijkstra shortest path tree is another major factor preventing the scheme from scaling to large wide-area networks because it requires intensive computing of the shortest path tree for all the active sources in a group. Finally, it is not efficient in the DVMRP that routers, which are not on the multicast delivery tree, still have to process truncated-broadcast packets periodically and perform the pruning of branches for all the active groups.

3.2. Core Based Tree

A Core Based Tree (CBT) uses one router as the core of the tree from which the branches emanate, as shown in Fig. 2. The nodes on the branches are made up of other routers which form the shortest path between a member host's directly attached router and the core router. A router at the end of a branch is called a leaf router in the tree. The major feature of CBT is that only one multicast tree is needed for each group. The cores can be placed in a heuristic way. For instance, the cores could be statistically configured throughout the backbone network[8]. Alternatively, any router could become a core when a host in one of its attached subnetwork wishes to initiate a group. Two distinctive routing phases can be identified in the CBT data delivery. Firstly, an unicast routing is used to route multicast packet to the core of the specified multicast tree. This is achieved by using the unicast address of the core in the destination field of a multicast packet. Secondly, once a multicast packet is on the tree, it is flooded on the tree corresponding to the packet's group identifier.

The major advantage of CBT is the improvement of scalability which has the scale factor of O(G). Furthermore, only routers in the path between the core and the potential group members are involved in the routing process. In comparison with the DVMRP, CBT needs not to broadcast or floods the truncating packets across the whole network. Finally, the construction of a CBT is independent of the unicast routing. The major disadvantage of the CBT tree is the concentration of all the sources' traffic at the core router which may result in network congestion at the core. Hence the CBT is also vulnerable to core failure which can partition the tree. Another problem in the CBT is that the core placement may not lead to the optimal paths between group members.

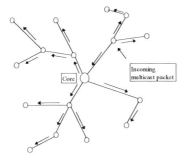

Fig. 2 Core based tree

The previous described multicast routing schemes have their advantages in different network configurations (e.g. DVMRP in regions where a group is widely represented, or CBT in network where bandwidth is universally plentiful). Recently, Deering *et. al.* developed a Protocol Independent Multicast (PIM) that tries to constrain the routing data so that a minimal number of routers in the network can receive it. The PIM is unique in the sense that it supports both types of trees i.e. SBT and CBT. It might be desirable to support both types of the trees such that the selection of tree types becomes a configuration decision within a multicast protocol[22].

3.3. Steiner Tree

Another multicast routing approach treats the routing as a Steiner tree problem[29,31,34,49,50]. The problem can be defined formally as following: For a given undirected network $G = (V, E, c)$ and a subset of vertices $X \in V$, find a tree T such that there is a path between every pair of vertices in X, and the cost of T is a minimum. Where V and E are set of vertices and edges respectively, c is the set of costs. Finding such a tree has been proved as an NP-complete problem[10,49]. Some heuristics can be used in practice for constructing a Steiner tree. Some heuristic algorithms have been shown to give near optimum results with respect to tree cost[29]. However, this routing scheme is not suitable for multicasting in a frequently changed group in which members joining and leaving will change the topology of Steiner tree frequently. Doar concluded that future work should focus on the ability to add and remove connections from a multicast tree and attempt to improve the routes in an incremental way, rather than in constructing monolithic solutions that may only be valid for an unprofitable short duration[23].

3.4. Multicast Routing in ATM Network

Recently, the extension of IP multicast over ATM has received a lot of attention in the Internet community. The draft version for implementing IP multicast over ATM is under intensive discussion by IETF. In IP multicast over ATM, two proposed routing topologies namely multicast mesh and multicast server have been implemented[5]. In the multicast mesh scheme, each sender is the root of a point-to-multipoint VC that has every other host in the group as a leaf; while in the multicast-sever scheme, all senders send their packets directly to a server that is located somewhere in the ATM cloud, which then retransmits copies to all group members. Another solution, an approach independent from IP multicast proposed by Chuang[18], tries to construct SBT and CBT over ATM network. Ammar uses another approach which tries to develop a new type of virtual path in ATM[4], namely the VP with intermediate exits, where a node that performs VP switching can copy switched packets to the local destinations. Based on the new type of VP, a SBT can be established for transmitting multicast packets.

A matrix topology, inspired from the parallel processing[25,28] shows great promise to support the N-way multicast communication in ATM network. The ATM virtual channels, both unicast and multicast, can be used to support 2-D matrix virtual topologies in following ways.

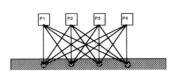

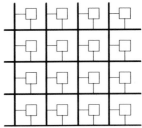

Fig. 3a. Four-way multicast connection   Fig. 3b. 4 x 4 matrix connection

Fig. 3a shows four processes, p1 through p4, are interconnected with a virtual bus by using a four-way complete multicast connection where one VC for each process to be used for sending and three VC channels for receiving. Fig. 3b shows how 16 processes are connected by a matrix of virtual buses. Established multicast connections in such a grid lets each process multicast to all other processes in maximum two-step message passing; first it sends to all the processes on the same row and then all receiving processes send to their respective columns. In such a topology, group members have identical multicast capability to each other that makes the possibility of the N-way multicast over ATM.

The multicast over ATM is still in its infant stage and is a fast evolving research area. Currently, ATM signaling specification[7] supports only point-to-multipoint VC's but does not support multicast address abstraction. A key of the multicast solution may lie on the ATM signaling which supports the group addressing. The merits of various ATM multicast routing approaches have to be evaluated before any concrete conclusion can be drawn.

IV. Multicast Group Management

The group management is an important function of a multicast protocol that manages the membership status and member joining or member leaving activities. There are two basic group management schemes: The distributed group management that allows local routers to manage the group membership in the directly attached subnetworks. While in the other extreme, the centralized group management scheme uses a group agent to coordinate all the group management activities. The distributed group management can be found in the early protocols such as Internet Group Management Protocol (IGMP)[20] and Process Group Management Protocol (PGMP)[41]. As the usage of computer network grows, network security becomes an important issue. The group members are distributed sparsely across a wider area that makes the traditional receiver initiated and broadcast-based multicast membership schemes inefficient. The trend of multicast membership management tends to be more and more centralized as described in several recent works[5,18,22,44,48]. This section examines the different schemes for distributed and centralized multicast group management.

4.1. Distributed Group Management Schemes

The multicast address is assigned as a logical group ID to a collection of users in the IGMP. Senders, without knowing all the receivers, simply use the multicast address as the destination address of the data packets for delivery to all the members of the group. Hosts can join and leave a multicast group in a transparent manner. They perform the joining and leaving action by notifying the attached routers, which in turn uses this information to prune or add branches to the multicast tree. The Internet Group Management Protocol (IGMP) is used by the routers to learn the membership of various groups in their directly attached subnetwork.

In the IP multicast, group management involves hosts issuing IGMP report messages either when these hosts perform a *JoinLocalGroup* or in response to an router's IGMP query. By periodically transmitting queries, IP multicast routers are able to identify which IP multicast groups have non-zero membership on a given subnetwork. All IP multicast hosts must issue *JoinLocalGroup* for the address during their initialization. Each host keeps a list of IP multicast groups it has joined. When a router issues a IGMP query on the address, each host begins to send IGMP reports for each group it belongs to. IGMP reports are sent to the group address so that other members of the same group on the same network can overhear the report. IP multicast routers conclude that a group has no members on the subnetwork when IGMP query no longer triggers associated replies.

Group management in CBT is a receiver initiated scheme in which the router uses acknowledgment for a joining host to establish a path from the joining host to the core. In CBT, whenever a router receives a "group membership report" from a host in the directly attached subnetwork, it will proceed the membership request by sending a *Join_Request* toward the core. This *Join_Request* is then repeated to the next-hop router on the path toward the core of the specified group. The Join-Request traverses until it reaches either a core or a router that is already part of the tree as identified by the group-ID. The *Join_Request* is normally acknowledged by a *Join_Ack*. All the intermediate routers traversed by the *Join_Ack* change their state to CBT-non-core routers for the group identified by the group-ID. It is the *Join_Ack's* that actually creating the span tree branches. Each router records its parent and child interface with respect to a particular tree. The parent interface in each CBT tree is where the *Join_Ack* was received while the child interface is the one over which a *Join_Ack* has been forwarded with respect to a particular group.

The distributed group management schemes shows a greater flexibility in managing the group membership. In IGMP for instance, it facilitates the implementation of a flexible multicast addressing scheme that allows any host to send to a group without knowing all the receivers. But it makes the security checking of group members more difficult to implement. The routers of the individual subnetwork can decide whether to grant a host's joining-request for a group even when the sender does not wish to. Furthermore, IGMP has no address allocation mechanism where addresses are assigned either by an outside authority or by each application. This may lead to address contention among multiple applications.

4.2. Centralized Multicast Group Management for ATM

The centralized membership management schemes have been widely adapted by many multicast protocols, such as in the Deering's PIM system[22], where the *Rendezvous Points* (RP's) are used for senders to announce their existence and by receivers to learn about new senders of a group. Recently, many researchers also work on implementing multicast protocols on ATM based networks[5,18,48]. Several typical centralized membership management schemes for ATM network are discussed in the following paragraphs.

In ATM, since the sender must have prior knowledge of each intended receiver and explicitly establish a VC with itself as the root node and the receivers as leaf nodes, centralized group management becomes more pragmatic. Armitage has described a protocol that supports IP multicast over ATM[5]. In his approach, a Multicast Address Resolution Server (MARS) acts as a registry of multicast group membership. The host address resolution entities query the MARS when a multicast group address needs to be resolved. It provides asynchronous notification of group membership changes by operating a point-to-multipoint VC to all the hosts that require multicast support. After receiving membership information from MARS, the sender can establish a point-to-multipoint VC to all the members of the group or use the multicast servers to distribute multicast packets to group members. The MARS may reside within any ATM host that is directly accessible by the hosts it is serving. It keeps an extended table of (Multicast address; ATM.1, ATM.2, ..., ATM.n) mappings. When a source has packets for transmission, and there is no outgoing VC established for the packets, the MARS is queried for the set of hosts currently constituting the group. The MARS will return the address ATM.1, ATM.2, ..., ATM.n to the source. Then, a point-to-multipoint VC can be established by the sender. Two messages *Mars_Join* and *Mars_Leave* are used to manage the host join and leave actions. The *Mars_Join* carries a multicast group address and the unicast address of itself. When *Mars_Join* is received by the MARS, it adds the specified ATM address to the table entry for the specified multicast group. The *Mars_Leave* message is processed by removing the specified ATM address from the table for a specified group. The *Mars_Join* and *Mars_Leave* messages are retransmitted to all the members of the group to ensure the membership changes are distributed timely.

Another similar centralized group management scheme for ATM can be found in Chuang's system which uses a hierarchical centralized group management architecture[18]. In the highest level, a directory system enables the groups to be registered. An entry in the directory system provides a convenient means to identify the multicast services and to locate the second level group management entity namely the Multicast Coordination Center (MCC). The MCC is an enforcer of group policies and manages the group access control.

Centralized group management has two important weak points that have to be solved. Firstly, all the group management activities are conducted by the single group management entity which may cause significant communication delay due to the heavy burden on it. Secondly, the single group management entity is vulnerable to the failure of the hosting site. An obvious solution to this problem is to create several backup group management entities.

V. QoS Definition and Implementation Techniques

As we mentioned before, the B-ISDN has to supply wide variety of services in dealing with different types of traffic. Some new applications, such as real time distributed control, multimedia collaborative work and video conferencing, require timely delivery of data while maintaining the causal relationship among the messages. Reliability and ordering are therefore important QoS (Quality of Service) to be supported by the multicast protocols. The multicast QoS can roughly be classified into data link level QoS (low level) and group level QoS (high level). The data link level QoS concerns the parameters that should be guaranteed by the communication channels. These parameters include minimal value, peak value, average values of throughput, maximum delay, and etc. The group level QoS defines reliability and ordering requirements for the multicast communication. This survey emphasizes on the guaranteeing the group level QoS schemes

5.1. Link Level QoS

Many solutions of link level QoS are for one-to-one communication but there is limited work done for the multicast communication[35,43,46]. ST-II is one of the pioneer protocol that supports link level QoS for multicast in Internet environment. It is a network level protocol that guarantees end-to-end bandwidth and delay for all connections. Negotiations of bandwidth and delay between sender, intermediate routers and receivers take place at connection set-up time such that the ST-II prevents the connections being set up unless there is sufficient resources for the expected traffics. In fact , ST-II operates by layering a virtual circuit service on top of IP that is not compatible with the datagram service of IP. This effectively reduces the number of ST-II users since they cannot use the reservation protocols for normal application.

RSVP is another protocol that guarantees link level QoS by implementing some important concepts, such as filters and receiver-oriented resource reservation. A filter, residencing in a intermediate node, specifies a subset of the data bounded to a designated receiver. The filters are distributed in the various intermediate nodes during a multicast session to facilitate the selective data transmission. It is natural that the receiver is responsible for the initiation and maintenance of the resource reservation. RSVP uses the lower layer multicast routing protocol to establish multicast tree and then the source sends path packets to mark all the routes from source to receivers. Once a path has been marked, a receiver can send a reservation request upstream toward the source. Each node on the path makes the reservation and relays the request to the routers are upstream toward the source. To adapt the changes of routing and membership, RSVP maintains "soft state" in the routers to enable repeat reservation at regular interval. However, this scheme cannot guarantee end-to-end QoS since the QoS request must be applied independently at each hop[14].

Both ST-II and RSVP do not address routing or make a simple attempt on routing. The ST-II builds a multicast tree from unicast routing table while RSVP relies on the underlying network for routing. Other related topics on link level QoS are hierarchical coding of multimedia data[43] and QoS negotiation[35]. Since guarantee link level QoS is relatively a new research topic and few results are presented, this paper will not investigate any further.

5.2. Group Level Multicast QoS

This section will first give the definitions of different QoS requirements and then examine several important solutions in guarantee these QoS in the multicast communication environment.

Best effort: is similar to UDP traffic in which a data packet can be delivered 0, 1, or more times to a destination without ordering guarantees on delivery.

Reliable: A reliable QoS guarantees that packets are delivered correctly to the intended receivers.

Due to the varying network delay in the multicast routes, multicast messages usually arrive at different points in time at the receiver site[36]. Without synchronization, individual receivers may receive messages ordered differently. Therefore, in some applications, the multicast protocol must provide guarantees of the order in which data packets are sent to the destinations. For instance, consider a deposit and withdrawal transactions for the same bank account in a computerized banking system, if the withdrawal is performed first an overdraft occurs and a penalty is charged. With the deposit first, no penalty is incurred and the balance of account is different. Similar examples can be found in the videoconference where ridiculous reactions may occur if a destination receives information in a reversed order.

> *Source ordering*: If message m_1 and m_2 are sent from the same source site and they are destined to the same multicast group then all the processes in this group should receive them in the same relative order and each message is delivered once to the members in the group.

> *Causal ordering*: It guarantees that each message, sent to a group G, is delivered to all active, i.e. both correct and faulty, receivers in G or to none of them, and are processed according to their causal order.

> *Total ordering*: If two messages m_1 and m_2 are delivered to the same multicast group, then all the addressed processes receive them in the same order even if they come from different sources.

Tracing back to the early multicast implementations such as the V system[17] and IP multicast[20], they implemented only the "best effort" delivery of multicast packets without further guarantee of message reliability and packets ordering. The ISIS system is one of the earliest protocol that provides causal ordering and total ordering[12]. It is implemented on top of a reliable multicast protocol which requires separate acknowledgments from each destination that limits the performance. Almost at the same time, many other multicast protocols emerged that provide various high level QoS's for multicasting[6,13,26,30,48]. Generally speaking, when the throughput of the network system remains the same, higher QoS levels increase the latency of the data delivery[48]. The techniques for QoS guarantee are discussed in following paragraphs.

To guarantee single source ordering of multicast packets is relatively straightforward and sometimes it is done by the underlying network protocols. The basic idea is to number the packets at the source and to have destination sites to order the incoming packets in a buffer. This method allows the receivers to detect missing packets.

To guarantee total ordering needs more effort. Many solutions, ranging from distributed to centralized controlled, have been proposed. One solution is to stamp each packet with an time-stamp that records the sending time, and then deliver packets in the time-stamp order. As illustrated in Fig. 5, if sources S_1 and S_2 send packets to group $G = \{c, d, e, f\}$. Assume that S_1 send to G packet P_1 with time-stamp T_1. When the destination c receives P_1, it can not forward P_1 immediately to the destination process. It must check for all the potential sources if there are other packets with smaller time-stamps. When c is certain that a packet has minimal time-stamp among all the undelivered packets does it deliver it.

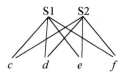

Fig.5 Two sources send to group $G = \{c, d, e, f\}$

Birman et.al. have proposed another solution based on the network wide priority number11. Each receiver maintains a priority queue. The sender sends the packet to destinations which assign their own priority numbers to the packet. This priority number is a system wide unique number higher than any given so far for that receiver. The packet is marked undeliverable and put in the queue. All the receivers return their priority number for the packet to the sender. The sender selects the highest priority number and sends them back to the receivers who replace their original number with the new one and mark the packet as deliverable. Each receiver reorders its queue and whenever the packet at the front of the queue is deliverable, it is delivered. This solution needs intensive exchanging information between sources and receivers that create high protocol overhead.

One of the early centralized multicast protocols that guarantees ordering QoS can be found in Navaratnam's work which uses a single token site to support total ordering and reliability39. It requires that each site send back a positive acknowledgment before the next packet can be sent. This solution is limited in scalability by the center site and is vulnerable to failure of the center site.

Chang and Maxemchuk16 proposed a more burden-shared approach in order to reduce the synchronization cost. Here all the sources send to a central site which assigns sequence number to the packets and then forwards them to the receivers. This center site is identified by a token and the token circulates through the receivers. This strategy reduces the burden on the single site that guarantees message ordering. Similar approaches can be found in the Reliable Multicast Protocol RMP48 and Aiello's work2 which are based on a modified version of Chang's token ring protocol. The RMP provides an N-way virtual circuits, namely token ring, between groups of processes connected by a multicast medium. It lets the reliability control to be shared by all the processes so that each process has the same role in the communication. The RMP uses the negative acknowledgment for error detection and retransmmission while limiting the necessary buffer space by passing a token around the members of a token ring.

In summary, QoS's are important service guarantee for various applications. Normally, certain level QoS can only be supported in the expense of efficiency because extra control messages have to be transmitted. The approaches based on the retransmission may degrade the performance of the protocol and give the high burden to receivers for dropping the redundant packets. The centralized token site approach has limited scalability and is vulnerable to token site failure. The multimedia applications have specific QoS requirements for different types of data stream. For instance, it is not necessary to have the fully reliable video stream for a videoconference, while the reliable is obliged for text transmission in update the distributed databases. Therefore, a multicast protocol should have the capability for the application to select appropriate QoS levels.

VI. Summary and Future Research Problems

Multicast communication has received more and more attention in recent years because it is a basic support protocol for many multiparty interactive multimedia applications. In this paper, a number of important multicast protocols and their significant features are surveyed. The important issues related to multicast are identified and examined. These issues cover multicast routing topologies, multicast group management schemes, and QoS guarantee techniques. The following conclusions are made.

- The development of multicast protocols started from supplying basic service, i.e. best effort to guarantee enhanced higher quality of services to applications. The multicast over ATM is still in its infant stage. Since the multimedia data and ATM architecture are different from traditional data and network respectively, new multicast protocols that support multimedia communication over ATM network have to be developed and the process for development will follow the similar development process as in other multicast protocols.

- Many multicast routing topologies have been used in different protocols and each of them has its merits in specific situation. The flexibility of ATM VC's could be explored to support various multicast routing topologies. The ephemeral routing solutions which provide optimum solution for a short life time are not practical in dynamic real world applications.

- Based on the characteristic of ATM network, centralized group management schemes are preferred.

- Certain level of QoS should be guaranteed for different multimedia applications. Normally, the QoS guarantee is at the expense of the efficiency.

Finally, it should be noted that there are still some research areas in multicast communication requiring further investigation.

- In ATM network, only point-to-multipoint unidirectional VC's can be established and the VC's do not provide reverse communication. Therefore, methods for sending back the acknowledgment to maintain certain level QoS have to be investigated.

- The ATM allows the integration of various multimedia traffic data. To support the transmission of selective data to receivers of different capabilities is a new topic for multicast communication.

- In most of the past multicast protocols, N-way multicast is not supported. Practical solutions for N-way multicast is still an open research area.

In future, we intend to propose a suitable ATM multicast service that supports real-time multimedia traffic (i.e. video and audio).

References

1. L. Aguilar, "Datagram Routing for Internet Multicasting," *ACM Comp. Comm. Rev.*, Vol.14, No.2, 1984, pp. 58-63.
2. R. Aiello, E. Pagani, G. P. Rossi, "Causal Ordering in Reliable Group Communications," *Sigcomm'93*, Ithaca, N.Y, USA, Sept. 93, pp. 106-115.
3. A. Alles, "ATM Internetworking," Cisco Systems, Inc. 1995.
4. M. H. Ammar, S. Y. Cheung, C. M. Scoglio, "Routing Multipoint Connection Using Virtual Paths in an ATM Network," *IEEE INFOCOM '93*, pp. 98-105.
5. G. Armitage, "Support for Multicast over UNI 3.1 Based ATM Networks," *Internet Draft*, Jan. 1995.
6. S. Armstrong, A.Freier, K. Marzullo, "Multicast Transport Protocol," *RFC1301*, Feb. 1992.
7. ATM Forum, "ATM User-Network Interface Specification Version 3.0," Pretice Hall, 1993.
8. T. Ballardie, P. Francis, J. Crowcroft, " Core Based Tree - An Architecture for Scalable Inter-Domain Multicast Routing," *Sigcomm'93*, Ithaca, N.Y, USA, Sept. 93, pp. 85-95.
9. J. J. Bae, T. Suda, " Survey of Traffic Control Schemes and Protocols in ATM networks," *Proceedings of the IEEE*, Vol. 79, No.2, Feb. 1991, pp.170-189.
10. L. Berry, "Graph Theoretic Models for Multicast Communication," *Comp. Net. & ISDN Sys.*, Vol. 20, 90, pp 95-99.
11. K. Birman, T. Joseph, "Reliable communication in the presence of failures," *ACM Trans. on Computer Systems*, Vol5, No.1, 1987, pp. 47-76.
12. K. Birman, A. Schiper, P. Stephenson, "Lightweight Causal and Automic Group Multicast," *ACM Transactions on Computer Systems*, Vol. 9, No. 3, Aug. 1991, pp. 272-314.
13. K. Birman, "The Process Group Approach to Reliable Distributed Computing," Communications of the *ACM*, Vol. 36, No. 12, Dec. 1993, pp. 37-53.
14. R. Braden, L. Zhang, D. Estrin, S. Herzog, S. Jamin, "Resource Reservation Protocol -- Version 1 Dunctional Specification," Internet Draft, 1995.

15. A. Campbell, G. Coulson, D. Hutchison, "A Quality of Service Architecture," *ACM SIGCOMM Computer Communication Review*, 1994, pp. 6-27.

16. J. M. Chang, N. F. Maxemchuk, "Reliable Broadcast Procotols," *ACM Transactions on Computer Systems*, Vol. 2, No. 3, Aug. 1984, pp. 223-233.

17. D. R. Cheriton, W. Zwaenepoel, "Distributed Process Groups in the V Kernel," *ACM Trans. on Computer Systems*, Vol. 3, No. 2, 1985, pp. 77-107.

18. S. C. Chuang, "A Flexible and Secure Multicast Architecture for ATM Network," Internet version, Dec, 1994

19. D. E. Comer, " Internetworking with TCP/IP," Vol. I, Prentice-Hall.

20. S. E. Deering, "Multicast Routing in Internetworks and Extended LANs," *ACM Computer Communications Review*, Vol.18 No.4 1988 pp. 55-64.

21. S. E. Deering, D. R. Cheriton, "Multicast Routing in Datagram Internetworks and Extended LANs," *ACM Transactions on Computer Systems*, Vol. 8, No. 2, May 1990, pp. 85-110.

22. S. E. Deering, D. Estrin, D. Farinacci, VanJacobson, C. G. Liu, L. Wei, " An Architecture for Wide-Area Multicast Routing," *ACM SIGCOMM 94*, London, Aug. 1994.

23. M. Doar, I. Leslie, "How Bad is Naive Multicast Routing?" *IEEE Proc. of INFOCOM '93*, pp. 82-89.

24. H. Eriksson, "MBONE: The Multicast Backbone," *Comm. of ACM*, Vol. 37, Aug. 1994, pp. 54-60.

25. A. J. Frank, L. D. Wittie, A. J. Bernstein, "Multicast Communication on Network Computers," *IEEE Software*, Vol. 2, No. 3, 1985, pp. 77-107.

26. H. Garcia-Molina, A. Spauster, "Ordered and Reliable Multicast Communication," *ACM Transactions on Computer Systems*, Vol. 9. No. 3, Aug. 1991, pp. 242-271.

27. B. Heinrichs, K. Jakobs, A. Carone, "High Performance Transfer Services to Support Multimedia Group Communications," *Computer Communications*, Vol. 16, No. 9, Sept. 1993.

28. C. Huang, P. K. McKinley, "Communication Issues in Parallel Computing Across ATM Networks," *IEEE Parallel & Distributed Technology*, Winter 1994, pp. 73-86.

29. X. Jiang, "Routing Broadband Multicast Streams," *Computer Communications*, Vol. 15, no. 1, 1992.

30. M. F. Kaashoek, A. S. Tanenbaum, S. F. Hummel, H. E. Bal, "An Efficient Reliable Broadcast Protocol," *Operating System Review*, Vol. 23, No. 4, Oct. 1989, pp. 5-19.

31. B. K. Kadaba, J. M. Jaffe, "Routing to Multiple destinations in computer networks," IEEE Trans. Commun. Vol. 31, No. 3, Mar 1983, pp. 343-351.

32. J. Kadirire, "Minimising Packet Copies in Multicast Routing by Exploiting Geographic Spread," *Computer Communication Review*, 1994, pp. 47-62.

33. B. G. Kim, P. Wang, "ATM Network: Goals and Challenges," *Comm of ACM*, Vol. 38, No. 2, 1995, pp. 39-44.

34. V. P. Kompella, J. C. Pasquale, G. C. Polyzos, "Multicast Routing for Multimedia Communication," *IEEE Trans. on Network*, Vol. 1, No. 3, June 1993.

35. L. Mathy, O. Bonaventure, "QoS negotiation for Multicast Communications," Proceedings on Multimedia Transport and Teleservices, Vienna, Austria, Nov. 1994.

36. E. Mayer, "An Evaluation Framework for Multicast Ordering Protocols," *COMM'92*, MD. USA, 92, pp.177-187.

37. P. K. McKinley, W. S. Liu "Multicast Tree Construction in Bus Based Network," *Communications of the ACM*, Vol. 33, No. 1, Jan. 1990, pp.29-42.

38. J. Moy, "Multicast Routing Extensions for OSPF," *Comm. of ACM*, Vol. 37, Aug. 1994, pp. 61-66.

39. S. Navaratnam, S. Chanson, and G. Neufeld, "Reliable group communication in distributed systems," *Proceedings of the 8th Int. Conf. on Dist. Comp. Sys.* San Jose, June 1988, pp. 439-446.

40. L. H. Ngoh, T. P. Hopkins, "Transport Protocol Requirements for Distributed Multimedia Information Systems," *Comput. J.* Vol. 32, No. 3, 1989, pp. 252-261.

41. L. H. Ngoh, "Multicast support for group communication," *Comp. Net.& ISDN Sys.*, Vol 22, 1991, pp. 165-178.

42. B. Rajagopalan, "Reliability and Scaling Issues in Multicast Communication," *COMM'92*, MD. USA, Aug. 92, pp.188-198.

43. N. Shacham, "Multipoint Communication by Hierarchically Encoded Data," *IEEE Proceedings of INFOCOM '92*, 1992, pp. 2107-2114.

44. D. H. Shrimpton, C. S. Cooper, "Multicast communication on the Unison network," *Computer Communication*, Vol.13, No.8, Oct. 1990, pp. 460-468.

45. W. Strayer, B. Dempsey, A. Weaver, "XTP: The Xpress Transfer Protocol," Addison-Wesley, 1992.

46. C. Topolcic, "Experimental Internet Stream Protocol, (ST-II)," *RFC 1190*, CIP WG, Oct. 1990.

47. D. C. Verma, P. M. Gopal, "Routing Reserved Bandwidth Multi-Point Connections," *Sigcomm'93*, Ithaca, N.Y, USA, Sept. 93, pp. 96-105.

48. B. Whetten, S. Kaplan, T. Montgomery, "A High Performance Total Ordered Multicast Protocol," *Intenet Draft Copy*, 1995.

49. D. W. Wall, "Selected Broadcast in Packet-Switched Networks," *Proceedings of the Sixth Berkeley Workshop on Distributed Data Management and Computer Network*, Feb. 1982, pp. 239-258.

50. B. M. Waxman, "Routing of Multipoint Connections," IEEE Journal of Selected Areas on Communication, Vol. 6, No. 9, Dec. 1988, pp. 1617-1622.

51. L. Zhang, S. Deering, D. Estrin, S. Shenker, and D. Zappala, "RSVP: A New Resource ReSerVation Protocol," IEEE Network, Sept. 1993.

Multimedia over narrowband networks

Frank Van Reeth, Karin Coninx and Eddy Flerackers
Applied Computer Science Laboratory
Limburgs University Center
Universitaire Campus
B 3590 Diepenbeek
Belgium

Abstract

Looking at the ever increasing success of the networked services offered by organisations alike CompuServe, AOL and Prodigy, it becomes evident that the future of multimedia will heavily be influenced by networking aspects. This trend is also visible on the public service networks (X.25, X.29 -and variants- and ISDN) offered by many telecom operators, where a migration is envisioned from the traditional (text-based) videotex online services towards multimedia online services [Mauth 95]. The paper elucidates the developments we are undertaking in the realization of a VEMMI (Videotex Enhanced Man-Machine Interface, an ETSI pre-standard for multimedia online services on existing videotex networks) terminal. Aside the developments at the system level - overall framework, communication with the server, local management of the multimedia objects and the GUI - a designer tool enabling interactive graphical specification of the GUI (with accompanying code generation) is also discussed. A short explanation on several trial applications is given. Aside the elucidation on the narrowband developments, an overview is given of the realizations within the broadband area.

1. Introduction

Especially within the European context, the online services of the last two decades have mostly been based upon the videotex standard. Its' purely text-based user interface, with limited interaction possibilities and no provisions for client-server functionalities (exploiting local intelligence) indicate that the videotex standard is around already for a relatively long period.

With the ever increasing competition of online services enabling multimedia content (the vast processing performance in today's micro-computers has enabled multimedia applications to appear on the desktop of almost everyone), it became obvious the videotex standard needed a facelift. Hence, the definition of a standard by ETSI (European Telecommunication Standardization Institute) enabling multimedia online services. The official ETSI document terms the ETS 300 382 standard: "Terminal Equipment; Enhanced Man Machine Interface for Videotex and Multimedia/Hypermedia Information Retrieval Services" [ETSI 95]. We utilize the short term VEMMI (coming from the original ETSI term "Videotex Enhanced Man-Machine Interface") throughout the text.

VEMMI is an open platform-independent standard enabling enhanced multimedia online services on the public service networks, including the existing videotex networks and less mainstream networks (e.g. CATV networks), as opposed to the online services of specific companies (CompuServe, Prodigy, AOL, ...) which are running on private networks.

In comparison with the traditional videotex standards, we can enlist the following improvements of the VEMMI standard:
- oriented around objects rather than around pages; these objects (display objects, resource objects and metacode objects, cfr. Section 2.2) enable terminal-independent definition of the interface on the client-side.
- integrated multimedia interface (text, data, images and sound) vs. text-based interface; the JPEG compression [Wallace 91; Pennenbaker 93] allows the utilization of still images within narrowband networks. For sound applications, PCM and ADPCM encoding techniques are utilized.
- the intelligence of the client-terminal (in our approach: a PC running MS-Windows) is exploited more than in the traditional videotex approach: indeed, VEMMI provides features enabling (and exploiting) 'intelligent' behaviour at the terminal side. This behaviour is intended to improve the response times on data links with lower data bandwidth. Firstly, interface objects which are frequently used within a given application can be stored at the terminal. When needed, these objects are automatically retrieved from the storage device therefore dramatically reducing the amount of data needed to be sent over the network. Secondly, as a result of user interaction, the client's options are two-fold : it can perform local actions by changing the state of objects already resident on the client. In this case, all these actions are treated locally without notifying the server. A second option consists of sending reports (possibly containing data) towards the server, which then will perform more complex actions.

In this paper, we address the relevant items in the realization of a networked multimedia infrastructure, based upon the VEMMI standard. Concretely, the implementation of the VEMMI standard on the MS-Windows environment is discussed. Attention is given to the way in which the standard is mapped to the environment at issue. As the VEMMI objects have a rather low level - and specific - format, a designer tool enabling interactive graphical specification of the GUI (with accompanying code generation) is developed. Moreover, a short explanation on several trial applications is given. These applications can fluently run on narrowband networks (from 2.4 Kbit/s up to 64 Kbit/s). Some applications, e.g. the transmission of MPEG [Le Gall 91; MPEG-1 93] video sequences over the network, naturally need higher bandwidth. Hence, aside the elucidation on the narrowband developments, an overview is given of the realizations within the broadband area.

In Section 2, the overall system architecture is elucidated; the VEMMI objects are explained and it is shown how these are mapped into MS-Windows. Section 3 discusses the designer tool we implemented that enables the interactive graphical specification of VEMMI GUI's. In Section 4, some typical demo-applications on the narrowband networks are given, whereas Section 5 contains the extensions towards broadband networks. Conclusions and directions for future research are given in the last Section.

2. Overall Architecture

2.1 General

Figure 1 gives an overview of the overall system architecture. A stream of encoded bytes which holds all the VEMMI commands and objects first passes through the VEMMI Encoder/Decoder. This process will convert this stream into command or object blocks which are sent on to the VEMMI Local Manager. If the stream of data contains invalid or not well defined data, an error will be sent to the application on the server and is not propagated to the local manager.

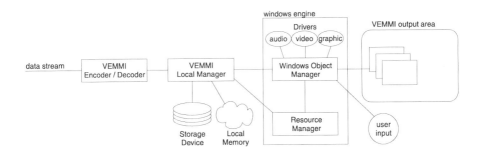

figure 1 : VEMMI terminal architecture (schematic)

The VEMMI Local Manager holds a platform independent definition of the various objects and their relationship with each other. It has the possibility to store resources and display objects onto local disk storage or to retrieve them from local disk. This storage/retrieval principle is also defined in VEMMI between two different sessions. Hence, resources and other objects need to be supplied only once across the network to the client side. Each of these stored objects is given a timestamp, so new objects can be sent to the client side with newer timestamps to replace old ones.

The platform independent definition of a display object will pass on to the Windows Object Manager which will map this representation on a windows object. Resource objects are passed on to the Resource Manager, which will convert these resources into windows resources, e.g., a font definition is converted into a windows font handle. The raw data are to be supplied in a format compatible with the VEMMI specifications, as they are managed and presented fully within the VEMMI terminal environment. An alternative approach can, e.g., be found in DEMON [Rosenberg 91, 93]. DEMON uses formats of commercial authoring and playback program, whereas VEMMI follows the specifications of the ETSI standard. (More prosaic, we could state: DEMON follows "the American way", whereas VEMMI follows "the European way").

User interaction on the displayed objects is retrieved through messages on the components of the display objects which are managed by the Windows Object Manager. These messages are if needed passed on to the Local Manager which will execute the actions associated with the component who triggered the action. The Local Manager is able to decide if a specific action has to be passed on to the application at the server side or if it can be treated at the client side. A VEMMI Open Object of a non-existing object at client side (either in memory or from disk), will produce a VEMMI Object Retransmission request which is sent to the server side.

2.2 VEMMI objects

VEMMI is a protocol that allows the programmer to create a user-friendly WIMP-interface for on-line applications. Implemented on a standard data transmission mechanism (eg. Videotex) it enhances the look and feel of its user interface. Originally defined as an extention to the existing Videotex protocol, it quickly emerged as a powerful development environment for interactive client-server multimedia applications.

The VEMMI environment provides a basic set of objects which help the programmer in the creation of user interfaces for interactive multimedia on-line services. These objects are quite versatile and can be created, modified and/or removed at any time during program execution. In VEMMI, four distinct categories of objects are defined.

The first group of objects consists of the so-called 'display objects' : these objects have an immediate (audio)visual effect on the user.

- application bar
  The application bar allows the programmer to create a menu in which the user is allowed to make a choice between a number of items. Upon user selection of a particular item, the client program takes control and performs actions as described above. Menus are well-known and commonly used in windows-based user environments.
- button bar
  The button bar provides the user with a set of choices which he can make at any time during the existence of the bar. Each choice is represented by a button which the user can click on. Upon user interaction, the client can perform local actions or send a report towards the server.

- popup menu

  The popup menu offers a set of choices and sub-choices which the user can select from. Its purpose is slightly different from that of the application bar and button bar as it can be dynamically provided in situations where current context is important.

- dialog box

  This is the display object where most of the interaction between the user and the VEMMI application takes place. In a dialog box, a collection of visual components (bitmap areas, text output areas, lines, frames) and input facilities (text input fields, buttons, check boxes,...) are provided which facilitate this interaction.

- message box

  The message box is used to display information, sent by the VEMMI application on the server towards the user in response to an unexpected event.

- sound object

  Sound can be embedded in sound objects. A sound object is processed when referenced (i.e. when opened).

- video object

  Video can be embedded in video objects. A video object is processed when referenced (i.e. when opened).

Most of these display objects contain one or more types of components of which each has its own specific properties (as already explained with the dialog box).

The second group of objects consists of the so-called 'resource objects': only when these resources are referenced by other (display) objects, they do have a visual effect on the terminal screen. Following resource types are provided :

- bitmap object
- font object
- text object
- videotex object

The third group of objects consists of so-called "metacode objects". A metacode object contains a collection of VEMMI calls. It can be executed by a call from one of the VEMMI objects during program execution. Metacode objects are especially useful in situations where repeatedly the same sequence of VEMMI commands is to be executed.

The last group consists of the so-called "operative objects". The most important instance of this group represents stand-alone programs which can be launched on the VEMMI terminal from within a VEMMI application.

2.3 Mapping of VEMMI objects onto MS-Windows

The implementation of the various components of VEMMI objects must insure a versatile mapping onto window objects. The VEMMI components should be able to contain their specific data and respond to actions defined by VEMMI. Some of the components also behave slightly different from the standard system global windows offered by the Windows environment. These components had to be implemented by using the standard windows as a basis to start from, otherwise all of the code to response to user input messages and display messages on these components had to be implemented as well.

In order to map the VEMMI components onto window objects, we used a technique called "window superclassing". A superclass is a class derived from another class, possibly a system global window class, like the standard "edit"-class.

Because superclassing registers a new window class, we can enlarge the number of bytes stored which each window. In these extra bytes we keep all the information relevant to the VEMMI component, which is not present in its base class.

This superclass also has its own window procedure, it can take three actions with a message : it can pass the message to the original window procedure of its base class (through CallWindowProc), modify the message and pass it to the original window procedure, or process the message and not pass it to the original window procedure. Using this technique we can easily create VEMMI components which react differently from the standard behaviour of window objects without having to create complete new objects.

We elucidate the above concepts by means of an example regarding a "Text Input Field" VEMMI-component. This component consists of a text label and an input area. The input area can have the constraint that only numeric characters (0..9,+,-,comma,dot,space) are allowed as user input. To achieve this goal we only have to inspect the various characters that are sent to the superclass window procedure and decide if they are allowed to pass through to the window procedure of the standard "edit"-class from which it has been derived.

In addition to the standard window-messages, the VEMMI components must be able to respond to a range of VEMMI-specific messages which do not have to be passed to the window procedure of its base class. These private messages are defined as (WM_USER + ...) message identifiers. These message identifiers are reserved by Windows to be used as application message identifiers. Special care has to be taken to define these messages, as the standard window classes from which some of the VEMMI components are derived also use some message-identifiers in the bottom part of (WM_USER + ...).

E.g.: a VEMMI component which has a value that the user is able to change, must have the capability to restore this value to its original value (the value it had on creation). To achieve this goal each superclassed window responds to the "WM_COMP_RESTORE_VALUE"-message, which is dealt with using the VEMMI specific data stored in the derived window.

3. Designer

3.1 Interactive specification of the VEMMI objects

In order to achieve user-friendly applications with additional integration of multimedia objects, a powerful tool is needed for the programmer implementing these remote applications. Hence, a fully interactive environment in accordance with the WYSIWYG principle is developed. Figure 2 depicts a snapshot from a screen in which the user interface of a VEMMI program is being defined.

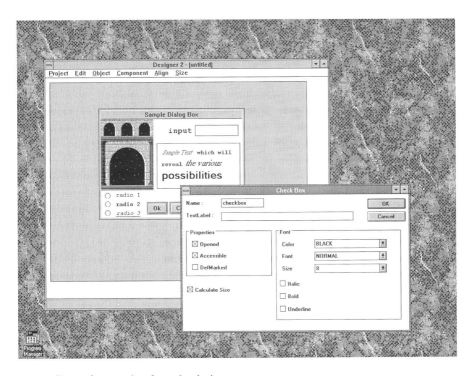

figure 2 : snapshot from the designer

In a first phase, all objects are straightforwardly defined : the VEMMI programmer quickly determines positioning and dimensioning of the desired objects in a graphical manner using mouse and/or keyboard input. Next, he/she can build up the look of the object using desired components which are selected and placed by only a few mouse

260

interactions. For each of these components, additional information can be supplied regarding its displaying behaviour.

Of course, should the programmer change his/her mind about the look, he/she can move and/or resize components at will. In addition, an extensive set of editing, alignment and resizing tools, all acting on a user-defined selection of components, has been supplied.

In a second phase, the programmer can define 'local behaviour' of the components which will interact with the user. For example, he/she can define how a push button should react when clicked upon by a user. When defining local behaviour, the programmer is supplied a list of possible actions a specific type of component can perform. He/she simply builds up a sequence of 'local actions' by selecting items from the list in the order he wants them to be executed.

Finally, when the programmer is satisfied with the look of his future application, he/she will call the VEMMI code generator which will translate the graphical environment in a piece of source code which will be fed into the compiler of the server on which the program will have to run. In addition all resource objects are created and stored at the server side. The reader should note that at this stage, only the interfacing part of the program is completed. Additional programming is still required from the programmer to define the actual behaviour of the program itself. Figure 3 depicts the above processes schematically.

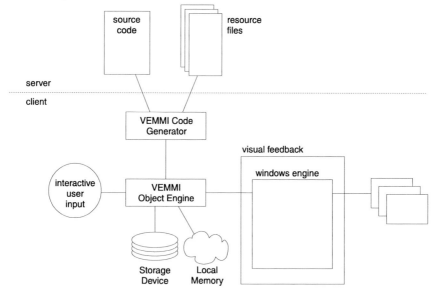

figure 3 : designer toolkit (schematic)

4. Example Applications

In this section, some of the trial applications are given. Figures 4-7 show the snapshots of some specific application screens.

4.1 Multimedia phonebook

An electronic phone directory : it contains personal information of a number of people. The user simply has to enter name and/or company of the desired person, after which he is supplied with a dialog box in which he can find the corresponding information together with a small photograph (fig. 4).

4.2 Art gallery

A remote auction in which users are allowed to select an art work from a list. They are then presented with a dialog box containing information about the chosen item, a picture of the art work, and the highest bid so far. Optionally, the users can make a bid themselves (fig.5).

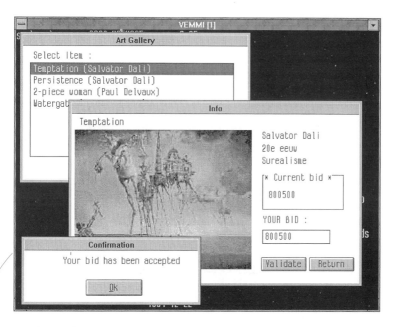

4.3 CD guide

A catalog of CD's, sorted by artist, which the user can browse through. For each CD, a dialog box is presented online with information, a picture of the cover and a music sample of one of the tracks. Also, the user has the opportunity to order the CD on-line (fig.6).

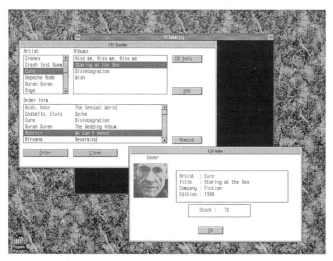

5. Incorporating broadband functionality

As a more advanced example application exploiting the intelligence locally available at the terminal client, we can consider the decoding of MPEG streams coming in over broadband communication lines.

In this application, the Windows PC acting as terminal hosts an MPEG decoder board, as well as a board (Ethernet or ATM) over which the broadband MPEG data stream is entering the terminal (we utilize the Transmission Control Protocol/ Internet Protocol (TCP/IP) protocol in both the Ethernet and the ATM implementation). Additionally an external Windows-program, driving the broadband communication board as well as the MPEG decoder board, has to be available. (Inbetween note: Should the external Windows program not be available locally, then VEMMI has the possibility to send it over from the server to the client-terminal).

The actual VEMMI program enabling this application hence uses the concept of "operative objects" (cfr. Section 2.2) for launching the Windows-program by the VEMMI terminal client under control of the server; VEMMI is solely used for the user interface implementing navigation. The application at hand clearly illustrates the possibilities of modularly expanding the range of potential online multimedia applications by exploiting the locally (at terminal side) available intelligence.

6. Conclusions and Future Research

In this paper, we elucidated the implementation of a networked multimedia system enabling interactive online services requiring treatment of text, data, images and sound. We aimed at providing an open system, according to the ETSI ETS 300 382 pre-standard on "Enhanced Man Machine Interface for Videotex and Multimedia/Hypermedia Information Retrieval Services (VEMMI)". Although some work has been done at the server (and network) side, most of the effort has been devoted to the client terminal development and the implementation of the designer toolkit enabling interactive definition and code generation of application GUI's. It is shown what the overall architecture looks like, what the various VEMMI objects are and how they are implemented on the MS-Windows environment. The relevant aspects of the toolkit are discussed and some example applications, developed on top of the developed system (and utilizing the designer toolkit), are elucidated. An overview is given of the way in which applications needing broadband communications are integrated into the system.

For future R&D, several topics can be mentioned. Firstly, it can be investigated how the VEMMI terminal implementation would be undertaken on other operating environments (e.g., Macintosh, X-windows, ...). Secondly, it would be worthwhile to investigate how VEMMI could be realized on CATV networks. Thirdly, it can be researched upon how the functionality of the designer toolkit could be extended to include 4GL features to access multimedia databases from within an interactive interface (aside the interactive specification of the application GUI's - including code generation). Lastly, interconnection of the VEMMI environment with the Internet world could be a topic worth investigating.

Acknowledgements

This work is funded by a grant from Belgacom, the Belgian national telecom operator: their support is fully acknowledged. At the implementational and editorial level, the work of several people in the Laboratory, especially of Koen Elens and Philip Schaeken, is greatly appreciated. The input of Peter Michiels at Alcatel Bell is also fully acknowledged.

References

Bucci, G., Detti, R., Pasqui, V. and Naviti, S. "Sharing Multimedia Data Over a Client-Server Network", *IEEE Multimedia*, Vol. 1, No. 3, 1994, pp. 44-55.

ETSI, "Terminal Equipment; Enhanced Man Machine Interface for Videotex and Multimedia/Hypermedia Information Retrieval Services (VEMMI)", *ETS 300 382*, ETSI, April 1995.

Le Gall, D. "MPEG: A Video Compression Standard for Multimedia Applications", *Comm. ACM,* Vol. 34, No. 4, 1991, pp. 45-68.

Mauth, R. "GUI Look Coming to Videotex Services", *Byte,* May 1995, pp. 40IS 3.

MPEG-1 "Information Technology - Coding of Moving Pictures and Associated Audio", *ISO/IEC 11172,* Int'l Standards Organization, Geneva, 1993.

Pennenbaker, W.B. and Mitchell, J.L., *JPEG Still Image Data Compression Standard*, Van Nostrand Reinhold, New York, 1993.

Rosenberg, J., Cruz, G. and Judd, T. "Presenting Multimedia Documents Over a Digital Network", *Proc. Int'l Workshop on Network and Operating System Support for Digital Audio end Video,* Springer-Verlag, Berlin, 1991, pp. 346-357.

Rosenberg, J., "Multimedia Delivery over Public Switched Networks", *The Bellcore Exchange*, Vol. 9, No. 1, 1993, pp. 20-24.

Wallace, G., "The JPEG Still Picture Compression Standard", *Comm. ACM,* Vol. 34, No. 4, 1991, pp. 30-44.

A Logical Basis for Continuous-Media Presentation with QoS

Makoto TANABE, Reiji NAKAJIMA

Research Institute for Mathematical Sciences
Kyoto University, Kyoto 606-01, Japan
{tanabe,reiji}.kurims.kyoto-u.ac.jp

Multimedia systems perform *continuous-media data* such as motion video and music sounds with requested quality. In this paper, a formal basis is introduced to discuss multimedia systems. The concept of computing and communicating resource capabilities amalgamated with their available time intervals is introduced, which is used to formally define the realizability of performances of continuous-media data with requested quality. The main contribution of the paper is the introduction of the deduction system of realizability, which makes possible the formal discussion of properties of multimedia systems, such as realizability of shared and synchronized performances under the constraints of QoS and limited available resources.

1 Introduction

In the area of multimedia information systems, the current situation is that almost every one is busy implementing application hardware and software without any general principle, formalism or underlying theory. It is similar to '60s when a tremendous number of spaghetti software proceeded and motivated studies of formal approaches and theories.

The work presented in this paper is intended to give a way of looking formally at what is being done in so called multimedia systems. More precisely, we want to provide a formal basis in which one can describe requirements of users and mechanisms to realize the requirements, although the formalism is not intended to serve directly as a tool for formal specification and verification in the conventional sense.

The main contributions we assert in the work include:

1. Formal representation of performances of continuous-media data using interval logic-like formalism.
2. Introduction of the notion of realizability of performances and its formalization.
3. Formalization of shared performances.

Several formal approaches to describing multimedia systems have emerged, e.g., object composition Petri-net [1], dual language approach [2], object-oriented approach [3] and an extension of CSP [4]. It is clear that more work must be done for formalization of multimedia systems, especially, to work out a formalism to deal with continuous-media data performances at an appropriately abstract level.

Overview of Multimedia Systems We wish to discuss how, or under what conditions, performances of media data could be *successfully realized* on a multimedia system. We say a performance of media data is successfully realized when all the constraints imposed on the performance are satisfied by the realization, where these constraints include:

(i) *Timing constraints among performances.*
Synchronized and/or sequentialized performances of several media data relate the timings of their realizations with one another.

(ii) *Requests for QoS.*
Requirements for realization of performances with intended QoS introduce constraints on usages of resources.

(iii) *Resource availabilities.*
Available computing and communicating resources for each user are limited, usually shared and, therefore, the availability may change as time goes by.

(iv) *Shared performances.*
For instance, suppose that nation-wide news must be shared by several local stations in the network. There, each station may impose constraints on its performances, in order to include it into its local programs.

Features of the Formal System PDS   In this paper, we introduce *PDS* (*Playability Deduction System*) as a basis of discussions on properties of multimedia systems. *PDS* features:

(i) *Interval-based Time Domain*
In order to treat performances of continuous-media data as an atomic notion, we adopt an interval-based time domain in our basis. Therefore, all the notions of multimedia systems are represented based on time-intervals, including performances of media data, physical resources and realizability of performances.

(ii) *Classification of Media into Two Categories*
Media are classified into two categories by whether they concern perception by users or not. The classification makes it possible to separate requirement specifications by users from analysis of resource availability by systems.

(iii) *Realizability of Media Data Performances*
The notion of realizability of media data performances is introduced as a relationship between two categories of media. Realizability of various perception media types, including continuous-media (such as audio and video) and static-media (such as text and still-image), is discussed formally in an unified way.

(iv) *Real-Time Constraints*
Real-time constraints such as interval-wise synchronization, sequential composition and resource competition among users can be formally described.

(v) Shared Performances

As a real-time system, a multimedia system requires unique timing-constraints if they allow performances shared by more than one users. We discuss the notion of shared performances using *PDS* .

(vi) Deduction of Performance Realizability

One of the main contributions of *PDS* is the introduction of the deduction system to establish realizability of performances. Realizability of composite performances can be discussed even when there are timing-constraints among components.

Additional Features and Limitations

(i) Global Clock

A large number of clock synchronization algorithms have been proposed for formal or informal modelling of distributed systems, among which use of global time is considered to be one of the widely supported technic[5]. Especially most of currently existing approaches to formalization of multimedia systems assume, implicitly or explicitly, the existence of global clock[1,2,4]. *PDS* also assumes the existence of global clock, for simplicity.

(ii) Static Cases

PDS does not deal with dynamic cases, e.g., user interactions and probabilistic events. We assert that the formalism is useful even if it is valid only for static situations. Firstly, there are many multimedia applications in which media data are performed statically, e.g, Quick-Time players[6] and broadcasting of programs. Secondly, we assert that the way of thinking derived from the formalism will possibly be useful in design phases of multimedia systems.

(iii) Application to Programming

There are only few proposals on how programming of multimedia systems should be done (one of them is "time advanced model"[7]). Therefore, one of the hopeful aims of the work is that the formalism will assist in designing multimedia systems or programming languages for their implementation.

The rest of this paper is organized as follows. In Section 2, we introduce by examples the basic concepts on which our formalization is based. We also explain how these concepts are formalized. Section 3 introduces *PDS* . We then describe the notion of shared performances using *PDS* in Section 4. Finally, in Section 5, we give some concluding remarks.

2   Basic Concepts and Their Formalization

There are a lot of notions and keywords concerning multimedia systems, e.g., QoS, networks, processes, schedulings and user interactions. Although all of them are important, in constructing a model of multimedia systems, we must carefully select only those which are necessary for describing systems in simple and essential ways. In this section, three concepts, *performances*, *processors* and *playabilities* are introduced as the fundamentals of *PDS* .

2.1 A Quick Introduction to PDS

As described in Section 1, in multimedia systems, the first objective of users' side is to enjoy playbacks of music, films and animations with intended QoS. As long as playback QoS is kept within their requirements, users do not care how ongoing realization is achieved. In terms of the example of media classification in Section 1, users are interested only in perception media, and all other media are implicit to them.

Now we introduce two terms: *performances* and *processors*. By *a performance*, we mean an instance of perception media. For example, "showing Superman on the screen", "a playback of Beethoven's Ninth Symphony", "writing sequences of animation frames of Donald Duck into a frame buffer" and "a display of warning message on a window" are performances. By *a processor*, we mean a unit of physical media and/or resources that can be used for realization of performances. For example, "(a use of) 64kbps (k-bit/sec) bandwidth of a local area network for 10 minutes", "an occupation of an audio device for 30 seconds" and "a read-access to an MMDB (multimedia database)" are processors. Each processor offers (possibly changing in time) computing and communicating resources over a time interval. We introduce descriptions to specify performances and processors, which we call as *performance descriptions* and *processor descriptions*, respectively. Performance descriptions have operators for synchronization, sequentialization and sharing of performances. Processor descriptions have operators for parallel and sequential concatenation and sharing of processors.

We say that a performance description is *realizable* on a time interval if a processor is available, using which a performance satisfying the description is realizable on the interval. The realizability relationship between performance descriptions and processors is extended to that between performance descriptions and processor descriptions, and it is called *playability* (Section 2.5). *PDS* is the formal system which deduces playabilities of composite performance descriptions from those of components.

2.2 Time Intervals

Most of the existing formal approaches to real-time systems adopt point-based time domains. Namely, they treat time as (total or partial) ordered sets [8].

Playbacks of continuous-media data, however, are realized over some time periods or time intervals. On the other hand, in other real-time systems, each instruction is usually assumed to be executed in a moment. We argue, therefore, that interval-based time domains are appropriate for treating performances of continuous-media data.

There are multiple ways of defining intervals [9,10]. We follow the formalization based on "chopping modality" in [10], because it is suitable to sequential and parallel composition of performances.

The time domain of *PDS* is $\langle \boldsymbol{I}, \oplus, + \rangle$, where $\boldsymbol{I}$ is the set of time intervals, $\oplus$ is a ternary relation on $\boldsymbol{I}$, and $+$ is an associative binary operator on $\boldsymbol{I}$. For $\boldsymbol{i}, \boldsymbol{i}_1, \boldsymbol{i}_2 \in \boldsymbol{I}$, $\langle \boldsymbol{i}, \boldsymbol{i}_1, \boldsymbol{i}_2 \rangle \in \oplus$ indicates that the interval $\boldsymbol{i}$ can be divided into adjacent intervals $\boldsymbol{i}_1$ and $\boldsymbol{i}_2$, where $\boldsymbol{i}_2$ follows $\boldsymbol{i}_1$. We use the notation $\boldsymbol{i} = \boldsymbol{i}_1 \oplus \boldsymbol{i}_2$ to mean $\langle \boldsymbol{i}, \boldsymbol{i}_1, \boldsymbol{i}_2 \rangle \in \oplus$. The operator $+$ stands for the addition of intervals. We assume that $\boldsymbol{i} = \boldsymbol{i}_1 \oplus \boldsymbol{i}_2$ implies $\boldsymbol{i} = \boldsymbol{i}_1 + \boldsymbol{i}_2$ and that, for any $\boldsymbol{i} \in \boldsymbol{I}, \boldsymbol{i} = \boldsymbol{i} + \boldsymbol{i}$. Although convex union may fit our intuition about "addition of intervals", we need not impose any more assumptions on $+$ and $\oplus$.

2.3 Performances

As described at the beginning of this section, when performances are requested by a user, their intended QoS are usually added to the request. For instance, a request for realization of an animation performance may contain the following QoS:

Duration	between 20 and 22 seconds.
Frame rate	more than 10 frames per second.
Colors	more than 256 colors.

By *a performance description*, we mean a specification (or, namely, a set) of certain performances together with its intended QoS. The main features of performance descriptions are:

(i) Formulas on Intervals

Performances are realized on intervals. Therefore, performance descriptions can be regarded as predicates on intervals.

(ii) Composition Operators

Timing constraints such as synchronization and sequentialization among performances are often enforced. Moreover, users may want to share common performances (Section 4). In order that performance descriptions may express these points, we introduce operators for sequential composition, parallel composition and shared performances as logical connectives.

Performance description has the following syntax:

$$\boldsymbol{D} ::= \boldsymbol{A} \mid (\boldsymbol{D}_1 \wedge \boldsymbol{D}_2) \mid (\boldsymbol{D}_1 \| \boldsymbol{D}_2) \mid (\boldsymbol{D}_1 ; \boldsymbol{D}_2) \mid \boldsymbol{D}^\mu$$

where $\boldsymbol{A}$ varies over atomic performance descriptions, where an atomic performance description consists of non-reducible performances. (We will come back this in Section 2.5.) On the other, μ is one of the identifiers which are superscripted to performance descriptions. Such identifiers impose restrictions on intervals of realization of superscripted performance descriptions. Namely, if several occurrences of (sub)descriptions are superscripted by the same identifier, they must be realized on the same interval.

Validity of each atomic proposition is supposed to be given as a *valuation* V, which is a relation between intervals and atomic propositions. $(i, A) \in V$ intuitively means A is realizable on i, which is formalized later in Section 2.5. We define the validity of performance descriptions as follows, where $(V, i) \models D$ stands for that a performance description D is valid on an interval i under a valuation V.

$$
\begin{array}{llll}
(V, i) & \models & A & \text{iff} \quad (i, A) \in V \\
(V, i) & \models & (D_1 \wedge D_2) & \text{iff} \quad (V, i_1) \models D_1, (V, i_2) \models D_2 \text{ and } i = i_1 + i_2. \\
(V, i) & \models & (D_1 \| D_2) & \text{iff} \quad (V, i) \models D_1 \text{ and } (V, i) \models D_2 \\
(V, i) & \models & (D_1; D_2) & \text{iff} \quad (V, i_1) \models D_1, (V, i_2) \models D_2 \text{ and } i = i_1 \oplus i_2.
\end{array}
$$

An Example: Post-Recording

Let $(M_1; M_2; M_3)$ be a performance description of a sequence of soundless animation performances:

M_1 : Tom speaks,
M_2 : Tom continues speaking and Jerry also speaks, and
M_3 : Jerry continues speaking.

Suppose that a performance description of sound

D_1 : Tom's voice

is prepared, and that we want to synchronize it with $(M_1; M_2)$, where Tom speaks, by post-recording. Here, the whole performance is $((D_1 \| (M_1; M_2)); M_3)$. And then, we prepare another performance description

D_2 : Jerry's voice.

and try to synchronize it, by post-recording, with $(M_2; M_3)$ where Jerry speaks. The whole performance description becomes $(D_1 \| (M_1; M_2^\mu)) \wedge (D_2 \| (M_2^\mu; M_3))$. Notice that two occurrences of the description M_2 denote the same performance, because the identifier μ is superscripted to both occurrences.

2.4 Processors

Let us give an example. Suppose that a performance description D specifies performances of an animation during about 20 seconds with a certain QoS such as colors, frame rate and resolution. In order to realize a performance which satisfies D, proper use of *processors* such as CPU allotment, network resources and access to an MMDB, is needed.

Processors can be viewed as amalgamated structures that have two dimensions: one is of resource availabilities and the other is of intervals. Namely, "how much and what kinds of resources can be used and on which intervals they are available", where the resource availability may change over the time intervals.

More formally, we define processors to be $\langle \boldsymbol{Pro}, \otimes, \boldsymbol{Pro\_I} \rangle$, where

Pro the set of all the processors.

$\otimes$ an associative and commutative binary operator on Pro.

Pro_I a function from the processors to the intervals.

Their intuitive meanings are as follows, where r, r_1 and r_2 are processors.

$r = r_1 \otimes r_2$ the processor r can be divided into two processors r_1 and r_2.

$Pro\_I(r) = i$ i is the interval on which the processor r is available.

By "*a processor description*", we mean a specification, or a set, of processors. For example, a processor of 'CPU allotment over certain intervals', satisfying the conditions below, may be required for realization of $\boldsymbol{D}$ in the example at the beginning of this section (2.4):

Duration of intervals	between 18 and 22 seconds.
Frequency of turns	CPU becomes available more than 10 times per second.
Duration of each turn	Once it becomes available, CPU is kept available for more than 10 milliseconds.

The following is another example of processor descriptions. We can specify availability of network resources and access to an MMDB by parameters below.

Duration	20 seconds
Available bandwidth	64 kbps (over the whole interval)
Access to the MMDB	read-permission for first 5 seconds

Remarks: Performances are instances of "perception" media and therefore viewed as *states* of "presentation" media on intervals. Processor descriptions can be considered as predicates on processors or sets of processors. Processors, however, are physical entities and can not be freely copied. Therefore, the formalization of processor descriptions follows the idea of *resource-sensitive*ness in linear logic [11].

Multiple operators on processor descriptions are defined (Figure 1). Let us give some examples. Let $\boldsymbol{R}_1$ and $\boldsymbol{R}_2$ be processor descriptions. Then, binary operators $\otimes$, $\bowtie$, $\updownarrow$, $\triangle$ and $\triangleright$ are defined as follows.

$$R_1 \otimes R_2 \equiv \{r \mid \exists r_1 \in R_1, \exists r_2 \in R_2, r = r_1 \otimes r_2\}$$
$$R_1 \bowtie R_2 \equiv \{r \mid \exists r_1 \in R_1, \exists r_2 \in R_2, r = r_1 \otimes r_2 \text{ and } Pro\_I(r) = Pro\_I(r_1) \oplus Pro\_(r_2)\}$$
$$R_1 \updownarrow R_2 \equiv \{r \mid \exists r_1 \in R_1, \exists r_2 \in R_2, r = r_1 \otimes r_2 \text{ and } Pro\_I(r_1) = Pro\_I(r_2)\}$$
$$R_1 \triangle R_2 \equiv \{r \mid \forall r_1 \in Pro, \forall r_2 \in R_2, \text{ "}r_1 = r \otimes r_2 \text{ and } Pro\_I(r) = Pro\_I(r_2)\text{"}$$
$$\text{implies } r_1 \in R_1\}$$
$$R_1 \triangleright R_2 \equiv \{r \mid \forall r_1 \in R_1, \forall r_2 \in Pro, \text{ "}r_2 = r_1 \otimes r \text{ and } Pro\_(r_2) = Pro\_(r_1) \oplus Pro\_(r)\text{"}$$
$$\text{implies } r_2 \in R_2\}$$

Use of these operators will simplify the presentations of some examples in the rest of the paper. Note that we use the same symbol $\otimes$ on processors as well as on processor descriptions, for it increases readability without any confusion.

272

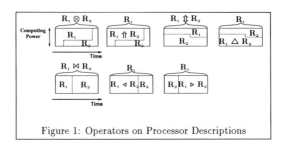

Figure 1: Operators on Processor Descriptions

Examples

Suppose that processor descriptions R and $Measure_{10}$ are given. R specifies the following usage of network resources:

Duration	between 25 and 30 seconds.
Bandwidth	more than 64 kbps.

$Measure_{10}$ specifies the processors with a duration of 10 seconds doing nothing:

Duration	10 seconds.
–	No ability

Here are examples of processor descriptions composed by operators.

Example I: $(R \bowtie Measure_{10})$ specifies such processors as

- have durations between 35 and 40 seconds.
- offer bandwidth of more than 64 kbps for durations between 25 and 30 seconds.
- do nothing for the last 10 seconds (probably waiting for an event).

Example II: $(Measure_{10} \triangleright R)$ specifies such processors as

- have durations between 15 and 20 seconds.
- offer bandwidth of more than 64 kbps for a period of 25 to 30 seconds, starting 10 seconds before the interval.

2.5 Playabilities

A *playability* is a relation between a processor description and a performance description. There are two typical kinds of relations.

(i) Universal Relations: If a processor satisfies a particular condition, it can realize some performance description.

(ii) Existential Relations: There is at least one processor that can realize some performance description. The processor is known to satisfy a particular processor description.

Correspondingly, we have two forms of playabilities: *box playability* with a modal operator "[ ]" and *diamond playability* with an operator "⟨ ⟩".

We assume the relation *Conf* between the processors and the atomic performance descriptions. Intuitively, $(r, A) \in Conf$ indicates that r can realize A on the interval $Pro\_I(r)$. It is out of the concerns of *PDS* whether or not each element (r, A) is in *Conf*. It is supposed to be justified by another lower level formalism which models more concrete levels of multimedia systems.

We say a valuation V is *generated from r* if

$$V = \{(\text{Pro\_I}(r), A)\} \text{ where } (r, A) \in Conf$$

or if

$$V = V_1 \cup V_2, \text{ where } r = r_1 \otimes r_2 \text{ and}$$
$$V_1 \text{ and } V_2 \text{ are generated from } r_1 \text{ and } r_2, \text{respectively.}$$

We say r *can realize D* if there exists a valuation V generated from r and an interval i such that $(V, i) \models D$.

Playability has the following syntax.

$$\boldsymbol{P ::= [R]D \mid \langle R\rangle D \mid P \wedge P}$$

where

$$
\begin{aligned}
[R]D &\equiv \forall r \in R, r \text{ can realize D.} \\
\langle R\rangle D &\equiv \exists r \in R, r \text{ can realize D.} \\
P_1 \wedge P_2 &\text{ iff } \text{ both } P_1 \text{ and } P_2 \text{ hold.}
\end{aligned}
$$

Note that these playabilities force allotment of processors and realization of performances to be on exactly the same intervals.

Examples of Playabilities

Now, we can express playabilities of various media types. Let us give some examples.

Example I: Static-Media Data (Figure 2)
> Let D_1 be a performance description requiring that a still-image data M is displayed in 32,000 colors for some duration. A processor is needed only at the beginning of the realization in order to write the data on the frame buffer.

Example II: Continuous and Compressed Media Data (Figure 3)
> Let D_2 be a performance description of an animation data, which are compressed and stored in a database. Therefore, in order to realize a performance satisfying D_2, uncompression is needed before their playback. It takes 10 seconds for uncompression.

It may be worth noticing that, in order to realize a performance on an interval, a processor on another interval may be needed. In Example I, a processor is needed only at the beginning of the realization of a still-image performance, while in Example II, uncompression of the animation data is needed beforehand. This disagreement between intervals of performances and processors has made it difficult to achieve synchronization among performances of different media data types.

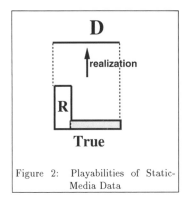

Figure 2: Playabilities of Static-Media Data

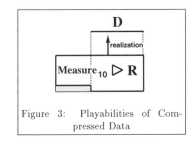

Figure 3: Playabilities of Compressed Data

Using the notion of playability, however, modalities borrowed from interval logic make it possible to describe playabilities of various media types in a unified way.

Playability of Example I: $[R_1 \bowtie True]D_1$

where R_1 specifies such processors that are needed at the beginning of the realization, and where $True \equiv Proc$, i.e., all the processors are in $True$. The playability $[R_1 \bowtie True]D_1$ indicates that systems only have to reserve a processor in R_1 at the beginning of the realization of D_1, and any processor can continue the realization after that.

Playability of Example II: $[Measure_{10} \triangleright R_2]D_2$

where R_2 specifies those processors which can uncompress the data and can realize D_2, and $Measure_{10}$ specifies those processors which spend 10 seconds doing nothing.

Then a playability $[Measure_{10} \triangleright R_2]D_2$ indicates that if a processor satisfying R_2 is prepared 10 seconds before a playback, it can realize D_2.

3 Deduction Rules of Playabilities

In this section, from among many possible rules, we give several rules for deducing playabilities of composite performances from those of components.

3.1 A Rule for Parallel Composition

$$\frac{[R_1]D_1 \quad [R_2]D_2}{[R_1 \updownarrow R_2](D_1 \| D_2)} \; [\, \| \,]$$

This rule deduces playabilities of $(D_1 \| D_2)$ from those of D_1 and D_2. Note that $R_1 \updownarrow R_2$ does not specify those processors which "can realize either, D_1 or D_2". It specifies those which "can realize both D_1 and D_2", as is seen from the "resource-sensitive" definition of processor descriptions.

Let us explain the rule more formally. Suppose $r \in R_1 \mathbin{\text{\ding{123}}} R_2$ be given. From the definition of $R_1 \mathbin{\text{\ding{123}}} R_2$, there exists $r_1 \in R_1$ and $r_2 \in R_2$ such that $r = r_1 \mathbin{\text{\ding{123}}} r_2$. Therefore, D_1 and D_2 are realizable on the same interval (without any interference between), because $[R_1]D_1$ and $[R_2]D_2$ are assumed, and $r_1 \in R_1$ and $r_2 \in R_2$ are on the same interval. Therefore, we have a playability $[R_1 \mathbin{\text{\ding{123}}} R_2](D_1 || D_2)$ as a consequence.

3.2 A Rule for Sequential Composition

$$\frac{[R_1]D_1 \quad [R_2]D_2}{[R_1 \bowtie R_2](D_1 ; D_2)} \; [\,;\,]$$

Similarly as Section 3.1.

3.3 Another Rule for Parallel Composition

Deduction rules which include diamond playabilities as a hypothesis are a bit more complicated.

$$\frac{\langle R_1 \rangle D_1 \quad [R_2]D_2 \quad R_1 \rightarrow (\,True \mathbin{\triangle} R_2\,) \; \raisebox{0.5ex}{$\vdots\,\pi$}}{\langle R_1 \mathbin{\text{\ding{123}}} R_2 \rangle (D_1 || D_2)} \; \langle \,|| \,\rangle$$

where $R_1 \rightarrow R_2 \equiv \{r \mid r \in R_1 \text{ implies } r \in R_2\}$ and $\genfrac{}{}{0pt}{}{\vdots\,\pi}{R}$ denotes that R is supposed to proved, i.e., proved to be equal to Pro, using a certain formal system of processor descriptions.

The hypotheses of this rule only assert that there exists a processor $r \in R_1$ that can realize D_1. Suppose for every processor $r_1 \in R_1$, there exists a processor $r_2 \in R_2$, such that r_1 and r_2 are on the same interval (that is what the third hypothesis asserts). Then, whichever processor r may be, there exists a processor in R_2 on the same interval as r. Therefore, the consequence holds.

The rules for sequential composition with modality $\langle\,\rangle$ are analogously defined.

3.4 An Example: Sequential Composition of Still-Image Performances and Compressed Animation Performances

Let us consider a concrete example. Suppose that a user requires realization of a performance of some animation data. It needs, however, uncompression before realization, and so still-image data is scheduled to be shown during uncompression. Let playabilities of still-image performances and of animation performances be given as the same as those of the examples in Section 2.5, i.e., given by $[R_1 \bowtie True]D_1$

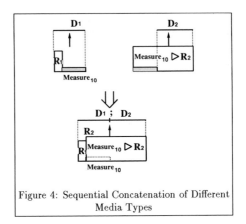

Figure 4: Sequential Concatenation of Different
Media Types

and $[Measure_{10} \triangleright R_2]D_2$, respectively. Then, what we want is a playability of the intented performances $(D_1; D_2)$. It is deduced as follows:

$$[R_1 \bowtie True]D_1 \quad [Measure_{10} \triangleright R_2]D_2$$
$$\vdots$$
$$[R_1 \bowtie R_2](D_1; D_2)$$

The deduction is achieved using composition rules as above and formalization of the nature of $Measure_{10}$, but the detailed explanation of each step is omitted due to the space limitation. Rather, we sketch the whole deduction as follows.

Let $r \in R_1 \bowtie R_2$ be given. By the definition of $R_1 \bowtie R_2$, there exists $r_1 \in R_1$ and $r_2 \in R_2$ such that $r = r_1 \bowtie r_2$. Moreover, since the duration of r_2 is longer than 10 seconds, r_2 is supposed to be divided into $r_m \in Measure_{10}$ and $r' \in Pro$, where $r_2 = r \bowtie r'$. Firstly, $r_1 \bowtie r_m$ can realize D_1, since $[R_1 \bowtie True]D_1$ is assumed, $r_1 \in R_1$ and $r_m \in True$. Secondly, $r' \in Measure_{10} \triangleright R_2$ is shown. In order to show it, we must show that for any $r'_m \in Measure_{10}$, $r'_m \bowtie r'$ implies $r'_m \bowtie r' \in R_2$. But by the nature of $Measure_{10}$, $r'_m \in Meazure_{10}$ and $r'_m \bowtie r'$ implies $r_m = r'_m$. Since $r_m \bowtie r' \in R_2$ holds, $r' \in Measure_{10} \triangleright R_2$ holds.

4 Shared Performances

As briefly described in Section 1, one of the main features of *PDS* is formal treatments of performance sharing. In this section, the concept and the formalization of performance sharing are introduced firstly, via an example.

4.1 An example: Broadcast Programs

As an example of performance sharing, let us consider broadcasting of TV news programs. Let "*Station_A*" be the central station and "*Station_B*" be one of the local stations. Suppose that $Station_A$ and $Station_B$ schedule to broadcast their respective news programs on the same period, while sharing nation-wide news among these programs.

$Station_A$ plans a news program specified by $\boldsymbol{D}_A \equiv (Global; Local_A)$, where a performance description $Global$ specifies broadcasting of the nation-wide news, and where $Local_A$ specifies a local news program produced by $Station_A$. $Station_B$ plans a news program specified by $\boldsymbol{D}_B \equiv (Global; Local_B)$, where $Local_B$ specifies a local news program produced by $Station_B$.

Two occurrences of $Global$, one is in $\boldsymbol{D}_A$ and the other is in $\boldsymbol{D}_B$, are supposed to be realized by the same newscast. A situation such as the above is called "*performance sharing*", in which more than one performance descriptions are supposed to be realized by realization of only a single performance.

Performance sharing is expressed in *PDS* as follows:

$$((Global^{\mu}; Local_A) \wedge (Global^{\mu}; Local_B))$$

Note that, in this example, two occurrences of $Global$ must be realized by the same newscast, as specified by $\boldsymbol{\mu}$.

4.2 A Sharing Rule of Playabilities

The following is the "[*sharing*]" rule of playabilities.

$$\frac{[R]D \quad \overset{\vdots \ \pi}{\mathcal{E}(R)}}{[R^{+a}]D^{\mu} \wedge \langle R^{-a}\rangle D^{\mu}} \ [sharing]$$

where $\boldsymbol{\mu}$ and $\boldsymbol{a}$ are identifiers of performance descriptions and processor descriptions respectively, and where choice of them is unique to each application of the rule. Also, $\overset{\vdots \ \pi}{\mathcal{E}(R)}$ denotes that $\boldsymbol{R}$ is supposed to be proved to be non-empty using a certain formal system for processor descriptions.

4.3 Applying the Rule to the Broadcasting Example

Applying the [*sharing*] rule to the broadcasting situation, we get the following deduction.

$$\frac{[Net]Global \quad \overset{\vdots \ \pi}{\mathcal{E}(Net)}}{[Net^{+a}]Global^{\mu} \wedge \langle Net^{-a}\rangle Global^{\mu}} \ [sharing]$$

where the processor description Net specifies those network resources which are needed to realize $Global$. The second hypothesis asserts that there exists such a resource.

Let us explain how it works. $Station_A$ prepares network resources satisfying Net, and broadcasts the news satisfying $Global$ using the resources. In other words, $Station_A$ is entitled to decide and prepare the processor among those which satisfy Net. On the other hand, $Station_B$ need not prepare any resource for the nation-wide newscast, or it does not know which processor satisfying Net will be used for the newscast.

According to the consequence of the rule,

$Station_A$ gets the playability $P_A \equiv [Net^{+a}]Global^{\mu}$.
$Station_B$ gets the playability $P_B \equiv \langle Net^{-a}\rangle Global^{\mu}$.

Let us explain the notation of these playabilities.

(i) Modalities of Playabilities

The modality "[ ]" of $\boldsymbol{P}_A$ indicates that $Station_A$ can decide which processor satisfying Net is to be used for broadcasting of the nation-wide news.

The modality "$\langle \ \rangle$" of $\boldsymbol{P}_B$ indicates that $Station_B$ only knows that broadcasting of the nation-wide news is realized by a certain processor satisfying Net.

(ii) Identifiers to Superscript Processor Descriptions

The identifier "$+\boldsymbol{a}$" in $\boldsymbol{P}_A$ indicates that $Station_A$ ought to prepare a processor satisfying Net in order to realize the shared broadcasting performance.

The identifier "$-\boldsymbol{a}$" in $\boldsymbol{P}_B$ indicates that $Station_B$ need not prepare any processor in order to realize the shared broadcasting performance, because $Station_A$ will do it on its behalf.

Let "$[Net_A]Local_A$", "$[Net_B]Local_B$" be the playabilities of $Local_A$ and $Local_B$, respectively. Then, the playability of the whole newscast $(Global^{\mu}; Local_A) \wedge (Global^{\mu}; Local_B)$ can be deduced as follows:

$$\frac{[Net_A]Local_A \quad \dfrac{[Net]Global \quad \mathcal{E}(Net)}{[Net^{+a}]Global^{\mu} \wedge \langle Net^{-a}\rangle Global^{\mu}} \vphantom{}^{\vdots\,\pi} \quad [Net_B]Local_B \quad \dfrac{}{(Net \rightarrow (Net' \vartriangleleft Net_B))}^{\vdots\,\pi}}{[Net^{+a} \bowtie Net_A](Global^{\mu}; Local_A) \wedge \langle Net'\rangle(Global^{\mu}; Local_B)}$$

where $R_1 \vartriangleleft R_2 \equiv \{r \mid \forall r_1 \in Pro, \forall r_2 \in R_2,$
"$r_1 = r \otimes r_2$ and $Pro\_I(r_1) = Pro\_I(r) \oplus Pro\_I(r_2)$" implies $r_1 \in R_1\}$.

5 Conclusion

We assert that the main issues of multimedia systems are: i) Realization of continuous media performances with given QoS, ii) Integration of various types of media, iii) Availability of resources and/or physical media, iv) Real-time constraints among performances, and v) Performance sharing among users. However, existing formalisms do not necessarily seem to adequetly deal with these issues, especially, integration of static media and continuous-media, the notion of shared performances, and the notion of realizability of performances. We have introduced *PDS* and explained how these issues can be dealt with upon *PDS* .

According to *PDS* , the main notions of multimedia systems are introduced as entities over time-intervals. We assert that this approach has the advantage of giving a highly abstract view of multimedia systems. We believe that *PDS* can be one of the candidates of models of multimedia systems. Finally, although it is important from the theoretical point of view, the problem of soundness of the proposed deduction rules is not addressed in this paper. It will be the topic of another paper. However, the proof of soundness should be rather straightforward. Only the rules, concerning shared performances, will require more work.

References

1. Miae Woo, Naveed U.Qazi, and Arif Ghafoor. A synchronization framework for communication of pre-orchestrated multimedia information. *IEEE Network*, pages 52–61, January/February 1994.
2. Howard Bowman Gordon Blair, Lynne Blair and Amanda Chetwyd. Formal support for the specification and construction of distributed multimedia systems(the tempo project). Technical Report MPG-93-23, Department of Computing, Lancaster University, 1993.
3. Simon Gibbs. Composite multimedia and active objects. In *OOPSLA*, pages 97–112, 1991.
4. Richard Staehli and Jonathan Walpole. Script-based QoS specifications for multimedia presentations. Technical Report 93-022, Oregon Graduate Institute of Science & Technology, 1993.
5. F.Panzieri and R.Davoli Date. Real time systems: A tutorial. Technical Report UBLCS-93-22, University of Bologna, October 1993.
6. Inc. Apple Computer. *QuickTime Developper's Guide*. Draft Developer technical Publications, 1991.
7. Roger B. Dannenberg and Dean Rubin. A comparison of streams and time advance as paradigms for multimedia systems. Technical Report CMU-CS-94-124, CMU, 1994.
8. Mehmet A.Orgun and Wanli Ma. An overview of temporal and modal logic programming. Technical report, Department of Computing, Macquarie University, 1994.
9. Johan Van Benthem. *The Logics of Time*, chapter I. Kluwer Academic Publishers, 2nd edition, 1991.
10. Yde VENEMA. A modal logic for chopping intervals. *Journal of Logic of Computation*, 1(4), September 1991.
11. Jearn-Yves Girard. Linear logic. *Theoretical Computer Science*, 50:1–102, 1987.

Chapter 7

Music Analysis and Performance System

LOOKING WHILE LISTENING: A MULTIMEDIA VISION OF MUSIC ANALYSIS

STEPHEN W. SMOLIAR

FX Palo Alto Laboratory, Inc.; 3400 Hillview Avenue, Bldg. 4
Palo Alto, California 94304, USA
Email: smoliar@pal.xerox.com

ABSTRACT

Music analysis is basically a problem in description. This paper examines three approaches to solving the problem, narrative, mathematics, and graphics, with an emphasis on graphics. The fundamental conclusion, however, is that no one descriptive technique is superior to all others. If we are confronted with the problem of describing music in a document, then the only way we can do justice to description will be if that document is a hyperdocument which takes advantage of the ability to link together a variety of presentations in different media. Therefore, we conclude by sorting out the different media which need to contribute to such documents and try to account for the nature of the links among them.

1. Music Analysis: A Problem in Description

When we think about multimedia applications in music, we generally think about systems which *compose* music,[21] although the problem of getting a computer to *perform* expressively is as much a problem of music generation as is automated composition.[1] However, *listening* to music is as challenging as generating it,[18] if not more so, since listening tends to be more directly involved with the medium of sound than are many aspects of composition or performance. One of the difficulties we must confront if we wish to have a computer listen to music is that we are not exactly sure what *people* do when *they* listen to music. Clearly, listening has a lot to do with music education. It even figures prominently in the professional literature as the discipline of *music analysis*; but there seems to be far less agreement about the tasks of music analysis than there is about those of composing and performing music. This is particularly ironic because much of music analysis has been reduced to the symbolic modeling of musical information and the manipulation of the resulting models.

In computer science when we think of constructing and manipulating symbolic models, we think of the capabilities afforded by programming languages such as LISP. In the humanities, however, the tradition of working with symbols is based not so much on symbolic calculi and their foundations in formal logic as it is on the foundations of *semiotics*, which is concerned more with the different *contexts* in which symbols are employed than it is with how those symbols are constructed and manipulated.[16] This broader contextual view argues that there is more to a symbol system, such as a natural language, than syntax and semantics; and one of its key tasks is to *describe* that system in a manner which illuminates just what the nature of that "more" is.

Music analysis is just such a problem of description: the description of the experience of listening to a musical composition.[22] The "more" of semiotics addresses the problem that description cannot be readily reduced to a simple exchange of symbolic codes. Thus, the description of a music experience cannot be reduced to some symbolic data structure, no matter how elaborate that data structure may be. This is because such data structures must respect certain *a priori* conventions concerning how symbols are used to communicate; but when I, as a human being, need to describe a music experience, particularly to other human beings, I cannot always assume that those conventions exist, let alone identify what they are.

What is required is a more agent-based view of music analysis. In particular the task of description, as it is applied to music analysis, is founded on *two* agents: the agent giving the description and the agent receiving it. Those two agents are rarely "of the same mind," so to speak. (They certainly do not have identical mental states, regardless what particular philosophy you choose to characterize the nature of mental states.)[14] Therefore, description is not so much a matter of the describing agent passing a code to the receiving agent as it is a matter of the two agents mutually negotiating towards a point where they have some confidence that they are both talking about the same thing.

2. Approaches to Description

John Roeder[16] has observed that there are three approaches to solving this problem of description: narrative, mathematics, and graphics. Let us briefly review the nature of the first two. Then we shall concentrate more specifically on the role of graphics.

The narrative approach is basically the most intuitive: the best way to describe music is simply to talk about it. Unfortunately, the very question of what it means to talk about music is highly complex—perhaps so complex as not to allow a single answer which can apply to all forms of music. Thus, if the music "tells a story," as in a tone poem or a setting of text, the narrative approach can begin with the story and attempt to explain how the music relates to it. However, it is unclear that this position can be generalized. Certainly not all music tells a story *explicitly*, and it is at least debatable whether music which does not tell one explicitly does so *implicitly*.

Another problem concerns just what it is that we are trying to describe. At one level music notation is a description, but that level has a highly variable degree of connection to what the *sound* of the music actually is. However, we can carry this reduction even further and argue that music is not so much the sounds which are produced as it is the *behavior* which leads to their production.[9] Thus, we are up against a broad class of problems concerning the description of behavior, many of which are far from being settled by psychology, the discipline which is supposed to worry about such problems of description.

Another approach to the use of narrative is to focus on communication through *poetic* devices, rather than those of expository prose. Robert Cogan[4] cites how Chinese music theorists of the Sung dynasty characterized an instrument sound as "dragonflies alighting on water" and another as "a cold cicada bemoaning the coming of autumn." However, his reaction to this approach is negative: "Although marvelously evocative, such images bring us no closer to sonic understanding—no closer, particularly, to the role of any sound in its sonic element." George Lakoff and Mark Johnson,[7] on the other hand, would take issue with Cogan's dismissal of the Sung use of metaphorical language as a basis for an ontology:

> Metaphor is for most people a device of the poetic imagination and the rhetorical flourish—a matter of extraordinary rather than ordinary language. Moreover, metaphor is typically viewed as characteristic of language alone, a matter of words rather than thought or action. For this reason, most people think they can get along perfectly well without metaphor. We have found, on the contrary, that metaphor is pervasive in everyday life, not just in language but in thought and action. Our ordinary conceptual system, in terms of which we both think and act, is fundamentally metaphorical in nature.

In other words the use of metaphor is far more than "marvelously evocative." Instead, as Lakoff and Johnson[7] demonstrate, the use of metaphor cuts very close to the "concepts that govern our thought" to the point where it may be the most appropriate approach to narrative description—for just about *any* subject matter—at our disposal.

Nevertheless, narrative is fundamentally an *informal* approach to description. This century has seen a variety of attempts to approach music with a much higher degree of formal rigor than has been applied in past centuries. The result has been increasing attention towards the expressiveness of mathematics.[10] Generally, this use of mathematics involves an *abstraction* of some set of properties which are represented by music notation and an *encoding* from the notational representation to some appropriate set of mathematical objects. The initial efforts in this approach usually involved the translation of pitches or intervals into integers which then served as domains for specific algebraic structures. However, as theorists became more enlightened to the fact that algebraic structures did not have to be defined over numbers, greater attention has been paid to the definition of abstract symbol structures and the operators which manipulate them.

When computer science was still in its infancy, Richard Hamming[6] gave us a memorable aphorism: "The purpose of computing is insight, not numbers." The same may be said of mathematics. Translating elements of music notation into mathematical structures is only useful to the extent that the mathematics will allow us to describe properties of the music which might not otherwise be evident. Furthermore, those properties should be significant not only by virtue of their underlying mathematics but also to the extent that they are related to how the music itself can ultimately be *heard*. This is the greatest challenge which the mathematical approach to description must face, although, as has been excellently demonstrated by David Lewin,[11] it is definitely capable of being met.

Graphic approaches to representation arise from a need to get away from both the limitations of narrative text and the constrictions of mathematical formalisms. The basic intuition here is that the non-verbal medium of sound should be replaced with the equally non-verbal medium of images. There is a potential danger here on biological grounds, however, since the path from ear to brain is decidedly different from that from eye to brain.[5] Nevertheless, graphics offers at least the *opportunity* for insights which might not be adequately abstracted by mathematical formalism or recognized in the course of narrative description. Furthermore, there is actually considerable *variety* in how graphics may be invoked in the interest of music description; so let us now try to gain some appreciation of the scope of that variety.

3. What Can Graphics Tell Us?

3.1. Musical Scores

The most obvious way in which graphics may serve the description of music is through the constructs of music notation. Certainly, these are the visual stimuli which are most commonly associated with music experiences; but they present some significant problems. Most important is that music notation is fundamentally *prescriptive*: It is more concerned with what performers are supposed to *do* than with what the listeners *experience*. Often this means that the notation assumes some underlying body of "background interpretation knowledge" on the part of the performer, which entails that what is specified by the notation is intentionally *incomplete*. For

286

example, the dynamic markings in the manuscripts of Wolfgang Amadeus Mozart are often so few that subsequent editors have inserted their own in order to provide more explicit instructions for performance.[17] Also, as the potential for *what* can be done in the course of a music performance has increased, particularly in the course of this century, the range of graphic constructs introduced to prescribe such behavior has grown at a prodigious rate.[3] Yet, in spite of this abundance of graphical constructs, there are still many critical aspects regarding both the performing and experiencing of music which

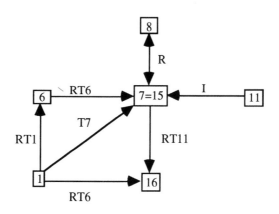

Fig. 1. Lewin's Mathematical Analysis of Dallapiccola.

notation simply cannot capture.[4] If description is what we seek, we are not going to find it strictly in music notation.

3.2. Abstractions of Other Descriptions

Often graphics are best put to use to supplement descriptions formulated in other terms. Thus, mathematical arguments frequently benefit from the use of diagrams which are either tightly coupled to the reasoning process or simply serve to make the conclusions clearer. We see an example of this in a mathematical description of music by Lewin, who constructed the diagram in Fig. 1 to illustrate his analysis of the first sixteen measures of a structurally sophisticated piano composition by Luigi Dallapiccola.[11] Each boxed integer represents a statement of a twelve-tone row which fills the entire measure (except for the first statement of the row, which fills the first five measures and is represented simply by the boxed 1). The arrows are labeled by "classical" transformations[a] of a row: T stands for Transposition, displacing all the pitches in the row by the same interval. (The displacement is given by the integer following the T.) R stands for Retrogression, playing the pitches in reverse order; and I

---

[a] These transformations are called "classical" because their origins may be traced back to Arnold Schoenberg's initial formulation of the use of twelve-tone rows in composition.[20]

stands for Inversion, playing each interval between the pitches in its opposite direction.[b] Regardless of the specific details of what the nodes and edges of this directed graph stand for, however, what is important is that the relationships among those transformations are more readily captured by the diagram than they could be by verbal explanation (which is also provided extensively by Lewin. In other words the mathematics may describe how this particular passage of music has been *structured*, but Lewin turns to constructing a diagram in order to communicate the *significance* of that structure.

One of the reasons this diagram is so effective is that it is more than just a summary of a set of elements (in this case twelve-tone rows) and the transformations which map one row into another. The *visual layout* of this directed graph is as important to Lewin's narrative as are the underlying mathematical relations. The node which stands for the one situation in which two measures both state the same row is deliberately central. Similarly, the symmetry of the lower-left corner of the diagram reflects a symmetry between the beginning and ending of the passage being analyzed. As a directed graph this diagram could have been drawn in many different ways, but the way in which it *was* drawn is a critical ingredient of its communicative significance.

Just as graphics may serve to clarify the abstractions of mathematics, they may be similarly employed as a means of clarifying what is represented in music notation. This often involves a process known as *score reduction*, in which a complex body of music notation is simplified, usually by abstracting away certain elements of the notation which may be interpreted as performing functions of embellishment or elaboration. For example in another analysis, Lewin[11] rewrites the sixteen extremely complicated measures of Karlheinz Stockhausen's *Klavierstück III* as a sequence of twenty-one measures of chord progressions. This abstraction is offered to the reader as an ear-training aid: If one can hear the chords in these progressions, one's ears will then be prepared to hear them in the original Stockhausen score.

This century has seen a long tradition of graphic approaches to score reduction. Heinrich Schenker used the technique to demonstrate how the masterpieces of tonal classical music exhibited "deep structures" involving very simple harmonic and contrapuntal progressions.[19] Schenker used graphics to represent the mapping of one of these simple structures through an entire composition through a series of transformations not unlike the rewriting rules of a context-free grammar. Eugene Narmour subsequently challenged Schenker's reductionism but replaced it with a similar notation which attempted to capture how melodic pitches form expectations which are either realized or denied.[13] However, like Schenker's, Narmour's notation attempted to represent that these relationships operated at several different levels of a hierarchy, ultimately reducing to the realization or denial of usually a single expectation. Finally, Fred Lerdahl and Ray Jackendoff have developed a suite of hierarchical graphic abstractions of musical scores which attempt to capture similar relationships of elaboration with respect to the primitives of both pitch and duration.[8] There is thus considerable variety in how graphics may be invoked to provide suitable abstractions of the representations of music notation.

3.3. Representing Sound

Yet another approach to the use of graphics arises from Cogan's alternative to the descriptive problems inherent in both narrative and music notation. For Cogan the graphic elements of greatest relevance are spectrographic traces:[4] If one wishes to

---

[b] Dallapiccola's use of twelve-tone rows is not particularly transparent. Consequently, specific examples from his score may tend to confuse more than enlighten. (There is also the problem of getting permission to reproduce such a score.)

describe the sounds of a music experience, then one should begin by *looking* at them in this form. His claim is that what the eye sees in such traces can supplement what the ear hears, perhaps even informing the mind of structural details which are not immediately apparent in the course of listening. There are several virtues in what Cogan has decided to do which deserve to be examined in some detail.

Most important of these virtues is what may be called his attempt to "conquer time." Sound cannot exist without the passage of time; but, during that passage, the sound goes as soon as it comes, so to speak. An instant cannot be scrutinized because, once scrutiny begins, the instant is gone. Cogan's images, on the other hand, are *traces* which remain in the present long after the sound has faded into the past; and, unlike the sounds themselves, those traces *can* be scrutinized in as much or as little time as the mind chooses to allocate. Music notation, of course, has the same advantage of timelessness; but these traces are an attempt to overcome the shortcomings of notation which have already been cited.

Another advantage to Cogan's approach is its scalability. By suitably compressing the time scale, one can take in the entirety of any sound event in a single glance. Of course, if that event happens to be all of an opera lasting several hours, that single glance is not likely to take in very much detail. However, if the sound source is a digital one and the spectrograph has been computed by digital signal processing techniques, it is an easy matter to construct a display in which the time scale may be adjusted in order to examine greater detail. Such an adjustable display is available in many commercial software products, such as SoundEdit 16.[12] The variable time scale is particularly important in that it provides an *implicitly hierarchical* view of the sounds of any musical experience which totally gets away from the symbolic representations of hierarchy which are found in Schenker,[19] Narmour,[13] and Lerdahl and Jackendoff.[7]

However, spectrographic traces are only one of many ways in which sound events may be represented visually. There is also the wave form itself: a display of how, for

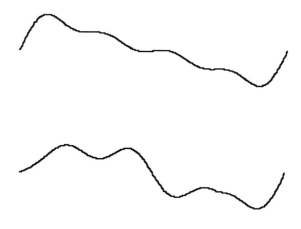

Fig. 2. Two Wave Forms Which Sound the Same.

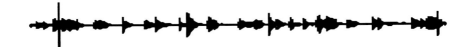

Fig. 3. Stockhausen's *Klavierstück III*.

example, a loudspeaker cone physically vibrates with the passage of time. This is again a display with the advantage of scalability; but, in this case, we have to be more careful about the scales at which we choose to examine the signal. When we get down to the millisecond level, we can see the actual periodic wave forms associated with isolated pitches. However, the *shape* of such a wave form depends not only on its *harmonic* content (as revealed by a spectrogram) but also on the *phase* associated with each of the component frequencies. The problem is that significant differences in phase do not necessarily imply differences in what is heard.[15] Consider, for example, the two wave forms in Fig. 2, each of which is represented by a single cycle. Both wave forms have the same harmonic content in identical proportions; but, in the second wave form, the second harmonic has been phase-shifted by 90°. However, in spite of the obvious differences in appearances, these wave forms are indistinguishable to the ear.

On the other hand if we view these wave forms at a *macroscopic*, rather than *microscopic*, level, they have at least the potential of being more informative. Fig. 3, for example, is the entirety of a performance of the *Klavierstück III* discussed above. This display tells us nothing about notes or pitch structures which may be modeled mathematically, but it *does* show how those notes are grouped into *gestures* and how the intensities of those gestures are modulated. In other words it provides some very direct relationships to what the ear is likely to hear when this particular music is performed.

4. What is Required: A Multimedia Architecture for Music Analysis

The "bottom line" of this exercise is that there is no one description which is superior to all others. If we are confronted with the problem of describing music in a document, then the only way we can do justice to description will be if that document is a hyperdocument which takes advantage of the ability to link together a variety of presentations in different media.[2] Therefore, we need to sort out the different media which need to contribute to such documents and try to account for the nature of the links among them.

Clearly, text is still necessary. The narrative approach cannot be sacrificed. However, when we think of text as a *printed* medium, we tend to think of it as *subordinating* other media, simply because most of those other media are less amenable to the printed page. We would do better to think of the text as actually being *narrated*—

delivered as a "real-time performance" during which it interacts with presentations in other media.

In the printed medium the other major element of musical description is the musical score. Certainly, when we *talk* about music, if often helps to refer to the notation; so links from the narrative into the notation reflect our general approach to discourse. Curious readers, however, may also want to follow such links *in reverse*. Thus, if one is preparing a particular passage for performance, it would be useful to be able to consult those elements of narrative description which are appropriate. Some performing editions do this by providing copious footnotes on the printed score pages, thus reversing the priorities of narrative text and music notation; but this approach is difficult for the reader who wishes to *begin* with the narrative. What would be more desirable would be to place narrative and notation on equal terms.

When we turn to the actual *sounds* of music, we depart from the capabilities of the printed page. These sounds are clearly tightly coupled to the musical score, but they can also be bilaterally coupled to narrative text. A text description which attempts to account for how a series of sonic events unfold in time should be aligned to those events. Similarly, the listener should be able to progress from a particular auditory experience to narrative which accounts for it, just as that listener may wish to identify where in the score that experience takes place.

Finally, there is the medium of images. Because this offers the greatest variety, it also requires the greatest complexity. Images such as wave forms and spectrograms follow the same time axis as the sound, so that particular connection is firmly and clearly defined. Similarly, score reductions are abstractions of the score itself; so there are usually straightforward links between a construct in a reduction and what has been abstracted from the score. Similarly, one may establish how different portions of a score are reduced according to different approaches to abstraction. Most problematic, however, are the diagrams which supplement mathematical descriptions. Often these diagrams refer to pitches or measures more as abstractions than as music events. Consequently, the primary links to mathematical diagrams will be more appropriately connected to explanatory narrative, since the primary role of those diagrams is to elaborate the narrative.

The relationships among these descriptive media may be summarized as in Fig. 4.

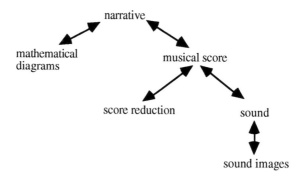

Fig. 4. Media for Describing Music.

This diagram has been represented as a tree to capture the "root" position of the role of narrative. The bidirectional edges are then intended to illustrate how both narrative and the other approaches to description tend to support each other. Furthermore, there is an implicit "horizontal axis" in the illustration which situates more abstract approaches to the left and more concrete ones to the right. Narrative is thus supported, in the abstract, by mathematical diagrams and, in the concrete, by the musical score. The score is, in turn, supplemented by diagrammatic abstraction, in the form of reductions, and by the actual sounds. Finally, the sounds may be associated with images of their wave forms and frequency content.[c] As a whole the diagram may be interpreted as a multimedia architecture for music analysis: If we wish to address that problem of how hypermedia texts about music theory should be authored, we need to begin by mapping out the scope of the domain which the authoring must accommodate. The diagram specifies what multimedia functionality will be required (particularly for the creation of graphic displays) for authoring to do justice to the domain of music theory.

5. References

1. D. P. Anderson and R. Kuivila, "Formula: A programming language for expressive computer music," *Computer*, vol. 24, no. 7, pp. 12–21, 1991.

2. N. D. Beitner, C. A. Goble, and W. Hall, "Putting the media into hypermedia," in *Proceedings: Multimedia Computing and Networking 1995* (A. A. Rodriguez and J. Maitan, eds.), pp. 12–23, SPIE, 1995.

3. J. Cage, *Notations*, New York, NY: Something Else Press, 1969.

4. R. Cogan, *New Images of Musical Sound*, Cambridge, MA: Harvard University Press, 1984.

5. J. J. Gibson, *The Senses Considered as Perceptual Systems*, Westport, CT: Greenwood Press, 1983.

6. R. W. Hamming, *Numerical Methods for Scientists and Engineers*, New York, NY: McGraw-Hill, 1962.

7. G. Lakoff and M. Johnson, *Metaphors We Live By*, Chicago, IL: The University of Chicago Press, 1980.

8. F. Lerdahl and R. Jackendoff, *A Generative Theory of Tonal Music*, Cambridge, MA: The MIT Press, 1983.

9. D. Lewin, "Music theory, phenomenology, and modes of perception," *Music Perception*, vol. 3, no. 4, pp. 327–392, 1986.

10. D. Lewin, *Generalized Musical Intervals and Transformations*, New Haven, CT: Yale University Press, 1987.

11. D. Lewin, *Musical Form and Transformation: 4 Analytic Essays*, New Haven, CT: Yale University Press, 1993.

12. Macromedia, *User's Guide: SoundEdit 16 for Macintosh*, San Francisco, CA, 1994.

13. E. Narmour, *Beyond Schenkerism: The Need for Alternatives in Music Analysis*, Chicago, IL: The University of Chicago Press, 1977.

14. H. Putnam, "The nature of mental states," in *Mind, Language and Reality: Philosophical Papers, Volume 2*, pp. 429–440, New York, NY: Cambridge University Press, 1975.

---

[c] One might wish to make a case that traces of wave forms may be viewed as more concrete, while Fourier spectra are more abstract; but it is unclear how sound such an argument would be.

15. J.-C. Risset, "Timbre analysis by synthesis: Representations, imitations, and variants for musical composition," in *Representations of Musical Signals* (G. DePoli, A. Piccialli, and C. Roads, eds.), pp. 7–43, Cambridge, MA: The MIT Press, 1991.

16. J. Roeder, "Toward a semiotic evaluation of music analysis," *Music Theory Online*, vol. 0, no. 5, 1993.

17. C. Rosen, "The shock of the old," *The New York Review*, vol. 37, no. 12, pp. 46–52, July 19, 1990.

18. R. Rowe, *Interactive Music Systems: Machine Listening and Composing*, Cambridge, MA: The MIT Press, 1993.

19. H. Schenker, *Der Freie Satz*, O. Jonas, editor, Vienna, AUSTRIA: Universal Edition, 1956.

20. A. Schoenberg, "Composition with twelve tones (1)," in *Style and Idea: Selected Writings of Arnold Schoenberg* (l. Stein, ed.), pp. 214–245, New York, NY: St. Martins Press, 1975.

21. S. W. Smoliar, "Computers compose music, but do we listen?," in *Multimedia Modeling* (T.-S. Chua and T. L. Kunii, eds.), pp. 73–77, Singapore: World Scientific, 1993.

22. S. W. Smoliar, "Comment on John Roeder's article," *Music Theory Online*, vol. 0, no. 6, 1994.

MUSICAL PERFORMANCE SYSTEM
USING 3D ACCELERATION SENSOR

SAWADA, Hideyuki;   OHKURA, Shin'ya;   HASHIMOTO, Shuji

Department of Applied Physics, School of Science and Engineering, WASEDA University
3-4-1, Okubo, Shinjuku-ku, Tokyo, 169, JAPAN
E-mail: 695L5113@cfi.waseda.ac.jp, shujivax@cfi.waseda.ac.jp

ABSTRACT

A musical instrument is a device to translate body movements into sound. Moreover, gesticulation is often employed in musical performance to express the performer's emotion. Therefore, many approaches have been proposed to analyze gesticulation or body movements for computer music systems. This paper describes a new musical system controlled directly by human gesture. The system consists of a three dimensional acceleration sensor, a MIDI sound source and a computer. The computer analyzes the kinetic parameters extracted from the acceleration vector sequence to recognize the human gesture. The recognition results can be used for both musical performance and timbre control in real-time. In performance control, the gesticulation is used as a sort of nonverbal command to direct the performance advancement, while in the timbre control, the kinetic parameters are associated with the sound parameters using the neural network to make a personal instrument. This allows private definition in the learning phase.

1. Introduction

Gesture plays an important role in our daily life as nonverbal media for emotional human communication. Therefore, if a machine can understand human gestures, it will be possible to construct a new man-machine interface with feeling.

In the field of musical performance, gesture is widely used. A conductor directs the musical performance by his baton movement. Conducting is a common nonverbal language globally used for music. On the other hand, musicians play musical instruments, which can be regarded as a kind of equipment to translate body movements into sound. In traditional musical instruments, the relationship between the action and the generated sound is determined by the physical structure of the instruments. The authors have developed a computer music system that can follow a human conductor[1] and a virtual instrument that generates sound according to a player's gesticulation by using a data glove and image processing techniques[2].

In this paper we propose a new musical performance system controlled in real-time by hand movements, using a three dimensional acceleration sensor. In previous works, body movements were measured by their positions or the trajectories of the feature points using position sensors or image processing techniques[3-6]. The most important emotional information in human gestures, however, seems to appear in the forces applied to the body. Therefore the system is required to respond to applied forces to achieve more impressive musical performance. Although there exist various methods for force measurement, we introduce a three dimensional acceleration sensor to make the

294

system simple and compact. Kinetic parameters of the hand movements are extracted from the acceleration vector sequence to translate human gestures. The recognition results can be used for both musical performance and timbre control in real-time. In performance control, the gesticulation is used as a sort of nonverbal command to direct the performance advancement, while in the timbre control the kinetic parameters are associated with sound parameters using the neural network to make a personal instrument which allows private definition in the learning phase.

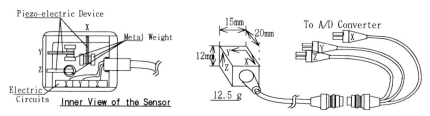

Figure 1. 3D Acceleration Sensor

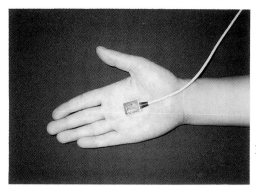

Figure 2. Picture of
Acceleration Sensor

2. Acceleration Sensor and Kinetic Parameters

2-1. 3D Acceleration Sensor

The acceleration sensor used in the proposed system is small enough to be attached to any points of the human body as illustrated in Figure 1 and Figure 2. The size is 20mm long, 15mm wide and 12mm high. It can sense independently three dimensional acceleration by the piezo-electric devices which cause the change of voltage according to the amount of acceleration applied to the sensor. The sensitivity is about 5mV per 1G in the range between -25G and +25G. Since the acceleration caused by human gestures easily exceeds 20G in the usual hand movements, this sensor is considered to be suitable for the use of gesture recognition. After passing through a 3 Hz low-pass filter to prevent the voltage signal from drifting, the acceleration data are amplified and fed to the computer through the A/D converter as 12 bit binary data.

2-2. Extraction of Kinetic Parameters

The three dimensional acceleration data $a_x(t)$, $a_y(t)$ and $a_z(t)$ are independently obtained in real-time, which correspond to the accelerations in x, y and z directions at time t, respectively. From the sequential acceleration data, gesture patterns have to be recognized. But one human gesture will not give the same sequential acceleration patterns, because sensor data have varying measurement errors and human movement can never appear the same, either, as seen in hand written characters. Consequently, simple pattern matching of sequential data won't work for a good recognition result.

To extract kinetic features from sequential acceleration patterns we use three projection vectors defined as,

$$\mathbf{A}_1(t) = (\ a_y(t), a_z(t)\ ), \quad \mathbf{A}_2(t) = (\ a_z(t), a_x(t)\ ), \quad \mathbf{A}_3(t) = (\ a_x(t), a_y(t)\ ) \tag{1}$$

where $\mathbf{A}_1(t)$ represents an acceleration vector on the y-z plane, as shown in Figure 4. In the same manner $\mathbf{A}_2(t)$ and $\mathbf{A}_3(t)$ represent the acceleration vectors on the z-x plane and x-y plane, respectively. The sampling rate of the acceleration data is set to 25Hz here. A succession of fifteen to thirty data set(the number of data are represented as s in the following equations), according to the duration of one gesture, are used for gesture recognition.

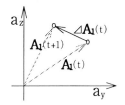

Figure 3. Difference of Acceleration Vector

Figure 4. Membership Function

Eleven kinetic parameters shown in table 1 are extracted from one sequence of each set of projected acceleration vectors in real-time for gesture recognition. These kinetic parameters were selected not only to satisfy the sufficient conditions for the discrimination of gestures to be recognized, but also to realize real-time processing.

Table 1: Kinetic Parameters

P d	Time Differences of Vectors
P g	Vector Products among Vectors
P r	Aspect Ratio of Circumscribed Rectangle
P a0 ~ P a7	Directional Characteristics of Vectors

Pd represents the total amount of acceleration differences in each plane given as,

$$P_d = \sum_{t=1}^{S-1} |\varDelta \mathbf{A}(t)|$$

(2)

Figure 3 shows the difference vector $\varDelta \mathbf{A}_1(t)$ obtained from successive vectors $\mathbf{A}_1(t)$ and $\mathbf{A}_1(t+1)$.

The rotating direction of hand movement is expressed in Pg which is calculated by the summation of vector products as,

$$P_g = \sum_{t=1}^{S-1} \mathbf{u}(\mathbf{A}(t) \times \mathbf{A}(t+1)), \quad \mathbf{u}(m) = \begin{cases} 1 & : m \geq 0 \\ 0 & : m < 0 \end{cases}$$

(3)

If acceleration vectors move in an anti-clockwise direction as illustrated in figure 3, value 1 is added to the parameter.

Pr is the aspect ratio of the circumscribed rectangle which is drawn around s-vectors in each plane, and has directional information given by the maximum vectors. Its calculation in the y-z plane is executed as below;

$$P_r = \frac{Vt^+ - Vt^-}{Hr^+ - Hr^-} \quad \begin{matrix} Vt^+ = \max_s \{az\}, & Vt^- = \min_s \{az\} \\ Hr^+ = \max_s \{ay\}, & Hr^- = \min_s \{ay\} \end{matrix}$$

(4)

The parameters Pa0 to Pa7 show the directional distribution of acceleration vectors to the eight main directions in every $\pi/4$ degrees. The membership function shown in Figure 4 is applied to each sequential acceleration data set, and the tendency to the main directions is determined by the equation below.

$$Pan = \sum_{t=1}^{S} F_n(\theta t)$$

$F_n(\theta t)$: Membership Function of n-th Main Direction

θt : Direction of $\mathbf{A}(t)$

$n = 0, 1, 2, \cdots, 7$

(5)

For example, for a vector whose angular direction is a little larger than $\pi/4$, the values f5 and f6, as shown in Figure 4, are assigned to the parameters Pa5 and Pa6, respectively, while the other Pa's are zero. Thus Pa's represent the tendency of the motion direction.

All the kinetic parameters are calculated in real-time from the sequential vectors $\mathbf{A}_1(t)$, $\mathbf{A}_2(t)$ and $\mathbf{A}_3(t)$ independently and are referred to for gesture recognition.

3. Gesture Recognition

3-1. Gesture Pattern Analysis

In gesture recognition, significant pattern data caused by human gestures have to be extracted from sequential acceleration data. In this system, the beginning of a gesture is perceived by the threshold manipulation, and then the gesture recognition procedure follows.

Gesture recognition is made by comparison with standard data acquired in the learning phase to make the system individually adaptive.

In the learning phase, the performer inputs gestures to be recognized by M times each. Then the average E_α^g and the standard deviations μ_α^g of the kinetic parameters are calculated for each gesture g as shown below, and stored as the standard pattern data. We selected M as 5 here.

$$E_\alpha^g = \frac{1}{5} \sum_{i=1}^{5} V_{\alpha i}^g \qquad \begin{array}{l} V : \text{Parameter Values} \\ \alpha = \text{Pd, Pg, Pr, Pa's} \end{array} \tag{6}$$

$$\mu_\alpha^g = \sqrt{\frac{1}{5} \sum_{i=1}^{5} (V_{\alpha i}^g - E_\alpha^g)^2} \tag{7}$$

In the recognition phase, the kinetic parameters V_α' are extracted and the evaluation value e_g is calculated for each standard pattern data as below,

$$e_g = \sum_\alpha \varepsilon_\alpha^g = \sum_\alpha \frac{(V_\alpha' - E_\alpha^g)^2}{\mu_\alpha^g} \tag{8}$$

Then the minimum e_g is selected as a candidate. In case it is smaller than a predetermined threshold value, the result of the gesture recognition is confirmed.

Some examples of recognized gestures are given in Figure 5 and Table 2, which show the acceleration trajectories in the y-z plane and their kinetic parameter values normalized as 0 to 1000, respectively.

Table 2: Examples of Kinetic Parameter values

	(a)Clockwise Rotation	(b) Single Shake	(c) Triangle Shape
Pd	547	235	472
Pg	0	458	667
Pr	126	389	231
Pa0	115	46	126
Pa1	102	111	52
Pa2	178	263	68
Pa3	163	303	244
Pa4	112	31	68
Pa5	91	20	206
Pa6	100	120	71
Pa7	139	106	165

298

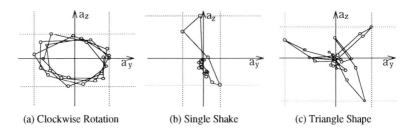

(a) Clockwise Rotation   (b) Single Shake   (c) Triangle Shape

Figure 5. Examples of Acceleration Trajectories

3-2. Musical Tempo Analysis

In the field of musical performance, a conductor directs the orchestra by showing his performance directions using a baton and gestures. Conducting can express a conductor's emotional feeling based on a conducting method, which are said to be a common nonverbal language globally used for music.

Frequency and amplitude of the acceleration caused by the performer's hand movements indicate the tempo and volume of music, respectively. Such physical information needs to be dealt with in a different way from the gesture recognition mentioned in the former section, since the temporal information is quite necessary here.

The conductor gives performance directions while facing performers, so we tried to extract tempo and volume information from sequential acceleration vectors $\mathbf{A}1(t)$ in the y-z plane. Here, beat points are detected in real-time according to the magnitude and phase patterns shown in the equations below.

$$\left| \mathbf{A}1(t) \right| = \sqrt{ a_y(t)^2 + a_z(t)^2 } \tag{9}$$

$$\arg \mathbf{A}1(t) = \tan^{-1}\{ a_z(t) / a_y(t) \} \tag{10}$$

Performers recognize the bottom point of the baton trajectory as a beat point. It means the musical beat is recognized just when a conductor brings down his baton. And the time between the beat points is perceived as tempo. We applied the acceleration sensor to the detection of hand movements of the conductor by setting it at the tip of the baton. In the measurement of acceleration, the maximum value is always found just before the baton reaches the bottom point, and the local minimum also exists at the bottom position. Observation of the maximum values tells us the beat points and is very useful for the tempo prediction in real-time performance.

We compared this acceleration method with the measurement of the trajectories using image processing employed in former research[1]. For position detection of the baton in the image frames, we attached a LED marker with acceleration sensor and took the image every 1/30 seconds. Figure 6 shows the vertical position change of the LED marker in the images together with the acceleration data. The method of image processing causes the delay of approximately 0.1 to 0.2 seconds, and also has a limitation that the performer moves his baton within the view field of the camera. Furthermore, it constrains the time resolution up to 30 Hz, on the other hand acceleration sensor can allow users to fix the data acquisition frequency just by setting the A/D conversion frequency. Consequently, the acceleration sensor made possible not only the simple composition of the system to detect the conductor's hand movements, but also more natural real-time tempo tracking.

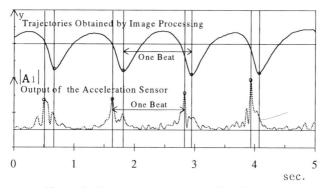

Figure 6. Tempo Detection by the Two Methods

4. Musical Performance System

There exist a lot of musical performance systems controlled by human performers' movements, some of which have been used in actual concert scenes so far. Such systems were, however, designed for specialists and have problems such as system volume, constraints in the practical environment, complexity of usage and so on. We constructed a musical performance system using a 3D acceleration sensor which anyone can easily use without any special knowledge of computers and music. The system view is photographed in Figure 7.

Figure 7.
Experimental Scene

4-1. Performance Control

The system diagram for the constructed musical performance is shown in Figure 8. MIDI instrument is used for sound generation and score information is given to the system in advance. Real-time gesture recognition is executed by comparing the obtained kinetic parameters with the standard data which has been acquired in the previous learning phase. And the music performance control progresses while MIDI information such as note on, off, volume and instrument selection are transmitted.

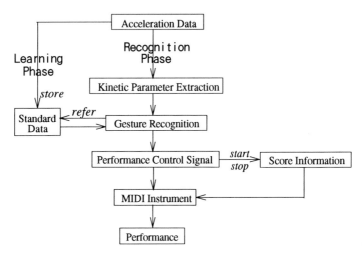

Figure 8. Diagram of Performance Control

First of all, in the learning phase, standard gesture patterns are generated and associated with the performance control commands. Ten gestures are currently used in the performance control. They are

shaking up and down, horizontal stroke, diagonal stroke, single shake,
star shape stroke, triangle shape stroke, heart shape stroke, directional indication,
clockwise rotation, anti-clockwise rotation and pause.

The performer also defines these gestures as associated with the performance commands such as the performance start, stop, tempo manipulation, volume change, selection of instruments, performer's judgments like Yes and No.

Then the recognition phase follows automatically and enables the performer to control the music by his gesture.

Table 3 shows the recognition results of 10 gestures mentioned above. It was tested in two ways. One is the case(A) that the test gestures are performed by the same person as the one who gave the standards, while the other is the case(B) that the test gestures are performed by a different person. 100 % recognition rate is realized in the former case, and fairly good results were also obtained in the latter case.

Table 3   Experimental Results of Gesture Recognition

	Case (A) Recognition Rate %	Case (B) Recognition Rate % (Mis-recognized as)
1. Up and Down	100	100
2. Horizontal Stroke	100	100
3. Diagonal Stroke	100	70(Triangle)
4. Single Shake	100	100
5. Star Shape	100	100
6. Triangle Shape	100	80(Anti-clockwise)
7. Heart Shape	100	100
8. Directional Indication	100	70(Single Shake)
9. Clockwise Rotation	100	100
10.Anti-clockwise	100	80(Triangle)

4-2. Tempo Tracking and Control

Musical tempo is determined by the beat points detected from the changing of acceleration of the conductor's hand movements. To create a computer music performance that follows human performers, the computer has to recognize and synchronize the musical tempo indicated by both human performers and the computer itself. For smooth performance the computer is required not only to calculate the human tempo but also predict the future tempo.

We adopted a tempo prediction model considering mutual interaction between the human system and machine system. Research on automatic accompaniment has been realized in several systems, in which a machine system simply follows a human. In such performances, however, the performer, especially an amateur performer, is obviously influenced by the machine performance. Considering the machine influence on human performers seems necessary for adaptive computer performance systems.

In the prediction equations shown below, M_i and K_i stand for event times of the i-th beat given by a human system and machine system, respectively. And m_i and k_i stand for interval times of human and machine between the i-th and (i-1)-th beats. α is a parameter representing the degree of the machine influence on the human system. Predicted beat event K_{i+1} is determined according to the equations below.

$$K_{i+1} = M_i + k_{i+1}$$
$$k_{i+1} = (1-\alpha)\sum_{j=0}^{r-1} b_j m_{i-j} + \alpha \sum_{j=0}^{s-1} c_j \cdot k_{i-j} \tag{11}$$

b_j and c_j are the linear prediction coefficients(lpcs) to predict human tempo and machine tempo, respectively. r and s are the degrees of predictors. In our experiment, r and s were set to 2.

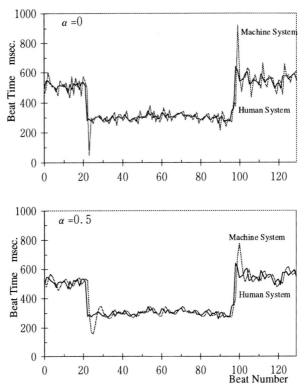

Figure 9   Predicted Tempo following Conductor

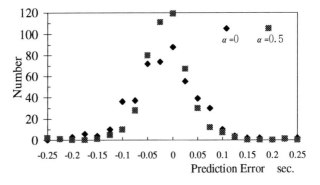

Figure 10   Distribution of Prediction Error of Tempo

We held two experiments in which parameter values of α were set to 0 and 0.5. The lpcs of b_0, b_1, c_0 and c_1 were 2, 2, -1 and -1, respectively, in which prediction will be given by the difference of the tempo. Figure 9 shows the comparison results of the parameter differences in the tempo tracking between human and machine systems. The human performer changed his tempo at the beat number 20 and 97.

Error distribution of tempo between human and machine system is shown in figure 10. In the case of $\alpha = 0.5$, a better result was obtained, compared with the $\alpha = 0$ which is the same model as the simple tempo tracking system without considering machine influence. The experimental result shows the existence of mutual interaction between human and machine system in real-time performance, and proves that a better accompaniment is accomplished using the interaction model of tempo tracking.

4-3. Timbre Control

4-3-1. Associative Neural Network

Musical timbre is related to many factors such as the spectra, attack time, decay time, sustain level and envelope figure[7,8]. We use white noise as a sound source and control the sound parameters, which include the envelope parameters and post filter characteristics, to modify the generated sound. An associative neural network (A-N.N.) is employed to interpret the kinetic parameters of the hand movement into the sound parameters as shown in Figure 11.

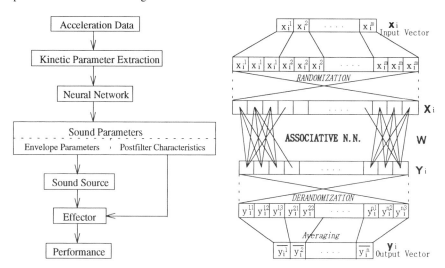

Figure 11. Diagram of Timbre Control

Figure 12. Associative Neural Network

The structure of the A-N.N. is shown in Figure 12. We assign the kinetic parameters of i-th gesture to the elements of the input vector $\mathbf{x}_i$, and the corresponding sound parameters to the elements of the output vector $\mathbf{y}_i$.

Let the input and output pattern vectors consist of m and n elements, respectively. Each element takes a continuous value in a certain range.

$$\mathbf{x}_i = (x^1_i, \cdots, x^m_i)^T$$
$$\mathbf{y}_i = (y^1_i, \cdots, y^n_i)^T \qquad i=1,2,\cdots,N: \text{Patterns} \tag{12}$$

To perform the quasi-orthogonalization of vectors, the input and output vectors are transformed as shown below:

$$\mathbf{X}_i = (X^1_i, \cdots, X^{k \cdot m}_i)^T = F (\mathbf{x}_i)$$
$$: \text{k·m elements for each pattern i}$$
$$\mathbf{Y}_i = (Y^1_i, \cdots, Y^{k \cdot n}_i)^T = F (\mathbf{y}_i)$$
$$: \text{k·n elements for each pattern i} \tag{13}$$

F expresses two operations. The first one is to increase the number of elements by k times duplication as,

$$X^{k \cdot p - j}_i = x^p_i \qquad p= 0, 1, \cdots, m$$
$$Y^{k \cdot q - j}_i = y^q_i \qquad q= 0, 1, \cdots, n \qquad j= 0, 1, \cdots, k-1 \tag{14}$$

and the second one is randomization by the element permutations. The associative information of the pattern pair is stored in the weight matrix $\mathbf{W}$ as,

$$\mathbf{W} = \{W_{rs}\} = \sum_{i=1}^{N} \mathbf{Y}_i \cdot \mathbf{X}_i^T \qquad \begin{matrix} r= 1, 2, \cdots, k \cdot n \\ s= 1, 2, \cdots, k \cdot m \end{matrix} \tag{15}$$

Then the pattern $\mathbf{Y}_o$ which corresponds to the input vector $\mathbf{X}_o$ is recalled as,

$$\mathbf{Y}_o = \mathbf{W} \cdot \mathbf{X}_o \tag{16}$$

The final output $\widehat{\mathbf{y}_o}$ can be recovered as,

$$\widehat{\mathbf{y}_o} = (\widehat{y^1}_o, \cdots, \widehat{y^n}_o)^T = G (\mathbf{Y}_o) , \tag{17}$$

where G includes derandomization and averaging manipulations, which correspond to the reverse operation of F. The averaging manipulation is given as

$$\overline{y^p_i} = \frac{1}{k} \sum_{j=0}^{k-1} Y^{k \cdot p - j}_i . \tag{18}$$

4-3-2. Timbre Control

Musical timbre is related to the various sound parameters. Our emotional impression on the musical sounds such as "solid sound", "heavy sound" and "light sound" are deeply affected by such parameters. On the other hand, we often express such feelings by our gestures. So we tried to correspond these emotional gestures to music controlled by sound parameters, by applying the A-N.N.

In this research we assigned the eleven kinetic parameters to the input vector elements of the A-N.N. And we also selected six sound parameters; attack, decay, sustain level, release, high-pass filter gain and low-pass filter gain, for the output vector elements.

The A-N.N. can be used to link the input vectors and output vectors so that the network can produce various kinds of sound by gestures. The advantage of using the A-N.N. is that the system can produce not only the patterns used in the training phase, but also produce patterns that fall within the parameters of the trained sets, through the generalization ability of the neural network.

5. Conclusions

In this paper we proposed a new kind of musical performance system together with the gesture analysis algorithm using a 3D acceleration sensor to measure the force of gesticulation. Unlike conventional musical instruments, performers can arbitrarily define the relations between gesture and sound to be generated, and can make an adaptive performance in real-time. By attaching another acceleration sensor at another part of the body, like head or arms, the ability of the gesture analysis can be easily improved to make the system more flexible and sophisticated.

The goal of this study is not only to provide a new type of musical system driven by emotional gesticulation without any special knowledge of musical instruments, but also to demonstrate the possibility of a new man-machine interface using gesture that realizes a system with emotion.

6. References

1. H.Morita, S.Ohteru and S.Hashimoto, "Computer Music System that Follows A Human Conductor", IEEE Computer, Vol.24, No.7, pp.45-53, 1991
2. A.Sato T.Harada, S.Hashimoto and S.Ohteru, "Singing and Playing in Musical Virtual Space", Proc. of International Computer Music Conference, pp.289-292, 1991
3. H.Katayose, T.Kanamori, K.Kamei, Y.Nagashima, K.Sato, S.Inokuchi and S.Simura, "Virtual Performer", Proc. of ICMC, 1993
4. M.V.Mathews, "The Conductor Program and Mechanical Baton", Proc. of International Symposium on Music and Information Science, pp.58-70, 1989
5. D.Rubine and P.McAvinney, "The Videoharp", Proc. of ICMC, pp.49-55, 1988
6. D.Keane and P.Gross, "The Midi Baton", Proc. of ICMC, pp.151-154, 1989

7. P.Hartono, K.Asano, W.Inoue and S.Hashimoto, "Adaptive Timbre Control Using Gesture", Proc. of ICMC, pp.151-158, 1994

8. H.Sawada, S.Ohkura, S.Hashimoto, "Gesture Analysis Using 3D Acceleration Sensor for Music Control", Proc. of ICMC, 1995

Chapter 8

JPEG and Model-Based Image Coding

Applications of JPEG Progressive Coding Mode in Distributed Multimedia Systems

Guojun Lu
School of Computing and Mathematics
Deakin University
662 Blackburn Road, Clayton, Vic. 3168
Australia
Email: lugj@deakin.edu.au

and

Hongjun Lu
Department of Information Systems and Computer Science
National University of Singapore
Singapore 0511
Email: luhj@iscs.nus.sg

ABSTRACT

In a distributed image database system, image data are transmitted from the server to the client for display in response to a query. When the network used to connect the server and the client is slow, significant amount of time is spent on data transmission between server and the client, leading to long system response time and affecting the system usability. In this paper, we propose to use JPEG progressive and hierarchical coding techniques to improve the system response time. These techniques allow images to be transmitted, decoded and displayed progressively to give users a perceived shorter response time. They also allow part of the image data to be transmitted, decoded and displayed if low image quality is sufficient for the application, leading to the saving of transmission time and cost.

In the paper, the JPEG progressive and hierarchical coding techniques are described. Some implementation details of progressive coding mode is given. Finally, our preliminary findings are reported.

1. Introduction

In a distributed multimedia system, the major issue is how to get the required information to the user within a reasonable amount of time, i.e. the system response time should be within an acceptable range. This issue becomes more acute when the communication network used is of limited capacity and when large number of users are sharing the communication network. Because the system response time determines whether the system is usable and viable, this issue has to be addressed in the distributed system design.

To improve the system response time and the efficiency of resource usage, Bulterman[1] presented a portable document structure. During the information (image) retrieval process, the client and server negotiate on amount of data and type of data to be transferred from the server to the client based on the current work load and capability of the server, the client and the communication network. For example, there is no need to transmit colour information to the client if it only has a black-and-white display. When the images are stored in JPEG format, the server would have two options in the way that it processes the client's request: It could decode the image locally using a fast parallel architecture and send the result over the network to the client, or it could send the encoded image to the client which would decode it upon receipt. The decision of which option to use will be determined based on the overall system response time.

In current release of Netscape navigator for WWW (URL: http://home.mcom.com/home/welcome.html), an increamental display approach is used. In this approach, part of image or document can be displayed while the remaining part is being transmitted and received. This improves the perceptual system response time. However, the whole display is divided into a number of displayeable parts and from the displayed parts it is hard to see the content of the whole image or document.

In this paper, we investigate the use of progressive and hierarchical image coding techniques to improve system response time and resource usage efficiency. In the progressive coding technique, images are coded into a sequence of "scans". Each scan improves the image quality on top of the previous scans. By organizing data in this way, images can be progressively built up while data are being received. The overall time of displaying a complete image may be similar to or slightly longer than when the image is coded using only one scan (called sequential coding), but the user can see the image building up process, giving the user a perception of shorter response time. Hierarchical coding can be see as one type of progressive coding. It has the advantage when a smaller version of the original image is required. We will explain this in detail in the following sections.

In next section, we look at the applications of progressive and hierarchical coding techniques in distributed multimedia systems. In section 3, the progressive and hierarchical coding techniques used in JPEG [2, 3] are explained. Section 4 presents our preliminary implementation and experimental results. Finally, Section 5 concludes the paper with a summary and a direction of further work required.

2. Operations of a Distributed Multimedia System

In a distributed multimedia system, there are a number of servers and clients interconnected via a communication network. In this paper, we are only interested in retrieval of images. So let us look at the image retrieval process.

The user issues queries using a user interface on the client which submits the queries to the appropriate servers. The server searches for relevant images in its storage. A list of relevant images is then returned to the client through the communication network. Upon receiving this list of relevant images, the client display them simultaneously, if possible, on a display window for the user to browse. At this stage, the displayed images are normally smaller version of the original images in order to display as many images as possible on one window. Only when the user is interested in a particular image, does he require the display of the full quality image.

In the above distributed image retrieval process, two operations are very important in determining the system response time: the image index and retrieval algorithms, and image data transmission from the server to the client. In this paper, we will not deal with image index and retrieval algorithms, though they are extremely important. The interested readers are referred to references [4, 5, 6, 7]. Rather, we assume that the relevant images have been identified using certain algorithm. We are interested in image data coding and transmission techniques to improve system response time.

As outlined above, images are displayed in two different ways: smaller versions are displayed for browsing and full size images are displayed for detailed inspection. In the browsing mode, there are normally many images to be displayed which are returned by the server as relevant images. Normally, not every returned images are interesting to the user. The user is normally interested in one or two, or a few of the returned images. For browsing and selection purpose, small low quality images are adequate. Thus, at this stage, if we can only transmit and decode part of the image data corresponding to the small low quality images instead of the full quality images, the system response time will be shorter and there will be no data which are transmitted but not displayed. This is possible if we use the progressive coding techniques which organize compressed data into a number of scans. All that we need to do is to transmit the data of the first few scans and at the client small low quality images are displayed based on these data.

When a full size high quality image is required, progressive coding techniques will allow the image to be built progressively to the full quality without the need for the user to wait for all the data to arrive, resulting in a shorter system response time.

It should be noted that decoding process is now more complicated than when the image is coded sequentially. Thus when the client is slow and the communication network is relatively fast, the use of the progressive coding may not gain much. But when the client is relatively fast and the communication network is slow, which is the case when a slow modem or a slow wide internet link is used, the use of the progressive coding techniques will gain significantly in terms of improved system response time. We use an example to show this point.

Example:

We assume:

    (a) Each image is compressed to a file size 20 kbytes

    (b) Decoding time of each scan (including sequential mode) is 1 second

    (c) Network transmission rate is 1 kbyte/s

    (d) 16 images are returned as relevant image for a query

    (e) 20% percent of data are required to obtain the small low quality image

    (f) The first scan has 10% per cent of the entire image data

Then:

    (1) In browsing mode 336 seconds are needed before 16 images are displayed when sequential coding technique is used.

    (2) 5 seconds are required to see the first image and 90 seconds are required to see all

    16 images at their low quality version for the browsing purpose using progressive coding.

    (3) In full image quality mode, 21 seconds are required before seeing the image when

    sequential coding is used, while 3 second is required to see the first scan when progressive coding is used.

The figures used in the above example are quite common when inter-country internet is used during working hours. The example shows the usefulness of the progressive coding techniques. In the next section, we will describe the progressive and hierarchical coding techniques specified in the JPEG standard.

3. JPEG Progressive and Hierarchical Coding

JPEG [2, 3] is now being widely used for still image compression. But only sequential coding mode is used in most cases. To many people, JPEG is a standard using sequential DCT-based coding. Actually, JPEG is much more than this. The above coding mode is called baseline coding system which must be present in all of the JPEG modes of operation. JPEG has a extended system in which lossless, progressive and hierarchical coding modes are specified. In this section, we first review the sequential DCT-based coding mode, then describe the progressive and hierarchical coding modes.

3.1 JPEG sequential DCT-based coding mode

The DCT-based encoding steps are shown in Fig.1. The source image data is normally transformed into one luminance component Y and two chrominance components Cr and Cb. Cr and Cb are normally down-sampled in both horizontal and vertical direction by a factor of two to take advantage of the lower sensitivity of human perception to the chrominance signal. Then each component is divided into blocks of 8x8 pixels.

A 2-dimensional forward discrete cosine transform (FDCT) is applied to each block of data. The result is an array of 64 coefficients with energy concentrated at the first few coefficients. These coefficients are then quantized using quantization values specified in the quantization tables. The quantization values can be adjusted to trade between compression ratio and compressed image quality. After quantization, there will normally be many zeros in the 64 coefficients.

The quantized coefficients are zig-zag scanned as shown in the figure to obtain a one-dimensional sequence of data for entropy coding. The first coefficient is called DC coefficient which represents the average intensity of the block. The rest coefficients (1 to 63) are called AC coefficients. The purpose of the zig-zag scanning is to order the coefficients in the order of increasing spectral frequencies. Since the coefficients of high frequencies (at the right bottom corner of the coefficient array) are mostly zero, the zig-zag scanning will result in most zeros at the end of the scan, leading to higher entropy coding efficiency.

314

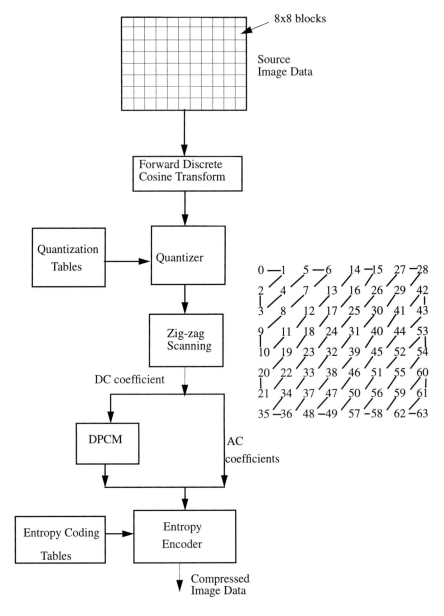

Fig.1 Sequential DCT-based Encoding Steps

The DC coefficient is Differential-Pulse-Code-Modulation (DPCM) coded relative to the DC coefficient of the previous block. DPCM coded DC coefficient and AC coefficients are entropy coded. In JPEG, both Huffman coding and arithmetic coding techniques are specified. Arithmetic coding is normally 10% more efficient than Huffman coding at the expense of the implementation complexity[2]. The output of the entropy coder is the compressed image data.

3.2 JPEG progressive coding mode

The DCT progressive mode of operation consists of the same FDCT and Quantization steps as that used by DCT sequential mode. The main difference is that each image component is encoded in multiple scans instead of a single scan. The first scan(s) encode a rough but recognizable version of the image which can be transmitted quickly in comparison to the total transmission time. The image quality is then refined by succeeding scans until reaching the level of picture quality that was determined by the quantization tables.

To achieve this requires the addition of an image-sized buffer memory at the output of the quantizer, before the input to the entropy encoder. The buffer memory must be of sufficient size to store all quantized DCT coefficients of the entire image. After each block of DCT coefficients is quantized, it is stored in the coefficient buffer memory. The buffered coefficients are then partially encoded in each of the multiple scans.

There are two complementary methods by which a block of quantized DCT coefficients may be partially encoded: spectral selection and successive approximation. In spectral selection the DCT coefficients are grouped into "spectral" bands of related spatial frequencies. The bands are coded in separate scans. The lower-frequency bands are usually more important to image quality and sent first. The DC coefficient must be the first scan coded separately. The number of bands (scans) is determined by the required image quality granularity and encoding and decoding implementation overhead.

In successive approximation the coefficients are first sent with lower precision and then refined in later scans. In the first scan, the DCT coefficients are divided by a power of two before coding. In the decoder the coefficients are multiplied by that same power before computing the inverse DCT. In the succeeding scans the precision of the coefficients is increased by one bit in each scan until full precision is reached. Spectral selection and successive approximation can be used separately, or mixed in flexible combinations.

3.3 JPEG hierarchical coding mode

The hierarchical mode provides a "pyramidal" encoding of an image at multiple spatial resolutions, each differing in resolution from its adjacent encoding by a factor of two in either the horizontal or vertical dimension or both. As an example, Fig.2 shows an image at three different resolutions. The original image O is at the bottom. The middle image M is obtained by down-sampling the original image by a factor of 2 in both horizontal and vertical directions. The top image T is obtained by down-sampling the middle image by a factor of 2 in both horizontal and vertical directions.

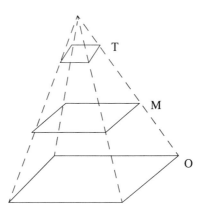

Fig.2 A set of pyramidal images used in hierarchical coding mode

The encoding procedure can be summarized as follows using the pyramid in Fig.2:

a) Filter and down-sample the original image by the desired number of multiples of 2 in each dimension, to obtain image T.

b) Encode this reduced-size image T using one of the sequential DCT, progressive DCT, or lossless encoding.

c) Decode this reduced-size image and then interpolate and up-sample it by a factor of 2 horizontally and/or vertically, using the identical interpolation filter which the receiver must use.

d) Use this up-sampled image as a prediction of the image M and get the difference bewteen this prediction and the image M. Encode the difference image using one of the sequential DCT, progressive DCT, or lossless encoders.

e) repeat steps c) and d) until the full resolution of the image has been encoded.

The encoded data of image T is stored first, then the encoded difference image as obtained in step d). During display, a range of images of different sizes can be displayed according to the application requirements. For example, if encoded data of image T is transmitted only, image T can be displayed. If coded difference image at resolution M is also transmitted, image M can be displayed. If all encoded data are transmitted, the image O can be displayed.

Hierarchical encoding is useful in applications in which a very high spatial resolution image must be accessed by a lower-resolution device, which does not have the buffer capacity to reconstruct the image at its full resolution and then scale it down for the lower-resolution display. In the distributed image database applications, hierarchical encoding is particularly useful. In the browsing mode, data correponding to a lower resolution image only is transmitted and displayed to improve system response time significantly.

4. Preliminary Implementation and Findings

We have so far implemented JPEG progressive coding using spectral selection. In this section, we report on our implementation details and preliminary results obtained.

4.1 Implementation of JPEG progressive coding using spectral selection

The implementation can be divided into four major steps: (1) To generate DCT coefficients for all blocks of an image to be encoded; (2) To select the number of bands and coefficients in each band; (3) To encode DC coefficients (the first band) with Huffman coding and (4) To progressively encode AC coefficients in subsequent bands with Huffman coding. In the following, we discuss these four steps. For further details, readers are referred to the JPEG standard specification [2].

DCT coefficients generation

The input image data are preprocessed into YCrCb colour space. Within each colour component, data samples are divided into 8x8 blocks. Image sample values are level-shifted to a signed two's complement representation. For 8-bit input precision the level shift is achieved by subtracting 128. For 12-bit input precision the level shift is achieved by subtracting 2048. Two dimensional FDCT is applied to each block of level shifted samples. The obtained DCT coefficients for all blocks are quantized and stored in the buffer memory for progressive encoding.

Spectral selection control

In spectral selection the zig-zag sequence of quantized DCT coefficients is segmented into bands. A band is defined in the scan header by specifying the starting and ending indices in the zig-zag sequence. One band is coded in a given scan of the progression. DC coefficients are always coded separately from the AC coefficients. With the exception of the first DC scans for the components, the sequence of bands defined in the scans need not follow the zig-zag ordering. For each component, a first DC scan shall precede all AC scans.

Encoding of DC coefficients with Huffman coding

The first scan for a given component encodes the DC coefficients. The DC coefficients are DPCM coded, i.e. the difference between the DC coefficient of the current block and the prediction of the DC coefficient of the current block based on the DC coefficient of the previous block is Huffman encoded. Note that all these DC coefficients have been quantized.

Progressive encoding of AC coefficients with Huffman coding

In each band, the quantized AC coefficients are Huffman encoded in a similar way to that used by the sequential encoding procedure. However, the Huffman code tables are extended to include coding of runs of End-Of-Bands (EOBs).

The end-of-band run structure allows efficient coding of blocks which have only zero coefficients in a particular scan. This is to take advantage of the fact that in high frequency bands, many blocks may have only zero value components. For example, an EOB run of length 5 means that the current block and the next four blocks have no nonzero coefficients in the band concerned.

4.2 Preliminary experimental findings

We here present our preliminary findings obtained from the above implementation. We will look at three aspects: (1) The compressed file size obtained using progressive coding compared with that obtained using sequential coding; (2) The data distribution among different bands; (3) System response time using progressive coding compared with that using sequential coding. The following is our findings and explanation.

(a) For the colour test image Lana of size 128x128, the file size using sequential coding with the standard quantization table is 4042 bytes. The file size using progressive coding with spectral selection at the same image quality (using the same quantization table as the sequential coding) is 4235 bytes when four bands are used. These four bands are as follows: The first band is for DC coefficients. The second band is for AC coefficients 1 to 4 in the zig-zag sequence. The third band is for AC coefficients 5 to 12 and the fourth for AC coefficients 13 to 63. The file size is slightly bigger because the overhead information needed for progressive decoding, but the increase is not very significant.

(b) Using the above band allocation, amount of data in each scan is shown in Table 1.

Table 1: Data Distribution Among Bands

Scans	Amount of data	Percentage of total
1st scan	237 bytes	5.6%
1st & 2nd scans	1682 bytes	39.7%
1st, 2nd and3rd scans	2872 bytes	67.8%
1st, 2nd, 3dr and 4th scans	4235 bytes	100%

(c) When a slow communication network, say 1 kbyte/s, is used, the decoding and displaying time will be insignificant compared with network transmission time. In this case, we will see the first scan of the Lena image within half of second when progressive coding is used, but it will take over 4 seconds to see the image when sequential coding mode is used. When image size is bigger, the difference will be even bigger. For example, if the image size is 512x512 instead of 128x128, and assuming the compressed file size increasing proportionally with the image size, then we will see the first scan within 8 seconds when progressive coding is used, but it will take more than 64 seconds for us to see the image when sequential coding is used.

(d) For browsing mode, the image quality obtained by decoding only the first scan and the second scan (about 40% of the total data) is adequate. By transmitting only these two scans, significant transmission time will be saved when many images are returned for browsing in response to a query.

(e) When a fast network is used for communication, the significant portion of time is spent on decoding and displaying image data compared with data transmission time. The improvement on response time will not be significant using progressive coding mode. In our experiments, we used a 10 Mbit/s ethernet. The results show that using progressive coding we will be able to see the first scan sooner than using sequential coding, but it takes much longer to see the complete image.

5. Conclusion and Further Work

In this paper, we show that progressive image coding techniques are needed in distributed image database systems, especially when the communication network is slow. We proposed the use of and introduced the JPEG progressive and hierarchical coding modes. We have implemented the JPEG progressive coding mode with spectral selection. Our experimental results show that using progressive coding will improve the system response time significantly when the communication network is slow relative to the image decoding time at the client.

The further work is to implement the hierarchical coding mode as it is more suitable for multi-image browsing. The code for progressive decoding needs to be optimized to decrease the decoding time.

Acknowledgement

We are grateful to the Independent JPEG Group for its sequential coding software, and to Teo Ee Hua, Ng Yeng Yong and Tham Kuo Feng for their work in implementing the progressive coding with spectral selection.

References

1. Dick C.A. Bulterman, "Retrieving (JPEG) Pictures in Portable Hypermedia Documents", Proceedings of the First International Conference on Multi-Media Modelling, Singapore, 9-12 November 1993, pp. 217-226.

2. William B. Pennebaker, Joan L. Mitchell, "JPEG Still Image Data Compression Standard", Van Nostrand Reinhold, 1993.

3. G. K. Wallace, "The JPEG Still Picture Compression Standard", Communications of ACM, April 1991, Vol.34, No.4, pp.30-44.

4. Gong Y et al, "An image database system with fast image indexing capability based on colour histograms", Proceedings of IEEE Region 10's Ninth Annual International Conference, 22-26 August 1994, Singapore, pp.407-411.

5. Chua T S et al, "A content-based image retrieval system", Department of Information

Systems and Computer Science, NAtional University of Singapore, submitted for publication.

6. Chua T S et al, "A concept-based image retrieval system", Proceedings of 27th Annual Hawaii International Conference on System Science, 4-7 January, 1994, pp.590-598.

7. Niblack W et al, "QBIC Project: querying images by content, using colour, texture, and shape", Storage and Retrieval for Image and Video Database, SPIE Proceedings Series, Vol.1908, 1993, pp.173-187.

APPLICATION OF GENERALIZED ACTIVE CONTOUR MODEL FOR MODEL-BASED IMAGE CODING

C. W. Ngo, S. Chan[*]

School of Applied Science, Nanyang Technological University
Nanyang Avenue, Singapore 2263
ascwngo@ntuvax.ntu.ac.sg asschan@ntuix.ntu.ac.sg

and

Kok F. Lai
Information Technology Institute
11 Science park Road
Science Park II, Singapore 0511
kflai@iti.gov.sg

ABSTRACT

In this paper, we present an approach for extracting, tracking and time sequence analysis of deformable contours. We apply the technique to motion estimation and the adaptation of 3D human facial model. These methods are the key-technologies for a model-based image coding system. For contour modeling, we combine a stable and invariant global contour model with local characteristics of the Markov random field. This, combined with an external energy field that attracts a contour to salient image features, turns boundary extraction and object tracking into energy minimization problems. In time sequence analysis, the transformation matrix and local uncertainty can be estimated from the current and previous extracted contours. They are used to describe the global and local motion of head movement and facial expression parameters in model-based facial image coding. Our method not only considers image analysis, but also integrates the action units (AU) described by Facial Action Coding System (FACS). As a result, this method improves robustness and accuracy in estimation. Finally, we have demonstrated with experiments how one can apply the above method to automatic facial feature extraction and tracking. Experimental results show that our method is particularly effective if appropriate prior knowledge can be incorporated and the range of allowable global transformations is known.

1. Introduction

1.1. Background Information

Coding of moving pictures system operating over a 64 kbits/s channel has been actively researched[1,2]. The goal of such coding is to extract a compact description of the scene for image data compression, recognition and reconstruction. However, conventional waveform coding methods[3] which are based on statistical correlation between neighboring pixels, are unsuitable for coding of moving pictures on very low bit rate visual communications. Recently, two new coding approaches, namely model-based image coding[4,5] and object-oriented analysis-synthesis coding[6], have been proposed to describe the image objects using physically based models. In contrast to traditional waveform coding, these two approaches treat the content of image in detail. As a result, the transmitted data are not the image itself, but the analyzed parameters. Hence, there is

---

[*]Please direct all enquiries to asschan@ntuix.ntu.ac.sg

a possibility of exploiting much more of the redundancy in sequence of images, and promise a dramatic reduction in bit rates. Table 1(a) shows the difference between various image coding methods and table 1(b) show their various source models.

Table 1(a).   Difference between image coding scheme

	Waveform Coding	Perception Based Coding	Model-based Coding	Object-oriented Analysis-synthesis Coding
Characteristics utilized	Statistical correlation	Human Visual System	A priori knowledge	Object structure knowledge
Form of transmitted information	Numerical data to represent signal waveform	Spatial frequencies based on threshold vision	Symbolic / numerical parameters components (components' movement, deformation)	Three parameter sets : motion, shape, surface color
Fidelity evaluation criteria	Mean squared error (MSE)	Rate-distortion theory	Subjective assessment	Objective / Subjective quality criteria
Compression Ratio	10 times	100 times	10^4-10^5 times	Make full use of transmission rate

Table 1(b).   Image Coding Techniques and Source Models

Coding Techniques	Source Models
Waveform Coding	Statistical model
Motion Compensation Coding	2D planar and motion model
Perception Based Coding	2D structure model (contours, texture)
Model-based Coding	3D model
Object-oriented analysis-synthesis Coding	moving rigid 3D objects / flexible 2D objects

Model-based facial image coding[7] has become popular for the application of videophone scene communications because it overcomes the problems found in traditional waveform coding. This application is constructed by preparing a 3D facial model on both transmitter and receiver sides. Therefore, the transmitter analyzes an input image and the receiver synthesizes an output image by transformation of a 3D model with the received parameters. A very low bit rate image transmission can be realized since only the required analysis parameters are sent. These parameters describe the facial motion and expression of a speaker. Currently, several 3D facial models have been developed to exhibit facial mimic action based on the Facial Action Coding System (FACS)[8] model of action units (AUs) introduced by Ekman and Friesen. Typical examples are Parke's model, Candide model and Aizawa's model[1].

1.2.   Motivation

Motivated by the data compression potential in model-based image coding, a great amount of effort has been put into developing algorithms that extract 2D contours[9,10] and estimate facial expression from various sources such as motion, shading and texture[7,11]. However, current techniques in contour extraction are mostly time consuming and they require human intervention. Contours have to be manually located for the first frame of the image sequence if automatic extraction fails.

In this paper, we describe the application of generalized active contour model (g-snake)[12] in model-based facial image coding. We begin by modeling and extracting facial feature contours directly and automatically from the first frame of image sequence. We then start motion tracking by replacing the previous extracted contours on the current image. In contrast to traditional contour extraction methods, our method is general and capable of representing any arbitrary shapes. It not only accounts for global changes due to rigid motion (e.g., head rotation), but also retains ability for local deformation (e.g., changes in facial expression).

We denote two energy functions, external and internal, to represent the goodness of fit between the contours and the desired image features. The internal energy is based on a stable and regenerative shape matrix which is invariant and unique under rigid motion. The external energy, combined with local characteristics of the Markov random field[13], models local deformation and attracts the contours to salient image features. Besides, we use an automatic and implicit selection of local regularization parameters based on minimax criterion[14]. As a result, our method is able to exert local control and is suitable for incorporation of global contour model for facial feature extraction.

In addition, we consider time sequence analysis of deformable contours based on generalized active contour model. The affine transformation matrix and local uncertainty can be estimated from the current and previous extracted contours. They are used to describe the global and local motion of facial mimic action. With these, we are able to estimate and perform human facial model transformation and adaptation.

The remainder of this paper is organized into six section. Section 2 presents the contour extraction and motion analysis procedures of our framework. Section 3 describes the basic concept of generalized active contour model and its application to model-based facial image coding. In section 4, we extend the work described to motion tracking and time sequence analysis of deformable contours. Section 5 explains the facial action units and the transformation rules of wireframe model. Section 6 demonstrates the experimental results for the above and section 7 concludes the paper.

2. Basic Framework

Figure 1 illustrates the general idea of our facial image sequence coding procedures. Motion pictures are input to the image processing part, in which Gaussian pyramid generation[15], edge detection, generalized Hough transform[16] and active contour model are implemented. Interframe facial actions are then estimated and calculated from time sequence analysis of deformable contours. These analyzed parameters are passed to the texture update part. The 3D human facial model is adjusted and deformed accordingly

Feature extraction is split into two stages. The first stage localizes the features in the image by generalized Hough transform (GHT). GHT is performed at the highest level of

Gaussian pyramid image so as to reduce search space and computational time. The second stage applies g-snake to find the accurate shape of each feature using simple knowledge about the feature. In order to increase robustness in motion tracking, motion prediction is carried out by exploiting the temporal motion information existing in the image sequence. In addition, a feedback mechanism is provided to handle error accumulation problem associated with the long sequence of motion tracking. Energy calculation will evaluate the closeness of actual and predicted contours. In this case, GHT will relocate the desired contour if it is necessary.

In this framework, some common knowledge is provided in the 3D facial model. This is typically related to Action Units (AUs) introduced by Ekman and Friesen, and relationship between the motion of different features. Since knowledge about the 3D shape is collectively expressed on the geometric model of human shape, 3D motion parameters can be determined using the depth values given by the model.

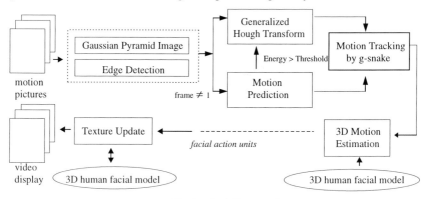

Fig. 1.   Basic Framework

3.   Image Analysis

The most important and difficult task of facial image analysis is to extract parameters required by the coding, such as positions of facial features and parameters of motion and deformation variance. Facial feature location is the first necessary step in automatically fitting the 3D model to a specific face. Moreover, this is a reliable cue in facial motion estimation. Facial motion can be further described as deformation variance of facial feature contour. For instance, the blinking of eye involves the deformation of upper and lower part of the eye rather than two corners of eye. Therefore, we consider facial image analysis as the problem of modeling and extracting arbitrary deformable contours from facial image sequence. Besides, we describe the shape of a contour based on an affine invariant global model, combined with Markov random field to model allowable local deformation variance.

3.1. Contour Model

A contour is a vector containing an ordered set of points, $V = [v_1, v_2, ..., v_n]$. Each v_i is defined on the finite grid : $v \in \text{IE} = \{(x, y): x, y = 1, 2, ..., M\}$, thus $V \in \text{IE}^n$. Denote U where each $u_i = v_i - g$ represents the displacement from an arbitrary reference point g. We can encode the shape of an arbitrary contour in the following shape equation :

$$AU^T = 0 \tag{3.1}$$

where

$$
A = \begin{bmatrix}
1 & -\beta_1 & 0 & 0 & .... & ... & -\alpha_1 \\
-\alpha_2 & 1 & -\beta_2 & 0 & ... & ... & ... \\
0 & -\alpha_3 & 1 & -\beta_3 & ... & ... & ... \\
... & ... & ... & ... & ... & ... & ... \\
... & ... & ... & ... & ... & ... & ... \\
0 & 0 & ... & ... & -\alpha_{n-1} & 1 & -\beta_{n-1} \\
-\beta_n & 0 & ... & ... & ... & -\alpha_n & 1
\end{bmatrix}
$$

is an $n \times n$ regenerative and stable shape matrix. The shape matrix is invariant and unique under affine transformation [12]. In other words, for a given A, if $\bar{U}$ satisfies $A\bar{U}^T = 0$, then

$$AU^T = 0 \Leftrightarrow U = T\bar{U} \tag{3.2}$$

where T is a 2x2 invertible transformation matrix which may describe rigid motions such as scaling, rotation, stretching and dilation. Moreover, displacement on the center of gravity, $\bar{g} + d$, has no effect on the shape equation.

Suppose the contour U exhibits small shape irregularities. To represent these random fluctuations in small localities, we define an internal energy :

$$E_{\text{int}}\{U\} = \sum_{i=1}^{n} \frac{E_{\text{int}}\{u_i\}}{\sigma_i^2} \tag{3.3}$$

where σ_i^2 is the deformation variance that allows assignment of location weightings on deformations.

$$E_{\text{int}}\{u_i\} = \frac{1}{l\{U\}} \left\| u_i - \alpha_i u_{i\alpha} - \beta_i u_{i\beta} \right\|^2 \tag{3.4}$$

where $l\{U\} = \frac{1}{n} \sum_{i=1}^{n} \left\| u_{i+1} - u_i \right\|^2$ is a normalizing constant, and

$$
i\alpha = \begin{cases} i-1 & ; i > 1 \\ n & ; i = 1 \end{cases} \quad \text{and} \quad i\beta = \begin{cases} i+1 & ; i < n \\ 1 & ; i = n \end{cases} \tag{3.5}
$$

Therefore, the conditional probability of u_i from g given the contour U is completely specified by the conditional probability of u_i given its two neighboring points, that is,

$$p(u_i | u_1, u_2, ..., u_n) = p(u_i | u_\alpha, u_\beta) \tag{3.6}$$

Hence, the local characteristic of Markov random field has been incorporated into the global contour model of g-snake.

3.2   Image Model

We define an image as the vector function $F: IE \rightarrow IM$. Depending on the datatype, either $IM = IH$ (intensity image or edge magnitude) or $IM = IH^2$ (2x1 intensity gradient vector). A template of a contour is the image $F = B_{U,g}$:

$$B_{U,g}(r) = \sum_{i=1}^{n} h_i \delta(r - u_i - g) \tag{3.7}$$

where $r = (x, y) \in IE$, δ is the delta function, $h_i \in IM$ and $|h_i| = 1$. In other words, a template $B_{U,g}(r)$ is a special image with values equal to h_i if $r = u_i + g$ but zero otherwise. For $IM = IH^2$, h_i is the unit vector which is normal to the contour.

A noisy image $F = f$ containing a contour can be modeled as follows:

$$f(r)|U, g = B_{U,g}(r) + \eta(r) \tag{3.8}$$

where $\eta(r): N(0, \sigma_\eta^2 I)$ is Gaussian, $I = 1$ if $IM = IH$; otherwise I is a 2x2 identity matrix. Consequently, $p(f|U, g)$ is Gaussian distributed and can be simplified to yield:

$$p(f|U, g) = \frac{1}{C} \exp\left\{ \frac{-f^T f + n - 2\sum_{i=1}^{n} E_{ext}(u_i, g)}{2\sigma_\eta^2} \right\} \tag{3.9}$$

where $C = (2\pi\sigma_\eta^2)^{M^2/2}$, and the external energy $E_{ext}(u_i, g) = 1 - h_i^T f(u_i + g)$.

3.3   Generalized Active Contour Model

The problem of extracting a contour with unknown deformation from a noisy image is equivalent to maximum a posteriori estimation under the Bayesian framework, where

$$\{U_{map}, g_{map}\} = \arg \max_{U,g} p(U, g | f)$$
$$= \arg \max_{U,g} p(U) p(f|U, g) \tag{3.10}$$

noting that $p(U, g) = p(U)$. Solving for the solution and ignoring constant, we have

$$\{U_{map}, g_{map}\} = \arg \min_{U,g} \sum_{i=1}^{n} \left\{ \frac{E_{int}(u_i)}{\sigma_i^2} + \frac{E_{ext}(u_i, g)}{\sigma_\eta^2} \right\}$$
$$= \arg \min_{U,g} \sum_{i=1}^{n} \left\{ \frac{\lambda}{1 - \lambda} E_{int}(u_i) + E_{ext}(u_i, g) \right\} \tag{3.11}$$

where

$$\lambda = \frac{\sigma_\eta^2}{\sigma_i^2 + \sigma_\eta^2} \in [0,1] \tag{3.12}$$

are the total regularization parameters which control the amount of local template deformation. From Eq. (3.12), posterior estimation turns into energy minimization in a generalized active contour model. When no prior knowledge is available, a parameter selection strategy based on minimax criterion can be used[14].

3.4. Shape Matrix and Regularization Parameters Learning

In model-based facial image coding, the objects to be coded are restricted to head movements and facial features. Since we have prior knowledge on the shape of a face and the individual facial features, the shape matrix A and regularization parameter λ_i can be trained from different samples.

Figure 2 shows the sequence of steps taken to train the shape matrix for mouth. The feature points that form the contour U, generally include locations of high curvature. An initial estimate of shape matrix A is computed from the first sample. Using this shape matrix and minimax regularization, the total energy is minimized and the shape matrix is then updated to A_1. By repeating the procedure for various mouth samples to obtain $A_1, A_2, \ldots, A_m$, the estimated shape matrix is,

$$A = \frac{1}{m} \sum_{j=1}^{m} A_j \qquad (3.13)$$

Fig. 2   Selects feature points, trains samples and generates ideal mouth contour

Similarly, we estimate parameters λ_i by learning the deformation and noise variance from the mouth samples. Based on minimax regularization, we estimate the deformation and noise variance of the first sample as follows :

$$\sigma_i = E_{\text{int}}(u_i) \qquad (3.14)$$

$$\sigma_\eta = \sum_{i=0}^{n-1} \sum_{j=0}^{n-1} F(i, j) \qquad (3.15)$$

where

$$F(i, j) = \begin{cases} f(u_i + g) - M(u); & u_i \in U \\ G(i, j); & otherwise \end{cases} \quad \text{and}$$

$$M(u) = \sum_{i=1}^{n} \frac{f(u_i + g)}{n}$$

$G(i, j)$ is the gradient operator that computes 2X1 intensity gradient vectors by fitting planes in 2X2 windows using the least squares method to image with m x n dimension .

By substituting Eq. (3.14) and Eq. (3.15) into Eq. (3.12), we can compute λ_i. We repeat the procedure for the rest of the samples. The estimated λ_i is the average value of all λ_i from each mouth sample.

Table 2. Results of training various mouth samples

u_i	α_i	β_i	λ_i
u_1	1.08	1.42	0.65
u_2	0.39	0.96	0.80
u_3	0.47	0.51	0.91
u_4	0.96	0.53	0.90
u_5	1.41	1.96	0.66
u_6	0.44	0.67	0.80
u_7	0.80	0.80	0.77
u_8	0.69	0.46	0.86

Table 2 shows the values of shape matrix and regularization parameters learned for various mouth samples in figure 2. In clockwise direction, u_1 locates at the left corner of mouth and u_5 locates at the right corner of mouth. They have higher values of α and β since they occupy high curvature areas. In addition, each u_i has their corresponding λ to represent their deformation variance.

4. Time Sequence Analysis

In[7,17], the basic shapes of the facial features are represented by characteristic or control points. These characteristic points are situated, respectively, on the eye, eyebrows, nose, mouth and outline of the face. Each feature consists of four characteristic points, that is, at two corners, uppermost and lowermost part. Therefore, interframe motion vectors are provided by detecting the coordinates of the characteristic points. Conventional methods usually depend on restricted conditions such as rigid-body motion to compute translation and rotation angles. The drawback of this method is that they cannot account for deformations which frequently arise from diversity and irregularity of shape. Generalized active contour model, in contrast, employ weak models which deform in conformation to salient image features. Basically, it measures deviation from an ideal contour and evaluates the match of the deformed contour with the underlying image. As a result, we can jointly estimate both global motion and local deformation. Unlike[7], the motion parameters in g-snake is taken by measuring the difference between the current and previous extracted contours. Hence, we can eliminate errors known as mosquito or blocking artifacts from block-oriented coder.

Denote $U(t)$ and $d(t)$ as the contour and displacement at time index t. We can model the evaluation of a contour as below :

$$U(t) = T(t)U(t-1) + \psi(t) \tag{4.1}$$

$$g(t) = g(t-1) + d(t) \tag{4.2}$$

where $T(t) = \begin{bmatrix} t_{11} & t_{12} \\ t_{21} & t_{22} \end{bmatrix}$ is a 2x2 matrix describing deformation, and $\psi(t)$ is local uncertainty. We can estimate $T(t)$ using least square methods. The solution is,

$$T(t) = U(t)U^T(t-1)[U(t-1)U^T(t-1)]^{-1} \tag{4.3}$$

$T(t)$ can be factorized in term of scale, rotation and other linear transformation. Modeling only scale and rotation, we write

$$T(t) = S(t)R(t) \qquad (4.4)$$

$$\Leftrightarrow \begin{bmatrix} t_{11} & t_{12} \\ t_{21} & t_{22} \end{bmatrix} = \begin{bmatrix} a & 0 \\ 0 & b \end{bmatrix} \begin{bmatrix} \cos\theta & \sin\theta \\ -\sin\theta & \cos\theta \end{bmatrix}$$

where $S(t)$ is scaling change indexed by a and b, and $R(t)$ is rotation matrix indexed by θ. By using least square methods, we have solution as follows :

$$\theta = \tan^{-1} \frac{w_1^T w_2^T}{\|w_1\|^2} \text{ where } w_1 = \begin{bmatrix} t_{11} \\ t_{22} \end{bmatrix} \text{ and } w_2 = \begin{bmatrix} t_{12} \\ -t_{21} \end{bmatrix} \qquad (4.5)$$

$$a = t_{11}\cos\theta + t_{12}\sin\theta \qquad (4.6)$$

$$b = t_{22}\cos\theta - t_{11}\sin\theta \qquad (4.7)$$

Subsequently, we estimate local uncertainty $\psi(t) = [\chi_1(t), \chi_2(t), \ldots, \chi_3(t)]$ as following:

$$\chi_i(t) = u_i(t) - T(t)u_i(t-1) \qquad (4.8)$$

Since the displacement vector, $d(t)$, has no effect on the transformation matrix, we can compute its value by taking the difference between the reference points of current and previous extracted contours. In very low bit rate communications, the transmitted parameters at time t include transformation matrix $(t_{11}, t_{12}, t_{21}, t_{22})$ and displacement vector (d_x, d_y). By factorizing the transformation matrix into scaling, rotation and local uncertainty, the receiver can alter the size, orientation, position and other local properties of the wireframe.

5.   Image Modeling

In order to represent the 3D shape of a human head and its facial features, a wireframe model consisting of a number of small triangles is employed. A large number of triangles are located in areas of high curvature and in areas which are important for the generation of facial expressions such as the eye and mouth. Figure 3 shows a typical example of the wireframe model, Parke's model, which is used in this paper. The model contains a full 3D description of the face object as well as parameters for controlling expressions. The facial expressions are described by action units (AUs). The action unit stands for a small change in the facial expression that is dependent on a small conscious activation of muscles.

FACS [8] classifies the facial expressions in terms of 44 action units involving one or more muscles. Each AU results in a visible change of the appearance of the face, e.g. the AU lip Corner Pull will pull the corners of the mouth up as well as generate wrinkles on the cheeks. With each AU, a weight is associated indicating how strong the AU is invoked by the person in the image. These weights form the parameteric representation of facial expressions.

Employing action units, 3D facial model can be expressed as,

$$\bar{s} = Rs + T + E\phi \qquad (5.1)$$

where R is the rotation matrix and T is the translation vector. They are used to specify global motions of the head. $\phi = (\varphi_1, \varphi_2, \ldots, \varphi_n)$ are local motion parameters that specify the facial expressions. The matrix E determines how a certain point s is affected by ϕ, and this is determined by action units.

In our implementation, R, T and ϕ can be directly determined. Five ideal contours are used to detect head, eyes, nose and mouth. We use generalized Hough transform to initialize the g-snake and capture the rough positions of head and facial features. Then, the precise contours and the correspondence motion parameters are tracked and extracted by Eq. (3.11) and Eq. (4.1). By factorizing the transformation matrix of Eq. (4.3) and computing displacement vector of Eq. (4.2), we can supply Eq. (5.1) the rotation matrix R and the translation vector T. Then, all points in the 3D facial model will be altered depending on translation, scale and rotation changes. Similarly, the procedure is repeated for each facial feature except that it only affects a certain group of points. In addition, ϕ is computed from $\psi(t)$ of Eq. (4.8) for each facial feature. Based on the value of E, the facial expression can be reproduced eventually.

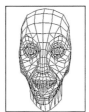

Fig. 3. Parke's Model

6. Experimental Results and Study

6.1. Feature Extraction

As shown in figure 1, Gaussian pyramid generation and edge detection are pre-processing steps of generalized active contour model. Gaussian pyramid helps in smoothing image and suppressing noise. Besides, it reduces search space for generalized Hough transform to quickly locate the rough contour of a feature. Figure 4 shows two levels of Gaussian pyramid for the 'Akina' image. The gradient images are computed by fitting planes in 2X2 windows using the least squares method. Hence, gradient direction vectors can be easily calculated to form the edge direction image.

After the rough contour is obtained from generalized Hough transform, the next step is to find the precise contour of each facial feature. Generalized active contour model will deform the rough contour and evaluate the match of the deformed contour with the underlying image. Figure 5 shows the features extracted. The white curves on each image represent the extracted contours of facial features. In general, our model can automatically identify facial features if appropriate prior knowledge, as shown in section 3.3, is incorporated.

Fig. 4. Two level of the Gaussian pyramid images(left), gradient images (middle) and edge direction images (right)

In figure 5(a), the shadow of the hair makes it difficult for g-snake to extract the exact shape of the left eye. Besides, the nose is incorrectly extracted because the boundary between nose and skin is often unclear. These situations, however, can be avoided if deformable surfaces instead of deformable contours are applied.

(a)   (b)

Fig. 5. The extracted contours by g-snake

6.2. *Feature Tracking*

In this section, we use an image sequence known as "Miss America" for lip and face tracking experiments. The processing flow is the same as that in section 2, except motion estimation and texture update are not included. The mouth and eye contours are trained as shown in section 3.3.

Figure 6 shows the experimental results for tracking the lip area from the 10th to the 29th frame. The sequence of images run from the left to the right. The white dots on each image indicate the points that form the contour. In some cases, the g-snake fails in locating the boundary accurately. This situation arises when the mouth is opened rapidly and the surrounding wrinkles generate misleading edge. To avoid this problem, a prediction algorithm[18] can be applied to adaptively predict the opening and closing of mouth.

334

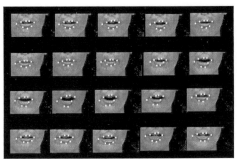

Fig. 6.   Lip tracking experiment

Besides, an experiment on human face and facial features motion tracking is conducted, as shown in figure 7. In this image sequence, apart from the changes in the shapes of eyes and mouth, the entire face moves once to the left and then returns to the original position. In other words, the positions of eyes and mouth do change with time. Our task is to track the motion of the head and extract the facial expressions. It can be seen from figure 7 that the positions and changes in the shapes of face, eyes and mouth are correctly extracted.

For the "Miss America" sequence, it is difficult to detect the left eye because of the existence of shadow. As a result, we use the extracted right eye contour to track the left eye so as to increase the probability of detection. Except from this case, it is possible to detect the right eye and mouth through almost the full sequence (150 frames).

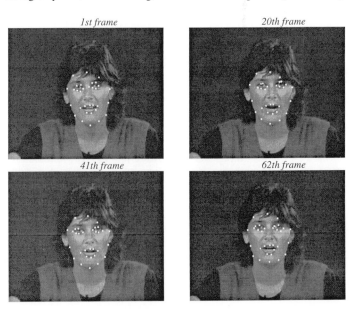

1st frame   *20th frame*

41th frame   *62th frame*

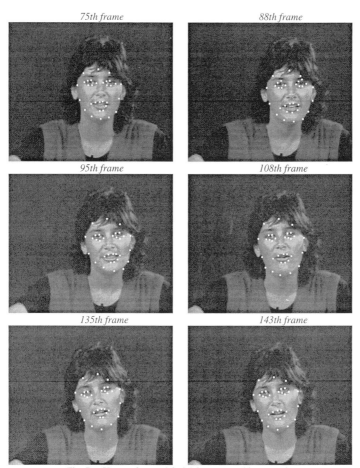

75th frame   88th frame

95th frame   108th frame

135th frame   143th frame

Fig. 7.   Human face and facial features tracking experiment

7.   Conclusion

We have presented the application of generalized active contour model in model-based facial image coding. To analyze the input image sequence, we consider the problems of modeling, extracting and tracking of facial features. Based on a regenerative shape matrix, both global and local deformation are integrated in our model. An internal energy function can incorporate a global model, and an external energy function can deform the resulting contour to match with the underlying image data. This led to a process where we can jointly extract and estimate global and local deformation of facial features from input motion pictures. Finally, we address the issue of automatic and efficient fitting of the wireframe to human face by using time sequence analysis of deformable contours.

In order to accurately perform feature tracking and extraction, we demonstrate with a learning algorithm on training of shape matrix and deformation variance from various mouth samples. The learned contour is eventually applied to the lip tracking process. Experimental results show that our method is robust if appropriate prior knowledge is incorporated. Besides, we also demonstrate with experiments how automatic feature extraction can be implemented in the first frame of image sequence.

Currently, our system is at the intermediate development stage. Work in automatic fitting of wireframe to human face is in progress. Future directions will include study on the inherent relationship between the global motion, local deformation and wireframe adaptation in 3D model-based image coding. Besides, the texture updating of luminance and chrominance information will also be incorporated in the near future. It is planned to integrate the above techniques and enhancements in a demonstration of videophone scene communications system.

References

1. Haibo Li, Astrid Lundmark & Robert Forchheimer, "Image Sequence Coding at Very Low Bitrates : A Review," *IEEE Transaction on Image Processing*, Vol. 3, No. 5, September 1994, pp. 589-609.

2. Musmann, Peter Pirsch & Hons-Joachim Grallert, "Advances in Picture Coding," *Proceedings of the IEEE*, Vol. 73, No. 4, April 1985, pp. 523-548.

3. Robert Forchheimer and Torbjorn Kronander, "*Image Coding - From Waveform to Animation,*" IEEE Transaction on Acoustics, Speech, and Signal Processing, Vol. 37, No. 12, December 1989, pp. 2008-2023.

4. K. Aizawa & H. Harashima, "*Model-based Analysis Synthesis Image Coding (MBASIC) System for a person's face,*" Signal Processing : Image Communication, Vol. 1, No. 2, October 1989.

5. W J Welsh, S Searby & J B Waite, "*Model-based Image Coding,*" Br Telecom Technol. J. Vol. 8, No. 3, July 1990, pp.94-106.

6. Musmann, M. Hotter & J.Ostermann, "*Object-oriented Analysis-synthesis Coding of Moving Images,*" Signal Processing : Image Communication, Vol. 1, No. 2, October 1989, pp. 117-138.

7. Masahide Kaneko, Atsushi Koike & Yoshinori Hatori, "*Coding of Facial Image Sequence based on 3D Model of the Head and Motion Detection,*" Journal of Visual Communication and Image Representation, Vol. 2, No. 1, March 1991, pp. 39-54.

8. Ekman P. & W. E. Friesen (1977), "Manual for the Facial Action Coding System," Consulting Psychologist Press, Palo Alto: California.

9. Michael Kass, Andrew Witkin & Demetri Terzopoulos, "*Snakes : Active Contour Models,*" Proceedings of First International Conference on Computer Vision, 1987, pp. 259-269.

10. Alan L. Yuilie, Peter W. Hallinan & David S. COHEN, "*Feature Extraction from Faces Using Deformable Templates,*" International Journal of Computer Vision, 1992, pp. 99-111.

11. Satoshi Ishibashi & Fumio Kishino, "*Color/Texture Analysis and Synthesis for Model-based Human Image Coding,*" SPIE Vol. 1605, Visual Communication and Image Processing : Visual Communications'91, pp. 242-252.

12. Kok F. Lai & R. T. Chin, "*Deformable Contours : Modeling and Extraction,*" International Conference on Computer Vision and Pattern Recognition, 1994, pp. 601-608.

13. R.Kindermann & J. L. Shell, "*Markov Random Fields and their Applications,*" American Mathematical Society, 1980.

14. Kok F. Lai & R. T. Chin, "On Regularization, Formulation and Initialization of the Active Contour Models (Snakes)," Asian Conference of Computer Vision, 1993, pp. 542-545.

15. Burt & E.H. Adeson, "*The Laplacian Pyramid as a Compact Image Code,*" IEEE Trans. on Commun., Vol. COM-31, No. 4, 1983, pp. 532-540.

16. Ballard, "*Generalizing the Hough Transform to Detect Arbitrary Shapes,*" Pattern Recognition, vol. 13, 1981, pp. 111-122.

17. T.Fukuhara & T.Murakami, "*3-D Motion Estimation of Human Head for Model-based Image Coding,*" IEE Proceedings, Vol. 140, No. 1, February 1993, pp. 26-35.

18. C.W.Ngo, S.Chan & Kok F. Lai, "*Motion Tracking and Analysis of Deformable Objects by Generalized Active Contour Models,*" Second Asian Conference on Computer Vision, 1995, to appear.

Chapter 9

3D Geometric Modeling

FEATURE BASED SCULPTING OF FUNCTIONALLY DEFINED 3D GEOMETRIC OBJECTS

VLADIMIR V. SAVCHENKO

Department of Computer Software, University of Aizu
Aizu-Wakamatsu City, Fukushima Prefecture, Japan
E-mail: savchen@u-aizu.ac.jp

ALEXANDER A. PASKO

Department of Computer Software, University of Aizu
Aizu-Wakamatsu City, Fukushima Prefecture, Japan

TOSIYASU L. KUNII

Department of Computer Software, University of Aizu
Aizu-Wakamatsu City, Fukushima Prefecture, Japan.

ANDREI V. SAVCHENKO

Hiwada Electronic Corporation, Pioneer Group
Adachi-gun, Fukushima Prefecture, Japan.

ABSTRACT

We present an approach to sculpting of functionally defined (or implicit) 3D geometric objects with arbitrary control points linked to features of an object. The displacement of these control points defines global space mapping. To interpolate displacements we use a volume spline based on the Green's function. We apply this technique to objects defined by implicit functions constructed in different ways: set-theoretic operations with R-functions, volume data interpolation, and depth data conversion. A splitting operation by a deformed halfspace is introduced to show the benefits of combining the implicit representation and set-theoretic modeling with sculpting.

1. Introduction

Deformation controlled by arbitrary points in 3D space is an important operation for many applications. For example, in some virtual environment systems the visitor would like to touch the scattered surface points of the virtual object for grabbing, pushing and sculpting. In CAD, it is also important to select features of an object to simulate the interactive distortion of the geometric objects. Methods of transformation of three-dimensional geometric objects have been widely studied in recent years. In the introduction to a special issue on interactive sculpting Rossignac[19] observes that "time has come for truly interactive and easy to use 3D sculpting systems."

Geometric objects defined by real functions of three variables (so-called implicit surfaces) have proven to be useful in computer graphics, geometric modeling and animation. We define geometric objects by implicit functions and just by a simple formula describe a complex object to manipulate it. Complex objects can be created with skeleton-based functions[3,30], so-called R-functions for set-theoretic operations[21], and by processing range or volume data. This paper extends power of the implicit representation by 3D sculpting. Sculpted objects can be then used as arguments of set-theoretic and other operations defined in terms of our shape modeling scheme.

The goal of this work is to extend the set of operations for design of free-form functionally defined shapes. This paper deals with a shape modeling scheme that, in the authors' opinion, combines high flexibility with easy numerical handling. We consider space mapping with arbitrary control points linked to features of an object. The displacement of these control points defines a global space transformation. The approach to mapping function construction is based on the scattered data interpolation. We emphasize that our scheme combines set-theoretic modeling with sculpting. This scheme allows us to generate new free forms by using set-theoretic, blending, offsetting and other operations, and to control global and local deformations. This scheme satisfies

341

a wide range of application needs. We introduce a splitting operation by a deformed halfspace and thus show the benefits of combining the implicit representation with sculpting. This operation can be applied in computer-assisted surgery training, CAD and animation.

The next section describes the related works. Section 3 provides basic information about our approach. Section 4 presents the results of experimenting with the algorithm. Section 5 provides concluding remarks. Details of the volume spline based on the Green's function are given in Appendix.

2. Related works

The following overview mentions several areas of related work, including shape transformation, feature-based modeling, volume splines and shape reconstruction. In recent years shape transformation techniques for 3D objects have achieved widespread use in geometric modeling and can be generally categorized as physically-based modeling[16,23], space mapping, shape transformation for polyhedral objects and skeleton-based modeling.

Free form deformations[20] are specified on 3D lattices and then transformation is applied to a geometric object. This process may prove difficult when the deformation is so complex that correspondence between the lattice deformation and the object deformation is not straightforward. Image warping (or morphing) techniques basically use 2D space mapping. Wolberg provides an introduction to image warping in[28]. This method relies on the user specified pairs of corresponding points in two images. While 2D warping is useful to create special effects for image transformation, 3D models can be used in design to create objects that combine features of the original objects. Continuous, invertible, one-to-one mappings between points of two objects provide topological equivalence of two objects and allow a user to control the deformation. Deformations allow the user to manipulate an object as if it was constructed from clay and to apply intuitive operations. Barr[2] introduced globally and locally defined deformations (bending, twisting, tapering). They are highly intuitive and are combined in a hierarchical structure, creating complex objects from simpler ones. Paper[4] presents a technique for computing space deformations that interpolate a set of user-defined constraints (displacements). The space deformation method is based on the following principle: the original and deformed spaces R^n are two projections of a higher dimensional space R^m. The deformation is defined by the composition of a function F: R^n -> R^m, that transforms the points of the original space R^n into points of R^m, with a projection T from R^m back onto R^n. Although all methods of space mapping based on control points are claimed to be model independent, they are practically applied to polyhedral and parametric surfaces.

Shape transformations for polyhedral objects fall into two steps. The first step is to establish a mapping from each point on one surface to some point on the second and the second step is referred to as the interpolation problem. The paper[11] presents a solution to the correspondence problem for Euler-valid, genus 0, polyhedral objects. There are problems though if self-intersection occurs during interpolation and user control. Skeleton-based modeling (blobby model[3], meta-balls[13] and soft objects[30] provides implicit surface transformations using arbitrarily placed control points.

The notion of a feature has been extensively discussed in[6,27,17,24,15,29,8]. A feature is a concept that relates form and function and we follow here the definition[6]: "A feature is a group of geometric and topological entities which have a functional meaning in a given context ". In our approach to space mapping we use control points on a surface that correspond to the user defined features.

Volume splines derived for multidimensional scattered data have been presented in[1,12,5]. A detailed discussion of techniques for extracting three-dimensional geometry from volume data can be found in[10]. This report compares methods of interpolation of scattered volumetric data. The compared methods are modified quadratic Shepard's method, volume splines, multiquadrics, volumetric minimum norm network and localized volume splines.

Shape reconstruction from given points can be thought as a special case of sculpting. We have applied an algebraic sum of a "carrier" solid with a volume spline to get a description of a reconstructed object[22]. This paper deals with shape transformation based on space mapping defined by volume splines.

3. Proposed solution

3.1 Representation of geometric objects

Although models of geometric objects can be of different types for applying 3D shape transformations based on space mapping, in our shape modeling scheme geometric objects are represented by the inequality: $f(P) \geq 0$, where f is a real continuous function of Cartesian coordinates P of a point. The function has negative values for points outside an object, positive values for inside points and zero values for points on a surface. Function representation of geometric objects can be useful for applying various kinds of transformations: set-theoretic operations, offsetting, blending, projection, sweeping, metamorphosis and hypertexturing[14]. Analytical descriptions of the set-theoretic operations using so-called R-functions have been discussed in[21]. Generally speaking, objects defined in this manner are not regularized solids as is required in Constructive Solid Geometry. In the simplest particular case the intersection of two objects defined by functions f_1 and f_2 can be described by $f_3 = \min(f_1, f_2)$ as mentioned by Ricci[18]. Of course, this description does not have satisfactory differential properties. Desirable C^1 continuity (excluding points where $f_1 = f_2 = 0$) can be provided with the set of R-functions presented below. If two geometric objects are defined as $f_1(x,y,z) \geq 0$ and $f_2(x,y,z) \geq 0$ respectively, then the following R-functions are useful : $f_3 = f_1 + f_2 - \sqrt{(f_1^2 + f_2^2)}$ for intersection and $f_3 = f_1 + f_2 + \sqrt{(f_1^2 + f_2^2)}$ for union.

3.2 Volume spline

In this work we use volume splines interpolating scattered data as a solution for creating mapping functions in a n-dimensional domain of arbitrary shape that contains a set of points $\{P_i = (x_1^i, x_2^i, .., x_n^i) : i = 1, 2, .., N\}$. This spline is based on the Green's function[25] and in the 2D case, it is the so-called thin-plate spline[1,5,12]. The coefficients of the spline (see Appendix) can be calculated by solving a system of linear algebraic equations. The only problem is operating with a dense matrix with diagonal elements equal to zero. We solve the system by the Householder method[9]. After defining the coefficients the spline $U(x_1, x_2, ..., x_n)$ can be calculated. This form of spline was chosen for two reasons:

• it was derived specially for the case of scattered points;
• it provides C^k continuity if $k < 2m - n$, where n is space dimension, and m defines a norm of a basis function.

3.3 Deformation

We discuss here space mappings driven by control points linked to features of an object. Our goal here is to define a deformation method that
• establishes one-to-one correspondence for all points in space;
• can be applied to n-dimensional spaces;
• does not depend on any regular structure of the control points data set.
Space mapping in R^n defines relationship between each point in the original and deformed object. Let an n-dimensional region of an arbitrary configuration be given and contain a set of arbitrary control points $\{Q_i = (q_1^i, q_2^i, .., q_n^i) : i=1,2,...,N\}$ for a nondeformed object and $\{D_i = (d_1^i, d_2^i, .., d_n^i) : i=1,2,...,N\}$ for a deformed object. By assumption, the points Q_i and D_i are distinct and given on or near a surface of an object. These points establish correspondence between features of two objects. The goal of the construction of the deformed object is to find a smooth mapping function that

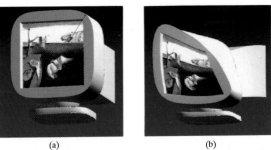

(a)   (b)

Fig. 1. Deformation of a set-theoretic object defined with R-functions. (a) An initial object with a red arrow indicating the control point displacement. (b) A deformed object. A picture deformed on a monitor screen after Salvador Dali's *The Persistence of Memory* (1931).

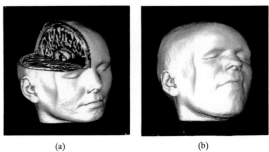

(a)   (b)

Fig. 2. Emulation of human face motion. (a) An initial volumetric head. (b) A deformed face.

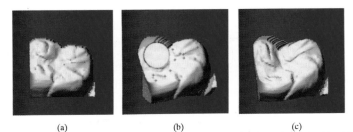

(a)   (b)   (c)

Fig. 3. Design of a tooth surface. (a) A standard tooth to be mapped onto a treated tooth with a drilled cavity (b). The red markers show 14 control points linked to corresponding features. (c) A recovered tooth after mapping the standard one.

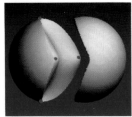

Fig. 4. Splitting a sphere in two parts according to a curve defined by four points.

approximately describes the spatial transformation. The inverse mapping function, that is needed to transform implicit surfaces, can be given in the form:

$$Q_i = U(D_i) + D_i, \qquad (1)$$

where the components of the vector $U(D_i)$ are the volume splines interpolating displacements of initial points Q_i. Note, since the algorithm does not use any regular grid, control points can be freely chosen by the user.

4. Experimental results

We have applied this mapping technique to different geometric objects defined by functions of three variables. These functions have been constructed in different ways:
• set-theoretic operations on implicitly defined primitives with R-functions;
• volume data interpolation;
• conversion of depth data.
We also illustrate this approach by a splitting operation. All the images presented in this paper were rendered on a Silicon Graphics Indigo[2] workstation by our experimental software written in C language.

4.1 Set-theoretic object

Figure1 illustrates the deformation of a 3D 'monitor' constructed from quadrics, superquadrics and blocks with set-theoretic operations defined by R-functions that allows us to get a single implicit function describing the object. Although the whole space is deformed, we define the deformation by a selected set of eight control points. Note that only one control point was actually shifted (see a red arrow in Figure1a). Another seven control points are located in the vertices of a box containing the object. These additional control points are used to localize the deformation.

4.2 Volumetric object

As Wang and Kaufman note in[26] volume graphics concerns manipulation of volumetric objects stored in a volume raster of voxels. For example, they consider constructive solid modeling at the voxel level. The application (Figure 2) was chosen deliberately to test the possibility of emulating human face motion and illustrates the sculptural flexibility of our algorithm to deform a muscle layer. The data of 150x200x192 voxels is used. We apply trilinear interpolation to it and subtract a given level value to define the implicit function. Figure 2a shows an initial volumetric object with a set-theoretic operation applied to show its internal structure. Five control points are placed inside the object and eight additional control points localize the deformation. Figure 2b shows how the skin layer is acted upon by the muscle layer. Deformation and polygonization of the deformed volumetric object took about 7 minutes.

4.3 Object represented by depth data

Many applications define the surface of a geometric object by depth data $z = d(x,y)$. The defining implicit function in this case can be represented as follows:

$$f(x,y,z) = (d(x,y) - z) \ \& \ box(x,y,z), \qquad (2)$$

where & indicates an R-function for the intersection operation and $box(x,y,z) = (a^2-x^2) \ \& \ (b^2-y^2) \ \& \ (c^2-z^2)$ with a,b,c setting the size of a bounding box. Consider the following practical problem, taken from a project in which the authors are involved (Figure 3). The problem is to design effective automation system for modifying a tooth occlusal surface. In order to obtain the proper surface of the treated tooth, a dentist may like to create and modify the surface interactively by using his own experience and results of a simulation of biting and chewing. On the other hand, it is necessary to keep topological features of the standard tooth presented by depth data. To provide this we can apply the proposed sculpting technique by establishing a correspondence between features (for example, ridges and ravines) of the standard tooth and treated one. Figure 3a presents the standard tooth that we would like to merge with the treated tooth with the drilled cavity (Figure 3b) using 14 control points linked to features. These points are marked by the red crosses. Figure 3c presents the recovered tooth after mapping the standard tooth. In practice, one can apply several consequent mappings to sculpt the desired surface.

4.4 Splitting operation

Fracon and Lienhard[7] investigated constructing metamorphoses of geometric objects by partition of geometric spaces into cells (vertices, edges, faces) to simulate natural phenomena. They use combinatorial maps and their extensions. Here we offer a splitting algorithm for functionally defined objects. It solves the problem arising in practice of splitting an object in two parts according to a curve or a set of points belonging to its surface. Figure 4 presents a simple example of splitting sphere. Four control points are placed on the surface. The following general scheme is used:
1) define an implicit function for the object;
2) define control points on or near the surface;
3) define projections of these points onto a reference halfspace, for example a plane or a hemisphere. The main problem is how to define the reference halfspace to provide one-to-one projection of the control points;
4) calculate a mapping function and apply it to the reference halfspace;
5) perform a set-theoretic subtraction of a reference halfspace from the initial object.
We plan to apply the splitting operation to remove undesirable parts of modelled teeth surfaces.

5. Conclusion

We have studied the possibility of using sculpting techniques for transforming of geometric objects described by real functions of three variables. It is clear that using implicit functions can be very computationally demanding, especially if interactive performance is desired. On the other hand, this approach has significant appeals. The shape modeling scheme combining implicit models and sculpting offers many advantages:
• various representational styles, including traditional implicits (quadrics, superquadrics, etc.), constructive geometry, volumetric and swept objects are supported;
• the definition of the sculpting technique is rather simple;
• arbitrarily placed points are used to control 3D deformation;
• deformed objects can be easily modified by further application of set-theoretic and many other operations;
• compactness of the representation allows us to implement application algorithms easily on parallel computers.
We suppose that the modeling process will be interactive with advances in hardware. The implementation of our software on a network of workstations has shown high processing speed. We intend to concentrate future research on applications for virtual environments, for example, to simulate the interactive distortion of a 3D object done by a virtual hand.

6. Acknowledgements

The authors acknowledge Professor Dr. Karl-Heinz Hohne for the volumetric data. We thank Professor Dr. John C. Dill for many suggestions and comments.

7. Appendix. Volume spline based on the Green's function

Data given:
- a set of scattered points $\{P_i = (x_1^i, x_2^i, ..., x_n^i): i = 1, ..., N\}$ in E^n ;
- values of a function $r_i = r(P_i)$.

The problem is to find a smooth function $U(x)$ so that $U(P_i) = r_i$. The Green's function is used as a basis function:

$$G_{m,n}(x, P_i) = \begin{cases} \|x-P_i\|^{2m-n} \ln\|x-P_i\| & \text{if n is even} \\ \|x-P_i\|^{2m-n} & \text{if n is odd,} \end{cases}$$

where $\|x-P_i\| = (\sum_{j=1}^{n} (x_j - x_j^i)^2)^{1/2}$, $x = (x_1, x_2, ..., x_n)$ is an arbitrary point of E^n. The coefficient $m \geq 2$ defines an applied norm. In practice, $m = 2$ can be used. For $m = 2$ and $n = 2,3$ the spline has the following form:

$$U(x) = \sum_{i=1}^{N+k} \lambda_i g_i(x, P_i),$$

where
$$g_i(x, P_i) = G_{m,n}(x, P_i), \quad i = 1, ..., N,$$
$$g_{N+1}(x, P_i) = 1,$$
$$g_{N+1+j}(x, P_i) = x_j, \quad j = 1, ..., k-1,$$
$$k = (n + m -1)! / (n!(m-1)!).$$

The spline coefficients λ_i are calculated using the system of $(N + k)$ linear equations:

$$A \begin{vmatrix} \lambda_1 \\ \lambda_2 \\ ... \\ \lambda_N \\ \lambda_{N+1} \\ \lambda_{N+2} \\ ... \\ \lambda_{N+k} \end{vmatrix} = \begin{vmatrix} r_1 \\ r_2 \\ ... \\ r_N \\ 0 \\ 0 \\ ... \\ 0 \end{vmatrix},$$

where the components of the matrix A are

$$A_{ij} = g_i(P_i, P_j), \quad i \leq N + k, j \leq N, i < j, i > j;$$
$$A_{ii} = 0; \quad i < N;$$
$$A_{ij} = g_i(P_i, P_j), \quad i \leq N, N < j \leq N+k;$$
$$A_{ij} = 0, \quad i > N, j > N.$$

8. References

1. P. Alfeld, in *Mathematical Methods in Computer Aided Geometric Design*, ed. T. Lyche and L. Schumaker (Academic Press Ltd, Orlando, England, 1989) 1.

2. A.H. Barr, *Computer Graphics* **18/3** (1984) 21.

3. J.F. Blinn, *ACM Transactions on Graphics* **1/3** (1982) 235.

4. O. Borrel and D. Bechman, *International Journal of Computational Geometry & Applications* **1/4** (1991) 427.

5. J. Duchon, in *Constructive Theory of Functions of Several Variables,* ed. A. Dodd and B. Eckmann (Springer-Verlag, Tokyo Berlin Heidelberg, 1977) 85.

6. B. Falcidieno, F. Giannini, C. Porzia and M. Spagnuolo, in *Proceedings of the IFIP WG 5.10*, ed. T.L. Kunii (Springer-Verlag, Tokyo Berlin Heidelberg, 1991) 125.

348

7. J. Fracon, P. Lienhard, in *Artificial Life and Virtual Reality,* ed. N. Magnenat Thalmann and D. Thalmann (John Wiley & Sons, West Sussex PO19 1UD, England, 1994) 23.

8. A. Gandhi and A. Myklebust, in *Proceedings of the Conference on CAD and Computer Graphics* (International Academic Publisher, Beijing, 1989) 245.

9. G.H. Golub and C.F Van Loan, *Matrix computation* (The John Hopkins University Press, Baltimore, 1984), p. 476.

10. A.E. Kaufman and G.M. Nielson, *Tutorial on volume visualization techniques and applications, Computer Graphics International '93* (Ecole Polytechnique Federale de Lausanne, 1993), p. 96.

11. J. R. Kent, W. E. Carlson and R.E. Parent, *Computer Graphics* **26/2** (1992) 47.

12. P. Lancaster and K. Salkauskas, *Curve and Surface Fitting an Introduction* (Academic Press Ltd, Orlando, England, 1988), p. 280.

13. H. Nishimura, M. Hirai, T. Kawai, T. Kawata, I. Shirakawa and K. Omura, *Journal of papers given at the Electronics Communication Conference'85* **J68-D (4)** (1985) (in Japanese).

14. A. Pasko, V. Adzhiev, A. Sourin and V. Savchenko, *The Visual Computer* (to appear).

15. S. Parry-Barwick and A. Bowyer, *Technical Report 098* (University of Bath, School of Mechanical Engineering,1992) p. 20.

16. A. Pentland, I. Essa, M. Friedman, B. Horowitz and S. Sclaroff, *Computer Graphics* **24/2** (1990) 143.

17. M.J. Pratt, *Int. J. Computer Integrated Manufacturing* **6/1&2** (1993)13.

18. A. Ricci, *The Computer Journal* **16/2** (1973)157.

19 J. Rossignac, *ACM Transactions on Graphics* **13/2** (1994)101.

20. T.W. Sederberg and S.R. Parry, *Computer Graphics* **20/4** (1986) 151.

21. V. Shapiro, *Computer Aided Geometric Design* **11/2** (1994) 153.

22. V.V. Savchenko, A.A. Pasko, O.G. Okunev and T.L. Kunii, *Computer Graphics Forum* **14/4** (1995) (to appear).

23. J.A. Thingvold and E. Cohen, Computer Graphics **24/2** (1990) 129.

24. D.G. Ullman, *Design Theory and Methodology, ASME* **DE-53** (1993) 91.

25. V.A. Vasilenko, *Spline-functions: Theory, Algorithms, Programs* (Nauka Publishers, Novosibirsk, 1983), p. 212.

26. S.W. Wang and A.E. Kaufman, *IEEE Computer Graphics and Applications* **14/5** (1994) 26.

27. J.R. Woodwark, *Computer-Aided Design* **20/4** (1988)189.

28. G. Wolberg, *Digital image warping* (IEEE Computer Society Press, Los Alamitos, California, 1990), p. 319.

29. R.F. Woodbury, *Computer & Graphics* **14/2** (1990)173.

30. G. Wyvill, C.Mc. Pheeters, and B. Wyvill, *The Visual Computer* **2/4** (1986) 227.

Interactive 3D Modeling System with Range Data

Takanori Hara*, Junji Sone**, Hiroaki Chiyokura***

*Graduate School of Media and Governance, Keio University,
5322 Endo, Fujisawa, Kanagawa 252 Japan
TEL 0466-47-5111, FAX 0466-47-5041, E-mail: hara@mag.keio.ac.jp

**Manufacturing Engineering Research Center, TOSHIBA Corporation,
33 Shinisogo, Isogo-ku, Yokohama, Kanagawa 235 Japan

***Faculty of Environmental Information, Keio University,
5322 Endo, Fujisawa, Kanagawa 252 Japan

Abstract

We present an interactive 3D modeling system using range data captured by a rangefinder that employs laser stripe technology. 3D CAD and 3D CG technology are now popular in the fields of manufacturing and entertainment. This technology will also play an important role in the service industry and education. Electronic museums are also expected, whereby digital representation of collections will enable many people to easily access museums. For the implementation of this system, it is necessary to represent the collection composed of digital information.

Our system has two major benefits that are unavailable with existing system. First, the smooth curve of lower degree can be generated because we pick up the points representing the curve shape using rectangles surrounding sequences of points. Second, we implement the interface in which a user can design the character line interactively. In our system, it is easy to generate the 3D shape from measurement data of the object in a computer.

1 INTRODUCTION

3D CAD and CG technology have advanced to the point where 3D objects can be produced by Numerical Control (NC) or Rapid Prototyping from a 3D shape model in a computer. On the contrary, it is not easy to generate the 3D digital representation of shape from the real world. Some systems, such as an electronic museum, need the 3D shape model of the object in the real world. The electronic museum can display the 3D digital shape data and its text information on Internet, where people around the world can access this system. Compared to a conventional museum, an electronic museum has two advantages. First, preservation of the shape data: If the object is preserved in poor condition or deteriorates, only the 3D shape data will be left. This shape data of the object in the computer enables a variety of simulations and modeling copies of the actual object. Second, support of education: we can make software that displays 3D motion of the object and text information of the museum collection. This software can be combined with multimedia technology such as a video and audio. These technologies allow people to make an effective material of a lecture and a class or to create a new computer world. These materials can work for help the understanding and creative design. For example, life that died out in ancient times can be seen as if it were alive, or the 3D shape data of artifact can be located in a different environment such as an old town, pyramid or castle, outer space that cannot be done in a normal display.

To develop these applications, the collection of 3D shape data from the real world is needed. We were motivated to develop a new modeling system using range data captured by rangefinder. We have to solve two problems to make a modeling system. First, since the point sequence of slit data has many errors and unwilling wave, we need to approximate it and make the smooth curve. The second is to make the 3D solid shape model from a lot of measured points.

The point sequence is captured by a rangefinder that employs laser stripe technology. If the curve passing through all points included in one slit is generated, the curve has an unwilling wave. There are previous approaches that modify the error and the wavelet of the curve. Cohen and O'Dell[1] find an initial parameterization for a spline curve that helps identify the corners. Fang and Gossard[2] proposed a method that simulates the deformation of a perfectly elastic beam under the application of spring forces. This method was presented for reconstructing a smooth curve from a set of unordered and error-filled data points. In our system, we generate rectangles to pick up the points depicting the curve shape, with the width of the rectangle specified by a user. Then the curve passing through these characteristic points is generated. As a result, the smooth free form surface with few unwilling waves can be generated.

There are other approaches to reconstruct 3D shape model from unorganized points: Hoppe and co-workers[3] make the marching cubes by an algorithm of graph optimization in order to construct the polygonal surfaces. Hagen and Santrelli[4] fit B-spline surfaces on range data by a weighted least-square approach. Tunk[5] combines multiple views of an object, captured by a range scanner, and assemblies these views into one unbroken polygonal surface by clipping overlapping polygons. With these approaches, although shape data composed of polygons is effective for a shaded model, it is difficult to change the form of the 3D shape data for further processing, especially if it was not generated correctly at the beginning. We want to generate the solid model based free form surfaces, but it is not easy to generate the smooth character line and to combine multiple viewrange data of an object automatically. Therefore our system does not generate the 3D shape data automatically. Rather we have developed a function for the user to make the character line interactively based on the shape characteristic image by watching the range data. In this system, we use NURBS Boundary Gregory Patch (NBGP)[6,7] to construct the solid model. In this patch the G^1 continuity between two surfaces can be simplified and the shape control for making the smooth surface can be easily realized. Furthermore, by satisfying the G^1 surface continuity, 3D solid model can be built.

Also, to demonstrate our system we have included an example, showing the 3D shape model of a famous earthenware called HANIWA. It has been used as a doll in Japanese toms for over two thousand years ago. We advertised the 3D shape model of HANIWA with its explanation on Internet browser, Mosaic.

2 Overview

Here is an overview of our method. A sequence of many points is captured from a rangefinder. The curve is generated by each stripe of point sequence. The system can avoid the reversing of the normal direction of the curve caused by the measurement error. Looking at the characteristic of the object from the range data, a user specifies the shape of this area to generate free from surfaces. This area must be set as a shape of quadrilateral in which the boundary curves on opposite side should be placed as parallel as possible. Finally, the boundaries are corrected to satisfy the G^1 continuity of neighboring surfaces, and the solid model is generated. We show the procedure of this surface generation in Fig.1.

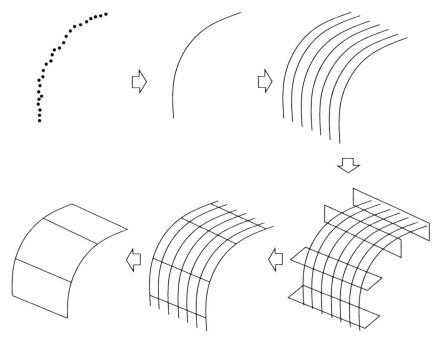

Fig.1 Flow of the surface generation

We used the Solid Modeling Kernel of RICOH, DESIGNBASE[8] to build our system. After modeling with range data, the local operations and the Boolean operations as functions of a solid modeler can be used for modeling a shape. Our system generates the NBGP from character curves automatically.

3   Generate reference curves and character curves

3.1   Find error points

The measurement data occasionally includes some points that are separate from the main data sequence due to laser measurement error. Such error points should be eliminated automatically. Our system finds the error points based on the distance of neighboring points. In Fig.2, since distances of DE and EF are substantially different from CD and FG, point E is eliminated.

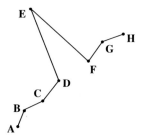

Fig.2 Find of the error point

3.2 Make the bounding box

The measured point sequences have waves of 0.1mm because of the laser property. If the curve for a given stripe is generated passing through all the points, this curve will have unwilling waves. Fig.3(a) shows the generated curve and its normal direction line. Note that some normal direction lines are reversed. If the curve has a lot of the reverses, it is difficult to eliminate these waves. To overcome this problem, our system identifies some points that characterize the curve shape and generate the curve based on passing through this modified data set. With this algorithm, we can get a low segment smooth curve that can be easily manipulated (see Fig3(b)). A characteristic point is selected by the rectangles surrounding one piece of the measured points. This filtering algorithm is as follows:

1. Make line between point[n] and point[n+m].

2. Calculate the maximum distance from the line to point[n], [n+1], [n+2]...[n+m]. The rectangle is specified by comparing the maximum distance and a width assigned by the user.

3. Repeat step 1 and 2 for the entire segment data.

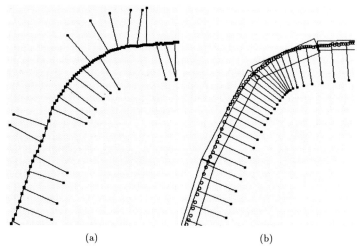

(a)   (b)

Fig.3 Make of the bounding box: (a)the curve passing through all of the measured points, (b)the curve passing through the characteristic points

3.3 Assign the tangent vector

Fig.4 shows the first tangent vector for a given measurement point sequence. Assigning the tangent vector the shape of the curve can be approached to the inside measured of the rectangle. Fig.4(b) shows generated curve using only characteristic points derived from the bounding box. The curve is out from bounding box. Fig.4(c) shows the generated curve constrained by tangent vector. These tangent vectors are calculated from the method of least squares to direct the middle position between one piece of data.

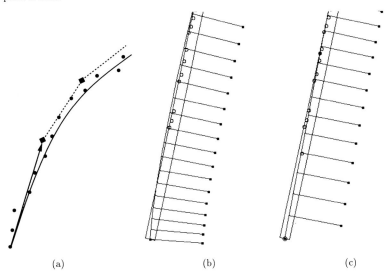

(a)   (b)   (c)

Fig.4 Set of the tangent vector: (b)set no tangent vector, (c)set the tangent vector

3.4 Correct the curvature

Using the above mentioned algorithm, we sometimes have unwilling waves. If the direction of the curvature should be constant, then, our system should correct the curve shape by moving the control point automatically. When the system tracks the concave direction of the control polygon, if it changes more than 180 degrees, then the curvature is reversed at that control point. Fig.5 shows a procedure to correct the curvature as follows:

1. Make a control polygon of the curve.

2. Check the direction of concave shape. In Fif.5, the concave shape around the point C is reversed.

3. Move the control point C to the middle point of the line BD.

4. Repeat step 2 and 3 for all control points of the curve.

If a curve has a lot of control points, it is difficult to correct the shape with this algorithm. In our system, it is easy to correct the curvature because the original control points are reduced to the characteristic points by the bounding box filter.

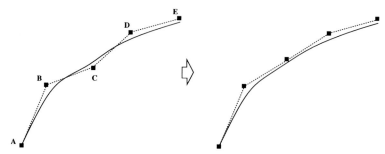

Fig.5 Change of the curvature

3.5 Generate the character curves

3.5.1 Create the cut face

After generating the reference curves, a user needs to divide the surface into rectangle areas which depending on the surface's characteristic. And a user makes a cut face on the overlapped area of two range data to combine the faces easily. We have developed the editing function to generate cut faces, parallel movement, rotate movement, expand and contract by dragging. At that time, this system can display the intersection points of curve group and cut faces, so a user can observe the intended angle and location easily.

We show the cut faces in Fig.6. After setting all the cut faces, the reference curve group is cut by cut faces.

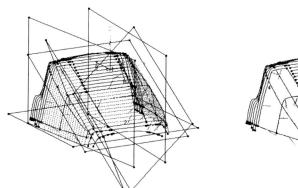

Fig.6 Set of cut faces   **Fig.7** Generation of initial faces

3.5.2 Generate of the initial face

When the boundary edge group that composes one surface is fixed, we generate the initial faces. Fig.7 shows some divided faces. The faces are constructed by cutting faces and reference curves. The characteristic curves are used for one side of boundaries. The other sides of boundaries, first and last reference curves are used. Another reference curves are registered and they are referred to make the control points of NBGP which procedure is described at the next section.

4 Surface generation

We explain the surface generation method from the character curves and the reference curves. First, characteristic of NURBS boundary Gregory patch is mentioned.

4.1 Characteristic of NURBS boundary Gregory patch

An NBG patch can represent a large surface bounded by NURBS[9] curves. As shown in Fig.8, eight sequences of control points define an NBG patch. Four sequences of control points $P_{0,j}$, $P_{3,j}$, $P_{4,j}$, and $P_{7,j}$ are NURBS curve control points that express surface boundaries. $P_{1,j}, P_{2,j}, P_{5,j}$, and $P_{6,j}$ determine the normal derivatives.

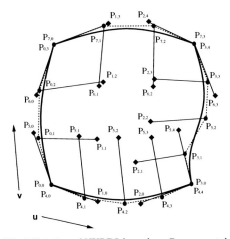

Fig.8 Notation of NURBS boundary Gregory patch

An NBG patch is an extension of the general boundary Gregory patch[10]. An NBG patch consists of three surfaces, S^a, S^b, and S^c, as follows:

$$S(u,v) = S^a + S^b - S^c.$$

S^a is defined by boundary curves and their normal derivatives The boundary curves and the normal derivatives are expressed by a NURBS. Similarly, S^b is represented by NURBS boundary curves and the NURBS normal derivatives. S^c is called a common surface of S^a and S^b, which is a cubic rational boundary Gregory (RBG) patch[11].

A NBG patch has the following features.

1. A Coons patch is well known as a surface that interpolates for piecewise boundary curves, while it is difficult to set the twist vectors on the patch. Since an NBG patch is represented only by control points, the expression of the NBG patch is easily understood.

2. On a NURBS surface, the number of control points, degrees, and knot vectors must be same on the two curves that face each other. On the other hand, the number of control points, degrees, and knot vectors of an NBG patch do not need be same among the four boundaries. Since the knot insertion is not needed, the amount of the data size of an NBG patch is smaller, than that of a NURBS surface.

3. The degree of the normal derivative on a curve is equal to that of the boundary curves of a NBG patch and the expression is simple. With this feature, the surface shape can be easily controlled with the normal derivative.

4.2   How to construct the surface

The surface is constructed from the character curves for the boundaries, the tangent vectors and the control points. The tangent vectors and the control points are calculated from the reference curves. We describe the method[12] to assign the tangent vectors and to fit the reference curves at the center.

4.2.1   Assigning of the tangent vectors

The quadratic normal derivative is used. Fig.9 shows the tangent vectors on the boundaries. These tangent vectors are defined from the equation:

$$\mathbf{S}_u(0,v) = 3\sum_{j=0}^{2} B_j(v)(\mathbf{P}_{1j} - \mathbf{P}_{0j}).$$

Here,$B_i(u)$ is a Bernstein polynomial. For the piecewise boundary curve, the length of the tangent vector is adjusting to the same length of the tangent vector that the cubic Bézier boundary curves have.

We may obtain a convex shape near the boundary, depending on the design. In such case, it is not sufficient to define the center tangent vectors from linear interpolation of both sides. Therefore, the tangent vectors should be given by the designer. Figure 10 shows an example of how to calculate the center derivative vector on the condition that the interpolation length takes half of overall section length(Vlen=1/2). A user is given the length(Vlen) that depends on the shape. The calculation procedure is as follows.

a) The points at u=1/6 are calculated from reference curves.

b) The cubic Bézier curve is used to interpolate the u=1/6 points and v=1/2 point is computed.

c) Similarly, points u=0 and v=1/2, u=1/3 and v=1/2, u=1/2 and v=1/2 are calculated.

d) The cubic Bézier curve can be generated passing through these points. Then we can get V_{p1} that is a passing value of the derivative function.

e) The control point $\mathbf{P}_1$ of the derivative function is calculated by the equation:

$$P_1 = \frac{V_{p1} - B_0(\tfrac{1}{2})V_{p0} - B_2(\tfrac{1}{2})V_{p2}}{B_1(\tfrac{1}{3})}$$

which is derived from the quadratic Bézier function.

f) The vector length is adjusting to the same length of the tangent vector that the cubic Bézier boundary curves have.

Fig.11 (a) shows NURBS boundary curves and tangent vectors V_{02} and V_{12} assigned from above method. Points P_1 and P_2 as starting points of the vectors. V_{00}, V_{01}, V_{10} and V_{11} are the tangent vectors of the boundaries at the corners. After fixing V_{02}, the normal derivatives interpolating V_{00}, V_{02} and V_{01} is defined as a cubic Bézier function. To construct a NBG patch, the boundary and its normal derivative are not only represented by the same degree, but also need have the same knot vector. Thus the normal derivative is subdivided. Fig.11(b) shows the control point determining the normal derivative.

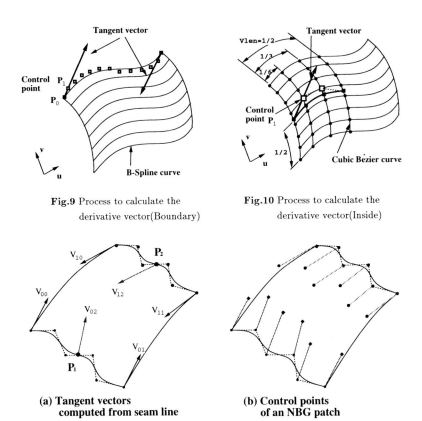

Fig.9 Process to calculate the derivative vector(Boundary)

Fig.10 Process to calculate the derivative vector(Inside)

(a) Tangent vectors computed from seam line

(b) Control points of an NBG patch

Fig.11 Construction of normal derivatives

4.2.2 Surface fitting at center area

Because three component's surfaces in a NBG patch are defined by only the boundary and its normal derivative, it is difficult to control the center area of the NBG patch. To get a freedom of the control, the degree of the common surface $\mathbf{S}^c$ is elevated. Although Fig.12 shows the control points of the common surface $\mathbf{S}^c$, Fig.12(b) show the a quartic RBG patch.

Then, we can have a control point $\mathbf{P}_{220}$ which enables to control the shape around the center. In our method, a designer assigns the parameters u_0, v_0 defining the center point $\mathbf{P}$. Point $\mathbf{P}(u_0, v_0)$ can be derived as follows. 1) Parameter u_0 points are calculated on the reference curves. 2) The cubic Bézier curve is used inapproximates of these points, and point $\mathbf{P}(u_0, v_0)$ is computed.

the control point $\mathbf{P}_{220}$ is determined by

$$\mathbf{P}(u_0, v_0) = \mathbf{S}^a(u_0, v_0) + \mathbf{S}^b(u_0, v_0) - \mathbf{S}^c(u_0, v_0).$$

From this procedure, surface shape at the center is adjusted to the reference curves.

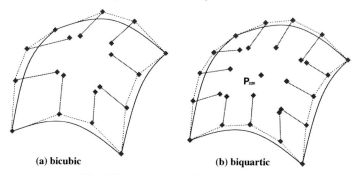

(a) bicubic　　　　　　**(b) biquartic**

Fig.12 Degree elevation of a common surface

5　Surface connection

The boundary curves of the connected surfaces are not coincident, because the positions of these curves have measurement error. In this case, boundary curves are corrected to satisfy the G^1 continuity. The topology of solid model is constructed. Finally, two surfaces is corrected to satisfy the G^1 continuity.

5.1　Connection of surface boundaries

First, two different boundary curves are averaged to make a new boundary curve that joints two connecting surfaces. The topology of the solid model is built. Finally, continuity is corrected for both sides of corner points on the duplicate boundaries. In our system, a user can select the direction of the character curves freely on the reference curves. Then, we have two methods that curves shapes are corrected to make a smooth connection.

5.1.1　The direction of tangent vectors are almost the same values

Fig.13(a) shows boundary face in which the directions of tangent vectors are almost the same values. To satisfy the G^1 continuity, The control points $\mathbf{P}_{11}, \mathbf{P}_{10}, \mathbf{P}_{21}$ and weights w_{11}, w_{10}, w_{21} are corrected from following equation:

$$(n_1 - 1)(w_{11} - w_{10}) = (n_2 - 1)(w_{21} - w_{10})$$

$$(n_1 - 1)w_{11}(\mathbf{P}_{11} - \mathbf{P}_{10}) = (n_2 - 1)w_{21}(\mathbf{P}_{21} - \mathbf{P}_{10}).$$

Here, n_1 and n_2 are the order of curves.

5.1.2 The direction of tangent vectors are different values

Fig13(b) shows boundary face in which the directions of tangent vectors are different values. To satisfy the G^1 continuity, the control points and weights are corrected from following equation:

$$(n_1 - 1)(w_{11} - w_{10}) = (n_2 - 1)(w_{21} - w_{10})$$

$$\frac{(n_1 - 1)w_{11}(\mathbf{P}_{11} - \mathbf{P}_{10}) \times \mathbf{C}}{\| (n_1 - 1)w_{11}(\mathbf{P}_{11} - \mathbf{P}_{10}) \times \mathbf{C} \|} = \frac{(n_2 - 1)w_{21}(\mathbf{P}_{21} - \mathbf{P}_{10}) \times \mathbf{C}}{\| (n_2 - 1)w_{21}(\mathbf{P}_{21} - \mathbf{P}_{10}) \times \mathbf{C} \|}.$$

Here, $\mathbf{C}$ is the tangent vector of the duplicate boundary which joint surfaces $\mathbf{S}^a$ and $\mathbf{S}^b$.

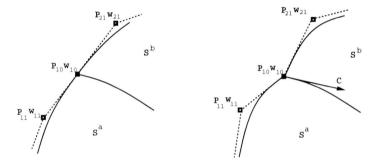

(a) The same tangent vector direction   (b) Different tangent vector direction

Fig.13 Correction of boundary continuity at corner

5.2 Joining two surfaces

The surface shape is controlled by normal derivative for NBG patch. Then, we can correct the normal derivative to make G^1 continuity of the two surfaces. In this method, the tangent vector can be transferred. If normal derivative is constructed by quadratic Bézier function, second tangent vector can be corrected. The number of the corrected tangent vector is calculated by subtracting one from tangent vectors degree. Then, the operation of surface connection can be simplified compare with the connection method of other type patches. We use the joining method[13,14] of Gregory patch. In this method, the normal derivative's degree of the connected surface is elevated. After corrected the normal derivative, control points of NBGP are calculated by subdivision which method is mentioned in above section.

6 EXAMPLE

The capabilities of our system are demonstrated by the HANIWA model shown in Fig.14. Fig.14(a) shows the measured points and Fig.14(b) shows the Mosaic window and the shape data modeled by using our system. We can see many small projections on the body and a sword on its hip. HANIWA is the earthenware that was offered in the tomb in Japan two thousand years ago. Before more, the people who had served a man of power had offered with him.

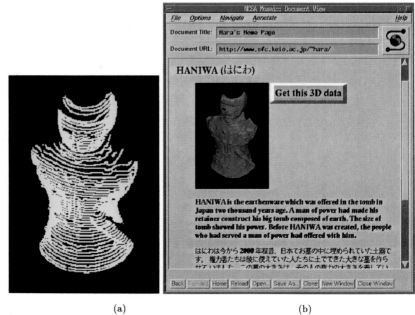

(a)   (b)

Fig.14 Example for Electronic Museum: (a) the measurement data (b) the shape data and the text information

7 CONCLUSION

The interactive 3D modeling system provides an improved algorithm for generating digital shape data from real world objects. This is accomplished by reducing the number of control points for the curve with the bounding box filter, assigning tangent vectors to the control points, and finally correcting any curvature reversals. These process result in more natural free-form surfaces compared to previous approaches. Also, the interactive feature allows users to modify the character curves while viewing the range data on screen. And the surface of 3D solid model can be constructed by NBGP. NBGP can be simplified connecting two surfaces to satisfy the G^1 continuity.

In addition, the generations of characteristic curves need further functions. The current system changes of the curvature radii and the inflection point automatically. So if the object has edge corners, these corners are blunted in our system. The processes that represent edge corners are necessary. And this system should appropriate the cut faces as free form surfaces to improve the specifying the area.

This system makes it easy to capture the object from a real world in a computer, and reserve the shape data. Combination of this modeling system and multimedia technology leads many effective educational softwares.

ACKNOWLEDGMENTS

We would like to thank AISHIN NEWHARD for the range data that was used in this research project.

REFERENCES

1 E.Cohen, C.L.O'Dell, A Data Dependent Parameterization for Spline Approximation, *Mathematical Method in Computer Aided Geometric Design*, T.Lyche and L.L.Schumaker, ed., Academic Press, Boston, 1989.

2 L.Fang, D.Gossard, Multidimensional curve fitting to unorganized data points by nonlinear minimization, *Computer-Adid Design*, Vol.27, No.1, 1995.

3 H.Hoppe, T.DeRose, T.Duchamp, J.McDonald, W.Stuetzle, Surface Reconstruction from Unorganized Points, *Computer Graphics Proceedings*, Annual Conference Series, 1992.

4 H.Hagen, P.Santarelli, Variational Design of Smooth B-Spline Surfaces, *Topics in Surface Modeling*, SIAM, Philadelphia,

5 G.Turk, M.Levoly, Zippered Polygon Meshes from Range Images, *Computer Graphics Proceedings*, Annual Conference Series, 1994.

6 J. A. Gregory, Smooth interpolation without twist constraints, *Computer Aided Geometric Design*, R. E. Barnhill and R. F. Riesenfeld, ed., Academic Press, New York, 1974.

7 J. Sone, T. Watanabe, S. Yamakawa and H. Chiyokura, Surface Control using a NURBS Boundary Gregory Patch, *Proc. CGInternational '94*, Melbourne, 1994

8 H. Toriya and H. Chiyokura, *3D CAD Principles and Applications* , Springer-Verlag, 1993.

9 W. Tiller, Rational B-splines for curve and surface representation, *IEEE CG & A*, 3, (6), 1983.

10 K. Konno, T. Takamura and H. Chiyokura, A new control method for free-form surfaces with tangent continuity and its applications, *Scientific Visualization of Physical Phenomena*, N. M. Patrikalakis, ed., Springer-Verlag, Tokyo, 1991.

11 H. Chiyokura, T. Takamura, K. Konno and T. Harada, G^1 Surface interpolation over irregular meshes with rational curves, *NURBS for Curve and Surface Design*, G. Farin, ed., SIAM, Philadelphia, 1991.

12 J. Sone and H. Chiyokura, Generation of a Single Gregory Surface from 3-D Measurement Data , *Computer Graphics and Application - Pacific Graphics '93*, S.Y.Shin, T.L.Kunii, ed., Seoul, 1993

13 H. Chiyokura, Localized surface interpolation for irregular meshes, *Advanced Computer Graphics*, Springer-Verlag, Heidelberg, 1986.

14 H. Chiyokura, *Solid modeling with DESIGNBASE: Theory and implementation*, Addison-Wesley, Reading, MA, 1988.

Chapter 10

Multimedia Systems and Applications

USING MULTIMEDIA IN LEARNING ABOUT PROCESSES; DEGREE: A SIMULATION-BASED AUTHORING SYSTEM FOR MULTIMEDIA DEMONSTRATION BUILDING

Roger Nkambou
Luc Quirion
Marc Kaltenbach
and
Claude Frasson

*Département d'informatique et de recherche operationnelle, Université de Montréal
Montreal, Quebec, H3C 3J7, Canada
E-mail: nkambou@iro.umontreal.ca*

ABSTRACT

Multimedia resources are viewed as essential ingredients in the design of Intelligent tutoring System (ITS). Adorning an ITS with multimedia resources is usually a tedious task. We propose a way to alleviate this problem through a new kind of Multimedia authoring system named DEGREE†. This system facilitates the building and testing of multimedia enriched demonstration scenarios for carrying out particular tasks on a simulated device. These demonstrations are used to teach by showing and explaining how tasks should be carried out on the real device. They are built by direct manipulation on the simulator. Once built, the demonstration scenarios are used by learners either in a passive mode or in an interactive mode, at their choice. Thus, a student learns how to execute a task on a device by watching or by practicing. Three learning modes are supported: self-demonstration, interactive demonstration and free practice. In addition, the simulator explains itself by a kind of "balloon help" on its components. This paper describes the authoring demonstration building environment, as well as the student used presentation environment.

Key words: simulation, multimedia, task analysis, authoring system, learning environment.

1. Introduction

Acquiring motor and cognitive skill for executing practical tasks is a major concern in many training processes. For example, in professional training, a way to acquire such skills is by observing a domain expert in action (Collin 1987), and to practice by carrying out tasks and/or solve problems (Lajoie et al. 1989).

---

† Demonstration Environment Generator for Real Expertise Experiencing

In many circumstances, possibly just for motivational reasons or memory support (Kaltenbach and Preiss 1994), it is important that the learning environment be reasonably close to the real environment in which learners will have to exploit their acquired knowledge. Of course, one must take into account the cost of building such simulators, as well as the constraints inherent to computer simulated environments. To build realistic simulations we have used VAPS (Virtual Application Prototyping System) (Virtual Prototype 1993) which is a dedicated simulation building system particularly well adapted to visually representing devices and model their behavior. In the following, the simulated (virtual) device resulting from a modeling effort in VAPS is called the simulator. The simulators we have built so far allow users to get a global views of the device as well as detailed views of their parts (Halff, 1993). The purpose of this paper is to describe an additional layer of functionalities allowing instructional designers and learners to carry out useful tasks with the device (Merrill 1991).

DEGREE allows non-programming task experts to build demonstrations and curricula on top of simulated physical devices. The handling of a device is explicitly represented and enhanced with multimedia elements (such as texts, sounds, images and videos). The exploitation of simulators in building learning environments is what distinguishes our system from authoring systems such as Authorware (Authorware 1988), Macromind Director (Macromind 1991), or SuperCard (Supercard 1989), etc. The demonstrations are built by direct manipulations of the simulator, leading to action traces that can be edited, reorganized and augmented by additional multimedia elements. The resulting presentation sequences are then placed in a structured library that can be exploited for various pedagogical goals. Thus, with teaching as its main intended use, DEGREE can be part of a larger course building environment and "Intelligent Tutoring System" (ITS) that needs demonstration scenarios.

The creation of edited presentation sequences by an instructional designer may have to be preceded by a task analysis on the chosen device by a specialized task analysis expert (Polson 1993). The task analysis expert extracts useful sequences adapted to various categories of learners, degrees of expertise, previous experiences, levels of motivation, etc. This is needed because many apparently simple tasks, in fact require quite complex cognitive mental activities to be learned. Goms is a task analysis method (Polson 1993; Bovair, Kieras and Polson 1990) we found quite appropriate for task analysis related to the use of physical devices. This task analysis can be enhanced with specific information on the tasks and the task performers (conceptual errors, etc.). we have applied the approach to perform an exhaustive task analysis on the device, an intravenous perfusion pump.

Structuring sub tasks into more meaningful units is not easy, possibly due to a large number of alternative and complex relationships among parts. Goms also provides some guidelines in this respect.

2. DEGREE Architecture

Figure 1 shows the general architecture of the proposed system, being composed of two main modules: an authoring environment that is the expert tool for demonstration building, and a presentation environment that represents the framework in which learning takes place.

The authoring environment includes a set of tools: the animated trace editor, multimedia element editors, and the demonstration editor. These tools enable the author to build a complete demonstration or just to store elements that will be used in the building of future demonstrations. These elements are stored in a structured library according to their type, which is also user designed. At present, the library includes simulator usage traces, texts, images, sounds, video sequences, and demonstration sequences. Once built, a demonstration can be presented to a learner in the presentation environment.

The presentation environment has several adaptation parameters allowing the choice of a demonstration mode (component explanations, non-interactive and interactive scenarios,...) and an adaptation to the student's level (novice, intermediate, advanced).

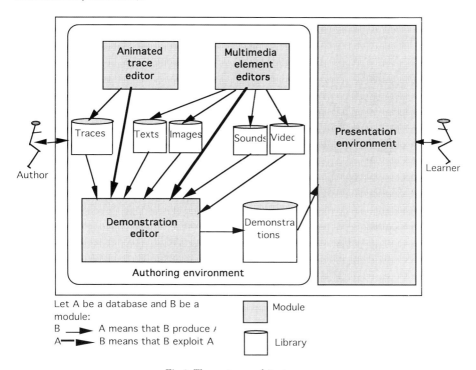

Fig 1: The system architecture.

DEGREE is composed of specifications for simulator design, a collection of editors to create/edit the objects in the demonstration libraries and the learner environment.

2.1. Simulator design specifications

The simulator design process includes physical and behavioral modeling. We have used the VAPS graphical object environment for modeling the physical appearance of the device and the automata-based language of VAPS for modeling the functional aspect of the device. This language is closely related to the ATN (Augmented Transition Network) paradigm (Woods 1970). When the device is functioning, each one of its functional components may pass through a set of consecutive states. The transition from one state to another is prompted by an event or combination of events coming from the behavior of another component, or explicitly generated by a user. Of course there are other ways of modeling the system behavior, such as user programmed specific constraints between parts, that would lead to more efficient simulations in terms of computer time; however, for DEGREE being designed for use by non programmers, it is necessary to spare them the trouble of coding in VAPS.

Thus we constrain the device behavior modeling to ATN based models. To each state of the device, we assign the possible events that it can receive, the possible actions that will be "fired" during the transition crossing, and the possible states in which the device can be after the transition crossing. The main advantage of this approach is that it gives access to the device state at any time and enables the capture of user action sequences on the simulator. If this constraint is satisfied, then DEGREE can be used on any kind of device simulator.

One simulator we have built is an intravenous perfusion pump (volumetric Flo-Gard 6201 of Baxter company (figure 2)). Figure 3 shows the simulated interface obtained. To insure that DEGREE is generic, we have also tested it on other VAPS based simulators, such as a bank automated cash dispenser.

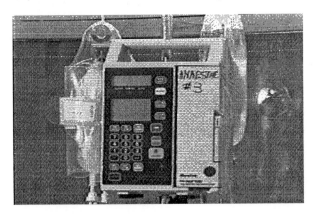

Fig. 2. The real infusion pump image.

The building of a simulator requires a thorough study of the real device and the completion of the following steps:

- Representation of the device physical components through graphical modeling (physical modeling).
- Study of the behavior of the given device:
  - Defining the graphs for the functioning automata.
  - Implementing of these graphs with the ATN language.
- Identifying the different uses of the device (by cognitive task analysis).

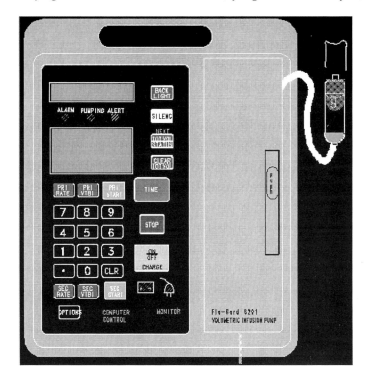

Fig.3. The front panel of the simulator interface.

2.2. The Demonstration authoring environment

As mentioned before, the authoring environment (figure 4) enables an author, interacting with the simulator, to build demonstrations based on the results of the cognitive task analysis. The building process is **done directly on the simulator and generates demonstrations intended for learners of different level of expertise**. It combines several tools for the creation of pedagogical components to include in a demonstration:

- an animated trace editor to build task segments by direct manipulation of the device. These segments will be later assembled in demonstration scenarios. The editor manages an animated hand so that human gestures (such as pressing on a button, turning a knob,...) can be easily included in a task demonstration.
- multimedia element editors (editors for texts, sounds, images and videos) are readily available to the demonstration author.
- an editor of demonstration scenarios is the main tool of our system, in the sense that the demonstration building effectively takes place there.

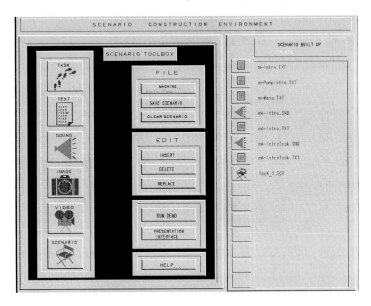

Fig. 4. The authoring environment interface.

2.2.1. Animated traces editor

This tool enables the author to record sequences of actions. The recording of actions is done by direct manipulation of the simulator. Each action in a sequence is coded, to be more meaningful than the original VAPS event codes. The sequence of filtered and coded actions is called a trace. When a trace is replayed, the coded actions in the trace are re-coded and fed to the simulator which executes them. Thus, the simulator receives events fired up by the re-coded actions, and responds to them as if it was being manipulated by the hand of an otherwise invisible user. In short, in the replay mode the simulated hand gives the impression that someone is manipulating the device.

The simulated hand trajectory is obtained concurrently with the direct manipulation of the simulator, thus creating what we call an animated trace. To compensate for human shaky movements or errors, the trajectories are automatically smoothed. This can be followed by further human editing of the animated trace. Thus in replay mode the hand movement from one device component to another can be given in variable speeds to reflect the timing of an expert performing the task.

The system allows the author to adjust the virtual hand size according to the simulated interface size, and to adjust moving speed. The speed assigned to the animation can be made to depend on the expertise level of the intended demonstration. In summary, to create an animated trace, the expert records the events constituting the task by direct manipulation of the simulator and then works with the resulting trace to improve it. We are going to see below how this trace can be further enriched with multimedia elements.

2.2.2. Editors of multimedia elements

Sound editor: The sound elements are used to add comment actions in an animated trace. The system sound editor (figure 5) allows the expert to record a sound component when watching an animated trace. These sound elements comment on the actions during their execution. Thus, the editor makes it easy to synchronize the added sounds with the sequence of corresponding actions of the animated trace.

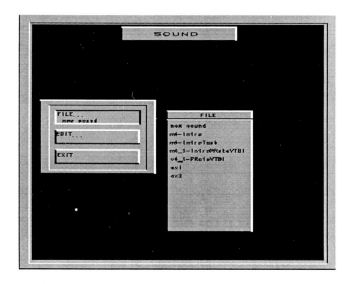

Fig. 5. The sound editor.

Text editing tool: This tool (figure 6) is for editing text components. It includes the possibility of creating hypertext links between text components. A text component can be "interactive" or "on-time".

An on-time text is displayed for a period of time specified at the edition time. An interactive text allows the learner to read it normally. This text is showed in a different window allowing the learner to change a page, stop the display, and continue the demonstration.

The text editing tool makes it possible to parametrize texts and to change these parameters at any time. This is achieved via a specialization of the general hypertext facility. One particular usage is to highlight concepts in a text in synchrony with the corresponding actions on the simulator.

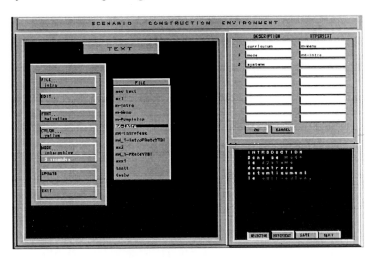

Fig. 6. The text editing tool.

2.2.3. Demonstration scenario editor

This editor is the major tool of our system. The previous tools mentioned are of course available in the demonstration editor if it is necessary to create demonstrations elements. The building of a demonstration means the building of its constituent scenarios. A scenario includes five element types: task components (animated traces), texts, sounds, images videos and scenarios. This is a recursive definition. These elements are organized in a semantic sequence defined by the author. We link a database (library) to each type of element (figure 1). Except for demonstration scenarios, we have shown already how these elements can be created by using available tools. Databases are accessible during the building of demonstration scenarios (including the demonstration library). The different parts of the demonstration scenario editing tool are showed in the figure 7. These parts include:

- A selection area, which is composed of a digital key for each type of element that make up a demonstration scenario,
- A building area where the demonstration building takes place; this area is extensible;
- A bloc of functions consisting of:
  - A function that allows the choice of the simulator on which demonstrations will be built;
  - A function that allows the expert to save a demonstration in the demonstration database;
  - A function that allows the expert to empty the building area;
  - A bloc of node editing functions; this allows the author to edit the nodes of a demonstration graph;
  - Two functions that allow users to test the demonstration
  - A help function.

During the building process, the author has the possibility to create other elements that are not existing in the databases, and put them in the demonstration sequence. For this, the system allows the author to access the necessary tools. There are two possible approaches to adding a new element in a demonstration sequence: top-down and bottom-up approaches.

In the top-down approach, when the type of element to be added is selected and put in the demonstration sequence, the building of this element is immediately requested. The appropriate tool comes up and the author creates the element. After this creation, the element is automatically inserted in the demonstration.

In the bottom-up approach, an element that is not ready can be nominally inserted in the demonstration; its creation is not required at this time. Thus, the author continues building the demonstration without stopping for this element. However, creation of the missing element will be requested automatically when the author has finished and wants to test or record the demonstration he has built.

A demonstration scenario can be recursive in the sense that demonstration element can also be a demonstration (hyper-demonstration concept). We have set up a way to manage this recursion by offering the possibility to expand a demonstration that is part of another one. When a demonstration that is already built is selected and added to demonstration sequence being assembled, it appears in the latter sequence as one compact element. Then, the author can ask to expand it. The expansion opens another working area where the body of this demonstration appears (figure 7). The author can also modify the demonstration. If some demonstration in the sequence is not already built (added by bottom-up approach), the working area that appears is empty, and the author can build it up. We have limited the recursion levels to three.

Once the building of a demonstration is completed, the author can switch to user mode in order to test and validate it.

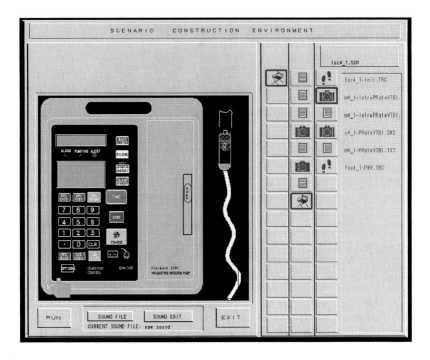

Fig. 7. Building a demonstration.

Completed demonstrations are put in a pedagogical database that can be exploited by a teaching system. We implemented a student interface in which the demonstrations can be chosen by the student.

2.3. Presentation environment

The presentation environment is where the learner views or interact with a demonstrations. This environment is composed of three parts (figure 8):
- A main window that contains the simulator,
- Two secondary windows that display the pedagogical components.

At the bottom of the screen, a button bar gives access to the set of functionalities from the presentation environment.

Three demonstration modes are available: self-demonstration, interactive demonstration and free practice.

In the self-demonstration mode, demonstration sequences are played on the simulator. The learner has no possibility to interact with it.

In interactive mode, the learner can interact with a demonstration being played using the following operations: forward, backward, make a pause, record a part of the demonstration, start the demonstration at different points.

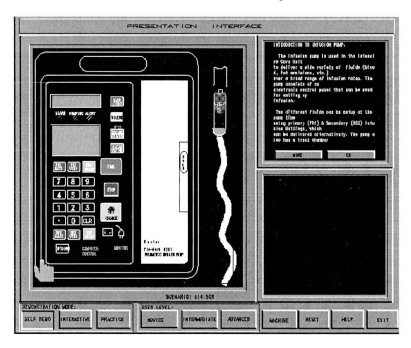

Fig. 8. Presentation interface.

In the free practice mode, the learner can manipulate the simulator without constraints. The advantage of this functionality is that, as for most existing simulators, it allows unsafe manipulations to be tested for their consequences that would rather be avoided as they occurred on the real device. In a job context, this functionality allows users to practice on the simulator before undertaking the task on the real device. Comments on unsafe actions can complement this functioning mode.

3. Using demonstration in an ITS

The demonstration library that DEGREE produces can be used in many contexts. We describe in this section examples of use of this library in the context of a full ITS. This ITS (Nkambou et al. 1995) includes several modules, in particular, a subject matter knowledge structure named *curriculum*, the role of which is to organize the learning material in a way that can be exploited for various teaching/pedagogical purposes. This curriculum can hold demonstration sequences produced by DEGREE. Thus the multimedia demonstration sequences become usable at a higher level of abstraction.

3.1. Using demonstrations in an ITS building environment

The demonstration library is available when an instructional designer builds a curriculum. In accordance with instructional principles, the designer can decide to assign a demonstration to an instructional objective, for instance, the acquisition of a *primary infusion* procedure. One of the resources that can be needed for the achievement of this objective is a demonstration that shows how a primary infusion task can be carried out on a Baxter pump. To do that, the instructional designer creates a link between this objective and the demonstration. Of course, if such a demonstration is not available in the demonstration library, the designer can create it by activating the DEGREE system.

3.2. Using demonstrations in the teaching / learning process of an ITS

The ITS architecture we have proposed includes also a Tutor module, a Planner and a Student Model. The Planner is the module that defines the current focus of instruction, according to the student knowledge represented in the Student Model (Nkambou, Lefebvre and Gauthier 1996). This focus (instructional goal) is then sent to the tutor which will try to access to the curriculum to extract all pedagogical resources that are related to this objective. According to the Student Model and the current performance of the student, the Tutor module can decide to present a demonstration which then starts up. In our model, a pedagogical resource is represented by an object that can receive massages such as: show, stop, evaluate, suspend, ...

When presented a demonstration, the student can interact with it. Several kinds of interaction are possible.

4. Interactivity during a demonstration

Scenarios that make up a demonstration are in the form of a collection of small pieces of code. The first aspect of interactivity deals with the choice of the pieces of code that will be included in the demonstration sequence. The student can:
- Access directly the piece that interest him.
- Review a particular segment
- Mark the steps of the demonstration that seem important to him.

The second aspect of the interactivity deals with the fact that the student can:
- Interrupt a demonstration flow
- Ask questions such as: *more detail, more slowly, ...*

5. Conclusion

We have presented a multimedia authoring tool for building task demonstrations on physical devices. These demonstrations are useful for learning purposes. Thus, in a teaching system, demonstrations can be considered as pedagogical resources contributing to the achievement of learning goals. Current work deals with refining the parametrizing of demonstrations so that they can be adapted to various levels of student expertise.

6. Acknowledgments

We would like to thank the MICST (Ministère de l'Industrie, du Commerce, de la Science et de la Technologie du gouvernement du Québec) for providing financial support of the SAFARI project where this work was undertaken. We also thank Daniel Phalp, Christophe Abadie, Thang Ho Le and Joseph Badette for their collaboration.

7. References

Authorware 1988 *Tutorial Lessons*. Authorware, Inc., Minneapolis, MN.

Bovair, S., Kieras, D., E. and Polson, P., G. 1990 The acquisition and performance of text-editing skill: A cognitive complexity analysis. In *Human Computer Interaction*, 5, 1-48.

Collins, A. 1987 A sample dialogue based on a theory of inquiry teaching. In C.,M., Reigeluth (Eds.), *Instructional theories in action: Lessons illustrating selected theories and models*. Hillsdale, NJ.

Halff, H. 1993 Supporting Scenario-andSimulation-Based Instruction: Issues from the Maintenance Domain. In *Automating instructional design: concept and issues*. ETD. Englewood Cliffs, N.J. pp. 231-248.

Kaltenbach M., Preiss, B. 1994 IconiCase: a visual system for rapid case review. In Ottomann, T. and Tomek, I (Eds): *Proceedings of EdMedia*, pp. 305-310, AACE.

Lajoie, S., Lesgold, A. et al. 1989 *A procedural guide to the avionics troubleshooting tutor development process*, Learning research and development center. University of Pittsburgh.

Lajoie, S., P., Sandrasegaran, N. et Bouchard, R. 1994 *Technicians Use of a Volume Infusion Pump: A Cognitive Task Analysis Approach*. Research report, Projet

SAFARI (Phase 1). Université de Montréal, Laboratoire Héron, Montréal, Canada

Macromind 1991 *Overview Manual*. MacroMind, Inc., San Francisco, CA., 1991.

Merrill, M. D., Zhungmin, L., Jones, M. K. et Hancock, W. 1991 Instructional transaction theory: transaction shells. In *Educational Technology*, Vol. 32 , No 6, pp. 12-26.

Nkambou, R., Gauthier, G., Frasson, C. et Seffah, A. 1995 Une architecture de STI avec une composante curriculum explicite. In *Environnement Interactif d'Apprentissage par Ordinateur,* pp. 315-327, Eyrolles, Paris.

Nkambou R., Lefebvre, B., Gauthier, G. 1996 A curriculum-based student modelling for ITS. Summit to the Fith International Conference on User Modelling.

Polson, M. C. 1993 Task Analysis for an Automated Instructional Design Advisor. In *Automating Instructional Design: Concept and Issues*. ETD. Englewood Cliffs, N. J. pp. 219-248.

SuperCArd 1989 *User Manual*. Silicon Beach Software, Inc., San Diego, CA.

Virtual Prototypes 1993 *VAPS (3.0) Conceptual Overview*. Virtual Prototypes, Inc., Montréal, Canada.

Woods, W. A. 1970 Transition Network Grammars for Natural Language Analysis. In *CACM*, Vol 3, No 10, pp. 591-606.

TELEOKE : A Multimedia Communication Karaoke System

Yong-Jun Song
Korea Telecom Software Research Laboratories
i7, Umyeon-dong, Socho-gu, Seoul. *137-792*, Korea
e-mail : yjsong@pine.kotel.co.kr

and

Myeong-Won Lee, Byung-Kyu Yoo, Young-Whan Kim

ABSTRACT

We are developing a multimedia client and server system to provide users with multimedia information services. As one of its applications, we have developed a multimedia communication karaoke system, TELEOKE. This system consists of a server system and several client systems that are connected to each other in a network such as LAN or PSTN. Using this system, users can sing a song while seeing the text of the song with images on a computer monitor, and listening a MIDI[1] music. In the TELEOKE system, the multimedia server system sends all the data of a music to client terminals so that the music is played with its text and background images. This paper presents the communication karaoke system including the multimedia client and server system.

Keywords : TELEOKE, multimedia, communication, karaoke, client, server, information coding, MIDI, JPEG

1. Introduction

Recently, karaoke systems are getting more popular in people's life. Traditional karaoke systems play mainly in a stand-alone type. As computer and network technologies develop, we can come to use multimedia in communication networks. In our laboratory, we have been developing a multimedia client and server system to provide users with multimedia information services through a network. As one of its applications we have developed a multimedia communication karaoke system, TELEOKE, so that we can enjoy singing a song using personal computer in a network.[2]

This paper presents the organization of TELEOKE in the view of a client and server model, and shows the execution examples of the system. Finally this paper describes our future work to improve the system so that it can be commercialized in KT(Korea Telecom) networks, and also its service prospects as a conclusion.

2. The Organization of TELEOKE
2.1. Overview

These days commercial karaoke systems are popularly used to enjoy songs with the text display. There are also home karaoke systems or karaoke programs to be operated on a computer. These karaoke systems contain all the necessary data inside, thus we can classify them as stand-alone karaoke systems. Some commercial karaoke systems play songs in a cable TV. Since they should have their own song data while playing a song, they can't be called as a communication karaoke system. There are business oriented communication karaoke systems that were developed using a network. All the song data are transferred from a central server. In this case, these systems needs the special hardware-typed karaoke system that can handle the received data. On the contrary, our systems is intended for an end-user to sing a song using his/her personal computer at home.

The basic concept of TELEOKE is that a server system provides several client systems with all the data for playing a song requested by an user. The sever and client systems are connected to each other in a network. The server stores the karaoke data in a database and manages their service. Whenever a client requests song, the server retrieves the song data and sends them to the client system. The text of the song is displayed on the background image while playing the music. Fig. 1 shows the conceptual organization of TELEOKE system.

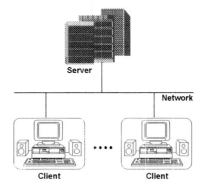

Fig. 1. The Conceptual Organization of TELEOKE

In the following sections, we will describe more details about the TELEOKE which has the three main components such as network, server system, and client system.

2.2. Network

We implemented TELEOKE in a local area network(LAN) that is connected to internet. This system can be easily changed to be operated in PSTN or ISDN which has low data transmission rate than LAN since this system uses only small size data such as MIDI, JPEG, and text whose size is below about 40Kbyte. In addition, it can be easily extended to a multimedia communication karaoke system which uses a full motion video display as a background when the B-ISDN is used in the near future.

2.3. Server System

2.3.1. The Structure of Server System

Generally a server system should have functions such as transaction processing, disk management, distribution processing, etc. However, the functions of the server system in TELEOKE are restricted to manage the data for karaoke, to retrieve them for a song requested, to encode them with a coding method we defined, and finally to send the encoded data to the client system. The server system is run on a SUN SPARCstation10. As seen in Fig. 2, the internal structure of the server system is composed of a database management system(DBMS), two encoders for information coding, and a communication module.

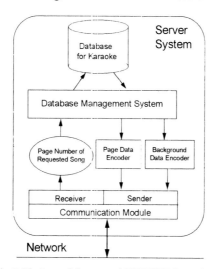

Fig. 2. The Internal Structure of TELEOKE Server System

2.3.2. Database Management System

A DBMS is used for storing and managing all the data for karaoke, and retrieving them whenever client system requests a song. For this purpose, we use UniSQL DBMS[3]. Fig. 3 shows the class hierarchy for constructing the karaoke database.

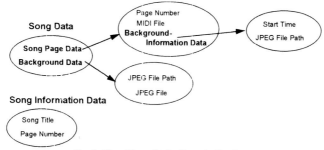

Fig. 3. Class Hierarchy for Karaoke Database

The karaoke database consists of song information data and song data. The former contains the title of a song and the page number which includes the song data, and when the server and client system are connected to each other the server system retrieves all these data using the DBMS to send them to the client system. The latter contains song page data and background data which is displayed while the song is played. In the system, the data for a song is stored and sent in a page unit to clients. The song page data consists of the number of page, MIDI data which has temporally synchronized song and text, and background information data which contains the start time when the background image will be displayed and the path name where the JPEG file is saved. Finally, background data consists of the path name of JPEG file and the JPEG file for actual image data which is processed with the background information data.

2.3.3. Information Coding[4]

When the client system requests a song using a page number of 4byte integer, the server system retrieves the song data with the page number and encodes the data by the following information coding : information coding is an agreement among systems when they store or interchange multimedia data, and it describes several kinds of media, temporal and spatial information for synchronization, and the commands for user interfaces. In TELEOKE there are song information data, song page data, and background data, and they should be sent from a server to client systems. We defined the information coding for the interchange of such data between a server and several client systems. The page coding is defined to interchange song information data and song page data, and also the background data coding to interchange background data.[5]

Therefore it is necessary for the server system to have the page encoder and background data encoder for each information coding. The reason that a song's data is divided into song page data and background data is that the size of background data is too large to be included in a page. So to speak, if background data is included in a page data it is inefficient to interchange the song data in a page unit. The server system sends the encoded song page data to the client systems first, and then sends the encoded background data one by one for its background image. When the encoded song page and background data for the first background are received, the client system starts to play the song and to display the texts and the background image, and in the meanwhile it receives the second encoded background data for the next background to display it at a specified time, and so forth.

In Fig. 4 and Fig. 5, the page coding and the background data coding are defined respectively.

```
<PageCoding>::=<TotalLen><ModeFlag><PageNum><NumOfElm><Element>⁺
<Element>    ::=<ElmType><ElmLen>{<SongData>|<SongInfoList>}
<SongData>   ::=<MIDIData>|<BackgroundInfo>
<MIDIData>   ::=<StartTime><FileName><MIDIFile>
<BackgroundInfo>   ::=<StartTime><FileName>
<SongInfoList>      ::=<NumOfElm><SongInfoElm>⁺
```

```
<SongInfoElm>        ::= <TitleLen><Title><PageNum>
<ModeFlag> ::= 0
<ElmType>     ::= <MIDIType>|<BackgroundInfoType>|<SongInfoType>
<MIDIType> ::= 0
<BackgroundInfoType>       ::= 1
<SongInfoType>      ::= 2
<MIDIFileData>       ::= Data of MIDI File
 <TotalLen>,<PageNum>,<NumOfElm>,<ElmLen>,<StartTime>,<TitleLen>
                     ::= 4Byte Integer
<FileName>    ::= 13 bytes String
<Title>        ::= String
```

Fig. 4. The Page Coding for the Song Information Data and the Song Page Data

```
<BackgroundDataCoding> ::= <TotalLen><ModeFlag><FileName><JPEGFile>
<TotalLen> ::= 4Byte Integer
<ModeFlag> ::= 1
<FileName> ::= String
<JPEGFile> ::= Data of JPEG File
```

Fig. 5. The Background Data Coding for the Background Data

On sending the data, the first 4byte always represents the total data length in order to let the client system know the size of the following data. The client system interprets the first 4byte integer, and then it processes the following data. When the client system receives the encoded data from the server system it is necessary to distinguish the song page data from the background data. It can be done by the <ModeFlag> in the coding method. In case that the <ModeFlag> value of the received data is 0, it means that the data was encoded by the page coding. In the other case that the <ModeFlag> value of the received data is 1, it means that the data was encoded by background data coding.

2.3.4. Communication Module

The communication module of the server system waits for the connection requests from client systems. Whenever it receives a connection request it creates a child process as a dedicated server system for the client system and then waits for another connection request from other client systems. After the dedicated server system made connection to the client system, it sends the encoded data to the client system and receives the song request from the client system. When it receives a disconnection request from the client system, it releases the connection and then exits the process. This module is implemented using the Berkeley socket.

2.4. Client System
2.4.1. The Structure of Client System

The client system is operated on MS-Windows 3.1 in an IBM compatible PC which has a MIDI compatible sound card such as Sound Blaster to play MIDI and LAN card. When user selects a song at the client system, the client system requests the song data to the server system. After receiving the data of the song, the client system plays the MIDI and displays text and the JPEG images for the users in order to sing it watching the text and backgrounds. The client system is composed of a communication module, two decoders for information coding, the MIDI player[6], the text processor, the JPEG decoder, and the song title manager as seen in Fig. 6.

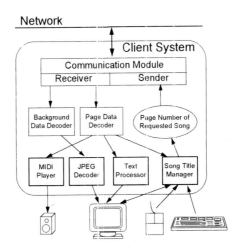

Fig. 6. The Internal Structure of TELEOKE Client System

2.4.2. Communication Module

The communication module of the client system sends the connection request to the server system. After the request is accepted, the client system is connected to the server system. And when the user wants to stop the service, the client system sends a disconnection request and then releases the connection. This module is implemented using winsock which is the socket in MS-Windows.

2.4.3. Song Title Manager
2.4.3.1. The Structure of Song Title Manager

As described before, when the client system is connected to the server system, first of all it receives the information about all songs which the server system manages. The song title manager in the client system manages such information for users to select songs. It consists of 3 lists such as 'Serviced Song List', 'Received Song List', and 'Reserved Song List', and 2 buttons such as OK and Cancel(Fig. 7).

Fig. 7. The Song Title Manager

2.4.3.2. Serviced Song List

'Serviced Song List' shows the titles of all the songs in alphabetical order which can be serviced by the server system, so that users can select a song by clicking one in the list with a mouse to enjoy the song. When the user selects the song, the song title manager checks whether the song was already registered in the 'Received Song List'. In the case of not yet being registered, the communication module sends the page number of the selected song to the server system to request the song data, and after receiving the data the client system decodes them to save in a local storage system and registers the song title in the 'Received Song List' and 'Reserved Song List' of the song title manager.

2.4.3.3. Received Song List

'Received Song List' shows the title of each song in alphabetical order whose data was received from the server system. Because the client system saves the received song data in a local storage system, it is unnecessary for the client system to request the song in 'Received Song List' to the server system. Instead of that, the client system only registers the song in the 'Reserved Song List' of song title manager so that the title of the song is appended as the last element of the list.

2.4.3.4. Reserved Song List

'Reserved Song List' shows the title of song which is currently being played and, if any exists, the titles of songs which were reserved to be played. The first element of the list is the song that is currently being played, and the newly selected song by user will be always appended as the last element of the list so that the songs are listed by the reserved order. After playing the first song ends, the first element of the list is deleted and the next element newly becomes the first element automatically, and at the same time playing the song begins. If the user wants to cancel the reservation of a song, it can be done by simply pressing the cancel button after selecting the song element in the 'Reserved Song List'.

2.4.3.5. Song Reservation

The client system doesn't wait to play a song until all the data of it are received from the server system but it begins to play the song as soon as the song page data and the first background data are received. The background data for the next backgrounds will be received during playing the song, and it will be displayed at the specified time in the song page data. As a result, TELEOKE can come to process the song data partially in real time.

2.4.4. Data Sending, Receiving, and Processing

The song data which is transmitted as a response of song request to the server system has the song page data which was encoded by the information coding as seen in Fig. 4 and the background data which was encoded by the information coding as seen in Fig. 5. Therefore the page data decoder and background data decoder are necessary for the client system to present the encoded data.

The song data is decoded after being received from the server system. It consists of background data, MIDI data which contains the music and the text, and their temporal synchronization information of both data. Generally both the start time of MIDI data and the first background data are 0, and it means that the background image will be shown at the same time when a MIDI processor begins to play the MIDI data. The music information in the MIDI data is translated and presented by the MIDI processor while the text and its temporal information in the MIDI data is translated and displayed by a text processor in synchronization with the song. And the background data is displayed by JPEG decoder at the specified start time.

2.5. TELEOKE Service Scenario

Until now this paper describes the server and client systems separately. In this section we illustrate the communication protocol between the server and client systems to provide users with a multimedia communication karaoke service(Fig. 8).

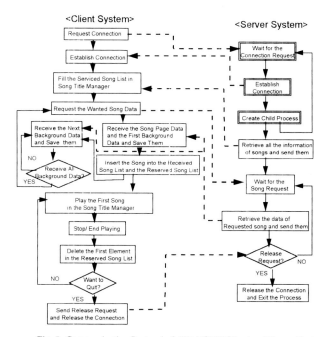

Fig. 8. Communication Protocol of TELEOKE Client and Server System

3. An Execution Example of TELEOKE
3.1. The Execution of the Server System

To use TELEOKE, first of all the server system should be run. The server system connected in a LAN should prepare an empty port for receiving request and sending data through the network, and the default number of port in the server system is 6400. Fig. 9 shows an execution example of the server program whose name is 'srv' with the default port. At the beginning of the server system's execution it waits for a connection request from client systems.

Fig. 9. Waiting for Client Requests in TELEOKE Server System

Fig. 10 shows the execution of the server system when it received the song request whose page number is 4. The server system retrieves the instance of song

data class whose page number is 4, and the next it encodes the song page data
which is included in the retrieved song data and sends them to the client system. At
this time the background data which are the attributes of retrieved song data object
aren't included in the song page data. They are sent separately after being encoded
by the background coding method as seen in Fig. 5. First the encoded song page
data are sent and the next the encoded background data are sent. In this figure, you
can see that 8 JPEG images are used for the backgrounds.

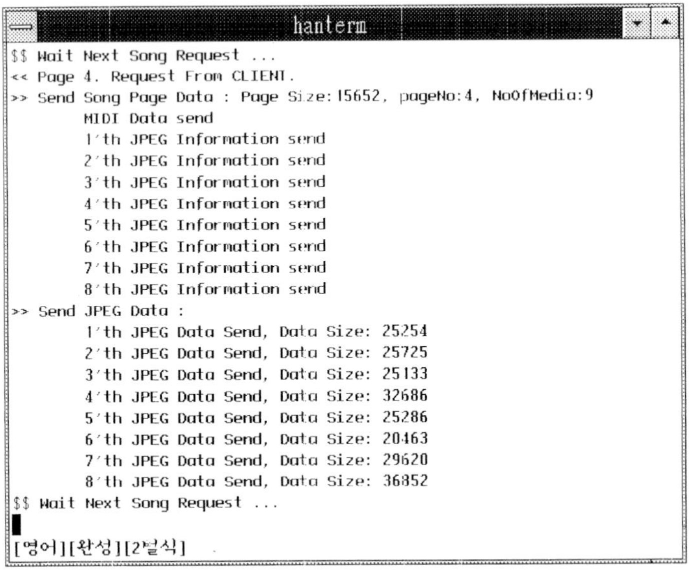

```
                           hanterm                              ▼ ▲
$$ Wait Next Song Request ...
<< Page 4. Request From CLIENT.
>> Send Song Page Data : Page Size:15652, pageNo:4, NoOfMedia:9
        MIDI Data send
        1'th JPEG Information send
        2'th JPEG Information send
        3'th JPEG Information send
        4'th JPEG Information send
        5'th JPEG Information send
        6'th JPEG Information send
        7'th JPEG Information send
        8'th JPEG Information send
>> Send JPEG Data :
        1'th JPEG Data Send, Data Size: 25254
        2'th JPEG Data Send, Data Size: 25725
        3'th JPEG Data Send, Data Size: 25133
        4'th JPEG Data Send, Data Size: 32686
        5'th JPEG Data Send, Data Size: 25286
        6'th JPEG Data Send, Data Size: 20463
        7'th JPEG Data Send, Data Size: 29620
        8'th JPEG Data Send, Data Size: 36852
$$ Wait Next Song Request ...
█
[영어][완성][2벌식]
```

Fig. 10. Data Transmission to the Client System from Server System

3.2. The Execution of the Client System

Several users can simultaneously enjoy songs with their own client systems.
Each client system has several menus related to connection, control, device, and
help as shown in Fig. 11.

Fig. 11. An Example of TELEOKE Client System Execution

The function of help menu includes user's manual and information about TELEOKE such as developer's name, version, date, and copyright, etc.

In the device menu, user can select a proper MIDI output device which makes sound using a sound card. The client system searches all the available MIDI output devices within the system and shows them to let the user select one MIDI output device. In our system, the MIDI mapper included in MS-Windows is used as a default MIDI output device.

The connection menu consists of the 'open' submenu for establishing a connection to the server system, and the 'close' submenu for releasing the connection.

If both systems are connected to each other, the client system first receives the information about all the songs which the server system can provide with. The song title manager in the client system manages them in the 'Serviced Song List'. Then the user can select a song in the song title manager to enjoy the music. Fig. 7 shows the song title manager at the time when the user selected 'Honesty' and click OK button. The selected song is automatically inserted into the 'Received Song List' and 'Reserved Song List'.

The client system starts to play the song when it receives the song page data and the first background data from the server system, while it receives the next background data continuously to display it at a specified time. The beginning scene of playing 'Honesty' in the client system is shown in Fig. 11.

An user can adjust parameters such as key, tempo, and volume using the control menu. The user can also control the status of a song such as play, stop, pause/resume, and replay. So we can say that the client system has most fundamental functions for a karaoke system using communication networks.

In addition to the above functions, TELEOKE provides users with reservation function so that users can reserve other songs as long as all the necessary background data for the current song were already received while one song is being played. In other words, when the network between the client and server system has no traffic, the network can be used to transmit the data for another song. Fig. 12 shows the song title manager after selecting 'Let It Be' and 'Without You' while the client system is playing 'Honesty'. The newly selected songs are inserted into the 'Received Song List' and 'Reserved Song List' and then reserved to be played.

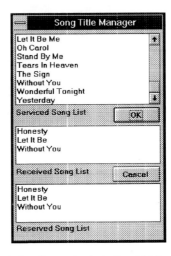

Fig. 12. Song Reservation in the Song Title Manager

When it finishes playing 'Honesty', the first element of 'Reserved Song List' is deleted and the next song 'Let It Be' becomes the first element in the list. The user can reserve the song again although the play is finished. In this case, it is unnecessary for the client system to request the data of selected song to the server system because the data of song which had been already requested has been stored in the local storage system of the client system.

4. Conclusion

This paper describes TELEOKE, a multimedia communication karaoke system, which was implemented using a multimedia client/server technology. Users can simply enjoy songs with a personal computer as the client system which is connected to the server system in a LAN. The characteristics of this system are that several client systems can be operated concurrently while only one server system manages the data of all songs. The maintenance cost of karaoke can be saved at both sides, a provider and users because the management and change of the data for karaoke are done only on the server system. It is more convenient for users to enjoy the up-to-date songs because they don't need to make hard efforts to get the data for themselves. Our system uses MIDI as music and displays the text in progress with the play of a song in the same manner as commercial stand-alone karaoke systems so that users can sing a song easily.

To provide the service of the system in PSTN, it is necessary to prepare data for many songs with good quality sound and background images. The more important thing is to keep users from waiting too long to enjoy a song. To do so, size of data such as MIDI, JPEG should be small to decrease transmission time through PSTN. In addition, the number of background images should be optimized considering the transmission rate in PSTN.

Hereafter commercial karaoke shops would use communication karaoke system which gets all the data for songs in LD or CD-Video from the remote server system through a exclusive line. The multimedia communication karaoke system such as TELEOKE would be used via PSTN at home in few years.

5. References

1. *MIDI 1.0 Detailed Specification Interim*, **ver.4.2**, MMA
2. Yong-Jun Song, Myeong-Won Lee, et al., *A Study on Multimedia Software Technologies*, TR (Korea Telecom 1994)
3. *UniSQL/X Users Manual*, **ver.2.1** (UniSQL, 1993)
4. J.F.Koegel Buford, Rita Brennan, *Multimedia Systems*, (ACM Press, 1994), Ch.14, p.323-340
5. Yong-Jun Song, Myeong-Won Lee, et al., *the Server System Construction for Multimedia Information Services*, **Korea HCI'95** (KISS, 1995)
6. Jong-Soo Kim, *Music World in IBM PC*, (Ohm, 1994)

On Storage Server Issues for Multimedia-On-Demand Systems

Lek Heng Ngoh, Huanxu Pan and Venugopal Reddy
Institute of Systems Science
National University of Singapore
Heng Mui Keng Terrace, Singapore 0511
contact e-mail: lhn@iss.nus.sg

ABSTRACT

In this paper, the various research and design issues of a storage server in the context of a multimedia-on-demand (MOD) system are explored. Using the research prototype currently being developed by the authors as an example, we first examine the data throughputs of various disk systems which can be used to form the basis of the storage server. Next we present a producer-consumer based dynamic disk scheduling scheme to retrieve multiple data streams simultaneously and deposit the data in the buffer memory of the MOD server for delivery to the respective clients. We show experimentally that the dynamic nature of the algorithm is more efficient and robust than the static disk scheduling algorithms which have been proposed elsewhere. We further demonstrate how by using the concepts of "multimedia capacity region" (MCR) the QoS-guaranteed service "capacity" of the storage server can be determined for admission control purposes. Finally the overall design of a typical MOD storage server and the various multimedia information browsing techniques are discussed.

1.0 Introduction

The potential usages of a Multimedia-On-Demand system (MOD) are boundless. For examples, besides providing the much-talked-about movies-on-demand and music-on-demand services, MOD systems can also be designed to provide instant information access for education, training and sales as well as other types of information-on-demand services. It is expected that MOD systems will play an important role in the information superhighways now being implemented in many parts of the world.

Practical deployments of MOD systems are now thought to be possible due to the continuing advancements in computer and communication fields. One of the remaining important research challenges for MOD, however, has been in the design of MOD server storage sub-system. The major challenge here is to design an economically viable MOD storage sub-system to satisfy as many users (or clients) as possible in terms of giving them the requested multimedia information within a reasonable time delay, and to maintain high quality play-back. Due to the still high cost of semi-conductor memory (approximately US$50 per megabyte), most researchers agree that MOD storage server should be implemented with information stored in large magnetic disks (currently sold for US$0.30 per megabyte) and a relatively small amount of semi-conductor memory acting as local cache (or buffer). For servers with very large capacity (one terabytes or more) inexpensive but slower tertiary storage devices such as tape and optical jukebox have also been proposed to add to from a "storage hierarchy". In the short-term this picture of storage server design is not likely to change.

The way that data is down loaded onto the magnetic disks from these tertiary storage devices is often done off-line and over a prolonged period of time. On the other hand, data is expected to be retrieved in real-time from the magnetic disks into server semiconductor memory. In this paper, we focus only the data movement between disk and memory.

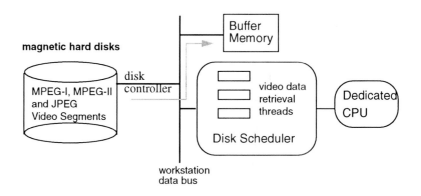

FIGURE 1. Storage Sub-System of a MOD Server

Figure 1. is a model of a MOD storage sub-system showing the way data is being retrieved using software from one or more hard disks via the disk controller into the buffer memory to be transmitted out to the networks. Compared with the other components of a MOD server such as the network, CPU and memory, the disk storage I/O is often the slowest in terms of its sustainable data throughput. An efficient disk storage system is therefore the most important issue in the design of MOD servers. Recent research efforts have largely focused on this topic[4,6,7,8,9,13,15,19,20,21] to mention just a few. On the whole, issues tackled in this area can be further divided into the following:

- Disk read scheduling algorithms for multistream data retrieval[4,6,7,15]
- The exact data layout (or storage placement) of multimedia information across one or more disks[19,20,21]
- Disk hardware design which results faster disk data throughputs

Besides the disk storage I/O, there are other areas of work concentrating in the following areas. It is important to note that these works are complementary and orthogonal to the various other work in storage sub-system listed above.

- The actual architectural design of such a hierarchical storage system [20]

- The distribution of multimedia data across multiple storage servers (e.g. "software" disk arrays[23])

- Databases and indexing tools which are required to manage and browse the entire multimedia data content[12]

Rather than to provide a general survey of these works, interested reader is requested to refer to the various references given in this paper for a detailed description instead. To provide some in-depth understanding we choose to present here the results of our work on the design of a storage sub-system module within the MOD server prototype and outline some other related research issues. Whenever possible, however, we will outline the merits and de-merits of our approaches as compared to the other related works.

The rest of this paper is organised as the follows. In the next section, the various research issues for disks to support multiple streams retrieval are presented. In Section 3., we focus on determining a suitable real-time disk data retrieval algorithm in order that multimedia data is read from the disks accordance to their respective quality-of-service (QoS) parameters. An experimental implementation and performance evaluation results of the proposed algorithm are also presented. Still on QoS, we show in Section 4. how the MOD storage server's "capacity" can be determined experimentally and the results used to provide real-time admission control. The related research issues for MOD storage server can be very wide-ranging, hence in Section 5., some of these topics are briefly introduced before conclusions are drawn in Section 6.

2.0 Disk Arm Scheduling for Multistream Retrieval

As mentioned earlier, the main objectives of the storage server design can be summarised as follows:

- To support as many users as possible.

- To ensure good quality delivery of audio/video information to each user.

- The time delay between the arrival of user request and the start of delivery must be as fast as possible.

- The whole system must be built economically in terms of system cost per stream delivery.

Given that these are somewhat conflicting objectives, challenging research issues and system design decisions have to be tackled. Today, a typical economically-viable system design is as shown in Figure 1. In this section, the various issues of this design will be discussed to give the reader an understanding of the trade-off involved. This will be followed by an in-depth discussion of our current research work on some recently identified issues in the next section.

First off, the raw retrieval throughput of the disk system will play an important role. Clearly the higher the disk throughput, the higher number of users can be supported potentially. Factors which influence the disk throughput are disk head seek time, read access time and disk controller bandwidth. For example, Table 1. shows the measured throughputs of the various disk systems. The numbers represent the throughputs obtained by reading the disk in contiguous fashion. These results were taken from a Sun Sparc-10 workstation running Solaris 2.3 operating system. All disks were connected to 10 Mbytes/sec SCSI-2 controllers. Perhaps the only surprising result is that the level-5 RAID system (with data stripe size of 8 Kbytes) has a lower than expected throughput number. This can be partly explained by the relatively small data stripe size used in our system.

TABLE 1. Disk Read Throughputs of the Various Disk Systems

Unix File System	1 x SCSI-2 (10 MBS)	2 x SCSI-2	Level-5 RAID Sys.
4.5 Mbytes/sec	6.5 Mbytes/sec	12.1 Mbytes/sec	7.0 Mbytes/sec

With the exception of the Unix example, the above experiments were carried out with a same retrieval pattern. In practice, however, when serving multiple stream requests which come in randomly to the server, the way that each data stream is retrieved from the disk has important impact on the overall disk data throughputs due to the overheads of disk arm movements. There has been much work done in the way disk arm is scheduled. Basically, disk arm can be scheduled in the following manners[22].

- **FIFO:** The read head is positioned to the desired disk partition according to the (random) order which the requests arrived. However, un-necessary disk arm movement overheads mean that it can suffer from low data throughput problem.

- **SCAN:** The read head starts at one end of the disks, and moves toward the other end, servicing requests as it reaches each track, until it gets to the other end of the disk. At the other end, the direction of the head movement is reversed and servicing continues. The head continuously scans the disk from end to end. This approach minimises unnecessary disk arm movements but has long response time.

- **C-SCAN:** As with SCAN, C-SCAN moves the head from one end of the disk to the other, servicing requests as it goes. When it reaches the other end, however, it immediately returns to the beginning of the disk, without serving any request on the return trip.

Note that besides the overheads due to disk arm movements, there is another software processing overhead due to the fact that a layer of software is needed to provide a proper file system (cf. the standard Unix operating system file structure). Care must be taken to preserve the overall throughput of the MOD storage server when designing an appropriate file system. There have been several proposals of such a software system[4,10].

Table 2. shows the throughput performance of each of the disk arm scheduling algorithms. These results are obtained by repeatedly reading (with a fixed size) the different raw disk partitions[1] using the above algorithms. Notice that the results show that SCAN algorithm can achieve the best performance. In practice. however, we need to consider the fact that C-SCAN can also operate as effective as SCAN if variable read size is allowed. And this does not have to be done with increased buffer space; as the scheduling algorithm would have taken this into consideration. The reason is that with SCAN the return path can take much longer time than the C-SCAN case. If fixed size data is used for both SCAN and C-SCAN then SCAN will be more efficient as we would use the return path to do work. In

TABLE 2. Disk Data Read Throughputs Using Different Disk Arm Scheduling Algorithms

Unix File System	Raw, FIFO	Contiguous, Raw C-SCAN	Contiguous, Raw SCAN
2.4 Mbytes/sec	3.25 Mbytes/sec	3.26 Mbytes/sec	3.31 Mbytes/sec

the case of the Unix file system, since Unix does not store large data in contiguous fashion[14] and that requests are served in FIFO basis, this plus the software overheads of the file system, the overall throughput is therefore relatively low.

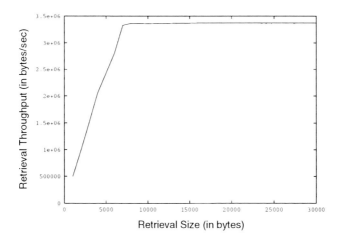

FIGURE 2. Single Disk Raw I/O Performance

The other experiment we conducted was to determine how the data raw read size can affect the overall disk throughput. Figure 2. shows the results of the obtained. Notice that when the read size is less than 5 Kbytes the overall data throughput does not reach the maximum. This can be explained partly due to the fact that at this amount the overheads of each disk read is significant in proportion to the amount of data[1].

---

1. SCSI-1 (max. throughput of 5 Mbytes/sec) disks were used in the experiments.

1. We also observed that the throughput in the inner tracks was not as good as the outer track. For example, the difference in throughput can be between 10-20% (i.e. 3.77 Mbytes and 2.97 Mbytes).

Last but not least, the choice of data placement policy over one or more disks is also an important topic. The basic objective here is still reducing the unnecessary disk arm movement overheads. Over the years, many schemes have been proposed for both within a disk[6] and across multiple disks[19,20,21]. For example in our prototype to be described later, content of each multimedia "object" has been stored in contiguous disk cylinders within a single disk. The data is further striped over multiple disks with a stripe size of 50 K bytes (this number was determined experimentally). The decision on the contiguously arranged data is based on the reason that MOD data is read-only and no editing required, therefore contiguous arrangement is feasible. Unlike some proposed work[6], we also do not attempt to address synchronisation between multimedia information streams at this level.

3.0 A Proposed Producer-Consumer Model for Real-Time Disk Data Retrieval

One of the most actively researched topics in recent years, however, is in the area of scheduling algorithm for disk data retrieval. This work essentially evolved from the disk arm scheduling work described in Section 2 when applying them in a real-time environment. Given that within a MOD system, there are real-time constraints for each of the retrievals, schemes such as SCAN and FIFO must be combined to work with real-time scheduling algorithms (e.g. earliest deadline first) in order to provide delivery with real-time quality of service (QoS) guarantees. So far many schemes have been reported on how to achieve this. However, most of these proposals do not take into consideration the variable-bit-rate (VBR) nature of the video data and therefore do not work well under this environment (see Section 3.1 for a detail discussion). In our prototype, we have used a producer-consumer model to understand this problem and propose a *buffer inventory based dynamic scheduling (BIDS)* approach to provide VBR video delivery.

We consider a MOD system as shown in Figure 3. In this system, when a *request* for a particular media (video or audio) stream is received, a *producer* retrieves from a disk the requested data stream and places it into a buffer. A *consumer*, on the other hand, reads the data from the buffer and sends the data through a communication network to the A/V player of the user (client) who has made the request. When there are many requests for the same or different streams being served, each request needs to be allocated a dedicated buffer and both the producer and the consumer have to be scheduled properly to handle all the requests so that their QoS requirements are met. The disk, producer and buffer together constitute a storage sub-system within a MOD server.

With BIDS the consumer transmits data to the user at exactly the same rate as the playback rate and the producer dynamically schedules data retrievals to feed the buffer according to observations of the buffer state as well as estimated playback rate. This approach has the following advantages: 1) the user needs only a small local buffer with a size large enough to carry out decoding and to absorb the network delay jitter; 2) the uncertainty effect in playback of a VBR stream is brought to the buffer at the MOD server and thus can be dealt with much more easily since the buffer state can be observed; 3) with the buffer separating the consumer and the producer, the consumer can concentrate on transmitting data in its convenient way according to the playback rate (say on the frame basis for a video stream) while the producer can retrieve data from the disk in a more flexible and efficient way according to the locations of the data to be retrieved (say on the disk track basis without worrying about frame boundaries).

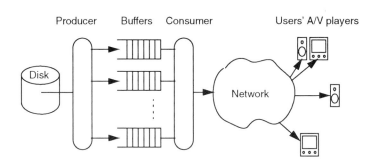

FIGURE 3. The Producer-Consumer Model

From now on, we shall refer to the data transmission rates from the MOD server to the users as *consumption rates*. Assuming that the consumption rates can be easily maintained as exactly the same as the desired playback rates of the users' A/V players and the network is consistent enough for its delay jitter to be absorbed by the users' local buffers, we shall focus on the scheduling issue of the producer, which is a key component in designing an MOD server. Our objective is to ensure that the consumer can always find data available in its buffers for consumption so that the continuity of media playback can be guaranteed, i.e., to maintain the *buffer inventories*, which we define as the amounts of data in the buffers, non-zero at any time. Meanwhile, we have to ensure non-overflow of the buffers as well to avoid data loss. We emphasize the different characteristics of this scheduling from conventional scheduling problems (say [17]) where the objective is often to maximize the overall system throughput, or to minimize the average job completion time.

There are two elements to be determined by a scheduling policy for the producer: one is the *retrieval size*, i.e., the amount of data to be retrieved in one access, for each request, and the other is the order of the retrievals. The former is actually associated with the concept of *retrieval cycle* within which only one retrieval is allowed for each request, and is to determine for each request the small data segment to be retrieved in the current cycle, while the latter is to determine the order of retrieving these data segments in the same cycle. For the order of retrievals, there are some common strategies such as *earliest-deadline-first (EDF)* under which retrievals are carried out in the order of the deadlines of the data segments to be retrieved in the same retrieval cycle, and *SCAN* under which the disk head moves from one end of the disk to the other and picks up the data segments to be retrieved for the cycle as it passes them until the last segment, and then reverses the direction of the movement for the next cycle. In [7], a *grouped sweeping scheduling (GSS)* strategy, which lies in between EDF and SCAN, was proposed, aimed at minimizing the buffer size requirement. GSS showed a limited gain over SCAN for the buffer requirement, at the cost of requiring a rather complex procedure for deciding on the optimal grouping and a corresponding solution for the retrieval size. For systems with a heavy load on the disk, as in the case of the MOD application, we believe that SCAN is generally the most efficient strategy when the retrieval sizes are determined. In this paper, we adopt the SCAN strategy and design a dynamic scheduling scheme that determines the retrieval sizes for heterogeneous media streams to ensure non-zero buffer inventories as well as non-overflow of data.

A complete description of the dynamic disk scheduling algorithm which we developed is found in[1,3] and will not be elaborated here. To describe this work briefly, let us introduce the following notation:

τ : maximum total seek time in a cycle;

μ : disk data throughput;

b_i : buffer size for stream i;

c_i : peak consumption rate of stream i;

A_i : retrieval size of stream i for the current cycle;

x_i : observed inventory level for stream i at the start of the cycle;

I : inventory target index for the cycle.

To achieve the inventory target, and meanwhile ensure non-zero inventory (i.e. no interruption on data consumption) throughout the cycle and non-overflow (i.e. no loss of data), it is sufficient to have A_i satisfy the following:

$$x_i + A_i - c_i T \geq c_i I, \qquad 1 \leq i \leq n$$

$$T \leq \min_{1 \leq j \leq n} \left(\frac{x_j}{c_j} \right)$$

$$x_i + A_i \leq b_i, \qquad 1 \leq i \leq n$$

It is proved in [3] that if

Load condition: $\rho = \dfrac{1}{\mu} \displaystyle\sum_{i=1}^{n} c_i < 1$

Initial inventory condition: $\min_{1 \leq j \leq n} \left(\dfrac{x_j}{c_j} \right) \geq \dfrac{\tau}{1 - \rho}$

Buffer size requirement:

$$b_i \ge \frac{2c_i\tau}{1-\rho}, \quad 1 \le i \le n$$

are all satisfied, the retrieval scheme determined by

$$A_i = \min\left\{b_i - x_i, \max\left\{0, \frac{c_i}{\rho}\left[(1+\rho)\min_{1 \le j \le n}\left(\frac{x_j}{c_j}\right) - \tau\right] - x_i\right\}\right\}, \quad 1 \le i \le n$$

guarantees non-zero inventory and non-overflow cycle after cycle, with I always kept above the level indicated in the initial inventory condition.

3.1 Dynamic vs Static Scheduling Algorithms

There have been a number of disk scheduling policies for MOD servers proposed in the recent literature. Most of them, say those reported in [5,6,7,9], are in the category of *static scheduling*, i.e., retrieve and transfer a fixed amount of data for each requested media stream in each cycle of fixed length. All of the mentioned papers assume constant consumption rates. To guarantee the continuity requirement, the fixed retrieval size should not be less than the amount that would be played out at the user site in one cycle. However, in the case of a VBR stream, problems can occur with a static scheduling policy. If the fixed retrieval size is just large enough to match the average playback rate, then from time to time when the playback rate reaches its peaks, insufficient data supply may cause interruptions in playback. If the fixed retrieval size is large enough to match the peak playback rate, then the over-supply of data during periods of low playback rate may accumulate to overflow the user's limited buffer space thus causing data loss. Therefore, it is hard to find an appropriate fixed retrieval size that can satisfy both no-interruption of playback and no-loss of data. Moreover, a static scheduling policy can not easily deal with situations of changing requests such as arrivals of new requests and service completions of existing requests, since such situations will break the strict balance between the retrieval and playback rates that a static scheduling policy is trying to maintain. Another type of static scheduling to deal with VBR streams is to retrieve for each stream in each cycle a predetermined block of data which has a variable size corresponding to a fixed playback time (cycle time) [16]. Such a scheme is not flexible since the optimal grouping of data into blocks depends on the number and types of the requests in service, and it will be tedious to implement the grouping since pointers or tables will be needed for finding the starting locations of the blocks. In [10], a similar approach to ours is presented, i.e., the producer and the consumer (different terminology is used in the paper) act on their own ways instead of being synchronized, and a dynamic scheduling policy for the producer is proposed. Although VBR streams are considered, the scheduling policy is to guarantee a minimum data rate, so that the transmission of data can be arbitrarily far ahead of the playback. The effect is actually the same as static scheduling for constant-bit-rate streams. The scheduling policy also involves complex computations at the beginning of each cycle and it is not clear how a certain operation at a cycle will affect the buffer state and then the feasible operations of the future cycles.

Our scheduling scheme is easier to implement compared with those mentioned above, since it needs fewer assumptions on both the system and the media streams, and all the parameters needed are easily identifiable. It is robust in the sense that even if the parameters are not accurately estimated, the observation of buffer states can always be used to make up this and adjust the scheduling decisions dynamically. It can also easily deal with the changing circumstances such as arrivals of new requests or service completions for existing requests. While simulations or analytical calculations are mostly used in the literature to evaluate the proposed scheduling policies, in [1], we experimentally compared our scheme with a generic static scheduling scheme and the results verified that our scheme to be more effective and robust.

3.2 Experimental Implementation

To verify the effectiveness of the proposed algorithm, a prototype software has been written to realise the system in order that experiments can be conducted to measure its performance. Figure 4. shows the schema of producer/consumer combination to transmit the data to the MOD clients. Producer and consumer communicate with each other by means of shared memory buffers. The implementation primarily contains two parts. First the *Producer*. This component is responsible for the following tasks.

- Admit new request or reject according to resources available

- Calculate the retrieval size for each stream in each cycle

- Schedule the requests and retrieve the disk data.

- Organize the retrieval of data from multiple disks.

For multiple disks, the data of an object is striped on different disks as described earlier in Section 2. The data is asynchronously read so as to speed up the disk retrievals. The producer submits a request to the *Disk Reader* and disk reader determines which part of the data is located on which of the disks and schedules an asynchronous read on those disks (one thread for each of the disks). The read is done in such way that there is minimal copying while recombining the data from all the asynchronous reads. Next the *Consumer*. It is implemented in multiple software threads to provide efficiency.This component is responsible for the following tasks

- Listen for the new client connections

- Communicate with the producer to admit the new client

- Schedule a retrieval from producer buffers for each client

- The frequency of retrieval is typically at 1/30 of a second for video data.

- Send the retrieved data (from producer to the clients)

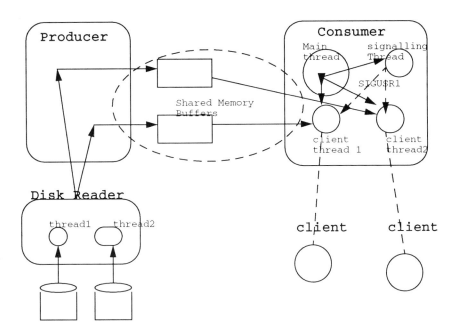

FIGURE 4. An Experimental Implementation of the MOD Server with BIDS Algorithm

3.3 Performance Evaluation

The implemented algorithm has been tested with sequences of video frames respectively from MPEG-I and JPEG resulting in an average consumption rate of 125Kbytes/sec (MPEG-I) and 200Kbytes/sec (JPEG) with a frame rate of 30 frames/second. In our experiments a buffer space of 1 and 3 Mbytes is reserved for each request. The streams retrieved are evenly distributed over the 6 partitions of the disk. Each stream has about 100Mbytes of data. Table 3. summarises some of the experimental results obtained. The results show that the maximum numbers of MPEG and JPEG streams can be retrieved (with QoS guaranteed, see next section) by the prototype are 31 and 22 respectively for a single disk case. Due to some low-level SCSI device driver inefficiency in handling simultaneous access on multiple disks, the corresponding numbers for 2-disk configuration are and 33 and 22 respectively. We expect these numbers to improve significantly if the disks are connected to a disk controller each. The above experiments were conducted using SCSI-2 disks and a multi-processor Sun Sparc-10 workstation running the Solaris 2.3 operating system.

TABLE 3. Performance Result of the Prototype MOD Storage Server

No. of Disks	Avg. Disk Retrieval Rate Used	MPEG Consumption Rate and Buffer Size	JPEG Consumption Rate and Buffer Size	Max. No. of MPEG Streams	Max. No. of JPEG Streams
1	6.2 Mb/sec	125KB/sec 1 MB	200KB/sec 1 MB	31	21
2	7.2 Mb/sec	125KB/sec 1 MB	200KB/sec 1 MB	33	22

4.0 QoS Guarantee and Admission Control

Thus far we have implied that as far as QoS for MOD data retrieval is concerned, a smooth, real-time delivery by the consumer in Figure 3. is desirable. In practice, however, users may be satisfied with a lower quality of service than the absolute smooth (i.e. no-interruption and no-loss guarantee). Therefore, we need to further define the QoS in general. As far as the MOD server is concerned, we consider users' QoS requirements from the following three aspects:

1) *the interruption rate*: the probability that the consumer finds no data available for consumption when it is invoked to take a consumption action (i.e., to transmit data) for a particular stream;

2) *the data loss rate*: the average amount of data being lost due to buffer overflow, out of a unit amount of data retrieved from the disk;

3) *the response time*: the time length since the arrival of a request until the first data retrieval for this request.

Of the three aspects, the response time is perhaps the least stringent with even many seconds often being tolerable. Besides, it is also the easiest to control as long as all the requests are served in a truly simultaneous way. The data loss rate can also be easily controlled with any scheduling scheme which makes use of buffer information and stops retrieving for a request whenever its buffer is full. Therefore we are mainly concerned with the interruption rate.

Given a scheduling policy and a set of QOS constraints, it is important, in the operation of the MOD service, to identify the region of load of various requests, within which all the requests can be scheduled with their QOS requirements being satisfied. This region is referred to as the *multimedia capacity region (MCR)* [2]. Based on the MCR, an admission control mechanism can then be built into the server to determine whether a new retrieval request should be admitted or rejected. As an example, Figure 5. shows the MCR of our one-disk prototype system which is described in the previous section. The QoS specification for all streams in this case is simply 30 frames/sec with zero interruption rate. Using the first set of MPEG and JPEG test data in Table 3. to conduct further experiments, the final MCR shows that the system can support a maximum of 31 MPEG or 21 JPEG streams, or any combination of MPEG/JPEG streams which falls within the MCR curve. Reference [2] further explains the rational behind MCR and shows how the MCR curves can be obtained experimentally.

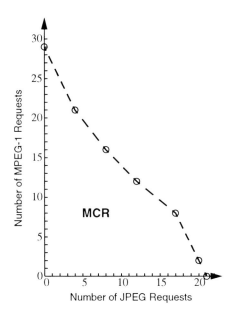

FIGURE 5. The Resultant "Multimedia Capacity Region (MCR)" of the System

5.0 Other Related Issues

Other outstanding issues of a MOD storage server which have not been covered so far are described briefly in this section.

First of all, given that the number of multimedia objects stored within the MOD storage server can be potentially large (say few millions). Plus the fact that MOD user's request should be allowed to have maximum feasibility in specifying the object (or combination of objects) of choice; techniques in graphical user interface design, multimedia information indexing, browsing and retrieval (i.e. multimedia database issues) should be exploited. This is an area of MOD research that just begin to gather momentum[12] and we will see a lot of active developments in the coming years.

Another related but important area of work is in the area of multimedia object editing and authoring. The issues here are mainly to do with building automated tools which can be used to create suitable object representation to facilitate later retrievals. An example is a hierarchical (tree) object representation of a news program in a news-on-demand system, selection of which news item(s) to view can be made by selecting a leaf or a node of the

Last but not least, one of the key objectives in storage server design is scalability. This means that the proposed server design must be able to expand to hold a much larger number of multimedia objects and user-base. Often this means connecting multiple servers over high-speed networks such as the up-and-coming Asynchronous Transfer Mode (ATM) networks. Figure 6. shows an example of a distributed MOD server architecture. Under this configuration, the various MOD servers can be either combined to operate as a very large server[13], or operate independently. In both of these cases, a network sub-system consisting of high-speed networks and supported by suitable multimedia (esp. audio and video data) transport protocols which is capable of synchronously delivering media information on time to the MOD clients will be needed. Current popular protocols such as TCP/IP and ATM can be enhanced to provide the necessary communication service.

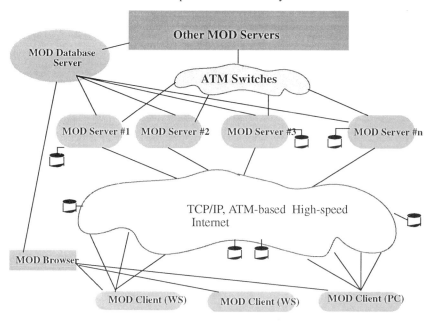

FIGURE 6. A Example Architecture of a Distributed MOD Storage Server

6.0 Conclusions

In this paper, we have examined the various research issues in the design of storage server for MOD systems. Using the research prototype, we explained the various important topics which are being worked on by other researchers and ourselves. In particular, we concentrated on the issue of disk scheduling and presented our proposed solution and demonstrated how it could be realised in practice as part of a MOD server. A scheme to provide real-time delivery and admission control was also described. Finally we briefly touched on the issues of multimedia authoring, databases and networking to show the wide-ranging topics in MOD storage server research. For further studies, the reader is referred to an excellent review paper[5] and its list of references for a further understanding of the issues discussed in this paper.

7.0 Acknowledgments

The authors would like to thank their colleague Pang Hwee Hua for the many thought provoking discussion on storage server designs. The Multimedia Capacity Region (MCR) work mentioned in the paper was a joint effort by Aurel Lazar, Anupam Sahai and one of the authors. This research is funded by the National Science and Technology Board (NSTB), Singapore.

8.0 References

[1]   H. Pan, L. H. Ngoh and A. A. Lazar, "A Producer-Consumer Model and a Robust Scheduling Algorithm for Multimedia-on-Demand Servers", Submitted to INFOCOM'96.

[2]   A. A. Lazar, L. H. Ngoh and A. Sahai, "Multimedia Networking Abstractions with Quality of Service Guarantees," *Proc. IS&T/SPIE Conference on Multimedia Computing and Networking 1995,* pp. 140-154, 1995.

[3]   H. Pan, L. H. Ngoh and A. A. Lazar, "A Dynamic Disk Scheduling Algorithm for Video-on-Demand Service," *ISS Technical Report*, TR94-164-0, 1994.

[4]   P. K. Lougher, "The Design of a Storage Server for Continuous Media", PhD Thesis, Lancaster University, Sept. 1993.

[5]   D.J. Gemmell, H.M. Vin, D.D. Kandlur, P.V. Rangan and L. A. Rowe, "Multimedia Storage Servers: A Tutorial", IEEE Computer, May 1995, pp. 40-51.

[6]   H. M. Vin and P. V. Rangan, "Admission Control Algorithms for Multimedia On-Demand Servers," *Proc. 3rd International Workshop on Network and Operating System Support for Digital Audio and Video*, pp. 56-68, 1992.

408

[7] P. S. Yu, M. S. Chen and D. D. Kandlur, "Grouped Sweeping Scheduling for DASD-Based Multimedia Storage Management," *Multimedia Systems*, vol. 1, pp. 99-109, 1993.

[8] Yee and P. Varaiya, "An Analytical Model for Real-Time Multimedia Disk Scheduling," *Proc. 3rd International Workshop on Network and Operating System Support for Digital Audio and Video*, pp. 315-320, 1992.

[9] H. M. Vin and P. V. Rangan, "Designing a Multiuser HDTV Storage Server," *IEEE J. Select. Areas Commun.*, vol. 11, pp. 153-164, 1993.

[10] D. P. Anderson, Y. Osawa and R. Govindan, "A File System for Continuous Media," *ACM Transactions on Computer Systems*, vol. 10, pp. 331-337, 1992.

[11] J. Gemmell and S. Christodoulakis, "Principles of Delay-Sensitive Multimedia Data Storage and Retrieval," *ACM Transactions on Information Systems*, vol. 10, pp. 51-90, 1992.

[12] L.A. Rowe, J. Boreczky and C. Eads, "Indexes for User Access to Large Video Databases", Proc. IS&T/SPIE 1994 Int'l. Symp. Electronic Imaging: Science and Technology, Int'l. Soc. for Optical Eng., P.O. Box 10, Bellingham, Wash., 98227-0010, 1994, pp. 150-161.

[13] H.H. Pang, "Data Retrieval in A Disk-based Multimedia Storage System", Submitted for publication. Available from the Author at hhpang@iss.nus.sg.

[14] S. J. Leffler, M.K. Mckusick, M.J. Karels and J.S. Quarteman, "The Design and Implementation of the 4.3BSD Unix Operating System".

[15] K.K. Ramakrishnan et. al.,"Operating System Support for a Video-On-Demand File Service", ACM Multimedia Systems Journal, pp. 53-65, Vol. 3 No. 2, 1995.

[16] E. Chang and A. Zakhor, "Variable Bit Rate MPEG Video Storage on Parallel Disk Arrays," *Proc. 1st IEEE Int. Workshop on Community Networking*, pp. 127-137, 1994.

[17] S. French, *Sequencing and Scheduling: An Introduction to the Mathematics of the Job-Shop*, Ellis Horwood Limited, 1982.

[18] J. Gemmell and S. Christodoulakis, "Principles of Delay-Sensitive Multimedia Data Storage and Retrieval," *ACM Transactions on Information Systems*, vol. 10, pp. 51-90, 1992.

[19] Y.J. Oyang, M.H. Lee, C.H. Wen and C.Y. Cheng, "Design of Multimedia Storage Systems for On-Demand Playback", Proc. of the 11th Int. Conf. on Data Engineering 1995.

[20] P.V. Rangan, H.M. Vin and S. Ramanathan, "Designing an On-Demand Multimedia Service", IEEE Communication Magazine, Jul. 1992.

[21] P. Bocheck, H. Meadows and S.F. Chang, "Disk Partitioning Technique for Reducing Multimedia Access Delay", Proc. of the ISMM Int. Conf. on Distributed Multimedia System Applications, Aug. 1994.

[22] A. Silberschatz and J. L. Peterson, *Operating System Concepts*, Alternate Edition, Addison-Wesley, 1988.

[23] F.A. Tobagi, J. Pang, R. Baird and M. Gang, "Streaming RAID -- A Disk Array Management System for Video Files", Proc. of the ACM Multimedia Conf., Aug. 1993.

Conference Organizing Committee

Conference Co-Chairs:
  Kunii, Tosiyasu L.(University of Aizu, Japan)
  Chua, Tat-Seng   (National University of Singapore, Singapore)

Technical Program Co-Chairs:
  Chua, Tat-Seng (National University of Singapore, Singapore)
  Pung, Hung-Keng (National University of Singapore, Singapore)

Tutorial and Audio Visual Chair:
  McCallum, John C. (National University of Singapore, Singapore)

Finance Chair:
  Toh, Sew-Kiok (National University of Singapore, Singapore)

Local Arrangements Chair:
  Chionh, Eng-Wee (National University of Singapore, Singapore)
  Chin, Wei-Ngan (National University of Singapore, Singapore)

Publicity Chair:
  Teh, Hung-Chuan (National University of Singapore, Singapore)
  Goh, Wooi-Boon (Nanyang Technological University, Singapore)

Exhibition Chair:
  Pung, Hung-Keng (National University of Singapore, Singapore)

Conference Secretary:
  Ho, Veronica (National University of Singapore, Singapore)

List of Sponsors

Organized and Sponsored by:
> Department of Information Systems & Computer Science,
>> National University of Singapore, Singapore
>
> IEEE Singapore Section, Computer Chapter
> Computer Graphics Society (CGS), Geneva, Switzerland

In Cooperation with:
> Association of Computing Machinery
> IEEE Computer Society
> Information Processing Society of Japan
> Inst. of Electronics, Information & Comm. Engineers of Japan
> Korean Information Science Society
> Singapore Computer Society

Corporate Sponsors:
> Chartered Electronic Industries (S) Pte Ltd
> CISCO Systems Ltd
> Hewlett-Packard Singapore Pte Ltd
> Silicon Graphics Pte Ltd

Book Exhibitor:
> Simon & Schuster (Asia) Pte Ltd

List of Technical Reviewers

Ahanger, G. (Boston Univ., USA)
Bulterman, D. (CWI, The Netherlands)
Coulson, G. (Lancaster Univ., UK)
Diaz, M. (LAAS, France)
Fry, M. (UTS, Australia)
Gibbs, S. (GMD, Germany)
Gu, J.Z. (East China Normal Univ., China)
Hardman, L. (CWI, The Netherland)
Hashimoto, S. (Waseda Univ., Japan)
Jansen, B. (CSIRO, Australia)
Kaeppner, T. (IBM, Germany)
Kunii, T.L. (Aizu Univ., Japan)
Lee, M.W. (Telecom, Korea)
Little, T.D.C. (Boston Univ., USA)
Magnenat-Thalmann, N. (Univ. of Geneva, Switzerland)
Ngoh, L.H. (ISS, NUS)
Masunaga, Y. (Univ. of Library & Information Sc., Japan)
Noma, T. (Kyushu Inst. of Tech, Japan)
Ooi, B.C. (NUS, Singapore)
Oren, T. (Compuserve, USA)
Pillai, R.R. (ISS, NUS)
Raghavan, R. (ISS, NUS)
Sahai, A. (ISS, NUS)
Schloss, G. (SUNY at Stony Brook, USA)
Schroeer, A. (IBM, Germany)
Senac, P. (ENSICA, France)
Shimojo, S. (Osaka Univ., Japan)
Shinagawa, Y. (Tokyo Univ., Japan)
Smoliar, S. (FX Palo Alto Lab, USA)
Suenaga, Y. (NTT, Japan)
Tanimoto, S.L. (Univ. of Washington, USA)
Teh, H.C. (DISCS, NUS)
Thalmann, D. (EPFL, Switzerland)
Venkatesh, D. (Boston Univ., USA)
Whang, K.Y. (KAIST, Korea)
Wu, J.K. (ISS, NUS)

Subject Index

Author Index

Citation Index

424

426